THE
RUSSIAN
SECRET POLICE

Muscovite,
Imperial Russian
and
Soviet Political
Security Operations

RONALD HINGLEY

SIMON AND SCHUSTER

NEW YORK

Contents

Preface

It is perhaps necessary to explain why 'secret' rather than 'political' or 'security' has been attached to 'police' in the main title of this book, for the fact is that the authorities concerned have conducted many of their activities openly, not to say blatantly—and often through the medium of officers wearing highly distinctive uniforms. There have, moreover, been occasions when Russian political security chiefs, both Imperial and Soviet, have explicitly spurned the term 'secret' as applied to their organisations. When submitting his project 'for the institution of a higher police' to the Emperor Nicholas I in 1826, for example, General Alexander Benckendorff rejected the whole concept of a *secret* police 'such as terrifies honest men, but is detected by scoundrels.'[1]

Over a hundred and thirty years later a similar idea was propounded by one of Benckendorff's successors as head of security—Yury Andropov, Chairman of the Committee of State Security (KGB). Speaking in December 1967, on the fiftieth anniversary of the founding of the first Soviet political police authority, he stated that: 'Only our enemies . . . portray the Soviet security service as some sort of "secret police".'[2] As this remark indicates, the Soviet authorities reject not only 'secret', but also 'police' (in Russian, *politsiya*)—a term which they do not recognise as applying to their own forces of domestic control, but employ only in descriptions of *bourgeois* (i.e. non-Communist) countries. There seemed, however, no more reason for following, on these pages, Soviet practice in the use of the word police than there is for accepting the curious term *bourgeois* as applicable to oneself and to the society in which one lives.

Chairman Andropov's claim, that Russian security transactions have fallen short of total secrecy, receives ample confirmation from the existence of so many books and articles devoted to aspects of Russian police affairs over the ages. The *Bibliography* of the present volume, for example, contains over three hundred titles—but remains highly selective. Should one wish to invoke a more comprehensive compilation, Edward Ellis Smith's bibliographical *The Okhrana* fills an entire volume and contains 843 items—yet confines itself to works bearing on the period 1880–1917.

For such reasons the titles 'political police', 'security police' or 'political security police' might have been preferred here. However, it has seemed on balance sensible to retain the generally accepted, if somewhat looser term 'secret police' as appropriate to a general study which covers more than four centuries' activity within a regrettably small compass. Despite extensive later leaks by escapees from Siberia, defecting OGPU men and so on, the organisation and policies of the various successive Russian police authorities have generally been shrouded in secrecy at the actual time of operations. Much of the material, indeed, still does remain buried in mystery. For example, the archives of the Third Section (1826–1880) have remained inaccessible to leading authorities on the subject (after certain periods of relaxation), just as do those of the Cheka, OGPU, NKVD, MVD and KGB. And yet an enormous amount is known, or can be reliably deduced, about all these organisations.

The present book is not primarily or even secondarily an administrative study of the secret police—an aspect of Russian history which might richly repay further investigation. At the moment adequate detailed administrative studies are unfortunately available only for limited areas of the field. Outstanding among such works are N. B. Golikova's *Politicheskiye protsessy pri Petre I* and P. S. Squire's *The Third Department*. Yet even Mr. Squire's excellent book deals only with the first thirty years of the Third Department (here called the Third Section), leaving the period 1855–80 uncovered. This and other phases, such as that of the Okhrana (1880–1917), await administrative historians equally scholarly and exhaustive—as does the whole Soviet period, though one must not say this without passing reference to E. J. Scott's admirable article on the Cheka, to Wolin's and Slusser's valuable manual, to Boris Lewytzkyj's helpful book, and to Robert Conquest's monumental *The Great Terror*, which touches on many aspects of NKVD organisation in detail inevitably horrific.

However, to have concentrated unduly, within so general a study as the present, on problems of organisation, demarcation, chain of command, recruiting, appointments and functions, would have been to risk being as dull as the above-mentioned authorities are fascinating—and without making any major impact on an aspect of police work which requires scrutiny in the minutest detail. The present study, by contrast, aims to describe secret police operations in general, concentrating on their influence on society at large as one of the most formidable forces at work within the Russian Empire and Soviet Union.

To avoid possible confusion it must be added that Russian espionage, as conducted in foreign countries, does not belong to the subject-matter of the present study. True, the security authorities here described, from Third Section to KGB, have all maintained spies and agents on alien soil, and some reference to such activities will be found below. They are, however, described only in so far as they were devoted to policing renegade Russian or Soviet citizens on foreign territory. Otherwise Soviet spies are mentioned only when their operations have been relevant to domestic security work—as has been true in varying degrees of Richard Sorge, Kim Philby, Rudolf Abel, Gordon Lonsdale, the Krogers and others.

To write a general study such as this is not necessarily to aim at 'popular' appeal in the bad sense of the word, or to admit a sensationalist and unscholarly approach. Scrupulous accuracy has been cultivated, though presumably missed in some degree, in a field where it is outstandingly difficult to attain, and a fairly extensive apparatus of references is therefore supplied in the *Notes* and *Bibliography*.

The following are a few points of detail.

Russian names are transliterated or otherwise rendered along lines laid down at length in the Prefaces to volumes i, ii, iii, v and viii of *The Oxford Chekhov*, edited and translated by myself and published by the Oxford University Press—except that, in the *Notes* and *Bibliography* only, the authors' (or their translators') own spelling of their names has been retained in cases where this diverges from the above. Here, too, female Russians regain the feminine grammatical endings of their surnames. In both text and *Bibliography* Czechoslovak, Hungarian, Polish and Serbo-Croat names have been robbed of their diacritical signs. Dates relating to Russian events preceding October 1917 are given in the Old Style—that is, in accordance with the Julian Calendar used in Russia until 1 February 1918. This means that, in the preceding twentieth century, dates lag thirteen days behind those used in western Europe, as by twelve days in the nineteenth and by eleven days in the eighteenth century. For the period October 1917 to 1 February 1918, Old Style dates have the New Style (Gregorian) equivalent added in brackets.

Finally, I am most grateful to Jane Grayson, Michael Nicholson and Dennis O'Flaherty for advice and/or loan of material, as also to Anne Johnston for secretarial help. Above all, I wish to thank my wife for making the completion of this book possible by her support and assistance.

RONALD HINGLEY

Frilford, Abingdon.

Introduction

The development of the Russian 'secret' or political police can only be understood against the background of Russian evolution as a whole. A brief outline must therefore be given at the outset of the general historical context in which many successive security organisations arose and became, in their various manifestations from the Oprichnina to the KGB, so outstanding as combinations of the horrific and the ludicrous.

As the Muscovy of earlier centuries, as the Russian Empire of 1721 to 1917, and as the USSR, Russia has a long and successful history of expansion under her ruling Grand Dukes, Tsars, Tsar-Emperors, Empresses and Secretaries of the Central Committee of the Communist Party of the Soviet Union. Reaching a level of about 230 million in the middle 1960s, the population had multiplied more than forty times from some five or six million at the end of the fifteenth century. This growing population was extremely varied—multinational, multilingual and multireligious around its core of Russians speaking the Russian language and subscribing in greater or lesser degree to an official State cult: first of Orthodox Christianity, then of Marxism-Leninism. Territorial expansion has also been a notable factor in Russian evolution. From a central nucleus of about sixty thousand square miles, in the early sixteenth century, Russian and (after 1917) Soviet territory multiplied nearly one hundred and fifty times in four centuries to its present size of 8,650,000 square miles.

The problem of policing an area larger than Brazil and Canada combined was especially intractable during the centuries when an imperial order, dispatched by courier from Moscow or St Petersburg, might take several months to penetrate the remotest corner of the Tsar's domains. Even with the advent of railways, telegraph, radio and airlines, vast distances have remained a special factor in the conduct of administration. In an authoritarian State the need for police terror is, perhaps, greater in proportion to the distance between the controlling centre and the remotest provinces.

Though rough parallels for Russian expansion may be found in the history of many other States, Russia remains unique among those belonging to the European and (through most of her history) Christian tradition in the extent to which an increase in population, area and international influence has been accompanied by the seemingly inexorable strengthening of centralised authority under a single supreme ruler. In other nations a diametrically opposed evolution is generally to be traced, power being disseminated among ever-widening circles of the population as absolute monarchies have gradually given way to ornamental monarchies or republics. While such development has been taking place elsewhere, the citizen of Imperial and Soviet Russia has beheld the triumphal march, little deterred by an occasional halt or retreat, of an absolutist autocracy in which his ruler's will was law, while the political police and other instruments of coercion waxed increasingly powerful. This onward surge of authoritarianism was hampered at times by the weakness of individual autocrats, and also by the failure of the last three Romanov Emperors, between 1855 and 1917, to carry conviction to the world at large, to many of their subjects, and even to themselves. In 1906 the autocracy gave way to what was technically constitutional government, but of an extremely restricted order, and under a Tsar who still retained the official title of Autocrat at the time of his abdication during the revolution of February 1917.

The second revolution of 1917, that of October, brought to power a Bolshevik or Communist government nominally dedicated to principles entirely different from those of the Tsarist absolutist autocracy. Yet this great upheaval signally failed to halt authoritarian tendencies such as had been maintained with difficulty since the middle of the nineteenth century, and had lapsed entirely between February and October 1917. Rather was the triumphal march resumed as Russia found herself once more under authoritarian, and then totalitarian, rule—nominally by a dictating proletariat, but in practice once again by supreme rulers, Lenin and Stalin, and later by a controlling oligarchy sporadically dominated by a Khrushchev or a Brezhnev.

In a country which has rarely lacked, and then only for the briefest periods, an individual supreme ruler during the last five centuries, the supreme duty of the political police has been to safeguard that ruler's person and the political system which he represents. Judged by this simple criterion the police of the Imperial period was less successful than its Muscovite predecessor and Soviet successor, since no less than five of the Tsar-Emperors concerned met a violent end by assassination or something approaching it (Peter III, Ivan VI, Paul I, Alexander II, Nicholas II), whereas the period 1547–1721 witnessed the slaughter of only two autocrats (Theodore Godunov and False Dmitry), whose claims or hold on the throne were never more than precarious. As for the Soviet period, despite attempts on Lenin's life, and possibly Stalin's too, the political police has proved an effective bulwark against assassination at the very highest level. It has also been outstandingly successful in containing any attempt to upset the Soviet form of government—by contrast with the Imperial Russian Okhrana, which so dramatically failed to prop up the fabric of Empire in 1917. Nor has the Soviet security police permitted popular uprisings of an earlier type such as sought to effect a change of rulers without necessarily changing the political system—those of the False Dmitrys (1605–10), Stenka Razin (1670–1) and Yemelyan Pugachov (1773–4) being the most dangerous. From palace revolutions, however, such as brought the Empresses Elizabeth and Catherine to the throne in the eighteenth century, the Soviet Union has by no means remained immune, since Nikita Khrushchev ousted his main rivals in 1957, but also fell from power himself in 1964, as the result of *coups* staged behind the scenes. Both of these successful *coups* were, significantly, supported in some degree by the political police of the day, the KGB—as will be discussed in due course.

Few indeed have been the major upheavals in Russian society, Imperial or Soviet, to which some secret police authority has not made a significant contribution—either by its active intervention in a developing crisis or else by its failure to function effectively at a crucial moment.

From the Oprichnina to the Decembrists
1565–1825

The first organisation which can conceivably be claimed as an institutionalised Russian political police force was the Oprichnina, set up in 1565 by Ivan the Terrible, the first Grand Duke of Moscow to be crowned as Tsar. For the Oprichniks, as members of this body were called, the best translation is perhaps 'outsiders'. The word is appropriate in the sense that this corps of six thousand men, carefully selected for their loyalty to the Tsar, was outside or above the law, being permitted and indeed encouraged to commit any crime, mass murder included, against non-Oprichniks with complete impunity. To emphasise their function as an instrument of terror, Oprichniks were clad in black from head to foot, rode black horses, and carried emblems symbolical of their role in sweeping away, sniffing out and crunching treason—a broom and a dog's head attached to their saddles.

Individual Oprichniks received extensive grants of land and peasants, the previous owners, being simply driven out. Thus large rural areas and entire towns quickly came under Oprichnik control, until these lands may have comprised about half the territory of Muscovy. Part of Moscow itself was given over to the Oprichnina, and inside this enclave the Tsar had a palace specially constructed, deserting the Kremlin for this new abode. Not that such seclusion entirely satisfied this monarch forever hounded by fear of his subjects' treachery. He also maintained a reserve headquarters at Aleksandrovskaya Sloboda, some seventy miles northeast of Moscow. In this grotesque stronghold, a combination of barracks and monastery, Ivan would carouse among a brotherhood of three hundred Oprichniks who masqueraded as members of a monastic order, dividing his time between strenuous religious devotions and visits to his torture chambers.

As these details show, the Oprichnina was in many ways a private army of licensed murderers which happened to be maintained by the legitimate hereditary sovereign, but which shows few of the traits of a police authority as the term is commonly understood. In aiming at the mass terrorisation of an entire population, however, rather than at the selective investigation and punishment of individual political dissidents, the Oprichnina closely anticipated an organisation generally accepted as the classic model of a twentieth-century political police—Stalin's NKVD, particularly as it operated during the great terror of 1937–8. Furthermore, the practice of uprooting the populations of whole areas, and of transferring them by force to some distant region designated by authority, was already an established Russian tradition by the time of Ivan the Terrible—one which foreshadows the mass arrests and expulsions of Balts, Poles, Volga Germans, Chechens, Crimean Tatars and others by Stalin's police in the 1940s. Both Ivan the Terrible and Stalin feared their own subjects, and each sought to forestall attempts against his own life and political system by the pre-emptive slaughter of all potential opponents. Under neither despot was the serious investigation of treachery a major consideration. Paying scant attention to such details, Russian Tsar and Georgian Secretary-General both based themselves on an intuitive feel for treason, whether of individuals, suburbs, cities or whole provinces. Stalin's NKVD was admittedly accustomed to frame its victims under an article, Number 58, of the Criminal Code—a mere formality where sentence *in absentia* and extortion of confession by torture were the rule—whereas the Oprichnina scorned even so flimsy a façade of legality. Not seeking to make the punishments which they lavishly imposed fit any crime as established in law, Ivan's Oprichniks simply punished. The Tsar could direct this body of highwaymen and gangsters wherever he wished, or safely leave it to the business of spontaneous plundering and slaughter when his energies were occupied elsewhere.

The bloodiest massacre carried out by the Oprichniks was mounted by Ivan personally in early 1570, when he unleashed these cut-throats and torturers on the city of Novgorod, suspected of collaborating with the enemy state of Lithuania. As with many of Ivan's most harrowing suspicions, his distrust of this, the second city of his realm, was based on little more than a hunch and per-

haps on a false denunciation, but tens of thousands of Novgorod-
ians were killed in a five-week orgy of cruelty, the bodies being
flung in the River Volkhov, while the surrounding countryside
was also devastated for many miles around. The clergy were a
particular object for attack by the Oprichniks, who plundered
monasteries, torturing and murdering monks. At the very beginning of the Novgorod expedition the marauders had found a
victim on the highest ecclesiastical level in the Metropolitan
Philip, who had once demonstratively refused Ivan his blessing
in the Uspensky Cathedral and denounced the Tsar's cruelties.
After sentence by fellow-ecclesiastics at a rigged trial—another
Stalinist touch—Philip was strangled in a monastery cell in Tver
by a leading Oprichnik, Malyuta ('Babe') Skuratov. Among many
other senior clerical victims Archbishop Leonid of Novgorod was
sewn up in a bearskin and hunted with hounds on the Tsar's
orders.

In about 1572 the Oprichnina was wound up, or at least the
name ceased to be used, but such an imprint had the organisation
made on popular imagination in the eight all too long years of its
existence that Oprichnik has passed into the Russian language as
a convenient name for the more terroristic minions of later
authority. It was used, for example, by the common people to
describe the gendarmes and Cossacks who acted as the punitive
arm of the nineteenth- and twentieth-century Imperial police.
Similarly, after the overthrow of the Imperial system, Lenin's and
after him Stalin's secret policemen—members, successively, of the
Cheka, OGPU, NKVD, NKGB, MVD, MGB and KGB—have
regularly been described, out of earshot, as Oprichniks by those
opposed to their methods. Not that Stalin himself by any means
regarded Oprichnik as a term of opprobrium. On the contrary,
he spoke of the 'progressive role' played by the dread Tsar's gang
of hoodlums. Ivan's fault was not ruthlessness but insufficient
ruthlessness, according to the great Soviet dictator, who once
pointed out with characteristic pawky humour that the Terrible
Tsar had wasted too much time praying when he might have been
usefully killing still more boyars.[1]

The liquidation of the aristocracy of boyars and princes, chief
rivals to the Tsar's authority, appears to have been one of Ivan's
motives in maintaining his reign of terror, but it is also true that
boyars and princes were among those recruited into the Oprichnina, as indeed were a number of foreigners. Ivan's attack on the
Church—another rival centre of power—may also be explained

by a desire to strengthen the authority of the centralised State, as vested in the person of its absolute ruler. However, neither this nor any other simple explanation appears to account fully for so bizarre a phenomenon as the Oprichnina. Often considered the greatest single problem in Russian historiography, it may well continue to defy rational explanation, being the offshoot of an individual's unhinged imagination. Yet, irrational as the method may have been, one overriding motive for the establishment of the Oprichnina was certainly Ivan's concern for his personal safety. Terrorised by his own fantasies, the Tsar sought salvation in plunging his whole realm into a reign of terror, while living apart from his subjects as a whole in a milieu policed by specially selected and trustworthy armed men. The nineteenth-century Russian historian Klyuchevsky was not stretching language unduly when he referred to the Oprichnina as an outright 'police dictatorship' and 'higher police concerned with treason'.[2]

That the Tsar should in course of time turn and rend his most enthusiastic henchmen was in the logic of his personality, and in the early 1570s he is found presiding over the execution and imprisonment of many of these former accomplices in terror. Ivan thus disposed of such discarded terrorists as Prince Afanasy Vyazemsky and the Basmanovs, father and son—just as Stalin was to liquidate his NKVD Commissars Yagoda and Yezhov nearly four centuries later.

Between the disappearance of the Oprichnina, in 1572 or later, and the year 1697, when the Preobrazhensky Office was empowered by Peter the Great to investigate political subversion, Russia lacked any institutionalised political police force. It would be impossible, however, to pass over these years in silence if only because of so many events which underlined the need to find some way of containing political upheaval. Nor did the lack of any regular security police authority prevent a variety of departments and individuals from discharging the functions of political investigation and repression on a more casual basis during this period.

The accession, in 1584, of the feeble-minded Tsar Theodore I seemed to offer a brief respite to the country previously ruled by his father, Ivan the Terrible, while *de facto* rule came to be exercised by the new Tsar's brother-in-law, Boris Godunov. This ambitious statesman was widely believed to see himself as the childless Theodore's successor to the throne. He faced an obstacle to any such ambition in a legitimate infant heir, the Tsarevich Dmitry—Tsar Theodore's half-brother and the only other surviving son of Ivan. It was, therefore, extremely convenient for Boris Godunov when, in 1591, report of Dmitry's sudden death reached Moscow from Uglich, the provincial town to which the boy had been exiled with his mother. The mystery surrounding this affair was not dispelled by an official investigating commission under Prince Vasily Shuysky, himself an ambitious intriguer, who was dispatched to Uglich and concluded that the Tsarevich had died accidentally, having suffered an epileptic fit while playing with a knife. The local people blamed Godunov's agents for the crime, and though the authorities tried to suppress this version of the incident by cutting out the tongues of gossip-mongers, the tale continued to spread, and Godunov was widely held responsible for the murder. During the next fifteen years Vasily Shuysky alternately disavowed and then reavowed his confirmation of the Tsarevich's death for purposes of intrigue, changing his mind no less than seven times in all. The most important political investigation of the late sixteenth century therefore augured ill for the integrity and truthfulness of the many political inquiries and trials which lay ahead.

Rumours of complicity in the Tsarevich's murder notwithstanding, Boris Godunov did in fact succeed to the throne in 1598— but only to preside over various calamities, the first being the terrible famine of 1601–3. Then, in 1604, a new chapter in Russian history began with the appearance of the first and most successful in a long series of seventeenth- and eighteenth-century Pretenders to the throne. Posing as the Dmitry who had probably died or been murdered at Uglich in 1591, the impostor invaded Muscovy at the head of a band of Polish adventurers. It was Simon Godunov, Tsar Boris's cousin and sometimes referred to as head of his secret police, who conducted the investigation which, rightly or wrongly, revealed 'Dmitry' to be a runaway serf called Grishka Otrepyev.[3] This revelation did not, however, prevent the invading Pretender from attracting to his banner an increasing number of Cossacks, now that he was established on Russian soil. These unruly citizens, largely of peasant origin, lived on the periphery of the realm, having fled from the oppressions of central authority in Moscow. From now on for well over a century they formed an essential complement to any Pretender, for neither a Pretender without Cossack support, nor Cossacks without a

Pretender's leadership, ever succeeded in threatening the State, whereas in combination the two were formidable indeed.

While False Dmitry's forces were already advancing on Moscow, Boris Godunov happened to die. He was succeeded by his sixteen-year-old son Theodore, who was brutally murdered after only six weeks' rule in the uproar which accompanied False Dmitry's triumphal entry into the capital. Then, after less than twelve months' rule, Dmitry himself was deposed and slaughtered, the body being burnt and the ashes fired from a cannon in the direction of Poland, whence he had come. His successor, Tsar Vasily Shuysky, presided ineffectually over raging chaos from 1606 to 1610, after which he was captured by Poles, dressed in a white smock and driven as a trophy into Warsaw in an open carriage. Invasion of Russia by Poland led to the two-year occupation of Moscow by these foreign invaders until, in 1612, the Poles were driven out and a new dynasty occupied the Russian throne in the person of Michael, first Tsar of the House of Romanov (1613–1917).

Little firm control was provided by the inert and passive Tsar Michael, who ruled from 1613 to 1645, nor was any specific department of political police set up under him or his immediate successors. Considerable attention was, however, attached to political investigation, conducted on a local level with officially sanctioned use of torture by regional Governors *(voyevody)*, or by whichever among the Offices of State, situated in Moscow and administering various territories or classes of the population, happened to have jurisdiction in a given instance. The most important cases found their way to the Tsar himself and his Council of Boyars.

During this reign Pretenders continued to proliferate and to meet a variety of fates. One—the four-year-old son of that curious double impostor who posed as the Pretender False Dmitry—was hanged at the Serpukhov Gate in Moscow in 1614. A False Timothy, purporting to be the son of Tsar Vasily Shuysky, created havoc at the head of a Cossack band, then fled to Constantinople, Italy and Vienna, respectively embracing Islam, Catholicism and Protestantism before being extradited to Russia from Holstein and put to death by quartering.[4] Various suspect priests were also investigated—by the secular authorities—and among them was Metropolitan Afony of Novgorod who had burnt, and thereby omitted to report to the authorities, an anonymous written political denunciation, such as were commonly left lying about the churches. The Metropolitan also received a public reprimand for failing to denounce certain 'unseemly remarks' made by one of his subordinates.[5] As this reminds one, *failure to denounce* has been throughout the ages a particularly serious Russian form of crime, a comparatively recent offender being the Soviet writer Anatoly Kuznetsov—rebuked by the KGB in 1963 for omitting to report a student who had approached him with a hysterical tirade describing the Soviet Union as a Fascist country.[6]

In the reign following Michael's—that of Tsar Alexis, who ruled from 1645 to 1676—failure to denounce was established in law as a major crime. It was now, in the new Law Code of 1649, that political offences were for the first time distinguished from civil crimes—an essential step forward in the early evolution of a political police. Henceforward attempts on the Tsar's life, treason, plots against the government and mass rioting were distinguished from other forms of crime, being made punishable by death and the confiscation of all property—as had been a common informal practice previously. At the same time the obligation to denounce such offences to the authorities was imposed on all subjects, including even serfs, who were otherwise not permitted to complain against their owners. By now a special procedure had been adopted whereby an informer made known his wish to utter a denunciation. He must shout aloud in some public place the formula 'Sovereign's Word and Deed', which obliged those present to report the affair to the competent authorities for immediate secret investigation. For all three forms of crime— treason, intention to commit treason and failure to denounce treason—the penalty was death.

Under Tsar Alexis the investigation and punishment of political offences continued on basically the same principles as before, but with an increased use of special investigating commissions, consisting of two or three officials and empowered to punish as well as to question offenders. Punishment and questioning were, in fact, intimately intertwined since the basic instrument of interrogation was physical torture. Such special commissions were used to deal with some of the many dangerous urban riots of the period, including those in Kursk and Veliky Ustyug in 1648, which they curbed with hanging, flogging and imprisonment. In 1660 such a commission was appointed to investigate unruly conduct on an individual level when a certain Ch. Sumarokov accidentally fired a bullet into the Tsar's quarters while shooting jackdaws near by, for which he was sentenced to amputation of the left arm and right leg. Such were the penal methods applied under a Tsar who gained the nickname Most Gentle.

More serious upheavals continued to involve investigation by the Boyar Council. These included the most dangerous disturbance of the reign—the great Cossack revolt of 1670–1. Its leader, Stenka Razin, was personally interrogated by members of the Council before execution in Moscow by quartering. Razin had carried a False Alexis (a pretended son of Tsar Alexis) on his staff, and also a False Nikon (a pretended Patriarch). Three years after his execution yet another Pretender, a False Simeon, whose real name was Vorobyov, was executed in Moscow, the investigation of this case also having been carried out by the Boyar Council.

Despite the variety of authorities engaged in combating political crime, the reign did also see, in 1650, the establishment of a body which dimly foreshadows the more specialised political police organisations of the future—the Secret Office. This was essentially a private secretariat of the Tsar engaged in administering whatever affairs most nearly concerned him, including the management of the elaborate falconry installations which were his main hobby. The Office also maintained a sporadic review of political cases, taking precedence over other departments owing to its status as a direct instrument of the supreme ruler. Among the activities of the Office was the furnishing of agents to supervise Russian ambassadors in foreign countries, and also Generals in time of war. Such agents were political commissars *avant la lettre* rather than spies, and often received large bribes from those whom they were sent to scrutinise.[7]

Important as it was, the Secret Office never became a regular security force, and was in any case abolished on the Tsar's death in 1676.

Not until the reign (1682–1725) of Peter the Great was an organisation established with a clear claim to be regarded as a Russian political police authority in a fuller sense than the Oprichnina. On the need for such an organisation Peter had received a sharp warning in infancy. Chosen as monarch by a national assembly just before his tenth birthday, the young Tsar had witnessed on 15 May 1682 a terrifying demonstration of the perils besetting his throne—a mutiny of the Streltsy, the soldier-traders who garrisoned Moscow and themselves functioned as a rudimentary civil police. Marching on the Kremlin with banners flying, this murderous mob rampaged through the royal apartments and butchered Peter's relatives. Though the boy-Tsar was not deposed in the upheaval, the mutiny undermined his position by elevating his feeble-minded half-brother to the throne as Ivan V—now co-monarch, but with senior status to Peter, whose half-sister Sophia became regent. She acted in this capacity until 1689, when Peter was able to muster sufficient support to depose her from the regency and force her to enter a convent. His half-brother died a few years later.

Thus, with *coup* and counter-*coup*, began the rule of Russia's most powerful Autocrat, who hated his capital city and its ancient traditions, being determined to drive Muscovy into the modern age along the path trodden by the advanced states of modern Europe. The most extreme symbol of this intention was the Tsar's foundation of a new capital city, St Petersburg, on marshes wrested from Sweden during the long war which gave Peter possession of the southern Baltic coast. The city dated its foundation from 16 May 1703, when work began on the Peter and Paul Fortress on an island near the centre of the future capital. Designed as a bulwark against Sweden, this stronghold was never used in any foreign war, but became a prison for the Tsars' domestic enemies. Its chief rival, as a notorious place of incarceration for victims of the Imperial political police, was the Fortress of Schlüsselburg, also captured from the Swedes by Peter and situated on an island about forty miles east of the new capital.

To build St Petersburg, defeat the Swedes, transform an army and create a navy, while fostering mines, wharves, foreign trade and countless connected activities, Peter savagely taxed his subjects, also conscripting them as labourers and soldiers on such a scale that his entire realm began to resemble a vast slave camp in which many of the inmates believed that their Tsar was destroying Russia. Peter's unpopularity owed much to his deliberate flouting of ancient tradition as he swept through his realm, snipping and taxing beards, mocking age-old religious rituals and putting his officials and gentry into heretical western European dress, while antagonising, executing, torturing and regimenting those who thwarted him, even his favourites being physically endangered by playful buffets, rib-crushing hugs and the obligation to quaff huge bumpers of brandy. Thus Peter aroused nationwide resentment and political opposition ranging from muttered grumbles to plots against his life, while rumour spread that the Tsar was Antichrist —no true son of the late Tsar Alexis, but a German changeling foisted on Russia as a baby by foreigners. Nor was rumour silent about the family life of one who forced his first wife into a convent under humiliating circumstances, had her lover impaled many years later and caused his own eldest son to be knouted to death.

Brutal as Peter was, his was a brutal age, and he showed himself a perfect master of its administrative idiom when he created a security organisation capable of keeping the population under firm control—the Preobrazhensky Office. This was first established for quite a different purpose—to administer two new army regiments, the Preobrazhensky and Semyonovsky Guards, which grew out of the units of militarised young contemporaries with whom Peter had experimented in the techniques of warfare as a boy. A versatile body, the Preobrazhensky Office also came to control the tobacco trade—as much the work of the devil as any of the Tsar's other concerns, according to conservative Russian thought. It was in 1697 that this organisation first undertook the regular investigation and judgement of political offenders, after Peter had abandoned Russia to conduct an eighteen-month tour of western Europe, leaving the head of the Preobrazhensky Office, Prince Theodore Romodanovsky, in charge of security at home. Prince Theodore continued to head the Office until his death in 1717, when he was succeeded by his son, Prince Ivan.

As chief political policemen of the realm, both Romodanovskys proved effective. Their organisation received almost exclusive jurisdiction in political cases, together with the right to investigate and question any citizen, regardless of age, sex and station, who might come under suspicion of treason. Romodanovsky's office thus obtained precedence over all other governmental bodies, since he not only had the right to summon individuals for questioning, but might also require their help, having the power to reprimand or flog those who withheld co-operation or attempted to exercise independent jurisdiction in matters of political security.

Since the staff of Romodanovsky's office consisted only of two chief clerks and between five and eight assistants, he made regular use of officers and soldiers of the Preobrazhensky and Semyonovsky Guards as couriers and to execute arrests. Prince Theodore thus anticipated General Benckendorff's position in the second quarter of the nineteenth century, when he headed the small Third Section stationed in the capital, but also commanded the far larger Corps of Gendarmes as his executive arm. Another parallel lies in the close personal interest taken by the Autocrat—by Peter in Romodanovsky's work, as by Nicholas I in Benckendorff's. The

Great Tsar frequently visited his political police headquarters and gave or reviewed judgements in many cases, thus helping to establish a stock of legal precedent. That he personally applied torture on the premises of the Preobrazhensky Office was widely rumoured, but is not confirmed by evidence.

Peter undertook his most savage bout of political repression in 1698 after receiving news of a revolt of the Streltsy—object of suspicion to the young Tsar ever since their previous rising had endangered his throne at the time of his accession. Reaching him in Vienna, this dire report forced him to cut short his tour of western Europe and hasten back to Moscow. By the time of the Tsar's return the revolt had been suppressed and its ringleaders were already executed, but he at once decided to reopen the case and to make such an example of the surviving Streltsy as should put an end once and for all to the possibility of further wide-scale mutiny within his realm. Peter did not, however, simply order the execution of all those involved, for he was also concerned to establish the origins of the revolt, and in particular the degree of complicity of the former regent, his half-sister Sophia.

The period recognised only one investigative technique for crime, whether civil or political—torture. As a general rule three stages were involved. First the victim would be hoisted aloft by his arms in a manner which dislocated them—the strappado— after which he was subjected to blows from the special flail-like whip of rigid leather called the knout. Roasting over a slow fire followed, and the triple process could be repeated, with intervals for recovery when necessary, until the interrogator was satisfied that he had laid bare the truth—for this, not the infliction of pain, was the chief purpose of the operation. In the case of the Streltsy the number of those involved was so great that special arrangements had to be made, thirteen torture chambers being set up in the Preobrazhensky Office, while twelve boyars were seconded to assist Romodanovsky. After prolonged ordeals, from which the Tsarevna Sophia's female servants were not exempt, information was obtained confirming that she had indeed sent a letter inciting the Streltsy to revolt in the first place. She was thereafter incarcerated in the same convent under closer guard, but not herself subjected to physical ill-usage. As for the Streltsy themselves, the Tsar ordained their public execution by the hundred in Moscow on 30 September 1698, and ordered that the bodies should be exposed for months afterwards by the walls of the Kremlin and elsewhere, three being placed directly opposite Sophia's cell window—a grisly reminder of the foolishness of fomenting revolt in the age of Peter I. Supplementary actions against the Streltsy continued over several years until the affair was overtaken by another mutiny, in the provincial town of Astrakhan, which led to further mass investigations and executions, comparable on a somewhat smaller scale to the vengeance wreaked on the Streltsy.

Appalling though these episodes were, they did at least represent terror applied on a more limited, rational, calculated and politically effective scale than the outrages committed by the Oprichnina over a century earlier. Compared to the terror administered by an Ivan the Terrible or a Stalin, the suppression of the Streltsy and of the Astrakhan mutineers was an operation of almost surgical precision in which the total number of those executed did not much exceed one thousand.[8]

The methods used to crush the Streltsy and the Astrakhan mutineers were also employed throughout the reign to investigate political crime on a lesser scale, from treasonable plotting down to gossip and careless talk. For the detection of such offences the Office relied almost exclusively on the method of denunciation by crying 'Word and Deed'—already a traditional procedure, but one which gained yet greater prominence under Peter. Once the deadly formula had been invoked the nearest local authorities were obliged to arrest the speaker and also the person against whom his accusation was brought, and to deliver both, fettered hand and foot, to the Preobrazhensky Office in Moscow, where they remained in custody until the case should be settled. Once again torture, principally by the knout, was the routine investigative procedure. Witnesses and informers were also subject to imprisonment and torture on exactly the same basis as accused persons, though there is evidence of class distinction in applying these severities, members of the gentry being less savagely used than peasants. Such were the means whereby the two Romodanovskys assured themselves that they had obtained the truth, though in some cases they may only have discovered which of the various competing victims was most sensitive to pain. Many of the accused had merely retailed items of gossip about the Tsar's domestic life, cursed him when drunk, or complained of the burden of taxation in private. There was also the occasional exhibitionist fanatic such as the monk Ivan, who appeared in Moscow naked except for a brass chain and cross, and publicly reprimanded the Great Tsar for shaving off his subjects' beards, consorting with foreigners and fostering alien heresy.[9]

Once the matter of guilt had been decided, it was the head of the Preobrazhensky Office who generally pronounced sentence. This might be to execution by quartering, breaking on the wheel, beheading or hanging. For lesser offenders knouting or whipping was prescribed, with two possible grades of severity—ordinary and merciless—the number of lashes in either case being left to the discretion of the official flogger. Various forms of mutilation were also practised—the cutting out of the tongue, ripping of nostrils and branding by needles on forehead and cheek with the words KAT (convict) or VOR (criminal), powder being rubbed into the wound to render it permanent. Exile to Siberia might follow, and the above punishments were applied in whatever combination the Romodanovskys judged suitable. For members of the clergy, who were particularly prominent (accounting for some twenty per cent of all cases handled by the Office),[10] a special form of beating was sometimes prescribed—with spade-shaped cudgels called *shelepy*. For the clergy, and on occasion for other citizens, imprisonment might involve confinement in a monastery, since many of these were equipped with suitable dungeons.

During some thirty years' activity as a security organisation, the Preobrazhensky Office handled many thousands of cases. There can be no doubt of its success in controlling subversive word and deed, even though many examples of grumbling, criticism and threats must have escaped the Romodanovskys' net, the rigours of investigation being such as to deter potential informers. On the other hand there were also powerful inducements to cry 'Word and Deed', not least the threat of drastic punishment which hung over individuals who might later prove—sometimes after an interval of several years—to have overheard treasonable talk without reporting it to the authorities at the time. Potential informers were also tempted by the practice of giving monetary and other rewards. For instance, a serf might hope to receive his freedom should he successfully denounce his master, but also risked severe chastisement if investigation should reveal his accusation to be groundless.

Powerful as the Preobrazhensky Office was, it did not maintain an absolute monopoly in political detective work, and it happens that the most notorious single security offence of the reign came under investigation by an independent commission specially established for the purpose—the Secret Chancellery. This was the affair of Peter's son and heir, the Tsarevich Alexis, who had turned out an addict of religious pursuits and other old-fashioned Muscovite ways, being also indolent, unwarlike and unco-operative. He attracted the hopes of all who secretly opposed Peter's policies, thus constituting a potential threat to his father even before committing the supreme crime of seeking political asylum abroad. It was in 1716 that the young Tsarevich escaped from Russia to the Holy Roman Empire. Traced to a fortress near Naples by his father's agent Peter Tolstoy, Alexis was tricked and bullied into returning to Russia. After an investigation lasting six months, the Tsarevich perished under the knout in the Peter and Paul Fortress, having dragged many of his associates down with him by revealing their names under interrogation.

The Secret Chancellery had now completed the main task for which it had been set up, but continued to function in St Petersburg on a temporary basis. Hitherto the new capital had lacked such a security organisation, for despite the transference of most other governmental departments from Moscow, the Preobrazhensky Office had remained behind in the old capital, perhaps because Peter still saw that ancient city as the fount of all sedition.

The five years following Peter's death in 1725 saw the end of the Secret Chancellery, which was abolished in 1726, while the Preobrazhensky Office followed suit—wound up in 1729, when Ivan Romodanovsky expressed a wish to retire. Neither body had functioned with its old effectiveness after Peter's death, when Russia was ruled by two short-lived monarchs who took little or no part in the business of government—his widow, Catherine I, and his grandson, Peter II. It was left to Peter's daughter, the Empress Anne (reigned 1730–40), to re-establish a regular political security organisation: the Chancellery for Secret Investigations, created by a decree of 6 April 1731. Headed by General Andrew Ushakov, a former member of the Secret Chancellery under Peter the Great, the new body was in many ways a reconstituted Preobrazhensky Office, especially as Ushakov himself reported direct to the Empress. Like the Romodanovskys before him, he was empowered to commission other government departments to undertake work on behalf of his organisation, and exercised a virtually exclusive right to investigate treason. The formula 'Word and Deed' remained in vogue, while denunciation and torture still provided the basic technique of investigation. Nor did the cruelties practised by Anne's executioners lag far behind those inflicted under her father Peter the Great. The new Chancellery did, however, mark a departure from the Preobrazhensky Office in various ways. It was based on St Petersburg (from 1732) instead of Moscow, but maintained an important branch in the old capital. It had an expanded staff of two secretaries and twenty-one clerks, and was not burdened with duties outside the field of political security—unlike the Preobrazhensky Office, which had also been heavily involved in military administration. The new Chancellery was therefore equipped to handle a large volume of work, and the Moscow branch alone processed cases affecting a thousand persons every year.[11] The cases handled by the Chancellery during Anne's reign included one of dual imposture when the Cossack settlements of southern Russia threw up a team of two pretenders posing as Peter the Great's sons Alexis Petrovich and Peter Petrovich (the one a victim of the knout and the other dead in infancy). After investigation on the usual lines the two impostors were beheaded, their bodies were burnt and the severed heads were exhibited on iron poles.[12]

The Chancellery for Secret Affairs might prove equal to dealing with long familiar phenomena such as Pretenders, even in double harness, but was less able to control two other flourishing Russian institutions. The first was that of the post-Petrine favourites—powerful, flamboyant intriguers who owed their position to the sovereign's personal favour. During Anne's reign three German potentates were particularly important—Field-Marshal Münnich, Count Ostermann and above all Ernst Biron, the Empress's lover, who became particularly notorious for his cruelty. These three overshadowed the political security chief Ushakov, who gained a reputation for ferocity combined with social charm, but did not enter the inner ring of the Empress's most favoured associates. Nor did his Chancellery succeed in keeping the guards garrison of the capital out of politics. Intimidation by officers of the Semyonovsky and Preobrazhensky Guards had helped to secure the election of Catherine I to the throne after Peter the Great's death. Between 1741 and 1801 groups of guardsmen mounted no less than three successful *coups*, each leading to the deposition and violent death of a reigning monarch. The first of these victims, Anne's successor and great nephew Ivan VI, was in no position to defend himself personally, being an infant of only fifteen months when the Tsarevna Elizabeth, the toast of the guards and Peter the Great's younger daughter, placed herself at the head of the Grenadier Company of the Preobrazhenskys on the night of 25-26 November 1741, moving suddenly and swiftly to place the infant Emperor under arrest.

Though Ushakov had not been a supporter of the usurping Empress Elizabeth, he contrived to maintain himself at the head of the Chancellery for Secret Investigations. Among the cases handled by him was that of Nataliya Lopukhin, a social rival of the beautiful Empress and renowned as one of her most attractive subjects. Implicated in 1743 in a plot to dethrone Elizabeth sponsored by the Austrian ambassador to St Petersburg, Nataliya was condemned, together with her husband and son, to death on the wheel—a sentence which the Empress commuted to knouting, tongue-slitting and exile in Siberia.[13] In the context this was an act of clemency, and is a reminder that Elizabeth had reputedly taken an oath on the night of her *coup d'état* never to sign a death sentence if she should succeed in winning the throne.[14]

Though no death sentences were in fact imposed during her reign, this did not unduly hamper the Chancellery for Secret Investigations, which continued to function under a new chief, Alexander Shuvalov. Meanwhile Stephen Sheshkovsky, a clerk in the Chancellery, was gaining an increasing reputation for ruthlessness and efficiency, and he eventually succeeded Shuvalov as head of the Chancellery.

On 21 February 1762 Elizabeth's successor Peter III issued a special manifesto declaring the Chancellery for Secret Investigations abolished. Its files were to be transferred to the Senate under seal and there committed 'to eternal oblivion'.[15] At the same time the formula 'Word and Deed' was declared invalid, punishment being prescribed for any who should invoke it in future.

Thus Peter III accomplished a not uncommon manoeuvre of supreme rulers—that of pretending to do away with a political police authority while in fact allowing it to continue under a new name and different auspices. Two weeks before issuing the manifesto winding up the Chancellery for Secret Investigations, Peter had already created its successor—the Secret Bureau. Though this was to be subordinated to the Senate—and thus received status inferior to that of the Chancellery for Secret Investigations, which had come directly under the monarch—no great changes were contemplated. The new institution was largely manned by officials transferred directly from the old, and was still headed by the feared Sheshkovsky—now appointed Secretary to the Senate.

Only six months after the accession of Peter III the new police organisation signally failed in its cardinal role of protecting the

Autocrat's person when he suffered deposition in a *coup d'état* mounted by the guards regiments of the capital with his estranged and ambitious wife at their head. Thus Catherine the Great became ruling Empress, being a far more flagrant usurper than Peter the Great's daughter Elizabeth, for the new sovereign was not even a Russian, but a German princess who chanced to have been selected as consort to the Russian heir eighteen years earlier. Catherine therefore had every reason to feel vulnerable after seizing power. She herself had just demonstrated how easily the throne could be toppled in a military *coup*, and she was in the position, unusual for an usurper, of grasping power at a time when no less than two legitimately appointed monarchs were still alive. Apart from Peter III, seized by Catherine's accomplices after the *coup d'état*, there was also Ivan VI, who had been held captive for over twenty years since being ousted from the throne in infancy by the usurping Empress Elizabeth.

Peter III survived his arrest and enforced abdication a mere seven days before being murdered in custody by Catherine's henchmen—not, however, with her complicity, so far as the evidence goes. The new monarch's position was greatly strengthened by the murder of the old, as it also was by the rich rewards which she proceeded to lavish on those who had helped her to power, including favours showered on the guards, recently insulted and ill-used by her imprudent husband. On 22 September 1762 a sumptuous coronation ceremony in Moscow helped to consolidate her position further. She also sought to enhance her popularity by confirming the terms of her predecessor's manifesto purporting to abolish the political police. Of abolishing it in reality she had even less intention than had Peter III, for she not only maintained the newly established Secret Bureau in being, but removed it from the control of the Senate as a whole—placing it directly under that body's Procurator-General. His was an office of the greatest importance during her reign, and one to which she would never appoint an official in whose loyalty she had not complete trust.

Within two years of Catherine's accession a lucky accident destroyed the captive Emperor Ivan VI, who was now held in solitary confinement under stringent conditions of secrecy in the Fortress of Schlüsselburg. An officer of the Fortress garrison, Lieutenant Mirovich, conceived the idea of liberating the 'nameless prisoner', as he was called, and of bringing him by boat to St Petersburg and proclaiming him Emperor. It happened, however, that Ivan's jailers were under strict instructions, confirmed by Catherine herself, to kill the prisoner on the spot if any attempt should be made to free him. Thus Ivan came to be stabbed to death before Mirovich could reach his cell, and Mirovich then had no alternative but to give himself up. He stood trial after elaborate investigation, and was publicly beheaded—the first death sentence to be carried out in St Petersburg for twenty-two years,[16] and an indication that the new Empress intended to be ruthless in defending her throne.

With two legitimate sovereigns slain, pretenders to the throne continued to menace the usurping Empress in varying degrees, one of them being outstanding as author of the most dangerous bid to seize power since the days of the False Dmitrys. This was Yemelyan Pugachov, leader of the great revolt of Cossacks and peasants in 1773–4, who gave himself out as Peter III, spoke of Catherine as his wife and set up a mock court of his own while his irregular armies scoured the south-east of European Russia, hanging landlords, burning manor houses and even threatening Moscow itself. Captured after betrayal by his associates, and brought to the old capital in an iron cage, the rebel leader was interrogated by Sheshkovsky before being publicly beheaded and quartered. Meanwhile, special investigating commissions were in action at the scene of the uprising. Empowered to punish offenders on the spot, and having their own troops under command, they sentenced over twenty thousand persons to flogging, exile and death.[17]

Of the Empress's determination to protect her throne from impostors, by-passing when necessary her political police, further evidence was provided when she arranged for the kidnapping, in Leghorn, of 'Princess Tarakanov'—a romantic adventuress who had laid claim to a series of noble titles during journeyings round Europe before committing the fatal indiscretion of passing herself off as a daughter of the Empress Elizabeth of Russia. She thus became one of the few female pretenders to the Russian throne, but perished in the dungeons of the Peter and Paul Fortress in St Petersburg to which she had been shipped by Catherine's agent, Admiral Alexis Orlov.

Meanwhile Sheshkovsky's sinister reputation continued to grow, and he was promoted from Secretary to Chief Secretary of the Chancellery for Secret Investigations. He captured the imagination of contemporaries to a greater extent than any other eighteenth-century Russian head of political police, and many tales were told about his methods of interrogation. His inquisitions often took place in a room festooned with icons, where the groans of knouted victims would mingle with the prayers of the Orthodox Church as chanted by their chief tormentor with a piety which recalls two earlier and more august torturers: Ivan the Terrible and Peter the Great. Sheshkovsky was renowned for his own skill in applying the knout, but confined his administrations to genteel victims, refusing to soil his hands on the lower orders. He commonly began his interrogations by hitting his victim on the jaw with a stick, and his headquarters is said to have contained a room with a special chair. The victim once seated, this device would sink into the floor, depositing the sitter in a cellar where the Chief Secretary's torturers were already waiting for him.[18] Describing himself as a faithful hound of the Empress, Sheshkovsky remained in constant touch with her, receiving detailed instructions in respect of the many political cases in which she maintained an interest. When irritated on one occasion by some misdemeanour of a Madame Kozhin, a Major-General's wife, the Empress told Sheshkovsky to abduct her from a masked ball which she was known to be attending, and to take her off to the Secret Bureau for a whipping before returning her to the ballroom with due courtesy.

The French Revolution of 1789 greatly shocked Catherine, casting over her last years a blight which the execution of Louis XVI in 1793 did nothing to relieve. Frequent references to 'the French mania', 'the French poison', 'the French infection' and so on in police reports and trial documents of the 1790s, as in the Empress's own jottings, show how deeply this impression had penetrated. To these fears of revolution must be ascribed the development of a new sphere of police activity, one which still remains especially characteristic of Russian political security operations: a concern with the activities of imaginative writers. Both under the late Tsar-Emperors and under Communist dictators, Russian writers have been a source of ideas, all too often imported from the politically tainted West, and in the late eighteenth century ideas were already replacing peasants' pitchforks as the main danger to Russia's supreme rulers.

Most important among several police operations of the period was the case of Alexander Radishchev—author of *A Journey from St Petersburg to Moscow*, published in 1790 and containing an outspoken attack on the institutions of autocracy and serfdom in the form of discursive travel notes. The censor having passed it without reading it, the work chanced to fall into Catherine's hands. She was especially horrified by a fragment from an *Ode to Freedom,* praising regicide and invoking Oliver Cromwell with approval. Nor was the great Empress mollified by another chapter which contained a violent satire directed against herself and her Court. Furious, she reprimanded the negligent censor, ordering Radishchev's arrest and consigning him to the terrible Sheshkovsky for interrogation. Radishchev appears to have escaped torture, perhaps because he immediately made full confession and expressed regret for his 'insane book'.[19] Chained like a common malefactor, he was tried and condemned to death by the St Petersburg Criminal Court, a sentence which the Empress graciously commuted to ten years' Siberian exile. Radishchev thus came to repeat his own 'journey from St Petersburg to Moscow', as the first stage of a far longer journey to Irkutsk and beyond. Ill, shivering, with fettered ankles and escorted by an armed sergeant, he jolted along the appalling road until a fast courier overtook the party, bearing an imperial order for the fetters to be removed and for the prisoner to be provided with clothing and money—the result of a further act of clemency won from the Empress by his friends.

Two years later another delinquent writer, Nicholas Novikov, was arrested on the Empress's order. He obediently answered a written questionnaire presented to him in custody by Sheshkovsky and containing seventy-five items, but refused to renounce his convictions. He was sentenced by imperial Ukaz to fifteen years' imprisonment in Schlüsselburg Fortress for his activities as a Freemason and publisher of works contradicting the tenets of Orthodox Christianity.

After four years in the dungeons Novikov, now broken in health, was released by order of the Emperor Paul, who came to the throne in 1796 on the death of his hated mother Catherine and celebrated his accession by undoing many of her ordinances. Radishchev was permitted to return from Siberia to more comfortable exile, under secret surveillance by the police, on his own estates in European Russia. Paul was, however, merely spiting his mother's ghost, not introducing an age of comparative freedom, and was soon finding victims of his own. Where Catherine had acted on comparatively rational, if over-severe, calculation of dangers to her person and realm, her emotionally unstable son was liable to interpret the accidental inflexion of an eyebrow or cut of a jacket as 'impudence' and to dispense savage, sudden arbitrary punishment in the course of a momentary tantrum. He was especially severe on officers who chanced to earn his displeasure during one of the many military parades from which he would despatch delinquents straight to Siberia or the dungeons of his fortresses. Paul did not abolish the Secret Bureau—a creation of his father Peter III, not of his hated mother—and it continued to function under the direction of his Procurator-General of the Senate. Meanwhile the Bureau had acquired a new head, Alexander Makarov, in succession to Sheshkovsky, who died in 1794. The new security chief was, however, a comparatively obscure figure who never attained the notoriety of his feared predecessor. Nor did he succeed in averting the unpopular Emperor's assassination in his bed chamber where Paul was battered with a golden snuffbox and strangled with a scarf by a mêlée of drunken officers at dead of night on 11–12 March 1801.

The abolition of the Secret Bureau was among the first steps undertaken by Alexander I on succeeding to the throne in 1801. In a manifesto of 2 April, issued within three weeks of his father's assassination, the new Tsar declared that 'in a well-ordered State all crimes should be embraced, tried and punished by common law. We have considered it expedient to abolish and destroy forever not only the name but also the actual operation of the Secret Bureau, ordering that all its cases should be committed to the State Archives to eternal oblivion.'[20]

Details extracted from the archives in question by M. N. Gernet, the chief Soviet authority on Russian prison history in the Imperial period, show that in March 1801 at least seven hundred detainees were held in custody or exile under the auspices of the Secret Bureau. The victims were distributed among five fortresses, two monasteries and other places of detention and exile in twenty-six provinces of European Russia and Siberia, as was recorded in registers drawn up under the new Tsar.[21] One striking feature to emerge from the review now undertaken of the defunct Secret Bureau was the frequency with which no record whatever could be found, either in the office of the Bureau itself or in any local place of detention, of the reason why a given prisoner had been consigned to the dungeons in the first place, sometimes several decades earlier. One victim was a craftsman from Barnaulsky Zavod, a certain Vityazev, who had been held in Yekaterinburg jail at the behest of the Holy Synod since 1757. Neither was any charge against him on record, nor could the man himself offer a lucid explanation of his presence in jail, having become senile and mentally deranged during more than forty years' imprisonment. Among the Secret Bureau's captives a fair number turned out to be army officers committed at the caprice of the Emperor Paul— this practice was particularly common in the last year of his reign, a period of galloping paranoia. Many of the officers in question were held for no reason which could be discovered, or on vague grounds such as 'impudence'. Religious dissenters were also prominent among the Bureau's prisoners, and these included over two hundred Dukhobors immured in the Fortress of Dunamünde. The same fortress also held a certain Kakhovsky, imprisoned for uttering criticisms of the taxation system and for other remarks tending to corrupt morals. His misdemeanours also included a comment on the assassination of Julius Caesar: 'If only our [Tsar] could meet the same fate!'[22] A serf pretender to the throne, who gave himself out as Peter III, was in the same fortress, as also was a Major Passek, author of an insulting lampoon directed against Catherine the Great in which the initial letters of each line made up the letters of her name.

Many of the seven hundred odd prisoners of the defunct Secret Bureau were now freed on the new Tsar's orders, but by no means all. For example, a daughter of the executed Pugachov failed to obtain her liberty. Originally incarcerated in Keksholm Fortress in 1774, she died—still exiled to Keksholm, though no longer in prison—sixty years later.

The abolition of the Secret Bureau was one of many indications that Alexander I was minded to preside over an era of political relaxation. One early act of clemency was his *Ukaz* of 27 September 1801 expressly forbidding the use of torture, which he issued on learning that the authorities in Kazan had subjected a suspected arsonist to such an ordeal with the aim of extorting his confession to a crime of which he was in fact innocent.[23] Yet many practices scarcely distinguishable from torture remained on the statute book and were frequently applied, sometimes on the Tsar's own direct instructions. They included passing through the ranks, a military punishment which might involve several thousand blows and often proved fatal. They also included the atrocious knout—and the branding of the faces of convicted criminals. Later in his reign Alexander abolished the practice of slitting nostrils. In theory he was prepared to consider doing away with the knout, but went no further than setting up a committee to consider the matter. Nor did he renounce the autocratic privilege of flinging recalcitrant citizens into his dungeons on impulse. In 1820, for example, a certain Moshchinsky was consigned to the Schlüsselburg Fortress for life. Having written a lampoon against the Tsar, he was officially designated as 'immoral, turbulent and beyond hope of improvement'.[24]

It was characteristic of Alexander I's well-known duplicity to proclaim the formal abolition of the Secret Bureau while permitting other secret police organisations to flourish under different guises. Even in the early, 'liberal', years of the reign such activity never entirely ceased. The Military Governor-General of St Petersburg had all along maintained a network of his own secret agents. In October 1802 he furnished a list of these to the Minister of the Interior, claiming that this 'secret police office' concerned itself 'with all objects, actions and speeches that tend toward the dissolution of the autocratic power and the security of the government, as for example: oral and written incitements, plots, wild or inflammatory speeches, acts of treason'.[25] Within a few years the Tsar had placed responsibility for political security under two specially constituted committees—those of 5 September 1805 and 13 January 1807. The latter body was put in charge of the Governor-General of St Petersburg's security force, and continued to function, at least nominally, until 1829, being to some extent a reincarnated Secret Bureau. Such activities remained repugnant to the liberal side of the Tsar's nature and he probably regarded them as a temporary expedient, necessary in order to keep the country under firm control during his absence with the Russian armies fighting against Napoleon. Yet Napoleon's defeat in the wars of 1812–15 only saw a further increase in Russian political police activity. Now apparently indifferent to the internal development of his Empire, Alexander had consigned its management to the all-powerful General Arakcheyev, who became a kind of domestic dictator. Alexander himself, renowned as the conqueror of Napoleon and a great leader on the highest levels of political and military strategy, entered a phase of religious mania in which his style of political leadership grew more and more apathetic.

Under these conditions police activity became an increasingly confused affair involving yet more competing organisations. From 1811 to 1819 a Ministry of Police functioned, one of its branches being a Special Chancellery devoted to political affairs. This Chancellery was placed under the direction of De Sanglen, son of a French émigré, while his superior as Minister of Police was a

Russian, General Balashov. Both Balashov and De Sanglen were transferred to other work in 1812, the year following the formation of the Police Ministry, but not before Alexander had made use of them to effect the sudden and dramatic arrest of his chief statesman Speransky, who had incurred widespread unpopularity in influential circles and was becoming a liability to the Tsar. Alexander conducted this affair with typical deviousness, insisting that the head of the Special Chancellery should spy on his own Minister as well as on Speransky, but leaving both the Police Minister and his Head of Chancellery in doubt until the very last moment as to who in fact faced arrest—Speransky or they.[26]

After functioning for only eight years the Ministry of Police was abolished and responsibility for the police reverted to the Ministry of the Interior—to which the Special Chancellery was transferred under its head, Maxim Von Vock. Meanwhile, outside the Ministry of the Interior, a variety of other security organisations continued to operate. In 1821 a special body of field security police was set up with the task of spying on the army, while the secret police of the Military Governor-General of St Petersburg still continued to function, as also did a security apparatus maintained by Arakcheyev.

While these bodies were busily engaged in thwarting each other, tailing each other's agents and hounding foreigners—for the period during and after the Napoleonic wars was one of acute official xenophobia—a major revolutionary conspiracy was all the time secretly gathering strength within the armed forces, though these were a special object of scrutiny by some of the police bodies mentioned above.

Owing to their unsuccessful *coup d'état* of December 1825 the conspirators in question have come to be known as Decembrists. Theirs was the first truly revolutionary movement in Russia, having political aims more sophisticated than those of the numerous revolts or palace revolutions of earlier times. Unlike the sponsors of such movements, the Decembrists did not merely aim to replace one Tsar with another more to their liking, but had sweeping institutional changes in mind, including the introduction of constitutional government and the abolition of serfdom. The most important single influence in forming their ideas was contact with western Europe obtained during the Napoleonic wars, an experience which made the Russian occupying forces painfully conscious of their own country's political, economic and social backwardness. Arriving home after the wars with the high hopes of domestic reform natural to returning heroes, they became bitterly disillusioned as they fell foul of the increasingly reactionary policies administered by Arakcheyev—a foretaste of the experiences which awaited the conquering Red Army of 1945 at the hands of Marshal Beria's NKVD. Far from enjoying any relaxation of discipline, Alexander I's victorious army was given over to an orgy of drill parades. Brutal floggings of soldiers remained in vogue, while the rank and file were still compelled to serve over twenty-five years with the colours, and even those lucky enough to be demobilised must revert to the status of serfs.

It was, therefore, in an atmosphere of growing dissatisfaction and intellectual ferment that Russian officers now began to form political secret societies. These split into two main groups. Based on St Petersburg and Moscow, the northern conspirators were the less extreme, while the southerners, headed by the forceful Colonel Pestel, inclined to radical solutions. The northerners plotted to set up a constitutional monarchy, the southerners wanted a republic. Some of them wished to begin operations by annihilating the entire imperial family, and at one time they proposed to recruit a suicide squad of assassins for this purpose.

The differences between the two groups were especially marked in their plans for the future of the police. Nikita Muravyov, chief theoretician of the northern group, proposed to dismiss the existing police, replacing it with an elected force. Pestel, by contrast, wished to have the citizenry of his ideal Russia dragooned by a 'higher' police set above the law and placed in control of the ordinary police, while operating a network of secret agents and a semi-military gendarmerie.[27] It is tempting to say that Pestel, like so many other revolutionaries, was less concerned to abolish tyranny than to transfer its exercise to his own hands. Be that as it may, his proposed police organisation foreshadows the Third Section and Corps of Gendarmes, as later set up by Nicholas I after the collapse of the Decembrist movement. By that time Pestel's plans had become known to the new Emperor, who was not averse to studying the views of political enemies, or to adopting the ideas of those whom he was engaged in crushing as individuals. Thus a revolutionary helped to inspire what was to become one of the autocracy's main instruments for suppressing revolution.

During the years preceding their attempted *coup* the Decembrists recruited new members and discussed their plans with a degree of immunity astonishing in a country riddled with spies. The explanation lies partly in the chaotic condition of the various competing police organisations, and partly in the Tsar's personal reluctance to sanction decisive measures. Typical of this attitude was his well-known comment, made in 1821 after the GOC of the Corps of Guards, Prince Vasilchikov, had submitted a report on the officers' secret societies which were already forming precise revolutionary aims. 'I have shared and encouraged these illusions and errors myself [Alexander remarked]. It is not for me to punish them.'[28] In the same year General Benckendorff, Chief of Staff of the Corps of Guards, submitted to Alexander a Memorandum on the Secret Societies, in which he named several leaders of the conspiracy. The Tsar showed little interest, however, and Benckendorff even incurred disfavour by this display of zeal.[29]

Towards the end of 1825 several circumstantial reports on Decembrist activities reached the authorities. One came from a certain John Sherwood, an Englishman born in Kent, whose father had come to Russia to help to install weaving machinery during the boy's infancy. Sherwood, an NCO in a regiment stationed in southern Russia, secretly denounced the conspiracy to the Tsar. He was ordered to rejoin his unit and continue his reports on the developing plot, now as an accredited police spy, but no more decisive action followed. Meanwhile several other informers were contributing further information on the plot, and the conspirators might have been arrested in time but for the sudden death of the Tsar, which occurred at Taganrog on 19 November 1825.

The Autocrat's unexpected decease seemed to offer the Decembrists a heaven-sent opportunity, such as was unlikely to recur, of ending the autocratic system altogether—all the more so as one of Alexander's most unfortunate legacies to Russia was a dynastic crisis which involved an interregnum lasting seventeen days in the capital. During this time it was not clear whether the new Tsar was to be Alexander's eldest surviving brother Constantine or the second eldest brother Nicholas. The hiatus began on 27 November, when news of Alexander's death reached St Petersburg, and lasted until 14 December, when the Grand Duke Nicholas at last decided to assume power and to signalise this by having the oath of allegiance administered to himself as Tsar. In deciding to assert his right to the throne at this stage Nicholas had delayed dangerously, for the Decembrists were feverishly seeking to exploit a situation which seemed to play into their hands. Conveniently for them it could be made to appear—incorrectly—that Nicholas was engaged in usurping the throne from the rightful Emperor

Constantine. The Decembrists were therefore able to persuade a number of military units to revolt in favour of Constantine and to marshal them on the Senate Square in St Petersburg. Their intention was to intimidate the Senate, the most august corporate institution of the Empire, into proclaiming a new, provisional government by representatives of the Decembrists. This plan might even have succeeded had not Nicholas anticipated the danger just in time. He arranged for the Senate to swear allegiance to himself at 7 a.m. on 14 December. This was two hours before dawn, and some four hours before the first mutinous unit under Decembrist control, a section of the Moscow Regiment, paraded in defiance on the Senate Square.

It is conceivable, though highly unlikely, that these few hours were instrumental in postponing the overthrow of the Imperial system by nearly ninety-two years—until February 1917. As it was, the new Tsar's artillery easily battered the mutineers into submission, after the failure of several attempts to talk them into surrender. A revolt by the southern Decembrists was crushed a few weeks later.

The Third Section under Nicholas I
1826–1855

The rising of 14 December 1825 became a crucial episode in the evolution of the Russian political police owing to its impact on the new Emperor Nicholas I, long feared in the army as a savage disciplinarian. On the night following the revolt he began a searching investigation into the conspiracy which had so rudely shaken his throne. Within hours of driving the mutineers out of the Senate Square in the evening dusk, the Tsar had set up an interrogation room in a hall of the nearby Hermitage, adjoining the Winter Palace. Arrests proceeded apace, and Nicholas was eager to question all the conspirators in person. They were brought in to face him with their hands bound, and he at once showed himself a police interrogator of considerable talent and flexibility as he hectored and insulted some of the prisoners, shouting and stamping his feet, but adroitly won the confidence of others by displays of sympathy. Anticipating the use of arc-lights in a more technologically advanced civilisation, he made one prisoner face a cluster of burning candles, glared into his eyes and demanded a complete confession. Such was the force of the young Emperor's personality or charm that some of the prisoners obediently admitted their part in the revolt. One impressive feature of Nicholas as interrogator was his persistence in continuing almost uninterruptedly round the clock—the Soviet 'conveyor' system in reverse, it might be claimed, since it was the interrogator, not the prisoner, who was deprived of sleep.

Among those personally questioned by the Tsar were some hundred and fifty arrested persons, whom he dispatched to the Peter and Paul Fortress with notes to the Commandant stating how each should be treated. Nicholas's prescriptions varied according to the degree of co-operation given by each individual. Some were flung into irons on his orders, the Tsar personally specifying whether ankle-fetters, handcuffs or both were to be used, while one individual who particularly displeased him was to be 'put . . . in chains so that he cannot move'.[1]

Though the new Tsar took such opportunities of venting his spite on certain victims, his chief concern was to unravel every thread of the revolutionary conspiracy. With this in view he set up an Investigating Committee which spent six months probing into the affair, Decembrist plans to assassinate the Emperor forming a central point in the inquiry.[2] That investigation completed, a Higher Criminal Court was appointed, consisting of seventy-two dignitaries of State and Church, who were to judge the main accused, numbering 121 persons. Tried *in absentia*, the Decembrists languished in solitary confinement in their dungeons, unaware that their case had even come before a court until they were suddenly summoned to hear an official proclaim sentence. That there should be death sentences Nicholas had decided in advance, and he also made it clear to the court in oblique but unambiguous terms that execution should be by hanging.[3] This was, in the context, an example of imperial clemency since the court's original sentence—pronounced on the five accused considered most culpable—had been to an even more barbarous form of death by quartering. Many death sentences originally pronounced by the court were commuted to terms of imprisonment. Five, however, still stood, and the Russian revolutionary movement thus gained its first martyrs in Pestel, Ryleyev, Sergey Muravyov-Apostol, Bestuzhev-Ryumin and Kakhovsky—hanged with scandalous incompetence on a bastion of the Peter and Paul Fortress on 13 July 1826. Over a hundred others received sentence of prison or exile, being submitted to the ordeal of civil execution by having swords formally broken over their heads. Their officers' uniforms were torn off them and burnt in their presence, after which they began the long journey to Siberia wearing the customary foot fetters and escorted by gendarmes. Such was the fate of the Decembrists proper—that is, of the officers and gentlemen who had led the revolt. As for the peasant soldiers who had followed their lead, those considered particularly guilty received sentences of flogging so severe (up to 12,000 strokes 'through the ranks') that they were the equivalent of the death penalty, while the mutinous units as a whole were mostly transferred to service in the Caucasus. In all, the Decembrist Affair provoked over three thousand arrests between December 1825 and March 1826.[4]

The Decembrists' conditions of prison or exile varied greatly and they remained a leading preoccupation of the Tsar's. He took sufficient interest in them, for example, to approve the design of a new prison in far-eastern Siberia containing windowless cells—a provision which caused an explosion of indignation in St Petersburg society and was later relaxed. Despite this characteristic detail, the Decembrists as a whole were never treated with harshness remotely comparable to that of a Soviet or Hitlerite concentration camp. As for Mazour's statement ('rarely has there been a judicial case in which defendants suffered more savage and inequitable punishment than that of the Decembrists')[5]—unhappily for humanity, such procedures have been anything but rare, as many later pages of the present study will show. Savage and inequitable though the Emperor's justice certainly was, he explicitly abjured the kind of witch hunt whereby ever-widening circles of suspects, entirely innocent of conspiratorial intent, tend to become implicated in guilt by association. In his manifesto of 13 July, issued in connexion with the execution of Pestel and his associates, Nicholas expressly stated: 'Let no one dare to make family relationship [with the accused] the subject for rebuke. This is forbidden by the civil law and even more so by the Christian law.'[6] Though the proceedings against the Decembrists were a gross mockery of a trial, the authorities were at least genuinely concerned to establish the complicity or non-complicity of individuals in the rising. Nicholas was not inaugurating a reign of terror for terror's sake, for which reason his Police State remained a primitive affair, judged by modern standards—while yet representing a considerable advance on the level attained under Alexander I.

Having stamped out the Decembrist conspiracy, the Tsar set up an organisation designed to make such episodes impossible in future. In the establishment of this new police authority General Alexander Benckendorff became prime mover. Like many other high-ranking officers of the Russian army, Benckendorff was of Baltic German origin, and had served as a fighting commander during the Napoleonic wars. On the day of the Decembrist Revolt he had earned the new Tsar's gratitude by his firmness in handling troops stationed on the Vasilyevsky Island, which faces the scene of the uprising across the River Neva. Impressed by Bencken-dorff's loyalty, the Emperor appointed him to the Investigating Committee set up after the revolt. When, therefore, in January of the following year, Benckendorff submitted to Nicholas a project 'for the institution of a higher police', his ideas were assured of a sympathetic hearing.

Benckendorff's proposal begins by rejecting the concept of a *secret* police, such as 'terrifies honest men, but is detected by scoundrels'. After a brief reference to the importance of intercept-ing correspondence—one lesson which the police of earlier reigns hardly needed to learn—he stated that the new organisation must operate from a known centre, being feared and respected for the 'moral qualities' of whoever should be its chief. That person should combine the offices of Minister of Police and Inspector of Gendarmes.[7] The Emperor, however, proved unwilling to re-constitute a Ministry of Police, such as had existed between 1811 and 1819, since he wished to have the new security authority under his direct personal control. He decided to make it a part of his personal Chancellery, a body which he considerably expanded on succeeding to the throne. An *Ukaz* of 3 July 1826 accordingly created the Third Section of His Imperial Majesty's Own Chan-cellery, Benckendorff being appointed as its head. A few days earlier Benckendorff had also been appointed Chief of Gendarmes. From the outset, therefore, the new 'higher police' consisted of two bodies distinct from each other, but united under the com-mand of a single individual. This dual authority was to answer for political security as a whole, since civilian and military per-sonnel both came within its terms of reference. As a 'higher' police the new organisation was to take precedence over the lower police, which continued to concern itself with ordinary crime under the Ministry of the Interior. An attempt—far from successful—was thus made to avoid the rivalry between competing authorities typical of Alexander I's days.

Of the two bodies constituting the new higher police, the Corps of Gendarmes remained an essentially military organisation, sub-ordinated to the Ministry of War for administrative purposes and partly recruited from the Gendarme Regiment which had sup-plied a military police force since 1815. New members were en-listed from the army, not among civilians. To distinguish the Corps from any kind of secret police, gendarmes were conspicuous in white gloves and a sky-blue tunic contrasting with the drab green worn by members of the civil service in general.

The gendarmerie was a far larger organisation than the Third Section. By the end of the reign the Corps numbered up to eight or nine thousand men, whereas the Third Section comprised only some forty officials, mainly civilians.[8] It was, however, the Third Section which formed the nerve centre of the higher police, and it has been said to have exercised executive authority over the gendarmerie, though such a question of precedence could not arise in acute form since the same officer always commanded both bodies. Thus, by virtue of the special trust reposed in Benckendorff by the Emperor, the Third Section became, almost overnight, the senior office of the State, outranking in effect all other governmental institutions. The senior status of the higher police naturally aroused the resentment of other departments, and not least of the Ministry of the Interior, which was responsible for the lower police. A running bureaucratic feud between Third Section and Ministry of the Interior continued throughout the period of the Third Section's existence, from 1826 to 1880. The tone was set for this competition only a few weeks after the establishment of the Third Section, when Von Vock, its Director of Chancellery, wrote to his chief Benckendorff to explain that plain-clothes agents of the lower police were keeping himself and his Third Section colleagues under surveillance. Even more insulting, a particularly low grade of operative had been chosen for the job—'blockheads pointed out by all the street urchins'.[9]

Despite such attempts by other institutions to assert themselves, the Third Section was able to maintain its pre-eminence. Universally acknowledged as the second most powerful individual in the Empire, Benckendorff was in regular contact with the Emperor and was his constant companion during the lengthy tours of inspection carried out by Nicholas inside and outside his realm. On these occasions the two men usually travelled in the same carriage. As a further sign of his affection and confidence, Nicholas always kept a bust of Benckendorff in his study.

By contrast with the Emperor, that ferociously energetic martinet, Benckendorff was a lackadaisical individual renowned for his absent-mindedness and even liable to forget his own name—there were said to be occasions when he had to refresh his memory on this point by consulting one of his visiting cards. Charming, courteous and urbane, he was a 'ladies' man' by vocation rather than a scourge of non-conformist citizens, and was generally judged neither particularly active nor particularly intelligent.

Some lack of perception on his part seems indicated by a remark made in connexion with the serious illness which overtook him in 1837, when he reflected complacently that he was 'almost the first of all secret police chiefs whose death people feared, and who have not been pursued at the edge of the grave by a single complaint'.[10] This was certainly an illusion, though it is also true that Benckendorff was never rated such a sinister figure as the various 'dreaded' secret police chiefs of the eighteenth century. He 'did not [one authority states] succeed in winning, let alone the affection, even the hatred of those whom the Third Department [Section] oppressed'.[11] Moreover, Benckendorff did at least impart an outwardly civilised gloss to higher police proceedings through the unfailing courtesy of his manner, though his politeness was often of the icy variety which expresses well-disciplined contempt.

Benckendorff died in 1844, after heading the Third Section for eighteen years. Only three other higher police officials attained comparable prominence under Nicholas I. Maxim Von Vock, a civilian official and—like Benckendorff—of German origin, was the only senior administrator to enter the new body with extensive experience of political police work under Alexander I. Von Vock was transferred to the Third Section in 1826 as Director of Chancellery after being head of the Special (i.e. political police) Chancellery of the Ministry of the Interior, and he brought some of his subordinates with him. Until his death in 1831, Von Vock functioned as Benckendorff's second-in-command, responsible for processing the vast quantities of denunciations and petitions which inundated the Third Section from all parts of the Empire. From these Von Vock would make extracts in legible handwriting for Benckendorff's consideration and for submission to the Tsar if necessary—as it often was, owing to Nicholas's passion for the endless minutiae of administration.

An important part was played by Lieutenant-General Leonty Dubbelt, who also appears to have been of partly non-Russian origin. After some years as gendarme Chief of Staff, Dubbelt became fully-fledged second-in-command in 1839, when he was also appointed Controller *(upravlyayushchy)* of the Third Section under Benckendorff as Head Controller, these new titles being introduced in the same year. Retaining this dual post until his retirement in 1856, Dubbelt was by common consent the most intelligent of the higher police chiefs of the reign, and was more generally feared than any other, though he too was outstandingly courteous in manner—even by the high standards of the political police. After Benckendorff's death in 1844, Dubbelt became *de facto* chief of the political police—but without rising to be titular head. That office passed to Count Alexis Orlov, Head Controller of the Third Section and Chief of Gendarmes from 1844 to 1856. Orlov was notoriously indolent. Lacking all vocation for security work, he is said to have remarked with regard to the political police that 'I do not comprehend the utility of this institution'.[12] He was more interested in diplomacy than in political investigation, and owed his appointment to his friendship with the Tsar. This was an eloquent tribute to Nicholas's refusal to entertain guilt by association, since Alexis Orlov happened to be the brother of a leading Decembrist, Michael Orlov. It was as if Stalin had put a relative of Zinovyev's in charge of the OGPU.

Whereas the Third Section remained a small though expanding office, functioning largely within the capital, the Corps of Gendarmes was a far-flung organisation designed to penetrate every cranny of the realm where sedition might rear its head. With this in view the Empire was divided into gendarme districts, of which there were five at first, and later eight, each under the command of a gendarme General and containing about ten provinces. In smaller centres officers of lesser rank acted as staff officers with wide—indeed, unlimited—discretionary powers to intervene in local affairs. Despite his relatively low rank, the gendarme staff officer of a province was empowered to overrule even his provincial Governor, who in all other respects could behave like an all-powerful satrap. Regional gendarme staff officers had mounted gendarme units under command, and they engaged their own secret agents to spy on the local populations. Their reports swelled the floods of paper reaching the Third Section from its own secret agents in St Petersburg.

It was in keeping with the militaristic atmosphere of the reign that gendarmes were recruited from the military—attracted by higher rates of pay and other privileges, but often repelled by the stigma which continued to attach to political police work. This continued despite successful attempts to attract into the gendarmes young officers of 'good family' and polite address whose interrogations of political suspects were commonly preceded by the offer of tea and a good cigar. Scented, cigar-smoking and often speaking fluent French, a gendarme officer thus tended to be at least the social equal of his quarry in an age when political subversion, now greatly reduced in scope, remained very largely the prerogative of the gentry.

According to official myth the higher police was less a scourge of subversion than a welfare association set up to protect widows and orphans. It was said that Benckendorff once asked the Emperor to give a directive for the activities of the Third Section, whereupon the Emperor reputedly held out a handkerchief, remarking: 'Here is all the directive you need. The more tears you wipe away with this handkerchief, the more faithfully you will serve my aims.'[13] Whether the story is true or not, the handkerchief is said to have been preserved for many years under a glass cover in the police archives.

Nicholas's higher police was not circumscribed in its operations by any narrow terms of reference, having a roving brief to enquire into 'all matters whatever'. Among them were legal processes, which were in a particularly confused condition, with some two million unsettled cases awaiting the judgement of the courts in 1826. The gendarmes were empowered to intervene and cut red tape in the courts and everywhere else, and also to deal with such problems as the counterfeiting of the currency and the activities of religious schismatics and sectarians, besides which extensive censorship responsibilities also fell to the higher police. When, in the 1840s, Russia embarked on building her first railway line of any importance—that between St Petersburg and Moscow—a squadron of gendarmes was detached to police this project, after which gendarme units were regularly used as railway police, their blue uniforms being a familiar sight on the stations.

Control of foreign visitors—always a source of deepest suspicion to the Russian official mind—naturally fell within the province of the political police. The movements of aliens within the Empire were under constant surveillance as the security authorities adopted practices eventually extended by the Okhrana and the Soviet secret police. In 1833 an American envoy was already reporting to his President that 'you can scarcely hire a servant who is not an agent of the secret police',[14] while intercepted correspondence was a normal phenomenon, often handled so carelessly that the police replaced broken seals with wax of a different colour. One Englishwoman reports an occasion when a large stack of wood was piled up outside a visitor's hotel room and contained a space where a man could keep the occupant under observation —a primitive 'bugging' device.[15] Nor was it easy for a foreigner, once inside Russia, to leave the country, since regulations required him to give notice of intention to depart by advertising in the newspapers at least three times. As a parallel to the surveillance of foreigners within Russia, the Third Section also maintained spies abroad, beginning in 1832 with the immediate intention of observing émigré Polish organisations, and then branching out into other departments of espionage. Russians were closely observed during their foreign travels, and one authority reports the amazement of such travellers when confronted on return with a full account of their doings in foreign parts. 'In the drawing-rooms of London and Paris he [the travelling Russian] dreads that the eye of the secret police may be upon him.'[16] The same informant also remarks that, where the secret police was concerned, 'its very spies are spied upon'—in which observation one seems to discern particularly distinctly the shape of things to come.

Such were the main activities of Nicholas I's higher police. Despite the emphasis on politeness, the gendarmes were feared and detested, while the Third Section was widely regarded as a resurrected form of the old Secret Bureau once so dreaded by the subjects of Catherine the Great and the Emperor Paul. But though the Third Section is often described as 'all-powerful', it was in a sense powerless, since it functioned essentially as an extension of the brain and will of the most autocratic of Russia's nineteenth-century sovereigns, being the chief instrument whereby Nicholas imposed discipline on Russia. It was, therefore, appropriate that this crowned martinet should have earned the nickname Gendarme of Europe. Nicholas was accustomed to keep his subjects 'up to the mark' by descending in person on offices, army units, schools and other institutions, dismissing the incompetent and praising the well-intentioned, then disappearing on another errand while the dust settled on the scene of his former visitation, leaving things very much unchanged. Such, too, was the function of the gendarmes, acting as an extension of the Tsar—and with equally little effect. Their staff officers numbered only a few hundred in a nation of fifty million administered by notoriously incompetent, corrupt, ill-paid, venal officials who might be briefly terrorised into postures of simulated activity or honesty when a Colonel of Gendarmes, resplendent in sky-blue serge, white gloves and plumed helmet rode up with a posse of his troopers. Such methods could not, however, effectively shatter the torpor of an Empire in which the majority of citizens were still peasant slaves. Nor did the Imperial Mounted Police acquire a reputation for always 'getting its man'—despite a bonus of ten roubles a head for doing so.

In containing subversion within the Empire, the higher police was generally successful—with certain exceptions great and small. Beginning with the Decembrist Revolt, the reign saw two sizeable further outbreaks in the Polish Rebellion of 1830–1, and the revolt of the Novgorod military colonists in 1831. The former event led to the extension of the gendarme system to Poland (part of the Russian Empire since the Partitions of the late eighteenth century and the Congress of Vienna). The outbreak in the Novgorod area was a mutiny of dissatisfied soldier-peasants. Both risings were brutally suppressed by military force. These events apart, revolutionary activity within the Empire remained at a low ebb, since so many political dissidents had been involved in the Decembrist conspiracy, and had therefore been immobilised in Siberian exile or prison at the outset of the reign.

Other conspiracies or outbreaks were of limited scope—for example, the circle of the Kritsky brothers in Moscow. They planned to start an uprising by distributing proclamations, and also intended to murder the Tsar and his family. This plan was a curious mixture of the vague and the concrete. On the one hand the attempt on the Tsar's life was to be postponed for ten years. On the other hand the assassins had already collected an armoury for use in the assassination, consisting of a shotgun, a dagger and a Turkish yatagan. Betrayed by an *agent provocateur*, members of the group—some mere youths—were severely punished, being scattered among the dungeons of the Empire.[17] Another mutiny of the period was planned in the depths of Siberia. The ringleader was the sentenced Decembrist Sukhinov, who had travelled all the way on foot, wearing foot-irons, over a period of eighteen months. At the Zerentuysk mine he plotted to raise a convicts' revolt, after which the mutineers would march on Chita and rescue the Decembrists imprisoned there—a plan which foreshadows the enslaved Colonel Mekhteyev's desperate bid to seize the Vorkuta concentration camp network in 1948. Sukhinov's slave revolt was betrayed by an associate, and he was sentenced to death. On the day before the projected execution he hanged himself with the strap of his foot-irons. His fellow-conspirators faced flogging or firing squad.[18]

Nicholas I's reign was remarkable for collisions between writers and police anticipated by the clash between Radishchev and Sheshkovsky in the late eighteenth century. In this renewed confrontation the adventures of Alexander Pushkin, Russia's greatest poet, played a revealing part. Between leaving school in 1817 and his death in a duel twenty years later, Pushkin was a constant concern of the security machine—first to that of Alexander I and then to the Third Section.

A precocious writer, this long-haired youth of partly Ethiopian descent early riled authority through his eccentricities of dress, irregular love affairs, spontaneous vitality and habit of saying or writing whatever first came into his head—all qualities calculated to provoke persecution by conformists. In 1820 he was exiled to southern Russia for writing such subversive lyrics as *Freedom* (1817) and *The Village* (1819). These and other scurrilous or revolutionary sallies could not be published, but circulated widely in manuscript. In 1824 police seized a private letter in which Pushkin expressed sympathy with atheism—an occasion for sending him to a quieter place of exile, on his family estate at Mikhaylovskoye in the Pskov Province of western Russia. Marooned in this backwater, Pushkin chafed at the boredom of country life. The end of 1825 brought new cause for alarm—that he might be implicated in the Decembrist conspiracy, for he had been the revolutionary movement's unofficial bard all along. Many of the conspirators were his personal friends, but they had deliberately not recruited Pushkin on a more regular basis, partly to spare so great a poet, partly to spare themselves—since he lacked the elementary discretion essential to any successful plotter.

Even in his rural retreat at Mikhaylovskoye, Pushkin was not forgotten by the police of the capital, especially after he had been secretly denounced for fomenting peasant unrest. A police agent, one Boshnyak, was dispatched to investigate, and set off for Pskov armed with a warrant granting him discretion to arrest Pushkin if he should judge it necessary. Adopting the cover of a travelling botanist, Boshnyak toured the Pushkin country, questioning innkeepers, landowners, peasants and clergy. The inquiry confirmed that the young poet was indeed behaving unconventionally, having attended a local fair wearing a broad-brimmed straw hat and a peasant shirt eccentrically belted with pink ribbon, besides carrying an iron rod as a walking stick. He had once asked a servant to turn his horse loose, since 'every animal should be free'.[19] No more sinister example of libertarian agitation came to light, however, and the bogus botanist therefore went his way, leaving Pushkin in peace.

Soon afterwards the tranquillity of Mikhaylovskoye was rudely shattered by a gendarme officer who bore peremptory instructions for Pushkin to present himself before the Emperor in Moscow, where Nicholas was still in residence after his coronation. The uprooted poet was ordered to cover the five hundred odd miles from his country retreat with all possible speed, travelling day and night, and accompanied by an imperial courier who could command a relay of the best horses. Arriving travel-worn and dirty four days later, Pushkin was brought before a monarch always impeccably dressed in military uniform, and the contrast between tall, icy sovereign and short, fiery poet must indeed have been striking. In this, the most celebrated interview ever to have taken place between Russian bard and Russian Autocrat, the Emperor is said to have inquired what Pushkin's attitude would have been had he chanced to find himself in St Petersburg on the previous 14 December. Pushkin replied frankly that he would have joined the Decembrists.[20] Dangerous though this reply may have seemed, the Tsar agreed to free Pushkin from exile if he would stop publishing subversive material. When Pushkin complained of the difficulty of publishing any material whatever owing to censorship restrictions, the Tsar promised that he himself would act as Pushkin's censor. The two parted on excellent terms, Pushkin little suspecting that he had fallen into a carefully baited trap, for it was Nicholas's intention to place him under the direct tutelage of the political police.

What followed was less an outright persecution of Pushkin than persistent niggling interference with the poet's life and work. The many written exchanges between Pushkin and Benckendorff maintained the lofty level of courtesy incumbent on gendarmes, but this did not conceal the true attitude of the police chief to Russia's premier poet—that of a nursemaid towards a disobedient infant. 'He is a very naughty boy [Benckendorff once wrote to the Emperor], but it will be to our advantage if we can direct his pen and words.'[21] Precisely this thought must have crossed many a Russian official's mind throughout the ages as he has contemplated the rich field of author-police relations, trying to assess the political profit and loss to be drawn from a Dostoyevsky or a Gorky, or from such lightweights as an Ehrenburg and a Yevtushenko.

The running battle between Pushkin and Benckendorff was a complex affair. One leading bone of contention was Pushkin's

verse play *Boris Godunov*. Barely had his concordat with the
Emperor been agreed before the poet was in trouble for infringing
its provisions—never precisely defined—by reading the play aloud
to circles of friends on several occasions. Then permission to publish the work was withheld for five years, involving Pushkin in
considerable loss of income. He also suffered the humiliation of
receiving the Emperor's advice, transmitted by Benckendorff, to
rewrite *Boris Godunov* as a novel in the style of Walter Scott—a
recommendation which the poet turned down with frigid deference. Further trouble arose from Pushkin's anonymously circulated blasphemous poem, *The Gabrieliad* (1818), in which the
Archangel Gabriel and Lucifer figure as rivals for the Virgin
Mary's favours, thus incidentally casting doubt on the paternity
of Jesus Christ.

Pushkin flatly denied authorship to a government commission
in 1828, but finally confessed his guilt in a letter to the Emperor,
after which Nicholas graciously decided to treat the matter as
closed.[22]

Pushkin was particularly irked by the repeated refusal of his
requests for permission to visit foreign countries. Irritating, too,
was Benckendorff's habit of reminding the poet that he must keep
the Third Section posted about all his proposed movements. This,
being Pushkin, he repeatedly forgot or omitted to do, incurring
particular displeasure in 1829 by absenting himself without leave
to journey through the Caucasus and visit the Russian army at
Erzerum, where it was engaged in fighting the Turks. That the
Emperor and Benckendorff learned of this affair only because
they chanced to read about it in a local newspaper, *The Tiflis
Gazette*, was an aggravation of Pushkin's offence.[23] Other repri-
mands included a criticism of Pushkin's turnout on the occasion
when he had sported a tailcoat at a ball given by the French
ambassador—Russian gentlemen were expected to wear a special
uniform for these affairs, and Pushkin was instructed to equip
himself accordingly. Nor did Benckendorff allow the announcement of the poet's engagement to Nataliya Goncharov to pass
without relaying certain heavily paternalistic comments from the
Emperor: 'His Imperial Majesty . . . has deigned to observe his
hope that you have . . . well examined yourself before taking this
step, and that you have found within you the qualities of heart and
character necessary to bring happiness to a woman, and in particular to one as charming and attractive as Miss Goncharov.'[24]

These were only a few among many humiliations which made

Pushkin write that he refused to become anyone's 'flunkey and buffoon'.[25] It was in a mood of injured pride and exasperation that he met his end at the age of thirty-seven in a duel provoked by insults to the honour of his wife. Nor did death itself end police interference with Pushkin, for there was reason to believe that the very obsequies of this one-time rebel might provoke political demonstrations. After the poet's study had been sealed by General Dubbelt of the Third Section, the coffin was removed from the Cathedral of St Isaac in St Petersburg, where it lay in state, to the cellar of another church so as to hide it from throngs of would-be mourners. Then it was placed in a peasant cart, covered with matting and straw, and whirled away through the night by relays of galloping horses under escort of four gendarmes for interment at Mikhaylovskoye.[26] A tradition had been founded, for the funerals of well-known writers have remained a concern of the Russian security machine ever since.

Within a month of the great poet's death the Third Section struck at his most gifted successor, Michael Lermontov, author of the obituary lyric, *Death of a Poet*, in which he attacked the Imperial authorities for driving Pushkin to his doom. The poem circulated widely in manuscript copies, and was brought to Benckendorff's notice on 22 February 1837. Three days later Benckendorff informed the Minister of War that the Emperor had ordered Lermontov's transfer from the Guards Hussars, in which he was serving as cornet, to a dragoon regiment. Lermontov was posted to the Caucasus—a fairly mild punishment for pillorying the Tsar's closest associates as 'butchers of freedom and of genius', especially as the poet was permitted to return to the capital after a year's disgrace on the fringe of the Empire.

Among the many literary-police scandals of the reign was that provoked by the philosopher Peter Chaadayev. In September 1836 his first *Philosophical Letter* had appeared in *The Telescope*, a Moscow publication. It contained a violent attack on the Russian Orthodox Church, and also on Russia herself as a nation too primitive even to be credited with having her own history. In a State where Orthodoxy, Patriotism and Autocracy formed the three main planks of official ideology, Chaadayev had denounced the first two and thereby defied the third. Police measures were not slow to follow. *The Telescope* was banned, its editor, N. I. Nadezhdin, was exiled to Siberia and the censor responsible for passing Chaadayev's article suffered dismissal. As for Chaadayev himself, his fate was to be officially branded as a lunatic. Benckendorff sent a resolution, emanating from the Emperor, to the Governor-General of Moscow, stating that the inhabitants of that ancient capital had at once realised that an article such as Chaadayev's could not have emanated from a compatriot in full possession of his mental faculties. For this reason Nicholas had given instructions that Chaadayev should be attended each morning by a capable doctor. This medico-police supervision was withdrawn in the following year, and has often been quoted as an Imperial precedent for the far severer Soviet practice, common under Khrushchev and Brezhnev, of confining political dissidents in mental hospitals.

The Telescope was not the first periodical to be closed down by the police. Two years earlier Nicholas Polevoy, editor of the *Moscow Telegraph*, had written a hostile review of a crudely patriotic play, *The Hand of the Almighty Saved the Fatherland*—the work of a certain Nestor Kukolnik. At a time when the review was already in print, but not yet published, Polevoy happened to visit St Petersburg and saw the play, but discovered to his dismay that it had an enthusiastic admirer in the Emperor, who had deigned to witness a performance, and had even decorated the author. Aghast, Polevoy tried to stop the publication of his review—too late. When the scandal broke Benckendorff sent for him, and asked what impulse had guided him in his remarks on the patriotic drama of Kukolnik. *'How could he express an opinion so contrary to the opinion of everybody else?'*[27] One may be forgiven for italicising a sentence so richly typical of the Russian and other political police throughout the years.

As Polevoy's and Chaadayev's misfortunes illustrate, Moscow had become the stage for scandals such as were less likely to break out in St Petersburg under the immediate eye of the Third Section and the Emperor. The 'absence of the Tsar' was prominent among various favourable conditions which, according to Alexander Herzen,[28] gained for Moscow University a leading place in Russian education of the 1830s, when he himself was a student there, and enjoyed an atmosphere of relative intellectual freedom. That Moscow was by no means immune from political police activity was, however, demonstrated when Herzen found himself arrested, in July 1834, for *not* having attended a party, to which he had *not* been invited at which some other students with whom he was barely acquainted had sung a scurrilous song combining criticism of the deity with abuse of the Emperor Nicholas.[29] After six years in the provinces, Herzen was permitted to reside in St

Petersburg, but was soon in trouble again—this time for repeating a news item judged unsuitable for dissemination by the Tsar, though it was already common knowledge: a policeman had killed and robbed a passerby near one of the many bridges in the capital.

Summoned to Third Section headquarters, Herzen was interviewed by three senior officials in ascending order of rank. First, Actual State Councillor Sagtynsky rebuked him—not (as might have been expected) for retailing politically undesirable gossip, but for being found out. Herzen should have made sure that his remarks could not be overheard by some 'bastard' of an informer, 'who asks nothing better than to come in here a minute later and denounce you'. Such was the contempt of the political police proper for the rank and file of its agents. Herzen was next passed on to Dubbelt, and remarks that he was surely more intelligent than all three sections of His Majesty's Own Chancellery put together. Interviewed finally by Benckendorff in person, Herzen records the police chief's expression as tired, kind and listless. He felt that Benckendorff had probably done less harm than might have been feared from the head of 'this terrible police standing outside and above the law'.[30]

Few if any notable Russian writers of the period escaped contact with the political police. Even the cautious Turgenev suffered arrest for a month and imprisonment on his estate for a year—as the result of another characteristic crime: publishing in the Moscow Press an obituary of Gogol, already banned by the St Petersburg censorship.[31] Gogol himself, the most important of all Russian prose writers to date, occupied an ambivalent position so far as the police were concerned. An extreme reactionary and bulwark of the autocratic system, he was one of the few authors of the period whom the Emperor could reckon an enthusiastic supporter. As such Gogol obtained several sizeable cash subsidies from the Tsar, directly or through the Third Section. However, the grotesque pictures of Russian life, contained in Gogol's novel *Dead Souls* and elsewhere in his work, made an opposite impression: that Gogol must be an opponent of the régime. It was in this capacity that he had earned for a time the admiration of Belinsky, one of Russia's first Socialists and also her greatest literary critic. Belinsky, too, nearly fell foul of the Third Section, for it is probable that only his early death in 1848 saved him from arrest—Dubbelt himself expressed his regret for the critic's decease, saying that 'we would have let him rot in a fortress'.[32]

One writing of Belinsky's was bound to provoke the political police—the famous open letter in which, now utterly disillusioned with Gogol, he denounced his former idol as a contemptible reactionary. Like so much else of a subversive nature, the document circulated in manuscript copies, and many literary-police threads were drawn together when, in 1849, it led to the arrest of Fyodor Dostoyevsky. Still a comparatively unknown young novelist, he was charged with 'disseminating a certain private letter full of impudent expressions against the Orthodox Church and Supreme Power', and also with attempting to spread anti-governmental propaganda.[33]

In the affair for which Dostoyevsky was sentenced writers played only a minor role, for this was a socially mixed group, also including students, army officers, civil servants and tradesmen. They eventually received punishment severe out of all proportion to that meted out to a Herzen or a Chaadayev—a sign that a more rigorous phase of repression had now set in. Of this indications had already been available in 1847, when the Society of Saints Cyril and Methodius, a Ukrainian cultural group with vague political aspirations, had been denounced to the Third Section and savagely repressed. The chief victim was the great Ukrainian poet Taras Shevchenko, sent to hard labour in Siberia, though not a member of the accused group. In 1848, shortly after this episode, the outbreak of revolution in several western European countries alerted the Russian Emperor and his police, disposing them to exaggerate still further the menace of such conspiracies as they were able to detect at home. Hence the importance attached to rooting out the association to which Dostoyevsky belonged and which was headed by M. V. Butashevich-Petrashevsky, a young official of the Ministry of Foreign Affairs.

Less of a secret society than a discussion group, the circle consisted of a few score young men, interested in current affairs, who took to holding an informal seminar on Friday nights in Petrashevsky's flat in St Petersburg, discussing political theory among dense clouds of tobacco smoke until the small hours of the morning, when a modest supper would be served. Opposed in varying degree to the *status quo* in Russia, they argued for the emancipation of the serfs and reform of the judiciary, but without having any concerted plan for starting a peasant revolt or burning down the law courts. A number of satellite circles had also begun to meet, and some members of these were more inclined to revolutionary violence than was the main body.

It is a sad reflection on the supposedly 'higher' Third Section that Petrashevsky's activities were unmasked in the end by the ordinary, 'lower' police operating under the Ministry of the Interior. The energetic Minister, Count Perovsky, sought to break the monopoly exercised by the 'higher police' in pursuing political criminals. He was abetted by Count Orlov, who complacently agreed to allow the Ministry of the Interior to handle the investigation of the Petrashevskyites. Thus the very head of the Third Section and Gendarmes co-operated in keeping an important political inquiry secret from his own organisation.

A high official of the Ministry of the Interior, I. P. Liprandi, controlled the detective work, his method being to penetrate Petrashevsky's Friday seminars with an undercover agent of his own. Since Petrashevsky took no security precautions whatever—leaving his door unlocked, for example, and his books and papers scattered about—the insinuation of an *agent provocateur* seemed to present no great difficulty. The problem was, rather, to find an operative on the books of the lower police who would not immediately attract attention in any civilised gathering by his uncouth demeanour and general stupidity. Eventually a young relative of Liprandi's, a former student called Antonelli, turned out suitable for the post. The young man was readily welcomed by Petrashevsky as a promising recruit, and was supplying detailed reports on the main circle and its satellites by early 1849.

In spring of that year St Petersburg was humming with rumours of the impending arrest of Petrashevsky and his followers. Only the higher police seemed blissfully unaware that anything was afoot until the Third Section was suddenly brought into the affair at the last moment, being instructed to make the arrests on the night of 22–23 April. Liprandi has recorded his embarrassment when the secret of the thirteen-month-old investigation, as carried out under his direction, was revealed to his old friend Dubbelt—for even that second highest policeman had been given no inkling of the matter, and seemed thunderstruck at the news.[34] The arrests were carried out according to plan. Dostoyevsky has described how he was seized in the small hours of the morning, according to best secret police tradition, by an officer wearing the sky-blue uniform and epaulettes of a Lieutenant-Colonel of gendarmes, accompanied (as was customary) by a representative of the lower police.[35] During the next eight months the arrested prisoners were held in solitary confinement in the Peter and Paul Fortress in St Petersburg—confinement broken only when they were brought before the official investigating commission for interrogation. They were tried under military law, though most were civilians, and eventually twenty-one received sentences of death by shooting.

The proceedings which took place on the morning of 22 December 1849 form an eloquent commentary on the Emperor Nicholas, who had determined in advance to commute all the death sentences, yet ordained that the grim farce of impending execution should be maintained up to the very last moment. On this cold but sparkling winter morning twenty-one condemned men, who had scarcely seen the light of day during the previous eight months, were conveyed in twenty-one cabs through the snows of the capital to the parade-ground of the Semyonovsky Regiment. Mounted gendarmes escorted them to this place of execution, where military units were drawn up in readiness together with a great array of high-ranking officers. The death sentences were proclaimed, the condemned were robed in white shrouds according to custom, a priest offered the last ministrations, and three of the victims, including Petrashevsky himself, were made to face the firing squad. The command to take aim had already been given when an officer galloped up on cue, and an announcement was duly made that the sentences had all been commuted to terms of imprisonment. Even then the proclamation was read out by a General Rostovtsev, who was a notorious stutterer . . . and must, surely, have been expressly selected for this very reason by an Emperor distinguished by the subtlety of his gallows humour?[36] Nervous ordeal by mock execution was, incidentally, by no means an invention of Nicholas I, who was reviving a common practice of previous Russian Emperors and Empresses, not founding a tradition of his own.

The main unmasker of this inflated 'plot', Actual State Councillor Liprandi, was indeed a political policeman by vocation. He had sought to expand the affair to even greater dimensions, seeking to present it as a vast conspiracy with ramifications throughout the Empire, though none of the judicial and investigatory bodies concerned would accept his interpretation. For example, the conclusion of the General Auditoriate, embodied in its report of 19 December 1849, was that: 'They [Petrashevsky's followers] did not belong to the category of organised secret societies, and there is no definite evidence that they had any contacts in Russia [as a whole]'.[37] Thus Liprandi, whom nothing less than an out-and-out witch-hunt would satisfy, proved far ahead of his time. He was not permitted to become the Yezhov or Himmler, or even the Senator McCarthy, of his age.

Commonly regarded as a fully fledged Police State, the Russia of Nicholas I represented only an embryonic and tentative early attempt at what was to be carried to perfection by later, more creative, political engineers.

3
The Third Section under Alexander II
1855–1880

The accession, in 1855, of Nicholas I's son as Alexander II greatly influenced the development of the higher police. Less self-reliant than his father, the new Tsar is found delegating real power to his security chiefs, among whom first Shuvalov and then Loris-Melikov exercised more political initiative than had fallen to any previous police official in Russia's history.

Alexander's rule began with a few years of widespread optimism and high morale. Much enthusiasm greeted the Emperor's benevolence in freeing the surviving Decembrists and followers of Petrashevsky, while making it easier for his subjects to travel abroad and to attend universities at home. Censorship was considerably relaxed, and on 30 March 1856 the Emperor made a firm declaration of his intention to emancipate the serfs—the greatest of his reforms, which was duly enacted five years later. Other innovations followed in the sphere of local government, military organisation and the law. It was the last-mentioned reforms, enacted in 1864, which most closely concerned the political police, recasting legal procedures on western models, introducing trial by jury, creating a Russian bar, and providing citizens with certain formal guarantees against arbitrary imprisonment and arrest. Other measures ordained a curtailment of flogging as a penalty which could be imposed by law. Unfortunately, however, the retention of 'administrative' measures—whereby officials could impose punishment without process of law—reduced the effect of the judicial reforms. In the relaxed atmosphere of the new reign's early years such extra-legal powers were invoked only on a limited scale, but were sanctioned in the

Note to Article One of the Code of Criminal Procedure—permitting the administrative power to take measures 'in order to prevent and limit the commitment of felonies and misdemeanours'.[1]

The reforms of Alexander II did not include the abolition of the Third Section—not, at least, until the year preceding the Tsar's death, after he had relied on the protection of the organisation, with decreasing confidence, for a quarter of a century. In the early years of the reign the Third Section was less prominent than under Nicholas I, partly owing to the resignation of the efficient Dubbelt from the joint offices which made him effective second-in-command of the higher police until 1856. Dubbelt's departure followed the retirement of his largely ornamental chief, Count Orlov. Though Dubbelt was offered the succession to Orlov's post as security overlord, he refused on the grounds that this exalted office should go to some wealthy and titled potentate.[2] The Tsar's choice accordingly fell on Prince V. A. Dolgorukov, a former War Minister, who duly assumed the twin appointments of Head Controller of the Third Section and Chief of Gendarmes on 27 June 1856.

During Dolgorukov's early years as chief security policeman political offences incurred penalties unusually mild. This was the period when illicit publications, many of them printed by the Free Russian Press in London, were privily circulated within the Empire, where Herzen's periodical *The Bell* had a wide readership. For issuing certain publications of this type on loan, in 1857, the employee of a lending library in the capital was arrested and taken to the headquarters of the Third Section—but punished only by exile under police supervision. At about the same time another offender suffered exile to northern Russia for reading aloud extracts from Herzen's *Bell* in a St Petersburg tavern. At a later date such offences would certainly have incurred penal servitude in Siberia, as one well-qualified contemporary observer remarks.[3]

Owing to an unhappy combination of circumstances the early 1860s witnessed a reversion to political persecution on an ever-increasing scale. By now the Reforming Tsar's reign had passed through its honeymoon period and was entering a phase of ever-greater severity, provoked by official fears of domestic unrest. The government faced dangers in three directions. On the periphery of the Empire the Poles rose against Russian rule in 1863, a revolution which attracted only limited sympathy from oppositionists in Russia proper, and was severely repressed by Russian military power. Another threat—easier to quell on a local level, but more dangerous in the long run—was continuing unrest at the heart of the Empire among its peasant population. The years immediately preceding and following the emancipation of the serfs were cursed with widespread peasant rioting such as was endemic in Russia, but had now attained unusually alarming dimensions.

Of more urgent concern to the security police than Poles or peasants was the situation in the capital, in Moscow and in certain provincial centres, brought about by growing disaffection among those touched by higher education—students, young people recently graduated or expelled from the universities, and high-school pupils. A section of these had begun to attract attention by cultivating eccentric manners and appearance—long hair for men, bobbed hair for women, blue spectacles, rugs thrown over the shoulder, loud voices and intolerant opinions, whether favouring feminism, atheism, materialism or utilitarianism in the arts. Though such postures at first impressed conservative Russians more as a joke in bad taste than as a serious menace, it was out of this material that the Russian intelligentsia now evolved as an oppositionist movement united in common hostility to the autocracy. These dissident adolescents were at first generally called 'new people' until Turgenev hit on the term Nihilists, a name which he was the first to apply to them in his novel *Fathers and Children* (1862).

It was in this atmosphere of growing disquiet that Michael Mikhaylov—poet, translator and defender of women's rights—became the first political exile of the new reign. He had smuggled into Russia six hundred copies of an illegal pamphlet published in London by Herzen's Free Russian Press. Entitled *To the Younger Generation*, this proposed freedom of speech, nationalisation of the land and the replacement of the Tsar by a salaried official. Mikhaylov was betrayed to the Third Section by a renegade Nihilist and underwent trial by a court of the Senate, receiving sentence of six years' penal servitude in Siberia. Before leaving for Siberia he suffered the ritual ordeal of civil execution, being taken to a public square in the capital, where his sentence was proclaimed on a scaffold and he was forced to kneel while a sword was ceremoniously broken over his head.

As the first political prosecution of the new reign, Mikhaylov's trial aroused a wave of protest among the intelligentsia. In September 1861, while the poet-pamphleteer was still in prison awaiting trial, the first of the St Petersburg university riots broke out, and included a political demonstration on the streets of the capital as a column of students marched to the residence of the Curator of the St Petersburg Educational District to demand the redress of various grievances. Mikhaylov's agitation of the younger generation was blamed for the disturbance, and when he was removed under gendarme escort to Siberia, the authorities took special precautions to forestall a rescue operation supposedly planned by a party of students. On the long journey to Siberia Mikhaylov was obliged to wear regulation convict's fetters, which clanked abominably, freezing and chafing his ankles. Then, when he reached Tobolsk in western Siberia, his chains were struck off as this pioneer political prisoner of the reign was fêted and received as a conquering hero. The Governor of the province later suffered dismissal for showing such indulgence to a condemned political criminal. As for Mikhaylov, he did not long survive the combined rigours of Siberian hospitality and the Siberian climate, but died in 1865. His memoirs shed light on many details of political police activity—confirming, incidentally, that the courteous tradition of Benckendorff and Dubbelt had by no means lapsed under Dolgorukov.

The political unrest of 1861–2 caught the Third Section unprepared, and Dolgorukov's proposals to counter increasing subversion reveal uncertainty and a tendency to bow to public opinion. One suggestion was that all political suspects in the capital should be summoned before the kindly Governor-General, Prince Suvorov, who would give each a fatherly admonition, warning them that they would be severely punished if they did not abandon political activity. The Tsar rejected this proposal on the grounds that it would give political dissidents a chance to destroy incriminating evidence. Nor was another proposal adopted—that of simultaneous police raids on all political suspects in the capital with the aim of mopping up the entire stock of illegal pamphlets in one fell swoop. But hesitant though the security authorities may have been in early 1862, they at least had a precise idea of their enemy's identity, as is shown in Prince Dolgorukov's report 'On Extraordinary Measures', dated 27 April and listing fifty names. The list is headed by Nicholas Chernyshevsky, political public enemy number one of the period.[4]

In May 1862 a series of devastating fires broke out in St Petersburg. Their origin remains obscure, but they were widely attributed to Nihilist students. The Nihilists for their part blamed the fires on police 'provocation'—a word which becomes increasingly common from now onwards to describe acts undertaken or instigated by the police in order to discredit and trap revolutionaries. That the fires were started by the police was maintained on the pages of Herzen's *Bell*. Whoever did or did not ignite the tinder, the result was a wave of revulsion against the Nihilists, which made it easier for the government to impose repressive measures. To assist in this campaign an Extraordinary Investigating Commission was set up in June under the chairmanship of Prince Alexander Golitsyn, with special powers to punish attacks on the social order. New restrictions followed and were chiefly directed against freedom of speech. Censorship regulations were tightened up, and Sunday schools—theoretically intended to teach reading and writing, but in fact centres of anti-governmental propaganda—were prohibited. The practice of holding lectures on private premises was forbidden, and the St Petersburg Chess Club, a hotbed of sedition, was closed down.

June 1862 also saw the suspension of the two outstanding radical journals, *The Contemporary* and *Russian Word*, for a period of eight months. Shortly afterwards Pisarev, a leading contributor to *Russian Word*, and Chernyshevsky (editor-in-chief of *The Contemporary*) were placed under arrest. Pisarev's crime was authorship of an untitled, unsigned manuscript. It was discovered by the police when searching the quarters of a student who named Pisarev as the author under interrogation. Incarcerated in the Peter and Paul Fortress, Pisarev awaited trial and sentence for over two years, being condemned to a further two years eight months' imprisonment. During this period he continued writing, and produced most of his important work in the cells.

The impulse for Chernyshevsky's arrest originated in London, when Herzen and Ogaryov sent to an associate in Russia a letter intercepted at the frontier by the Russian police. It suggested that *The Contemporary*, the suspended radical journal which Chernyshevsky had edited, might be printed in London or Geneva by themselves. Herzen's letter was sufficient to provoke Chernyshevsky's arrest, but the authorities found it hard to pin a charge on him. True, Chernyshevsky strongly approved of revolution in theory and was personally acquainted with many conspirators and authors of illegal pamphlets, but so far as can be established he was not personally involved in any specific plan to engineer an upheaval.[5] Though he might have been exiled without form of trial, the government was still sensitive to public opinion. It was perhaps for this reason that the Third Section forged an incriminating document allegedly in Chernyshevsky's hand—'evidence' purporting to show him as author of an illegal proclamation inciting the peasantry. This frame-up has been described as 'one of the greatest judicial crimes in Russian pre-revolutionary legal history'.[6]

While the case against him was still under preparation, Chernyshevsky was writing in his prison cell the work which gained acceptance as the Nihilist Bible—the long, didactic novel *What is to be Done?* The most influential, but also—arguably—the worst Russian novel ever penned, it provided a model for Socialist living devotedly copied by many young people of this and later periods. It was sent out of the fortress, perfectly legally, was duly passed by a variety of censoring officials, and was serialised in *The Contemporary*, now freed from suspension—a sequence of events eloquently illustrating the laxity of political controls at the time. Since the main reason for Chernyshevsky's trial and condemnation was his influence on the younger generation, the authorities committed a grave blunder when they permitted him to compose in his cell a work more subversive of youth than all his other writings put together. Official revenge was prolonged over a quarter of a century's imprisonment in Siberia and exile under particularly harsh conditions.

A further example of official casualness was the case of P. G. Zaichnevsky, who wrote a blood-curdling revolutionary pamphlet, *Young Russia*, in a Moscow jail, having been arrested for another offence, and then smuggled it out for distribution through the agency of a warder.

The authorities were not always so lax. They could also show excess of zeal in pursuing the flimsiest of rumours, as was shown by the investigation of another, more illustrious, writer who fell under suspicion of disseminating illegal pamphlets at the time—Count Leo Tolstoy, the future author of *War and Peace*. One reason for this imputation was the hospitality which the Count was accustomed to offer students and other suspect persons who helped to run his school for peasant children. Acting on information received, a Colonel Durnovo, staff officer of gendarmes, swooped on the novelist's estate at Yasnaya Polyana with a posse of soldiers and officials on 6 June 1862. They spent two days prodding walls and ceilings, rummaging in cellars and ferreting through Tolstoy's study and his sister's bedroom, but without finding any incriminating matter. As their official report to Prince Dolgorukov read: 'In Count Tolstoy's house . . . no secret doors and staircases, no lithographic materials or telegraph came to light.'⁷ Furious at this invasion of his privacy, Tolstoy protested to the Tsar—but obtained little satisfaction.

By the middle 1860s the misdemeanours of novelists, poets, publicists, agitators, thinkers and pamphleteers faded into the background as a new and more urgent danger arose with the first stirrings of organised Russian political terrorism. A secret society, Hell, was formed with the aim of assassinating the Tsar, and one of its members—Dmitry Karakozov, a student who had been expelled from two universities—acquired a revolver with which to accomplish the deed. He also wrote a manifesto explaining the project in advance, since he feared that it might be misconstrued by the common people. This incriminating document was brought to the notice of the St Petersburg Governor-General's office, but no action followed. A few weeks later, on 4 April 1866, Karakozov waylaid the Tsar as he was about to mount his carriage after a walk in the Summer Garden in St Petersburg. The assassin fired and missed, becoming first in a long line of luckless Nihilist marksmen. Seized by onlookers, he was taken to the Third Section headquarters, and on the following day Prince Dolgorukov ominously reported to the Tsar that 'all means' would be used to uncover the truth.⁸ The interrogation of Karakozov and his associates was indeed stringent by the standards of the time. It employed techniques regularly practised in the Soviet period—deprivation of sleep and food, threats of torture—but also included a form of pressure not generally employed under Lenin or Stalin: the obtrusive ministrations of an Orthodox priest, who plagued the prisoner with religious exhortations and ritual.⁹ The inquiry eventually yielded material for several hundred more arrests, while Karakozov himself appears to have become insane under interrogation—if indeed he had not been so all along. He suffered public execution by hanging on 3 October 1866.

The assassination attempt made a deep impression on the Tsar. It partly diverted his mind from thoughts of further reform to the techniques of self-preservation, fostering a new political climate and opening the way for reactionary statesmen. Prince Dolgorukov insisted on resigning now that Karakozov's attempt had proved the ineffectiveness of measures taken by his Third Section and gendarmes for the Tsar's protection. He proposed as his successor Count Peter Shuvalov, who had once been his subordinate as second-in-command of the higher police. Appointed Chief of Gendarmes and Head Controller of the Third Section, Shuvalov swiftly attained heights of power denied to any previous security overlord. One of his first steps was to engineer the dismissal of Prince Suvorov, the easy-going Governor-General of St Petersburg. At the same time the governor-generalship was put into abeyance, and Shuvalov secured the appointment of a close ally, General F. F. Trepov, to the key post of police chief, or City Prefect, of St Petersburg.

The influence of the Shuvalov-Trepov team increased in 1867, when the Tsar became target for a second unsuccessful assassination attempt, in Paris. Terrified of unseen perils, though courageous in the direct face of danger, Alexander ruled henceforward as a virtual prisoner of his own police. 'The real rulers of Russia were ... Chief of Gendarmes Shuvalov and the St Petersburg Chief of Police Trepov. Alexander II carried out their will, was their instrument. They ruled by fear. Trepov had so scared Alexander with the spectre of a revolution just about to break out in St Petersburg that, should the all-powerful police chief be a few minutes late in the palace with his daily report, the Emperor would make enquiry whether all was calm in the capital.'[10] Though these are the words of the Anarchist Prince Peter Kropotkin, whose judgements are not always temperate, the omnipotence of Count Peter Shuvalov during the years 1866-74 is attested by contemporary observers of many political hues, ranging from Kropotkin through the liberal Ministers P. A. Valuyev and D. A. Milyutin to the conservative and Slavophile Prince Meshchersky.

Nicknamed Peter the Fourth, which well emphasises the extent to which he had assumed control, Shuvalov exuded a bland and reassuring confidence on which Alexander came to rely. Should the Emperor hesitate to sanction repressive measures, Shuvalov could always bring him into line by harping on the constant danger of revolution, the fate of Louis XVI of France, and the need to 'save the dynasty'. Thus Shuvalov's influence transcended police operations in the narrow sense, as when he secured the dismissal of two liberal statesmen—the Ministers of the Interior and of Justice—persuading the Tsar to replace them with reactionaries.

Early in his administration Shuvalov reorganised the Corps of Gendarmes by abolishing the system whereby the Empire was split into eight huge commands for political police purposes. Of these only Warsaw, the Caucasus and Siberia now remained, while elsewhere smaller Gendarme Administrations were set up to coincide with the boundaries of individual provinces or districts of the Empire.[11] This did not, however, lead to any great degree of co-operation between provincial Governor and gendarme staff officer at local level, for each continued to operate independently in repressing political offences—an example of the lack of co-ordination between political police and Ministry of the Interior which continued to hamper administration as a whole. These and other measures adopted by Shuvalov do not reveal any creative flair for administration, and remind one that many contemporaries rated his powers to thwart others higher than his ability to take his own initiatives. However, Shuvalov at least emerges triumphant when tested by the rule-of-thumb criterion which may be applied to any chief of secret police: during his period of office no assassination attempt was made—not, at least, on Russian soil—either on him or on his imperial master. Whether Shuvalov himself deserves the credit or not, his eight-year spell as Chief of Gendarmes coincided with a relatively quiescent phase in the development of the Russian political opposition—a time when revolutionaries remained more addicted to verbal than to physical violence. Even the greatest political *cause célèbre* of the period—the trial of Sergey Nechayev—revolved around the murder of a humble fellow-conspirator, not of a high official.

A skilled tactician when face to face with the Tsar, Shuvalov appears to have been less discreet behind his master's back, and there is evidence that he once referred to Alexander in private conversation as 'an idiot incapable of statesmanship'.[12] If indeed the Chief of Gendarmes was so outspoken, he was wrong in assuming that his status as supreme political policeman necessarily exempted him from surveillance by secret agents reporting over his head. Shuvalov also made the mistake of antagonising Princess Catherine Dolgoruky, the Emperor's young mistress (and later morganatic wife, after changing her name to Princess Yuryevsky).[13] The Chief of Gendarmes reputedly thwarted certain shady dealings by her associates in the sphere of railway construction—a field notoriously ripe with pickings for the unscrupulous. Nor was Shuvalov himself immune from accusations of sharp practice such as aroused little surprise in an age when all Russian officials, high or low, were accustomed to exploit their office for purposes of private gain—similar accusations had been levelled against Benckendorff and Dubbelt, who had both dabbled extensively in 'business'. Whatever the exact reason for his dismissal, Shuvalov had overreached himself in his relations with the Tsar by 1874, for in that year Alexander is suddenly found 'congratulating' his most powerful favourite on appointment as ambassador in London. In this way Peter the Fourth received his *congé* as head of political police.

From 1874 the Third Section begins a period of steep decline as a sequence of relatively undistinguished Head Controllers takes office—three succeeding each other within four years, and continuing to combine the office with that of Chief of Gendarmes. The announcement of Shuvalov's immediate successor, General Potapov, aroused amazement. Recording the appointment of this 'bird brain' with his canary-like intellect, Valuyev adds an exclamation and question mark in his otherwise restrained Diary,[14] while another Minister, D. A. Milyutin, welcomed the new higher police boss for his very insignificance. At least Shuvalov's entire gang would now fall apart, Milyutin predicted —a political swing so fortunate as to be scarcely credible.[15]

The bird brain did not last long in office, being succeeded in rapid succession by two other comparative nonentities (Mezentsov and Drenteln)—a downgrading of the political police unwise in a period of growing revolutionary activity. But though the revolutionary movement was expanding fast, this was an expansion within a minuscule framework—at the beginning of the decade the revolutionaries had been numbered in hundreds, and by the end they might be reckoned in thousands. Another change concerned their attitude to political violence. In the early 1870s the Russian revolutionary mind was chiefly fixed on peaceful propaganda, particularly among the peasants who formed four-fifths of the Empire's population. The hope of converting these benighted muzhiks to Socialism led hundreds of young revolutionaries to take part in the 'pilgrimages to the people' of 1873 and 1874. Going out into the villages in these summers, sometimes disguised as peasants, such hopeful girls and boys met general lack of understanding. Their mission of talking rural Russia into revolution turned out a fiasco and many of them were arrested, denounced on occasion by the very Dark Persons whose enlightenment they had pursued at such personal inconvenience.

Farcical though they may have been, the pilgrimages to the people of 1873–4 caught police and legal authorities unprepared.

Many arrests were made, and complex investigations were undertaken, involving nearly two thousand people.[16] Trials followed, of which the monster 'Case of the 193', heard in St Petersburg from 18 October 1877 to 25 January 1878, was largest. Some of the accused had been in custody for three years or more before facing their judges, and though conditions of detention were unenviable, they were not such as to halt political activity. On the contrary, some of the prisoners were able to mount a running seminar on revolutionary methods and aims—all at the government's expense. In the end nearly half of the accused were acquitted, which by no means deterred them from resuming revolutionary work as free men and women.

By now the revolutionaries were feeling their way towards newer policies. Abandoning the countryside, they concentrated on work in the towns, at the same time establishing a clandestine central organisation to co-ordinate their activities. Under the name 'Land and Freedom' this became the most influential Russian revolutionary group during the years when it functioned, 1876–9. These years also witnessed a drift towards more violent methods as revolutionaries progressed from their original conception, of exhorting farm labourers on an individual basis, to the more ambitious project of murdering an Emperor as members of a compact group subject to conspiratorial discipline. By 1878 terrorism had been adopted as a policy by a significant section of the movement. Thus it came about that the rule of Alexander II, which had begun with such high hopes in 1855, ended a quarter of a century later in a flurry of revolutionary violence and police repression sparing neither Chiefs of Gendarmes nor revolutionary leaders, and culminating in the slaughter of the very Autocrat.

A scandal created in July 1877 by General Trepov, Shuvalov's nominee as St Petersburg City Prefect, provided the initial stimulus for the three years of terrorism 1878–81. As head of the 'ordinary' police in St Petersburg, Trepov also exercised jurisdiction in political police affairs owing to the absence of any exact demarcation between the functions of his office and those of the Third Section. It was during an inspection by Trepov of the St Petersburg Remand Prison that a condemned political prisoner, Bogolyubov, insulted the august visitor by refusing to bare his head. Trepov flew into a rage, knocked Bogolyubov's cap off his head and gave orders for him to be flogged—a command which was executed in a corridor of the prison. Common though flogging remained as a punishment inflicted on peasants, it was unprecedented since the days of the Emperor Paul as applied to political prisoners, since so many of these belonged to the estate of the gentry, and were treated with comparative politeness.

In revenge for this outrage to the Nihilist cause a young revolutionary girl, Vera Zasulich, made an attempt on Trepov's life on 24 January 1878, ambushing him with a revolver in the room where he was accustomed to receive petitioners. She succeeded only in seriously wounding the General in the left side, but further scandal was to follow at her trial—before a jury which acquitted her contrary to all evidence. The verdict was a slap in the face for authority and a serious blow to the prestige of the political police. Nor did the gendarmes even accomplish the comparatively simple task of taking Zasulich into administrative custody after trial, as would have been possible had friends not spirited her away in the demonstration and scuffle which developed outside the courtroom. She managed to escape abroad. As for her disabled victim, he was obliged to resign office and virtually disappeared from public life.

The date of Zasulich's acquittal, 31 March 1878, happened to coincide with the first sitting of a committee established to deliberate measures against the growing revolutionary movement: the Special Conference. Under the chairmanship of P. A. Valuyev, Minister of State Domains, the Conference included the Ministers of the Interior, Justice and Education, and also the Head Controller of the Third Section—General N. V. Mezentsov, successor to Potapov. The establishment of this new organ was another sign of growing official dissatisfaction with the Third Section's operations, which were handicapped—as Mezentsov did not fail to point out—by inadequate finance. Though Mezentsov himself did not survive to benefit, his plea was successful to the extent that the annual funds made available for secret police expenses were increased from under 200,000 roubles in 1877 to nearly 600,000 roubles three years later.[17] Over half of this last sum went to patriotic propaganda (in effect advertising copy) in the press, and brochures appealing to peasant loyalty in pseudo-folksy style.

On 30 January 1878, less than a week after the attempt on Trepov, the revolutionary Ivan Kovalsky, custodian of an illegal printing press in Odessa, pioneered a new custom which was to be followed by many others—that of resisting arrest by force of arms—when he defended himself against the police with revolver and dagger. Two days later, revolutionaries murdered the police informant Akim Nikonov in Rostov-on-Don. On 23 February a revolutionary fired his revolver at the Public Prosecutor of Kiev— an attempt which might have succeeded had the bullet not lodged in the victim's greatcoat. It was in Kiev, too, that Gregory Popko stabbed to death Baron Heyking, Captain of Gendarmes, on a street corner on 25 May.

Though northern Russian terrorism had so far lagged behind, 4 August 1878 saw an assassination in St Petersburg so spectacular that it put all the activities of southern killers in the shade—the slaughter of no less a person than the Gendarme Chief and Third Section Head Controller General Mezentsov by the flamboyant revolutionary S. M. Stepnyak-Kravchinsky. Between 9 and 10 a.m. on the fateful day the Chief of Gendarmes was taking his morning constitutional with a subordinate when Kravchinsky darted out of an entrance and fatally stabbed him in the abdomen. The General's escort, Lieutenant-Colonel Makarov struck the assailant on the shoulder with an umbrella, an eloquent comment on the depths of feebleness to which the once dreaded secret police had now sunk.[18] Nothing deterred, Kravchinsky leaped into a fast drozhky and escaped abroad, having liquidated the supreme police overlord in broad daylight on a main street of the capital. No more damaging blow could have been aimed against the security apparatus, even if Mezentsov himself rated as a nonentity, being considered more of a *bon vivant* than a scourge of terrorism.[19]

Revolutionary terrorists now seemed to be making all the running, and many of the government's counter-measures resembled hastily improvised reactions to individual acts of terror more than items in a co-ordinated scheme to deal with the problem as a whole. Among steps to strengthen authority after Mezentsov's assassination was the law of 9 August 1878, providing for the trial of political crimes by Military District Courts, even though the accused might be, and generally were, civilians. One purpose of this measure, described as temporary, was to avoid fiascos such as had attended the trial of Vera Zasulich before a soft-hearted jury antipathetic to high-ranking officers. Another aim was to facilitate the imposition of the death penalty, since this could be awarded under military, but not under civil, law. Shortly afterwards, on 1 September, regulations were issued whereby gendarmes and other police officials could investigate treason, execute arrests and impose administrative exile—all without the sanction of the Public Prosecutor's department, as previously required at least in form. On a non-penal level, the government appealed to the population, especially students, to avoid violence, and on 20 November the Tsar addressed representatives of the various social classes, asking them to help the government 'to halt erring youth in its fatal path'.[20] Such pleas fell on deaf ears, however, for the population as a whole seemed indifferent to the life and death struggle waged between a few hundred revolutionaries and political policemen.

Neither further tightening of the laws, nor the appointment of General Baron A. R. Drenteln as supreme political policeman in succession to Mezentsov, could halt the wave of accelerating violence—small as its scale was by comparison with the political killings and executions which were to follow in the 1900s. However, in a country where no important political assassination had taken place for nearly eight decades, relatively mild standards were still the rule. The year 1879 therefore made an especially harrowing impression as the terrorist season opened with the murder of the Governor of Kharkov, Prince Dmitry Kropotkin. A cousin of the well-known Anarchist Peter Kropotkin, he was shot down in his carriage by the terrorist Gregory Goldenberg on 9 February.

Soon afterwards St Petersburg became the scene of further outrages which caused particular concern in police circles. On 13 March General Drenteln was driving down the street flanking the Swan Canal on his way to a meeting of the Committee of Ministers when a horseman drew alongside his carriage, brandishing a revolver, and fired twice through the window before galloping off. Unscathed, Drenteln at once ordered his coachman to whip up and set off in hot pursuit, but his assailant—a twenty-year-old Pole, Leon Mirsky—managed to outdistance the Chief Gendarme's carriage on his English thoroughbred mare Lady. He was caught later, receiving sentence of penal servitude for life. Mirsky's attack was followed three weeks later by another yet more alarming to supreme authority—a third attempted shooting of the Tsar. On 2 April a young revolutionary, Alexander Solovyov, ambushed Alexander as he came out for his morning walk in the Winter Palace grounds, firing five shots which the Emperor managed to dodge. Solovyov was tried and hanged in the Smolensk Field on the outskirts of the capital before a crowd of over four thousand spectators.

The Tsar's response to this assault, the first against his person for eleven years, was an administrative disposition which further reflects his growing dissatisfaction with a political police apparatus focussed on the Third Section. The new course involved a switch to decentralisation, wide additional 'temporary' powers to deal with political offences being granted to Governor-Generals in the existing governor-generalships of Moscow, Kiev and Warsaw, while three new or revived temporary governor-generalships were set up in other large areas centred on Odessa, Kharkov and St Petersburg—and equipped with these same wide powers. Thus Russia had now acquired six regional proconsuls, or local dictators, empowered to take all measures necessary for the maintenance of public order on the spot. To the three new governor-generalships were appointed military generals who had distinguished themselves in the Russo-Turkish War of 1877–8: Totleben to Odessa, Loris-Melikov to Kharkov and Gurko to St Petersburg.

The reactions of the three war heroes to their new offices were by no means identical. In St Petersburg Gurko resisted his appointment on the very proper ground that no clear-cut chain of command was proposed, for the new Governor-General and the Head Controller of the Third Section were both charged with combating political disorder in the capital, yet without either being subordinated to the other. Moreover, while the Third Section was to bear the brunt of surveillance, arrest and investigation, it would fall to Gurko to decide which cases were to be prosecuted within his fief, besides which it would also be his duty to confirm or commute sentences of death and imprisonment. Gurko therefore felt himself liable to incur odium without responsibility, and would accept the new post only when the Tsar himself promised to adjudicate any demarcation dispute between Governor-General and Head Controller.[21]

In Odessa Governor-General Totleben delegated extensive powers to his ferocious assistant Panyutin, becoming notorious as a bloodthirsty tyrant, since he staged no less than eight out of the total sixteen executions for political crime which took place throughout the Empire between April and December 1879.

More subtle methods were in vogue under Loris-Melikov in Kharkov. Recently commander-in-chief of the Russian armies fighting the Turks in the Caucasus, this energetic Armenian warlord fully accepted the need for stern measures to hold back revolutionary unrest—but attempted to combine them with conciliatory techniques. Meanwhile more and more revolutionaries were swinging to the policy of terrorism by assassination, as was signalised by the formation of People's Will, a new political secret

society. Containing the extremist wing of the earlier Land and
Freedom, which was about to disband, People's Will was founded,
in effect, at a conference in the provincial town of Lipetsk in June
1879. On 26 August of the same year members of this new
political underground met in a forest and pronounced formal
sentence of death on the Emperor Alexander II.[22] Many members
of People's Will—including two especially important leaders,
Andrew Zhelyabov and Sophia Perovsky—were former moderates
who had embraced terrorism only after their other attempts to
influence society had ended abortively.

Inspired by such varied motives or feelings, members of
People's Will mined the railway track between the Crimea and
Moscow at two places over which the Tsar was to pass on his way
from his residence in Livadia to the capital in November 1879.
On 18 November one bomb, laid near Aleksandrovsk in southern
Russia, failed to explode for unexplained reasons, and another,
fired on the following night in a suburb of Moscow, did indeed
hit its target—a train which turned out to contain a consignment
of imperial jam, but no Emperor.

If one asks why the assassination of the Autocrat should have
commended itself so strongly to these young people, no clear
answer is forthcoming. One hope was that the murder of the Tsar
might provoke a mass uprising. Another expectation, no better
founded, was of putting heavy pressure on the slaughtered
monarch's successor to revert to the policy of liberal reforms.
Whatever reasons may have swayed individuals, the urge to slay
the Emperor was to many an emotional rather than a rational
drive, deriving from the revolutionaries' long-standing inability
to influence society effectively in any way at all. *Something*, surely,
was bound to happen after the Tsar's assassination, and whatever
form the change might take it must surely be for the better in the
present parlous condition of the Empire—or so some of the
revolutionaries incorrectly reasoned. Finally, to some of the conspirators, who revealed the most extreme eagerness to perish for
the cause, political conspiracy appears to have appealed as an
excitingly ostentatious way of committing suicide.

Shortly after the explosion in Moscow a police search in St
Petersburg turned up two rough plans of the Tsar's Winter
Palace containing mysterious markings. These naturally aroused
suspicion that some further attempt on the Emperor might be
under preparation, but Alexander himself scorned the suggestion,
telling General Drenteln that there was no need to search the

building. Nor was the competing police authority under Governor-General Gurko permitted to keep the Tsar's chief dwelling under effective surveillance. The reason for this almost fatal laxness was the presence of Alexander's young mistress, Princess Yuryevsky. She had taken up her abode in the Winter Palace when growing threats of assassination had made it impracticable for her imperial lover to visit her apartment in the city—since even a Russian Emperor boggled at conducting his illicit liaisons flanked by a squadron of Cossacks in their gaudy uniforms. Unfortunately the obligation to feign official ignorance of the Princess's presence in the palace—in fact an open secret—frustrated effective security measures, for even in the most illustrious of homes it is hard to trap a determined assassin while simultaneously turning a blind eye to the occupants' domestic arrangements. At least a gendarme post was set up in the cellar and some sort of search was made—one which failed to uncover the store of explosive which the carpenter Stephen Khalturin, a member of People's Will, had been secretly accumulating piece by piece over the weeks, and kept hidden under his pillow in a room below the Emperor's private dining-room. He eluded all detection, surviving even the friendship of an amiable corporal of gendarmes who tried to arrange a match between his daughter and the secret dynamiter.[23] Timing his delayed-action fuse for the hour when the Emperor was to be at dinner on the evening of 5 February 1880, Khalturin left the palace. At twenty minutes past six he was watching from the square outside when the explosion rocked the great building. It killed and wounded many soldiers of the guard, but the Emperor remained unhurt since he happened to be late for his meal that night.

Once again the Tsar's luck had held, and once again he responded to a terrorist act by ordering administrative change—setting up a Supreme Executive Commission on 9 February under the chairmanship of Count Loris-Melikov, who had distinguished himself as Governor-General of Kharkov by an approach to political security more flexible than that of his colleagues in Kiev, Odessa and elsewhere. The new organ was not just one more government committee, being rather the cloak for a personal dictatorship by Loris-Melikov, whose colleagues played a purely consultative role and rarely met as a body. Meanwhile Loris-Melikov virtually controlled all aspects of government except foreign policy. Nor was he slow to sample the perils of supreme office at first hand. On 20 February the revolutionary Mlodetsky fired a revolver at the dictator, but once again an assassin's bullet failed to penetrate his victim's clothing. The assailant was tried and hanged within forty-eight hours.

The appointment of the second dictator or deputy Emperor of the reign marked a reversal of decentralisation, as adopted in the previous April with the establishment and strengthening of the governor-generalships. These were now subordinated to Loris-Melikov, as was every other police and judicial authority. In the new dictator's view the chief reason for the government's failure to turn back the rising tide of revolutionary terrorism was lack of co-ordination, and he therefore proceeded to unify and streamline the forces of counter-revolution. As part of this campaign he secured the dismissal of General Drenteln, who made no attempt to oppose the new plans as Loris-Melikov took over the Third Section and gendarmes in person by an *Ukaz* of 3 March 1880, appointing Major-General Cherevin as his acting Head Controller.

An investigation into the Third Section conducted in the summer by a Senator Shamshin revealed a parlous state of affairs. Important documents, relating to political cases under review, turned out to be missing. Or they were discovered after repeated inquiry in the homes of officials—in one case behind a cupboard. One area only of the Third Section's activities turned out to be organised on an efficient basis—that concerned with the supervision of high dignitaries of the State.[24] There was a vast backlog of unsettled political cases, no less than 1,087 being under review on 1 March 1880.[25] At the same time about twelve hundred political suspects were reported as administratively exiled, while nearly seven thousand persons in all were under some form of police supervision in connexion with suspected political activity. Not that these figures were reliable—nothing connected with the Third Section was, it seemed. In many cases the police supervision of individuals was nominal, and evasion was all too easy—for example, Sophia Perovsky found no difficulty in eluding the escort of two gendarmes one night at a provincial railway station, escaping to become a leading architect of terrorism and chief assassin of the Tsar. At all levels lack of co-ordination was the norm. Provincial gendarme staff officers held their own lists of political suspects—at variance with others compiled for the same territory in the local provincial Governor's or Governor-General's office. Similar confusion existed in the capital, where the Third Section itself competed with the ordinary police and the Governor-

General's or City Prefect's department in investigating political offences. Under such conditions it was hardly surprising if, as Loris-Melikov reported: 'The Tsar of the Russian land, the master of ninety million subjects, could not consider himself safe in his own residence.'[26]

Loris-Melikov's solution to these problems was an *Ukaz* issued on 6 August 1880, abolishing the discredited Third Section and assigning its functions to a new Department of State Police. This was to be subordinated to the Minister of the Interior, who was also to be Chief of Gendarmes, for there was no intention of disbanding the gendarmes along with the Third Section which had hitherto controlled it. At the same time the Supreme Executive Commission was abolished, on Loris-Melikov's suggestion, but since he himself now became Minister of the Interior, while remaining Chief of Gendarmes, the change merely marked a regularisation of his status as internal dictator of Russia, not a diminution of his powers.

The period of Loris-Melikov's ascendancy saw an increase in 'cloak-and-dagger'· activity arising from the struggle between police and revolutionaries. Among the personnel transferred to the Department of State Police from the defunct Third Section was a confidential clerk, Kletochnikov. Valued for the neatness of the handwriting in which he transcribed reports from the Third Section's secret operatives, Kletochnikov was all along an undercover agent of People's Will who kept his revolutionary comrades constantly informed on the dispositions of the political police. He furnished lists of police agents and informers, and gave advance warning of police raids. Such penetration was not a one-way affair, for the police also had their own agents among the revolutionaries. The identity of these was no secret to the conspirators while Kletochnikov remained undetected, and in at least one case a police agent, uncovered by him, was promptly 'executed' by terrorists. This was a certain Reinstein, who posed as a revolutionary and betrayed to the police a secret printing press in St Petersburg. The police swooped, seizing the press and some of its operators, after which Reinstein—betrayed in his turn to the terrorists by Kletochnikov—was invited to a revolutionary meeting in an empty apartment, where he was done to death. Notice of his execution was given by People's Will in a bulletin published on their secret printing press, and from now on the slaughter of police agents within revolutionary ranks became a common proceeding.

Kletochnikov's services also helped to minimise the damage done to People's Will by a major betrayal which threatened to destroy the organisation entirely. Having assassinated Prince Dmitry Kropotkin early in 1879, Gregory Goldenberg had eluded arrest until November of that year. Caught while transporting a load of dynamite from Odessa, this highly-strung assassin was processed in a manner which reveals a growing sophistication in political police procedure. First a fellow-revolutionary—in fact a police 'stool-pigeon'—was put in the same cell. The unsuspecting Goldenberg blithely confided in this false friend certain incriminating details, on the basis of which he was next interrogated in depth by the sympathetic Captain Dobzhinsky of the Gendarmes. The Captain posed as a liberal, and persuaded the prisoner that only revolutionary terror stood between Russia and the enactment of sweeping reforms, for which reason it was Goldenberg's duty to give the names of all his comrades. Goldenberg naïvely agreed, supplying full details of terrorist organisation and methods in the pathetic belief that he was acting as a bridge between government and revolution. When he finally realised how he had been tricked he tore a towel into strips and hanged himself in his cell.[27] The relationship between Goldenberg and Dobzhinsky—the assassin who helped the police, the policeman who sympathised with assassins—foreshadows the more intricate examples of policeman-terrorist symbiosis to be considered in the later history of the Empire.

Many arrests followed Goldenberg's indiscretions, though Kletochnikov's warnings enabled some of the designated victims to avoid capture. Valuable as his information was, however, it could not always be up to date—as was demonstrated when he himself walked into a trap on 28 January 1881, having gone to warn another revolutionary of his impending arrest. Had Kletochnikov been in less of a hurry to leave his desk, he might have discovered that the arrest in question had already taken place and that the police had followed their normal practice by staking out the suspect's apartment in order to apprehend later visitors. Thus People's Will's master-spy was caught at last. The terrorists had lost an invaluable source of intelligence on police activity and the net seemed to be closing on their whole conspiracy.

Meanwhile Loris-Melikov's policy of iron hand in velvet glove seemed to be working successfully, since the year 1880 had passed without political assassinations and the problem of terrorism seemed on the way to solution. Loris-Melikov did not abandon the severities practised under earlier security chiefs, maintaining the policy of administrative exile, continuing to insist that political prisoners to Siberia should be fettered and have half their heads shaven, and increasing the severity of the régime in the special prisons for political offenders on the River Kara in Siberia. Nor did the hangings cease, for in November 1880 two terrorists, Presnyakov and Kvyatkovsky, went to the scaffold in St Petersburg. Such measures were, however, accompanied by attempts to conciliate moderate opinion. Censorship was relaxed, certain political exiles were reprieved and the notorious reactionary Count Dmitry Tolstoy was dismissed from his post as Minister of Education. Most encouraging of all, Loris-Melikov obtained the Emperor's provisional consent for a plan to admit persons elected by the public, or by elective local government authorities, to certain commissions appointed to advise on legislation. This seemed to offer, however distantly, the prospect of an eventual constitution based on popular representation. Whether or not such a development would have taken place within the next years will never be known, since before Alexander II could enact the proposal he was assassinated on the Catherine Quay in St Petersburg in the early afternoon of 1 March 1881—victim of a crudely constructed hand-grenade. The killer was Ignatius Grinevitsky, member of a four-man squad of bomb-throwers commanded by Sophia Perovsky.

Despite his initial success, outstanding ability and unflagging energy, Loris-Melikov had turned out the first and only Chief of Gendarmes ever to permit the slaughter of his Emperor.

4

The Nineteenth-Century Okhrana
1880–1900

Far from destroying the autocracy, Alexander II's assassination only served to consolidate the Imperial system, at least in the short term, ushering in a period of two decades during which the authorities kept political terrorism at bay, but without crushing the revolutionary underworld out of existence.

Once again political police affairs took their colour from a new sovereign whose policies differed from those of his immediate precursor. Alexander III's political thinking did not stray far outside the formula 'Orthodoxy, Autocracy, Patriotism', which had so aptly expressed the official ideology of Nicholas I's reign. The new Emperor was, however, less of a natural leader than his grandfather Nicholas I had been. In particular, Alexander III leaned heavily on a powerful favourite who came to the fore. immediately after the accession—Constantine Pobedonostsev. As Chief Procurator of the Holy Synod—in effect, Minister of Religion—this former tutor of the new Tsar retained considerable though fluctuating influence over his ex-pupil and also over the Tsarevich and future Tsar Nicholas II. Pobedonostsev accordingly cast his shadow over Russia during the last two decades of the century, channelling appointments to like-minded potentates and fostering repressive policies far outside the ecclesiastical sphere which was his nominal province. The most notorious reactionary in Russian history, he helped to inspire the series of 'counter-reforms' which were enacted under Alexander III—but without by any means undoing all the achievements of Alexander II.

After the imperial father's murder the physical safety of the son became the most immediate concern of Russian high officials.

Pobedonostsev himself considered the problem in detail, writing to the new Tsar ten days after his accession to stress the importance of careful security precautions within the palace. He pointed out the need to test the bells each night in case the leads might have been cut by lurking conspirators and also recommended looking underneath the furniture for concealed assassins.[1] On 27 March the new Emperor took the additional precaution of withdrawing to a remote palace at Gatchina. This gloomy edifice, situated about thirty miles south of St Petersburg was now under heavy guard by troops, cavalry and plain-clothes police.[2]

Among the humbler inhabitants of St Petersburg the first assassination of an Emperor for eighty years caused some commotion, and led to occasional scuffles on the streets—as when loyalist citizens manhandled long-haired youths thought to resemble Nihilists. For a time university students found it prudent not to wear their official uniforms. A more serious by-product of the assassination was the outbreak, in spring 1881, of anti-Jewish pogroms, largely in the Ukraine. For these the Imperial authorities, including local police organisations, were partly to blame—if not for directly instigating such outrages, at least for conniving at them. The violently anti-Semitic Baron Drenteln—former head of Third Section and Gendarmes, but now Governor-General of Kiev—was prominent in condoning pogroms within his new fief. Permitting a mob to sack Jewish shops and bazaars in a three-day riot, he himself looked on without intervening. So did troops specially summoned to suppress the disturbance—as is recorded in the memoirs of General V. D. Novitsky, head of the Kiev Provincial Gendarme Administration at the time.[3]

Pogroms recurred over several years, but the nation as a whole seemed to shrug off the sovereign's assassination, relapsing into political apathy—while the running fight between police and revolutionaries continued behind the scenes. The advantage was now with the police, partly as the result of success in exploiting disillusioned or gullible revolutionaries. Some were subverted by trickery, including Gregory Goldenberg, whose disclosures continued to assist in rounding up People's Will after 1 March. Other informers were renegade Nihilists who turned State's evidence in the hope of saving their necks, among whom Nicholas Rysakov was particularly important in the weeks following the assassination. Arrested as a bomb-thrower on the Catherine Quay on 1 March, this nineteen-year-old youth proceeded to betray every conspiratorial detail known to him, yet did not escape the gallows.

Another defecting terrorist of the period was a certain Merkulov, who patrolled the streets of St Petersburg pointing out to detectives all the revolutionaries whom he knew by sight. By such methods the police had seized some fifty members of People's Will, including Sophia Perovsky, by the end of March.

When terrorists still at liberty wrote to Alexander III offering an armistice in return for an amnesty and the promise of constitutional government, the authorities replied by hanging five conspirators, including the helpful Rysakov and the defiant Sophia Perovsky. Driven through the capital on a lofty tumbril to a scaffold on the Semyonovsky Parade Ground, the tsaricides were dispatched by a drunken executioner whose bungling overfulfilled even the customary norm, and was witnessed by massed troops, sightseers and foreign diplomats. So disgraceful a pageant could only bring disrepute on Imperial authority, as the government itself clearly realised, for this was the last public execution ever to be staged in St Petersburg. Secret executions were, however, to mount to tens or hundreds of thousands in the same city over the next seventy years.

By May 1881, when police captured the terrorists' secret printing press, all leading members of People's Will were under arrest or had fled abroad. Only one active representative of the conspirators' Executive Committee remained at liberty on Russian soil—the celebrated Vera Figner. Inspired by her efforts, the broken remnants of the organisation fled from the police of St Petersburg, transferring their headquarters to Moscow in summer 1881, and attempting to resume activity.

Loris-Melikov resigned as Minister of the Interior within two months of an assassination which could not but discredit his dispositions as police overlord. The occasion came on 29 April 1881, when the Tsar published a manifesto written by Pobedonostsev and inflicting a twofold slight on Loris-Melikov: it was issued without him being consulted, and it affirmed the autocratic principle in terms so forthright as to repudiate his modest proposals for constitutional reform, made at the end of the previous reign. He therefore had to step down, as he did in favour of Count N. P. Ignatyev, who was possibly put forward by Pobedonostsev, like most other important new appointees of the period.

The new Minister of the Interior reversed the policy of centralising police affairs in the capital. In a circular of 9 June 1881 he released the provincial gendarme administrations from subordination to local provincial Governors, as ordained by Loris-Melikov, thus restoring to the gendarmerie independence such as it had previously enjoyed. This measure was followed by the Statute of 14 August 1881 laying down conditions whereby a State of Emergency, or of Exceptional Emergency, could be declared within any area of the Empire particularly menaced by revolutionary unrest. Granting additional powers to Governor-Generals and gendarmes to order summary arrest, to forbid public and private gatherings, to issue special decrees for the maintenance of public order and so on, the statute fully restored these regional proconsuls to the power which they had enjoyed before Loris-Melikov's brief dictatorship. In theory the new 'measures for the protection of state security and public order' were temporary, but like many other such regulations in Imperial Russia they remained in force for many years, being renewed again and again until they lapsed in 1917. Other police measures included the establishment of special units for the investigation of political crime in St Petersburg, Moscow and Warsaw. These were termed Protective Sections (*okhrannyye otdeleniya*) and were subordinated to the Police Department. Headed by experienced officers, they could claim standards of professionalism beyond the ken of the old Third Section. From the introduction of these units in 1881 dates the loose but commonly accepted use of the word Okhrana to denote the Russian political police as a whole in the last thirty-six years of the monarchy.

Ignatyev also sponsored the law of 12 March 1882 on the supervision of administrative exiles—giving police the right to search their dwellings and forbidding exiles to teach or enter State service, but also providing modest financial support for those otherwise destitute. However, despite his energy in reorganising the police, Ignatyev fell into disfavour owing to his sponsorship of a National Assembly such as might conceivably have led to a semblance of constitutional government. On 30 May 1882 he was replaced by Count Dmitry Tolstoy. As the second most notorious reactionary in the country after Pobedonostsev, Tolstoy could be relied upon not to repeat the error of Ignatyev, and of Loris-Melikov before him: that of raising the spectre of representative rule.

Official security measures following Alexander II's assassination were accompanied by the semi-official recruiting of loyalist vigilantes for the new Tsar's protection. The first such body was set up by Major-General Baranov, appointed City Prefect of St Petersburg one week after Alexander II's death, and active in detecting imaginary plots in various parts of the capital. Baranov enlisted a Temporary Council of loyalists to provide the new Tsar with a bodyguard, forerunner of a more elaborate association—the Sacred Brotherhood, established in June 1881. With its Council of First Elders, initiation ceremonies and accent on ritualistic mumbo-jumbo, this might have been modelled on the American Ku Klux Klan, especially as it was dedicated to violence—fighting revolutionary terrorism and trickery with counter-terrorism and counter-trickery. An aristocratic body based on St Petersburg's exclusive Yacht Club, the Sacred Brotherhood came to number over seven hundred members. On a more plebeian level it also recruited a Volunteer Guard, fourteen thousand strong, to protect the Autocrat's person.

The Sacred Brotherhood planned, but did not carry out, the assassination of certain Russian revolutionaries active in emigration—Leo Hartmann, a former political dynamiter, and the Anarchist leader Peter Kropotkin. It also published, in Geneva, a periodical entitled *Truth (Pravda)*—the same title, by coincidence, as that of the later Bolshevik daily. The editor was a former police officer, and his aim was to discredit revolution by advocating violence so extreme as to be unacceptable even to a Russian political terrorist—a prime example of 'provocation'. The publication was duly smuggled into Russia—there to be destroyed, often enough, by other members of the Sacred Brotherhood in the belief that they were confronted with genuine revolutionary propaganda. The Sacred Brotherhood also sponsored clandestine negotiations with People's Will, seeking an armistice to cover the Emperor's coronation. By the end of 1882, however, People's Will was clearly a spent force, and negotiations were broken off. Then the Sacred Brotherhood was itself dissolved when Pobedonostsev reported it to be a greater menace to the Emperor than the revolutionaries.[4] The satellite Volunteer Guard lasted until Alexander III's coronation in Moscow on 15 May 1883, when it too was dissolved.

Little credit for crushing sedition belongs to these monarchist organisations—or to Count Dmitry Tolstoy either. As Minister of the Interior he held overall responsibility for political security, but was no police chief by vocation, his energies being concentrated on other aspects of home affairs. If possible he would have preferred to divest himself of the police duties which made him a target for assassination. Obliged to remain Chief of Gendarmes, and to retain the newly formed Department of Police within his purview, he assigned direct responsibility in these areas to General Orzhevsky, his Deputy Minister. When another colleague protested against this delegation of political security to a deputy, Tolstoy is said to have replied pithily: 'Let them shoot him and not me.'[5]

Increasing influence on police affairs was exercised by V. K. Pleve—appointed Director of the Police Department in 1881, and promoted Deputy Minister of the Interior alongside Orzhevsky three years later. Pleve retained this post until 1892. One authority describes him as effective head of the entire ministry under Dmitry Tolstoy and Tolstoy's successor I. N. Durnovo, both of whom 'took little part in its [the ministry's] affairs although they jealously preserved all their privileges as Ministers'.[6]

The depleted forces of People's Will had by no means abandoned the policy of assassination, and General Strelnikov, an outstandingly cruel prosecutor active in the military courts of southern Russia, attracted their attention as a suitable target. It was Vera Figner who selected him as murder victim. In her memoirs she accuses Strelnikov of implicating whole sections of the population in treason through extorted denunciations—of pioneering, in other words the 'pre-emptive' arrest of those thought likely to commit crimes of which they were actually innocent. Given a free hand, Figner indicates, he might have launched a mass terror—such as she herself lived to witness under Stalin before dying in her ninetieth year during World War II. She claims that Strelnikov 'practised mass searches and arrests, wreaking absolute havoc, seizing persons entirely unconnected with revolutionary activity and having only the flimsiest links with those who had implicated them. This was done . . . systematically according to the General's rule that it was better to seize ten innocents than to let one guilty person escape. Serious charges were brought against the prisoners —belonging to a secret society, attempted assassination of officials and so on. One and all were told outright that they would not be freed until they gave evidence against So-and-so or confirmed whatever was required.'[7] Nor did Strelnikov's rough soldierly manner compare favourably with the traditional courtesy of the

Corps of Gendarmes, for when a weeping mother came to plead with him he was apt to boast of his intention to hang her son. Like Liprandi, who had tried to whip up an empire-wide witch-hunt in 1849, Strelnikov was a man born before his time. That he should also die before his time was Figner's resolve, and she accordingly went to Odessa to investigate her victim's daily routine. An experienced agent, she quickly obtained the nécessary information, and the committee sent a suitable killer to take over —Khalturin, who had dynamited the Winter Palace back in February 1880. On 18 March 1882 the General was duly slaughtered, but Khalturin and an accomplice were arrested on the spot, and hanged within a few days. Figner herself faded away, after learning that the renegade revolutionary Merkulov, who knew her by sight, was prowling about Odessa, hoping to betray her to the police.[8]

Another pioneer of police techniques, but one who foreshadowed the 1900s rather than the Stalinist age, was Lieutenant-Colonel Gregory Sudeykin, an officer of the St Petersburg Okhrana. Where the coarse Strelnikov dealt in brutal threats, Sudeykin employed subtlety, posing as a former revolutionary sympathiser and student of Marx who aimed to set up a liberal régime in Russia, using the Okhrana as his springboard for this ambition. If only terrorists and political police, both specialists in violence, could combine forces, they might be able to impose their own terms on the defenceless Empire. Fantastic as this projected alliance of predator and prey may have sounded when first mooted, such collaboration was later to become a commonplace. In any case, which was hunter and which was hunted? In the context of terrorism police agents played both roles—as also did the terrorists. Each side was therefore well equipped to understand the other, for they shared professional interests and skills from which outsiders were excluded.

Sudeykin needed the help of a leading terrorist with similar mentality, and such a person became available in Sergey Degayev —not the first revolutionary to turn police informer but the first figure of any consequence to do so. Degayev had taken part in the mining operations preceding the assassination of Alexander II and had become prominent in the rump of People's Will. In his own eyes he was the senior surviving terrorist, and as such helped to keep Sudeykin under observation in early 1882, when a decision had already been taken to liquidate him. In winter of the same year Degayev is found operating a clandestine printing press in Odessa, only to be arrested there in December. He contrives to send a letter from prison to Sudeykin, who hastens to Odessa and finds Degayev a partner after his own heart.

Sudeykin now plans to launch terrorists headed by Degayev against leading state officials, including Dmitry Tolstoy. A botched killing of Sudeykin himself will also be arranged, thus making confusion worse confounded, and one crucial item in the programme is Sudeykin's resignation from his police post. This will be timed to provoke his recall by a terrified Emperor as the new Minister of the Interior. He will receive dictatorial powers—for who else can save Russia from the mysterious wave of terror in fact mounted by himself? So much for the future. For the time being Degayev's role is to reveal his fellow-conspirators, who might otherwise interfere with Sudeykin's grand design. He obligingly complies, giving names, cover names, addresses and other details against a promise that his friends will remain unmolested—an undertaking soon proved worthless by numerous arrests. The most important victim was Vera Figner, seized on 10 February 1883. At some stage even Degayev began to suspect that he was valued more as an informer in the present than for his promise as a future duumvir, but he was permitted to vanish from custody while under transfer from one prison to another. Such mock escapes were often essential when a revolutionary had agreed to become a police spy.

In May Degayev went to Geneva with instructions to contact the prominent émigré terrorist Leo Tikhomirov, and lure him to Germany for kidnapping and removal to Russia. Degayev was, however, a person of extreme verbal incontinence, besides having reason to believe that Sudeykin had deceived him all along. Instead of compassing Tikhomirov's destruction, he therefore anticipated the Khokhlov-Okolovich confrontation of 1954 by addressing his victim-designate with one of those lengthy confessions which come so easily to the Russian tongue. From this tirade various amazing details of Okhrana procedure emerged. The illegal publication *People's Will* had, it turned out, been printed for a time with type supplied by Sudeykin at police expense, having been subjected in effect to police censorship, besides which the Okhrana had also been supplying revolutionaries with their false documents. The entire terrorist organisation had, in fact, been taken over by the police—an event unprecedented in revolutionary history, according to Tikhomirov,[9] though such a situation was to become almost normal in the later development of Russian police-terrorist collaboration.

In Degayev's presence Tikhomirov found it easy to pose as a strong, silent man. He heard the story out in impassive silence after the speaker had expressed contrition, offering to exculpate his offence against the revolutionary movement by making whatever amends Tikhomirov might suggest. The confession completed, Tikhomirov gave his verdict—Degayev must now return to Russia and assassinate Sudeykin. Such, substantially, is the account of these transactions given by Tikhomirov himself. He appears a reliable witness, but it must be remembered that his narrative is based on the fantasies of one compulsive intriguer as related by another, besides which both Sudeykin and Degayev were clearly masters of artistic exaggeration *(vranyo)*.

Be that as it may, Degayev duly returned to Russia—but was in no hurry to compass Sudeykin's doom. Not until 16 December 1883 did he lure the Okhrana chief to a flat in St Petersburg and shoot him down, leaving two accomplices to finish him off with blunt instruments. The chief murderer himself contrived an escape to America, embarking on a second career as 'Alexander Pell', a genial college professor. He died in 1921, having reputedly come to deplore the Bolshevik Revolution.[10]

Despite continuing efforts by terrorists the political trials of the 1880s were smaller, less openly scandalous affairs than those of the previous decade. The government was now taking steps to avoid publicity such as had attended the acquittal of Vera Zasulich and the Trial of the 193, at which the revolutionary Ippolit Myshkin had screamed abuse at his judges until physically suppressed. No further use was made of the jury system in political trials, and cases were heard virtually *in camera*, the spectators being a *claque* carefully vetted in advance—a foretaste of the Stalin and post-Stalin periods. Thus judicial proceedings came to resemble more closely the parallel technique of imprisoning and exiling treason suspects administratively—on the orders of officials and without trial at all. Open scandal was also discouraged by abandoning public execution, whether this involved the death of the condemned, or only the 'civil' ceremony of breaking a sword over his head. Finally, the numbers involved were now smaller—the total of those sentenced for political offences in the 1880s has been calculated at 154, by contract with the 193 arraigned at only one of several mass hearings in the previous decade.[11] There was, however, some increase in severity in proportion to the numbers tried, for no less than 74 persons were sentenced to death in the 1880s, though the death sentence was actually carried out in only seventeen cases. As for the overall scope of political police activity in the 1880s, the records of the Police Department show a total of over 4,000 persons in all as having been interrogated in connexion with political matters.[12]

Among terrorists sent to the scaffold during the decade one merits particular attention—Alexander Ulyanov, whose younger brother Vladimir was later to become the most famous of all revolutionaries under the political cover-name of Lenin. A young zoology graduate, the elder Ulyanov took part in a plot to liquidate the Tsar on 1 March 1887, sixth anniversary of his father's assassination. Ulyanov's group sought to revive the glories of the past, calling themselves the terrorist section of People's Will, though that organisation was now destroyed in all but name. The plot came to light when the Okhrana intercepted a letter written on 20 January by one of the conspirators and predicting the outbreak of a new and merciless wave of terror in the immediate future.[13] Thus alerted, the police placed the writer, one Andreyushkin, under surveillance, and were able to arrest him on 1 March as he lurked on the Nevsky Prospekt in St Petersburg, carrying a bomb and poised to ambush the monarch. The police also picked up two other bombers and two lookout men. Some of the arrested men turned State's evidence and further arrests followed, involving several score of persons in all. Investigation revealed Alexander Ulyanov as the group's chief ideologist, who had also helped to prepare the bombs—remarkable objects in themselves, since they contained pellets of strychnine in addition to the conventional explosive charge, besides which one had been ingeniously disguised as Grinberg's *Dictionary of Medical Terminology*. For this unsuccessful attempt five condemned assassins went to the gallows in Schlüsselburg Fortress on 8 May 1887. The episode had an important influence on the development of Russian revolution, if indeed it is true that Lenin himself—now a seventeen-year-old youth—solemnly swore to take vengeance on the Imperial authorities for his brother's hanging.[14]

In 1890 yet another trial took place—that of Sophia Ginsburg and her associates. After joining a terrorist circle in Switzerland, she had entered Russia bearing a false passport and bent on political assassination. She was seized before proceeding to any specific outrage, having chanced to mislay a handbag which contained a draft manifesto explaining the proposed slaughter of the

Emperor in language suited to the understanding of the common people. Ginsburg received sentence of penal servitude for life, and hers was the last Russian political trial of the nineteenth century.

In the development of Russian political opposition foreign-based activity had played an important role since Herzen's emigration in 1847. Switzerland, England, France and other western European countries continued to offer revolutionaries political facilities unavailable at home, and it was natural that other leading oppositionists, including Lavrov, Plekhanov and Lenin, should eventually follow Herzen into exile, permanent or temporary. Their number was increased by runaways from imprisonment or Siberian exile, among whom Bakunin, Peter Kropotkin and Trotsky were prominent, until the total of Russian expatriates in western Europe approached five thousand in the last decades of the Empire.[15] Their activities ranged from study in the British Museum to the manufacture of explosives in clandestine workshops. They continued to maintain printing presses and to smuggle illicit writings into the mother country, as they came and went illegally over the laxly guarded frontier.

The assassination of Alexander II further boosted such émigré activity when the slump in terrorism at home persuaded many revolutionaries to transfer their activities to western Europe. It was therefore inevitable that the Imperial authorities should further develop political security work conducted in France and nearby countries. For this purpose a special centre was established—the Foreign Agency of the Police Department. Modestly accommodated in two small rooms on the ground floor of the Imperial Russian Consulate in Paris, the Agency operated against émigré revolutionaries in Switzerland and England as well as in France, and also at times in Germany, Austria-Hungary and elsewhere. From its modest beginnings in 1883, when it took over the operations of the defunct Sacred Brotherhood on alien soil, the Foreign Agency flourished until February 1917. The Russian Provisional Government of that year allowed the political émigré V. K. Agafonov to examine the Agency's secret files, on which he published a useful study in Petrograd in 1918, after which they found their way to their present home, the Hoover Institution at Stanford University, California.

The Foreign Agency employed a dual system of supervision

similar to that adopted in political police operations on home
territory. For 'external' observation—tailing suspects, detective
work, bribing *concierges* and so on—plain-clothes operatives,
termed *fileurs*, were used, and included hirelings of French and
other nationality as well as Russian citizens. The other form of
surveillance was 'internal', consisting of espionage by police spies
posing as revolutionaries. Many of these penetration agents had
begun as genuine revolutionaries before betraying their cause,
whether disillusioned, tempted by rewards, or blackmailed with
threats of imprisonment and exile.

The first important head of the organisation was the ambitious
and ingenious Peter Rachkovsky, who arrived in Paris as a minor
official of the Russian Police Department but soon took charge
of the whole Agency, expanding his activities far and wide. On the
night of 20–21 November 1886 he scored a notable *coup* by raiding
the People's Will printing press in Geneva. Three of his strong-
arm men gained access to the premises, destroyed quantities of
subversive literature, and broke up the current number of a
journal, *The People's Will Herald*—scattering the type stock of the
press, several hundredweight of it, about the city streets. Shortly
afterwards the same press was re-established, but Rachkovsky's
men successfully raided it again.

The year 1889 saw a further setback to Russian émigré activity
on Swiss territory—a fiasco which took place without any intervention by Rachkovsky. On 22 February Dembo and Dembsky—
Russian revolutionaries who might, from their names, have been
billed as a 'variety turn'—were experimenting with bombs near
Zürich when an accidental explosion occurred, a common enough
event in the crude dynamite laboratories operated by Russian
political assassins. Dembo lost both feet and died shortly afterwards in hospital—having confessed his activities as would-be
dynamiter. His story alarmed the Swiss authorities, who conducted an inquiry into Russian émigré activities and expelled a
number of undesirables from the country. Many of them departed
for Paris, thus moving directly into Rachkovsky's parlour.

In the French capital Russian police agents were already busy
manufacturing a scandal of their own—one designed to discredit
the émigré terrorists with their hosts. Using the name Landezen,
and masquerading as an apostle of extreme violence, a spy of
Rachkovsky's had wormed his way into an émigré circle in Paris.
He persuaded his dupes to prepare the assassination of the Tsar
Alexander III from French territory, providing funds allegedly

given by a rich uncle—who was in fact Rachkovsky. The group set up a bomb factory and Landezen himself helped to manufacture the product in the Forest of Raincy, while Rachkovsky kept the French Minister of the Interior in touch with the developing conspiracy. At a well-judged moment the *agent provocateur* vanished from the scene, and the other plotters were arrested by the French police. A sensational trial saw some sentenced to prison and others expelled from France, while Landezen himself—condemned in his absence to five years' imprisonment—was already safe in Belgium. He was eventually to succeed Rachkovsky, at one remove, as head of the Foreign Agency. Meanwhile the scandal provoked in Paris made its impact on high politics. Severe sentences, imposed on the terrorists by the French, pleased the Russian Emperor, inclining him to favour the Franco-Russian alliance which was sealed in 1891.[16] This sample of police 'provocation' is a reminder that Russian revolutionaries alluded to all Okhrana spies as *provocateurs*. They did not trouble to distinguish agents engaged merely in gathering information from those more actively involved, as was Landezen, in plotting outrages. The police name for those pilloried by the revolutionaries as *provocateurs* was 'secret collaborators', a term which has survived for low-grade agents of the Soviet political police.

A *bon vivant* and suave, expansive operator, Rachkovsky was no ordinary spy-master. He maintained a luxurious villa in St Cloud, staged lavish banquets, consorted with French deputies, Ministers and police chiefs, and was always ready to place his extensive knowledge of Parisian night life at the disposal of distinguished Russian visitors. He also recruited French journalists to the cause of Russian counter-revolution, and founded the *Ligue pour le salut de la patrie russe*, which offered French citizens an opportunity to co-operate with the Russian police—thus anticipating the Societies for Friendship with the Soviet Union of a later age. In the end, however, he overreached himself by attempting to warn the imperial family against the French hypnotist, spiritualist and charlatan Philippe, who had so commended himself to Nicholas II and his consort that they imported him into Russia as a domestic seer. Rachkovsky's intervention in this affair led to his dismissal from police service in 1902, but he was readmitted three years later.

The 1890s were not distinguished by spectacular police initiatives on home territory, partly because the two Ministers of the Interior concerned, I. N. Durnovo and Ivan Goremykin, preferred to administer affairs unobtrusively. Under their jurisdiction (1889–95 and 1895–99) political offenders were prosecuted with strict avoidance of publicity. Charges of subversion, such as had been judged in the open or semi-open trials of the 1870s, were now handled administratively, and the decade therefore witnessed no important political court cases—a far cry from the demonstrative 'civil' executions and public hangings intended to function as a deterrent in the 1870s. In 1893 the very category of political prisoner was officially abolished, after which no administrative distinction was made between 'politicals' and those sentenced for common crime.

To claim that police affairs proceeded without scandal in the 1890s would be to exaggerate, however. One such episode brought the dismissal of P. N. Durnovo (who happened to share a surname with the Minister of the Interior, and was himself to become a notable Minister of the Interior). In 1884 this able official succeeded Pleve as Director of the Police Department, but after some years in office committed the gross indiscretion of using police facilities to investigate his mistress, a Madame Dolivo-Dobrovolsky, whom he suspected of being unfaithful to him with the Brazilian *chargé d'affaires*. A police agent penetrated the Brazilian's household, ransacked a desk and brought the contents to the jealous Durnovo, who taxed the young woman with infidelity, producing her purloined letters as evidence. Then Durnovo was himself investigated by the city police of St Petersburg—they were delighted to have a handle against an official so high in political security counsels. When Alexander III heard of the Police Department Director's indiscretion he gave the order to 'get rid of this idiot at once'.[17] Durnovo's career thus suffered a serious setback—which shows how little a Director of the Police Department, even under a notoriously reactionary Emperor, resembled the all-powerful satrap of popular imagination.

In less trivial scandals the 1890s also abounded. The great famine of 1891–2 was followed by a serious cholera epidemic and widespread peasant rioting. Private individuals and voluntary organisations undertook famine relief more successfully than the government—which further strengthened a growing feeling among educated Russians that the autocratic régime had become a gross anachronism. The accession of a new Tsar, Nicholas II, in 1894 did little to diminish such impressions. Happier in a domestic setting than when arbitrating affairs of Empire, the young Emperor behaved with scandalous tactlessness during the coronation celebrations in Moscow in May 1896, when a mass stampede occurred in the Khodynka Fields near the city. Out of a great throng of citizens assembled to receive traditional gifts from the Emperor, over twelve hundred were trampled to death, but this did not prevent Nicholas and his Empress from attending a ball given on the same evening by the French Ambassador. Though neither the Khodynka catastrophe nor the great famine seriously menaced the fabric of State, they helped to create a climate favourable to radical reform or revolution.

In 1895 the prospect of the Tsar visiting Moscow had provoked an assassination plot organised by one Ivan Rasputin (who had no connexion with the later, more notorious Gregory Rasputin). The first Rasputin's band consisted largely of Muscovite students, and wished to revive the tradition of Tsar-bombing. Scheming to drop an infernal machine on the monarch from some belfry or from the window of a convenient house, they sought information on the imperial party's proposed route through the city. Experiments in bomb manufacture proving unsatisfactory, it was intended to obtain instruction in handling explosives from an Anarchist group in Berlin—when, on 4 May, members of the circle were suddenly arrested. No trial was held, but administrative sentences of prison and exile, proposed by the Ministry of Justice and Police Department, were confirmed by the Tsar.

The last years of the century saw a resumption of the duel between the political police and Leo Tolstoy, who was now Russia's best-known citizen as well as her most celebrated living author. As an advocate of non-violence, Tolstoy wrote to Alexander III in March 1881, asking him to pardon his father's assassins. Though the Tsar did not heed this appeal, he is said to have ordered that Tolstoy himself should not be subject to serious police molestation.[18] This immunity was also maintained under Nicholas II, during whose reign the great novelist continued his vigorous campaign against established authority in religion and government—as against many accepted conventions of human conduct in general. Such now was Tolstoy's eminence that the disadvantages of imprisoning him would surely have outweighed any conceivable gain. However, though Tolstoy was able to defy Imperial authority in a degree impossible to lesser mortals, his writings yet remained as subject to censorship as those of any minor scribe. He therefore arranged for his controversial work to be published illicitly, beginning with *Confession*—written in 1878-9, but first brought out by a foreign-based Russian press in 1883. Some of his writings were issued and distributed by revolutionaries. Tolstoy himself fell under occasional police surveillance, while his personal immunity from arrest by no means extended to his associates. In the 1890s the anti-Tolstoyan police campaign became more intensive owing to the master's support of a persecuted religious sect—that of the Dukhobors, who commended themselves to the militant champion of non-violence by conscientious objection to military conscription. Tolstoyan sympathisers of the Dukhobors had their letters intercepted, and were subjected to eavesdropping Okhrana detectives posing as cab-drivers, a common form of cover. For assisting the Dukhobors two of Tolstoy's disciples, Chertkov and Biryukov, suffered exile.

Another eminent victim of the *fin-de-siècle* Okhrana was Vladimir Ilyich Lenin, as yet only a junior revolutionary. Younger brother to Alexander Ulyanov—hanged in 1887 for plotting to assassinate Alexander III—Lenin had already attracted police attention in 1893, when he moved to St Petersburg, joined Marxist groups and conducted propaganda among factory workers. Lenin's early conspiratorial career well illustrates the mildness of police procedures in the 1890s. Already a suspect under close surveillance, he was permitted to leave the Empire for four months in summer 1895, though the police were presumably aware of his intention to visit Russian revolutionary centres in western Europe. Returning with the customary batch of illegal literature, Lenin eluded detection when re-crossing the frontier in September, and resumed activity in St Petersburg. He began work on a new illegal periodical, *The Workers' Cause*, but at the end of the year he and his circle were betrayed by a Dr Mikhaylov, who combined the professions of dentist and police spy, and was later mysteriously murdered—a fate common among secret police collaborators. Imprisoned in a St Petersburg jail, Lenin was permitted to borrow books in quantity and to begin systematic work on a major economic treatise. After a year's fruitful study in his cell he was administratively sentenced to three years' Siberian exile and was permitted to make the long journey at his leisure, travelling as a free man and at his family's expense. Comfortably ensconced in southern Siberia, Lenin continued his economic studies, which were published under the pseudonym V. Ilyin as *The Development of Capitalism in Russia*, in 1899, the author's last year as a political exile. To this lengthy revolutionary's study the censors raised no objection, though Ilyin's true identity was known to the police.[19] As this episode reminds one, Marxists still seemed less like harbingers of an Empire's doom than harmless eccentrics obsessed with obscure economic dogma. Even so basic a cult work of their creed as Karl Marx's *Capital* had appeared in Russian translation in 1872 (the first volume) without being prohibited by the censorship. By the end of the century the political police had come to regard Marxists with less disfavour than other brands of revolutionary. Their bitter quarrels with each other and with competing subversives helped to split the revolutionary movement as a whole. Furthermore, they rejected assassination as a revolutionary tactic, which naturally made them less undesirable in the eyes of authority than competitors in subversion who were about to revive the use of dynamite and revolvers on an extensive scale.

5

The Okhrana in the Age of Assassinations 1901–1908

Near the turn of the century the two main revolutionary groups each set up a centralised party to replace the amorphous 'circles' of the earlier period. The first to do so was the Marxist group to which Lenin belonged, founding in 1898 the Russian Social-Democratic Labour Party—ultimate ancestor of the present-day Communist Party of the Soviet Union. In 1903 the Social Democrats split into the two factions of Bolsheviks and Mensheviks, consisting of hard-line and soft-line Marxists respectively. As for non-Marxist revolutionaries, their main grouping was the Socialist Revolutionary Party, founded in 1902, though the term Socialist Revolutionary had already been used informally for several years by those who considered themselves revolutionary Populists or heirs to the defunct People's Will. Both clandestine in essence, the Social Democrat and Socialist Revolutionary organisations each maintained some degree of legally permitted activity throughout the late years of the Empire.

The Socialist Revolutionaries differed from the Social Democrats in two main respects. Firstly a section of the Socialist Revolutionaries practised terror by political assassination, whereas the Social Democrats rejected this tactic. The second point at issue was the role of the peasantry. Scorning the revolutionary potentialities of the Russian muzhik, the Social Democrats put their main hope in the factory workers of the towns, whereas the Socialist Revolutionaries considered the countryside to be pregnant with political upheaval. Yet the Socialist Revolutionaries operated principally in an urban environment except at times of widespread rural unrest. In such arguments the Police Department was extremely well versed, maintaining its own specialists on varieties of revolutionary doctrine.

At the turn of the century the rumblings of the 1890s gave way to an escalation of violence culminating in the unsuccessful 1905 Revolution. A rapid turnover in Ministers of the Interior was symptomatic of the new unrest. During the five years 1902–6 this supreme police post was held by six persons (Sipyagin, Pleve, Svyatopolk-Mirsky, Bulygin, P. N. Durnovo and Stolypin), of whom the first two and the last were assassinated while in office. Many, too, were the assassinations, dismissals and transfers among senior police officers during this disturbed phase, which was much influenced at the outset by an enterprising Okhrana chief, Sergey Zubatov.

Zubatov first made his mark as head of the Moscow Okhrana in the 1890s, having begun his career as a schoolboy revolutionary —a common apprenticeship for a budding police official. The system of fingerprinting and photographing suspects was first adopted under his jurisdiction, while he also improved methods of detection in general, raising standards of police professionalism all round. He concentrated particularly on the techniques of 'provocation', penetrating revolutionary groups with agents who stimulated excesses entailing the arrest of duped extremists. In moments of frankness Zubatov was apt to tell revolutionaries that 'we shall provoke you to acts of terror and then crush you',[1] but he did not invent police provocation, since this had already been pioneered by Rachkovsky and many others. Zubatov's main innovation was, rather, Police Socialism—the organisation of trade unions under Okhrana control.

A period of rapid economic development in Russia of the 1890s had been accompanied by a steep increase in industrial unrest among factory workers—still a proportionately small community of some three million, but fast growing and finding a new sense of solidarity. Towards the end of the century many strikes broke out, provoked by harsh labour conditions which factory legislation had done little to ease. Believing the workers to be more concerned with material conditions than with changing the Empire's political structure, Zubatov championed their economic interests. He thus hoped to detach them from revolutionary agitators pursuing political aims—for with shorter hours and better pay a worker could surely be as happy under an autocracy as under a revolutionary republic. The workers seemed to agree, flocking to join the Moscow Mechanical Production Workers' Mutual Aid

Society—Zubatov's first police-controlled trade union, established in May 1901. In this enterprise Zubatov was backed by two superiors, the Grand Duke Sergey Aleksandrovich and D. F. Trepov—Moscow's Governor-General and Chief of Police respectively. So popular was the new alliance between labour and authority that fifty thousand workers joined a procession led by the Governor-General and marched to Alexander II's monument in the Kremlin on 19 February 1902 in memory of the serfs' emancipation decreed forty-one years earlier by the Tsar-Liberator.

By contrast with these marching workers, university students were growing increasingly disaffected. Objecting to an announcement by their rector that he did not propose to tolerate the misbehaviour traditional at the annual celebration on 8 February 1899, outraged undergraduates of St Petersburg University protested in the streets, where mounted police charged them down, slashing their whips. Never before had the government used public violence against Russian students, and their reply was a nationwide university strike. In their turn the authorities issued the severe 'temporary rules' of 29 July 1899, whereby rusticated undergraduates were called up for military service. This further outraged scholarly youth, and the academic protest movement reached its climax on 1 February 1901 when an ex-student, P. Karpovich, shot and killed the Minister of Education, N. P. Bogolepov. It was the first political assassination since the shooting and clubbing of the Okhrana chief Sudeykin in 1883, and introduced an orgy of political murders which lasted for several years.

This spasm of violence came on gradually. Not until 2 April 1902 did the second assassination occur, the victim being D. S. Sipyagin, Minister of the Interior and thus overall head of the entire police apparatus. Sipyagin's killer was another student, S. V. Balmashov, who came from a base in Finland—conveniently removed from Russian police jurisdiction, though forming part of the Empire. Disguised as an imperial aide-de-camp, the youth obtained audience with his victim in the Maryinsky Palace on 15 April 1902, handed him a 'sentence of execution' and shot him dead. This murder marked the beginning of operations by a new and particularly dangerous group—the Socialist Revolutionaries' Fighting Organisation, in which Balmashov was only a minor cog, the leader being G. A. Gershuni. It was with this, its first terrorist act, that the Fighting Organisation acquired status as a body virtually independent of the main Socialist Revolutionary Party.

Sipyagin's successor as Minister of the Interior and Chief of Gendarmes was V. K. Pleve—a former Police Department Director. Even by other bureaucrats Pleve was criticised for lumping moderate oppositionists and militant terrorists together and suppressing both with equal zeal.[2] Pleve was also obsessed with the dangers presented to the State by statisticians working for the zemstvos (rural district councils)—and not without reason. Many a zemstvo employed such statisticians on a scale unjustified by the statistical yield, they were well poised to spread rural sedition, and one such official had so far forgotten the peaceful nature of his calling as to discharge a firearm four times through the windows of Pobedonostsev's flat in March 1901—without, however, injuring that arch-reactionary.

Pleve retuned the political police by establishing Okhrana sections in many large towns in addition to St Petersburg, Moscow and Warsaw, where they had existed since 1881. He also made important new appointments, transferring Zubatov from Moscow to be head of the Department's Special Section with control of all political investigation throughout the Empire.[3] Under Pleve's protection Zubatov became the Empire's most influential security official. Zubatovite trade unions—resembling the Moscow Mutual Aid Society and similarly based on Police Socialism—were founded in the capital and southern Russia, where Zubatovite aims included equal rights for Jewish workers. Thus was created a far-flung organisation wherein Tsar, Tsarist police and loyalist workers seemed united in a scheme to extort concessions from a common enemy—the industrial employers. There were instances when labourers suffered injury at work but could not obtain compensation until Zubatov's police intervened, compelling the employers to pay substantial sums. Such episodes naturally made Zubatovite Socialism popular, but involved interventions by the police in industrial relations already chaotic and caused friction with other government departments.

The perils of Police Socialism were eloquently demonstrated in summer 1903 when Zubatov's representative in Odessa, a Dr Shayevich, somehow allowed the police-inspired workers' movement in that city to break free from control. A general strike spread through southern Russia, where local, non-Zubatovite police were drawn in to curb arrest. Now discredited, Zubatov was abruptly dismissed and himself placed under police supervision. Though he was not one of those many ambiguous figures whose ultimate allegiance remains in doubt—for he was certainly a supporter of authority—his posture was puzzling, and the suspicion inevitably arose that he was a crypto-revolutionary exploiting police techniques to further the cause of subversion.

In 1903 the arrested Gershuni was succeeded as commander of the Socialist Revolutionary Fighting Organisation by Yevno Azef, another seasoned rebel—at least in the eyes of his fellow-conspirators. They were not to suspect what was in fact the case, that Azef had been in police pay for some ten years. Azef was born in 1869, son of a poor Jewish tailor, and began his career as a police spy in Rostov-on-Don.[4] He moved to Karlsruhe in Germany in 1892 and studied electrical engineering, putting himself through the local polytechnic on a retainer paid by the Russian Police Department for reporting the activities of émigré Russians. After serving as such a humble police spy for some seven years, Azef was summoned to Moscow in 1899 and initiated into the refinements of 'provocation' by Zubatov himself. Thus primed with the latest techniques, Azef attached himself to the Moscow branch of the Socialist Revolutionaries, being readily accepted on the strength of his revolutionary record in Karlsruhe. He persuaded his new friends to transfer their illegal printing press from Finland, where the Russian police could not easily lay hands on it, to Tomsk in western Siberia. Careful precautions were taken during the transfer by revolutionaries unaware that their newest recruit was reporting every detail to the police. Soon the uprooted press and many conspirators had been seized, steps being taken to ensure that no one should suspect Azef's part in the affair.

In 1901–2 Azef took part in the negotiations, conducted on foreign soil, which led to the establishment of a single Socialist Revolutionary Party for the Russian Empire. He also became a founder member of the Socialist Revolutionary Fighting Organisation before succeeding Gershuni as its head. So high did Azef rise in party counsels that he received a succession of increases in his police stipend, which leaped from an original fifty to five hundred roubles a month. It was an unprecedentedly high figure for a secret collaborator, apart from which Azef also received lavish bonuses and expenses—these infusions of cash being the main justification of political terror in his eyes. Both as master-assassin and police informer he was chiefly concerned with the pickings in terms of money, perquisites and riotous living. He is found, for example, spending the night of 5 January 1903 at Stoyetsky's, the priciest brothel in Moscow, heedless of the skilled plain-clothes men stationed in the street throughout the freezing winter night to guard and check his comings and goings.[5] Nor was the police Azef's sole source of income. He bled extensive Socialist Revolutionary funds deriving from the donations of rich businessmen, as also from 'expropriations'—armed robberies undertaken in order to replenish the party exchequer.

In a calling which involved him in simultaneous deceit on two fronts, Azef retained an unusually strong vocation for duplicity. The art was to keep the police content by feeding reliable information—yet not to tell enough to enable them to destroy a given revolutionary organisation entirely, and thus kill the goose which laid the golden eggs. Conversely, as head of the Fighting Organisation, Azef must engage in terrorist operations with sufficient zeal to retain his leadership—yet without bringing about so devastating a series of assassinations as to injure his standing with the police. In an age of mounting terror, Azef was arguably a restraining influence, since he sought to keep revolutionary and counter-revolutionary violence within such bounds that he could extract maximum benefit from both. Though he often pretended to lose his temper, he was a self-disciplined and discreet individual, contrasting with other revolutionaries apt to betray themselves out of sheer exuberance. He carried conviction with both sets of colleagues, remaining a valued police collaborator even when evidence showed that he was not disclosing all information, while within the revolutionary underground he was hero-worshipped despite growing indications that he was playing a double game.

Azef held his own political views which—as a sound professional man—he did not allow to influence the discharge of his duties. He was, improbably enough, a moderate liberal, as he would admit in conversation with his spymasters. He may even be plausibly regarded as one of the less dishonourable individuals on either side. Despicable as he was in betraying his associates through greed, many other contestants—bloodthirsty idealists or venal protectors of autocracy—were surely on a yet lower moral level than this prince of confidence-tricksters.

The Fighting Organisation's first major task under Azef's leadership was to assassinate Pleve—who, as Minister of the Interior, took responsibility for the very police organisation which was paying his chief murderer. Heartily detested by revolutionaries, Pleve became an object of rivalry between competing killer groups when a southern Socialist Revolutionary branch, led by one Sophia Klichoglu, decided to by-pass Azef's Fighting Organisation and liquidate the hated Minister unilaterally. Apprised of this threat to his prestige, Azef denounced Klichoglu to the police, who arrested her while the great double agent went ahead with his own schemes. These reached fruition on 15 July 1904, after many alarms, excursions and delays, when the terrorist Igor Sazonov, acting on Azef's instructions, threw a bomb at the window of Minister Pleve's carriage and blew him to pieces.

To what extent was Azef the active author of Pleve's assassination, and to what extent did he feign co-operation with the assassins while covertly seeking to thwart the outrage? The security chief Gerasimov, Azef's later Control, maintains that the great dissimulator gave the police adequate information on the projected assassination to have enabled a more efficient organisation to avert it.[6] On the other hand, Azef may have intended Pleve to die all along—indulging, for once, in personal animus. Himself a Jew, Azef was known to speak of Pleve with utter loathing,[7] which may have derived from the Minister's reputed responsibility for the terrible Kishinyov pogrom of 6–8 April 1903.

Pleve's possible involvement in the Kishinyov disaster raises the complex issue of Okhrana–Jewish relations. Though pogroms had been held in check since the early 1880s, Russia's Jews had not been free from molestation in the interim. Most of them belonged to categories confined to the Pale of Settlement in the western and southern provinces of the Empire. They were subjected to a harsh quota system governing admission to schools and universities, also suffering a host of other severe restrictions. The most flagrant anti-Semitic measure of the late Empire was the sudden expulsion of up to thirty thousand Jews from Moscow, as ordered on 29 March 1891—the first day of the Passover. Police, gendarmes and Cossacks swooped on Jewish homes at dead of night and marched off the occupants, fettered and in the company of criminals,[8] while the sick were removed on stretchers, receiving no other consideration on grounds of health. This was accordingly the nearest approximation in the history of the declining Empire to the great Soviet deportations of Germans, Poles, Balts and others—not excluding Jews—to be described below.

Anti-Semitism was encouraged by the last two Emperors. Though neither Alexander III nor Nicholas II was a Himmler or an Eichmann, they created a climate in which an unscrupulous police officer might hope to further his career by fomenting pogroms. Tolerators and inciters of massacres, such as P. G. Kurlov (Governor of Minsk) and D. B. Neidhart (Odessa Police Chief), received promotion. The Okhrana official Komissarov obtained the award of 10,000 roubles from a special fund after causing great scandal by inciting anti-Jewish riots with material printed on a press set up expressly for that purpose within the very Police Department. Inflamed by such agitation, pogroms flared up sporadically during the late Empire, being further assisted on numerous occasions by police connivance on the spot. The police did not openly start pogroms, for these commonly proceeded as follows. First a rabble of drunken Gentiles loots the Jewish quarter, while troops and police watch impassively. Then, as the Jews try to fend off the raging mob, troops and police swing into action against them, but signally fail to check the raping, maiming, beating and killing. The final touch comes when surviving Jews are arrested for disrupting the peace by defending their homes. Yet, bestial as they were, these episodes tended to number their victims in units or dozens, and at no stage approached an exercise in genocide as practised in the twentieth century.

To pogroms were added attempts to saddle the Jews with guilt for ritual murder, a campaign which led to the trial of Mendel Beilis, framed in Kiev in 1913 on the charge of murdering a Christian boy. Held in prison for over two years before trial, Beilis was found not guilty by a jury of twelve peasants, despite determined attempts by an anti-Semitic judge and officials to pervert the verdict.[9] It must be added that the *Protocols of the Elders of Zion*—the notorious and widely circulated document ascribing to the Jews a plan for world domination—may have owed its first inspiration to the fertile brain of Peter Rachkovsky, head of the Okhrana's Foreign Agency.[10]

In fostering hatred of the Jews the Imperial authorities aimed to divert popular dissatisfaction from themselves to a convenient scapegoat. Hence the encouragement given by authority, from the Emperor downwards, to ultra-rightist anti-Semitic groups—successors to the Sacred Brotherhood—which included the extreme nationalist Union of the Russian People or Black Hundred. Besides baiting Jews, such organisations also assassinated certain left-wing politicians. They thus became a problem to the Okhrana, though the activities of the ultra-left still remained that organisation's main concern. To the extent that Okhrana-hounded Jews became increasingly active revolutionaries, anti-Semitic forces within the political police had only themselves to blame for making enemies unnecessarily.

Among the many ambivalent figures of the period was the priest George Gapon, a disciple of the Okhrana chief Zubatov. Gapon set up in St Petersburg the Assembly of Russian Working Men—a police-financed trade union based on the principles of Zubatovite Socialism. The murdered Pleve had now been succeeded as Minister of the Interior by Prince P. N. Svyatopolk-Mirsky, whose appointment marked a swing from repression to conciliation of the political opposition. His gentler approach proved as unsuccessful as Pleve's hard line, however. So disoriented did authority become that Father Gapon continued to operate his police-controlled trade union long after Zubatov himself, the inventor of such organisations, had suffered disgrace and exile—and without handing over to any effective successor. Meanwhile Gapon's union burgeoned, attracting between six and eight thousand members.[11]

What future awaited a police-sponsored union from which effective police sponsorship had been withdrawn? The events of January 1905 were to show. Bringing out his members on strike after a minor dispute, Gapon sparked off a more widespread stoppage in the capital. He then decided to lead tens of thousands of workers on a massed march through St Petersburg on Sunday 9 January. From rallying points in the suburbs the processions would converge on the Winter Palace, whereupon Gapon would hand the Emperor a petition calling for an improvement in workers' material conditions. The document also made radical political demands inconsistent with the aims of Police Socialism and inserted by genuine agitators who had infiltrated the movement, thus fighting police provocation with revolutionary counter-provocation.

Out of this explosive situation official bungling produced an appalling disaster, for though the authorities had advance warning of Gapon's monster demonstration, they took neither of the two rational courses open to them. The Tsar might have stayed in the capital and received the petition at possible risk to his life—instead of leaving, as he did, for his palace at Tsarskoye Selo on the eve of the event. Alternatively, the affair might have been scotched at the outset, had Gapon and the other leaders been arrested beforehand, and had the authorities given advance notice of their determination to halt the march by military force. As it was the workers paraded in festive mood on what was to become Bloody Sunday. They carried icons and sang patriotic songs, unaware that troops had been ordered to halt the march by force of arms. The columns marched on—and were mown down in various parts of the city, the fatalities probably numbering up to one thousand, while many times that number were wounded. The victims even included policemen—escorting the marchers on official instructions, but themselves in ignorance of the order to open fire.[12]

Gapon was protected by the Socialist Revolutionary Rutenberg, who marched by the priest's side as he strode along holding a cross aloft, but threw him violently to the ground when the troops opened fire, thus saving his life. Rutenberg further aided Gapon's escape by cutting off his beard with scissors, disguised him in borrowed lay attire, and hid him in the flat of the revolutionary author Maxim Gorky—who himself suffered several weeks' imprisonment in the Peter and Paul Fortress for his part in these events. Gapon escaped abroad, basking in his notoriety as revolutionary leader, writing memoirs, embarking on strenuous love affairs, gambling in Monte Carlo and in general behaving like a spoilt celebrity. He later returned to Russia, and was murdered with the connivance of his former saviour Rutenberg for offering his services as a police spy.

Svyatopolk-Mirsky resigned from the Ministry of the Interior after Bloody Sunday, giving way to A. G. Bulygin—the first in a sequence of less conciliatory domestic overlords. D. F. Trepov, Chief of Police in Moscow, was translated to St Petersburg in the appointment (now reconstituted) of Governor-General, and was also made Deputy Minister of the Interior, being granted extensive powers to suppress revolution. He had not been many days in the capital when grave news overtook him. The Moscow Governor-General, Grand Duke Sergey Aleksandrovich, had been assassinated—blown to pieces on 4 February in another operation half launched, half thwarted by Azef as head of the Fighting Organisation, but carried out by one I. I. Kalyayev. Incensed by police failure to protect the Grand Duke, Trepov burst into Police Director Lopukhin's office in St Petersburg and screamed 'Murderer' before retiring and slamming the door behind him— an event unprecedented in Russian police annals.[13] Lopukhin was transferred to the less delicate office of Governor of Estland.

Lopukhin had recently appointed Colonel, later Lieutenant-

General, Alexander Gerasimov as head of the St Petersburg Okhrana. In this sensitive office Gerasimov went from strength to strength, unaffected by his chief's disgrace. He acquired greater influence than any other Okhrana head owing to the trust reposed in him by Governor-General Trepov, and also by P. N. Durnovo and Peter Stolypin, Bulygin's successors as Ministers of the Interior in October 1905 and April 1906 respectively. Stolypin combined the post of Minister of the Interior with the key office of Chairman of the Council of Ministers (in effect, Prime Minister) from 1906 until his assassination in 1911, taking a close interest in police matters, on which Gerasimov reported to him regularly in person.

Gerasimov owed his influence to professional competence, common sense and hard work—qualities far from universal among high-ranking Okhrana officials. A hard-liner by instinct, he was well equipped to lead an aggressive counter-attack against the revolutionaries. At the time of his appointment, as it happened, a powerful terrorist group was busily plotting a new outrage, of which vague intelligence had already reached Governor-General Trepov. The plan was to stage a great explosion on 1 March, after a commemoration service for Alexander II in the Peter and Paul Cathedral. Four key figures were to perish in a single holocaust at the moment of leaving the building: Governor-General Trepov, Grand Duke Vladimir Aleksandrovich, Bulygin and P. N. Durnovo. The scheme sustained a deadly setback when one of the plotters, Maximilian Schweizer, blew himself up while manufacturing bombs in St Petersburg's Hotel Bristol, being registered under the exotic cover-name of McCullough. Though the police could not at first identify the bogus Scot's dismembered remains, they eventually traced his associates, aided by Nicholas Tatarov—a young revolutionary who turned informer. On the night of 16–17 March the police arrested a score of conspirators—a great anti-terrorist *coup*. The press termed this event the 'Mukden of the Russian Revolution', alluding to the recent rout of the Russian army by the Japanese at the opposite end of the Empire.

Among the terrorists investigated by Gerasimov was a beautiful, rich and socially eligible young woman, Tatyana Leontyev, the daughter of a Vice-Governor of Yakutsk, who used her family house as a secret dynamite store. This deadly girl planned to sell flowers for charity at an imperial ball, and intended to offer a bouquet to the Emperor while shooting him with a revolver concealed in the blooms. Frustrated in this major project, she slipped over the frontier and emptied a Browning revolver into a wealthy Parisian in the restaurant of the Hotel Jungfrau in Interlaken— mistaking him for the hated P. N. Durnovo, whom he happened to resemble.[14] Another sequel to the Mukden of the Russian Revolution was the unmasking of the police informer Tatarov by the revolutionary group which he had betrayed. On 22 March 1906 he was killed in Warsaw as retribution for destroying a large section of the terrorist movement.

Though Gerasimov could claim much credit for halting political assassination, his efforts were heavily concentrated on protecting the highest personages in the land—the Tsar himself, the Grand Dukes and the Ministers. During Gerasimov's term of office, from February 1905 to October 1909, these potentates did indeed remain immune—excepting only the Grand Duke Sergey, whose murder occurred on the day following the new Okhrana chief's appointment, and was obviously not attributable to his negligence. Gerasimov saved these high personages by insisting that they remain closeted in their closely guarded residences at times when his spies informed him that they were in particular danger. He was, however, in no position—nor was it his function —to halt nationwide revolutionary unrest accompanied by the assassination of hundreds of officials of medium to low rank.

The Revolution of 1905, sometimes called the dress rehearsal for 1917, was no close-locked struggle between authority and subversion, but a series of sporadic riots and strikes in different parts of the Empire. They included military mutinies on the Trans-Siberian Railway by troops returning from defeat in the far east— only to be flogged into submission by punitive expeditions steaming in the opposite direction. There were also naval mutinies in Sevastopol and Odessa, the best-remembered episode being that of the Battleship *Potemkin*, which fell into insurgent hands. As if sensing that the key to a more formidable revolution, in February 1917, would be the defection of troops stationed in the capital, Gerasimov arranged regular conferences between St Petersburg garrison commanders and police representatives. His efforts helped to save the city from armed insurrection such as raged in Moscow in December 1905. This was put down by armed might, including artillery and punitive raids on the workers' quarters by Semyonovsky Guards under the ferocious Colonel George ('Wild Dog') Min.

Though St Petersburg escaped serious armed conflict, it was the stage for intense verbal violence—especially after Russian universities had received autonomy in August of the revolutionary year, and lecture-halls were given over to rowdy political meetings conducted with freedom of speech hitherto unknown in Russia. Gerasimov would have suppressed such indiscipline at once, and claimed that he could end unrest in the capital by arresting seven or eight hundred individuals and closing down the revolutionary presses.[15] His more conciliatory superiors Trepov and Durnovo disagreed, putting their faith in the Tsar's momentous Manifesto of 17 October 1905 in which he at last abjured—albeit by implication and in limited degree—the principle of autocracy. From now on a kind of parliament with narrowly restricted powers, termed the State Duma, was to be elected by the population at large on a franchise calculated to ensure conservative supremacy.

Immune from the general optimism, Gerasimov particularly deplored another key event of that winter—the establishment, on 13 October, of the St Petersburg Soviet, an assembly of Workers' Deputies whose leading spirit was Leo Trotsky. The Soviet comported itself as an alternative government, even commissioning its own police force—the militia. Wearing special armbands, members of this motley organ attempted to supplant the regular police. On one occasion, in Gerasimov's absence, two representatives of the Soviet gained access to the St Petersburg Okhrana offices and were permitted by a naïve underling to inspect the premises and, probably, even the papers on Gerasimov's desk.[16] Meanwhile the very policemen, both ordinary and political, and including the many *agents provocateurs*, were infected by the fashion for improvising trade unions and holding political meetings. Some Okhranniks went on strike, others feared for their lives—and for their jobs too under the new régime which threatened now that authority was collapsing on all sides.

Impatient with the St Petersburg Soviet, Gerasimov would have clapped the entire assemblage in prison at the outset, but it was not until 3 December that his superiors gave him permission to act. His men closed in on a session addressed by Trotsky, and took all the delegates into custody. Many other arrests followed in the city at large, numerous illegal printing presses came to light, and some four hundred bombs were confiscated.[17]

During the revolutionary year Azef's contacts with the Okhrana had lapsed, but Gerasimov managed to reactivate them—and with good reason, for Azef still commanded the Socialist Revolutionary Fighting Organisation, the most dangerous terrorist group of all. In a 'cloak-and-dagger' world full of bungling dilettantes it must have been a relief to each man to find himself dealing with a fellow-professional. Now happily co-operating with a spymaster more competent than any of his previous controls, Azef gave the police better value than had been received when Pleve and Grand Duke Sergey were blown up with his guarded assistance.

Despite the tactical advantage which he now enjoyed, Gerasimov decided not to arrest all the members of the Fighting Organisation betrayed to him by Azef. Were he to yield to that temptation, he reasoned, other volunteers would only come forward and found a new Fighting Organisation such as might prove impervious to police penetration. Gerasimov's and Azef's joint strategy was, accordingly, to keep the existing Fighting Organisation in being, while unobtrusively thwarting all its successive enterprises—thereby disillusioning the terrorists and gradually weaning them from the policy of assassination. To facilitate this collaboration a special conspiratorial apartment—known only to Azef, Gerasimov and a single servant—was maintained in St Petersburg. Here the Okhrana and the terrorist chief would meet for bi-weekly conferences over the samovar. Gerasimov always wore plain clothes and his erratic movements so puzzled his landlady that she once reported him to the police as a suspicious character.

Thus the St Petersburg Okhrana held the equilibrium of terror, protecting the Tsar—against whom an elaborate plot was mounted in 1907—and also the highest officials of State: all this through the virtual monopoly over attack on the most exalted personages conceded by the terrorists to their idol Azef. Gerasimov also encouraged Azef to disrupt the Socialist Revolutionary party by making inroads on its finances—a prompting utterly superfluous, for on the technique of squandering money Azef needed no advice.

Gerasimov reorganised St Petersburg Okhrana routine on professional lines. On assuming office he had been aghast to observe gross breaches of security—as when a police spy would report openly at headquarters in person, risking his cover as a pretended revolutionary. Gerasimov accordingly established safe apartments where meetings between agents and their controls could take place without fear of exposure. Many such hideouts were required, for Gerasimov developed counter-revolutionary espionage, already fostered by Zubatov and others, on a yet wider scale. At the height of his power he maintained up to a hundred and fifty spies

inside the oppositionist parties, and had further specialised counter-revolutionary operations, so that the individual groupings—
the Socialist Revolutionaries (the most dangerous), the Bolsheviks,
the Mensheviks, the Anarchists and even the liberal Kadets were
each under scrutiny by police experts on their theory and practice.

In 1906 the Maximalists—breakaway Socialist Revolutionaries
—brought new urgency to the practice of terrorism, for they
believed in going in for the kill without detailed advance preparation such as was cultivated by their senior colleagues in the
Fighting Organisation proper. Amongst other gruesome exploits
they staged a huge explosion in Stolypin's suburban villa on
Aptekarsky Island on 12 August 1906. Three Maximalist desper-
adoes, each carrying a briefcase stuffed with explosive, were
challenged as they advanced on the heavily guarded building, but
contrived to throw their bombs all the same, perishing in the
explosion along with over a score of others. Stolypin himself was
unhurt. The Maximalists also carried out a spectacular expropriation on the streets of the capital on 27 October 1906, using bombs
and Browning pistols to attack a vehicle conveying six hundred
thousand roubles from the customs. Wild uproar ensued, horses
being killed and sacks of money tossed into a getaway carriage
occupied by a well-dressed, veiled lady conspirator. This incident
reflected no credit on Gerasimov, who had received a tip-off, and
had arranged to ambush the expropriators—an attempt which
failed even though he packed the area with detectives. Shortly
afterwards, however, the culprits were rounded up and from the
end of 1906 onwards the main danger came from other groups.[18]

Such a body was headed by one Silberberg, who maintained a
hideout in a tourist hotel by the Imatra Falls in Finland, only a
few hours' journey from St Petersburg. On 3 January 1907 a member of this gang attacked the City Prefect of St Petersburg,
Vladimir Von der Launitz—detested for his cruelty in suppressing
peasant rebellion as Governor of Tambov in 1905. The assassin
shot him dead as he came downstairs after attending a service of
dedication in a new medical institute, then turned his weapon on
himself and died immediately. Unable to establish the gunman's
identity, the police had his head amputated and placed on show
in a bottle of spirit. It was the ever-helpful Azef who informed
Gerasimov that the head was that of 'Admiral' Kudryavtsev, a
member of Silberberg's group.

Despite the success of the Gerasimov-Azef axis in containing
terrorism at the most exalted level, the years 1905–7 saw an

epidemic of humbler political assassinations—numbered in hundreds, and occurring in the provinces as well as in St Petersburg and Moscow. They included attacks on local officials from provincial Governors downwards, police and gendarme officers being favoured victims. Many of these attacks were reprisals provoked by official brutality—as was the shooting, mentioned above, of City Prefect Von der Launitz in St Petersburg. Von der Launitz's former right-hand man in repressing the Tambov peasantry, Luzhenovsky, had been attacked by the young terrorist Maria Spiridonov on 16 January 1906. Running the tyrant to earth in the railway station at Borisoglebsk, she shot him dead, and was herself nearly beaten to death by Cossacks—but survived trial, prison and exile to challenge Lenin's authority in the Soviet period, embarking on further tribulations. Another revolutionary reprisal was the assassination of Colonel Min, who had turned his Semyonovsky Guards on the workers of Moscow while suppressing the revolutionary rising of December 1905, when a hundred and fifty people were reputedly killed out of hand. In 1906 Min fell victim in his turn to avenging terrorists, as did his subordinate Reimann.

In response to revolutionary violence the authorities developed counter-terror, employing the death penalty on a scale never before imposed by Imperial judicial organs. The system of bringing political offenders before Military District Courts, first introduced in 1878, had now been resumed. At the height of the troubles, terrorists were also made subject to trial by Field Courts Martial empowered to dispense justice yet more dubious and summary. The Field Courts Martial functioned for less than a year, from 19 August 1906 to 20 April 1907, but the number of those sentenced to death—and often hanged or shot within twenty-four hours of sentence—may have been over a thousand, since 629 executions are acknowledged even in the suspect official figures for August 1906–January 1907 inclusive.[19] Field Courts Martial took place in about a hundred localities of the Empire, ranging from Vladivostok to the Baltic. Warsaw topped the list with 59 executions, closely followed by Riga with 57—an indication of the extent to which terror and counter-terror now gripped the western, non-Russian periphery of Empire.

In St Petersburg itself trial by Field Court Martial took place inside the Trubetskoy Bastion of the Peter and Paul Fortress—the only place in the capital where the court could rely on conducting its peremptory business without interference. Escorted by gendarmes, the condemned were shipped down the River Neva by night to be hanged at Fox Cape on the Island of Kronstadt on a special gallows which could be assembled and dismantled as required. Facilities for execution by firing-squad were also maintained there. Meanwhile the Military District Courts were awarding capital punishment as well, and some five thousand death sentences were pronounced in 1907–9, according to official figures. During the same three-year period tens of thousands of persons also received sentences of penal servitude and exile.[20]

Thus, in the early twentieth century, the Imperial authorities came nearer to operating a political reign of terror than on any previous occasion, and their Cossack riot squadrons were sometimes compared with Ivan the Terrible's Oprichniks by terrorised victims. To the vast numbers of summary executions must be added the many beatings and shootings carried out informally by punitive detachments. However, to compare the repressions carried out under Nicholas II with those of an Ivan the Terrible, a Lenin or a Stalin would be to lose all sense of proportion. Lamentable as they were, the casualties under Nicholas II amounted only to thousands, being comparable in the number killed and injured to the proportion of sufferers from traffic accidents in any advanced country of the mid-twentieth century. It must also be stressed that the Imperial authorities were at least reacting— however incompetently and cruelly—against terrorist attacks directly menacing themselves, as was hardly the case with Ivan IV's Oprichnina or Stalin's NKVD.

6

The Decline and Fall of the Okhrana
1908–1917

From 1908 onwards Russian revolutionaries largely abandoned the policy of assassinating officials, the police regained control, and it was as a nation comparatively stable and united—at least on the surface—that the Empire entered the years preceding the 1914 war. In 1908–9 general disillusionment with terror was encouraged by the exposure of Azef by Vladimir Burtsev. A veteran revolutionary himself, Burtsev specialised in uncovering police spies within revolutionary ranks, and the unmasking of Azef was only the greatest among many such *coups* carried out by this one-man counter-provocation bureau. As often happened with Burtsev's denunciations, he at first met disbelief among the accused man's revolutionary colleagues. To his fellow-Socialist Revolutionaries Azef remained a hero, and Burtsev's charges at first recoiled on their author, who seemed to be wantonly slandering the acknowledged titan of terrorism. Burtsev managed to prove his case in the end with the help of A. A. Lopukhin, who—as a former Director of the Police Department—could speak with authority on Azef's contacts with his office. He refused to retract his testimony even after Azef had implored him to do so in person, visiting St Petersburg in November 1908 in a last bid to maintain his position. After travelling to London, where he met leading émigré Socialist Revolutionaries, Lopukhin confirmed Azef's status as a police spy of long standing. For divulging official secrets in this matter, Lopukhin was tried and exiled, but later pardoned. Azef escaped abroad, using false papers supplied by the Okhrana. Acquiring world-wide notoriety in the grand scandal which erupted around his exposure, he yet escaped 'execution' as so often meted out by betrayed revolutionaries to police spies. He dabbled in stocks and shares, and established a fashionable corset shop in Berlin, but was arrested during the War by the German police and died in 1918 shortly after being released.

Though political assassination was generally abandoned after Azef's exposure, the year 1911 saw one spectacular act of violence. At a gala performance in the Kiev opera house on 1 September, in the presence of the Emperor and his suite, a young man took a revolver from his tail-coat pocket and fired two shots, mortally wounding Peter Stolypin, Prime Minister and Minister of the Interior. The gunman was Dmitry Bogrov, a Jewish agent of the Kiev Okhrana who so integrally combined the roles of police spy and revolutionary that his true affiliations have never been established, and may even have been unclear to the man himself. Nor has the motive for the deed ever been clarified. Was it vengeance against Stolypin for supposedly fostering pogroms? Or an attempt by the assassin to assert his claims as a revolutionary and purge himself of guilt for working with the Okhrana? A more sinister theory has it that Bogrov was acting as the tool of illustrious persons connected with the Court and opposed to Stolypin's influence—now in any case on the wane. On this interpretation the assassin had been primed by General Kurlov, who was responsible for the Tsar's safety during the Kiev visit, and who held the dual post of Deputy Ministry of the Interior and Chief of Gendarmes. After Stolypin's death Kurlov was retired from these offices, and his activities became the subject of an official inquiry. This was abandoned, however—and on the Tsar's insistence. The question of Kurlov's complicity therefore remains undecided, the assassin having been conveniently hanged only a few days after the outrage, so that his evidence was no longer available. Since Stolypin had sponsored the infiltration of revolutionary parties by police agents such as Bogrov, he fell victim (like Pleve before him) to a system which he himself had fostered—and to the weapon of a junior subordinate.

The Okhrana devoted particular attention to stimulating and encouraging the activities of the Bolsheviks at the expense of other revolutionary factions or parties. One reason for this policy was the comparative harmlessness (as it seemed to the police) of a group which at no time before mid-1917 looked like a serious contender for power. The Bolsheviks were, on the contrary, a comparatively small organisation dominated by one seemingly eccentric individual—Lenin—who was given to the violent denunciation of rival revolutionaries. Seeking to build a nucleus of underlings blindly loyal to himself, he appeared to weaken the revolutionary movement as a whole by his strident refusal to cooperate with the many other foes of Tsarism who sought to sink their differences in a common campaign against the government. Hence the Okhrana's favourable attitude to Lenin, and hence an informal and unacknowledged alliance between Lenin and a political police organisation bent on destroying revolutionaries as a whole, but not greatly concerned at any consequent accretion of power to a section of the movement as minor as Bolshevism.

The chief link between Lenin and the Okhrana was the police spy Roman Malinovsky, the only traitor to the revolutionary cause whose operations rivalled or eclipsed those of Azef. Malinovsky was a petty criminal who had done time for burglary. As an undercover Okhrana agent, he became secretary of a St Petersburg trade union, posing as a Social Democrat who hovered between Bolsheviks and Mensheviks, while already reporting the activities of both to the police. Then he threw in his lot wholeheartedly with the Bolsheviks and stood for election to the Fourth State Duma in 1912 as their candidate for a Moscow ward. Always eager for its spies to rise to the top, the Okhrana supported Malinovsky's candidature by suppressing his criminal record and arresting rival candidates. The plan succeeded well, for Malinovsky not only became a Social Democrat deputy to the Duma, but even headed the six-man Bolshevik faction among the thirteen Social Democrat deputies as a whole. In the Duma, Malinovsky made the first political declaration on behalf of the combined Social Democrats, Bolsheviks and Mensheviks, whom he soon managed to set against each other, thus carrying out the splitting policy favoured by Lenin. A gifted orator, Malinovsky frequently addressed the Duma, his speeches being anything but impromptu. Many of them were drafted, written or vetted by Lenin, and then further revised by S. P. Beletsky—Police Department Director and one of the Okhrana officials later to be shot under Lenin's rule. The Police Department increased Malinovsky's stipend from fifty to seven hundred roubles a month as he continued to send detailed reports. They included accounts of intimate conferences with Lenin, a great enthusiast for this 'outstanding workerleader'.[1] Protected both by Okhrana and revolutionaries, Malinovsky easily commuted across the frontier to consult Lenin, now established in the Cracow area. Malinovsky became treasurer of the newly founded Bolshevik newspaper *Pravda*, supplying the police with data on the paper's finances, and with lists of its contributors. Nor was he hindered by the paper's editor, Miron Chernomazov, since Chernomazov too was a police agent. Dissatisfied with the political line taken by *Pravda*, Lenin sent first Sverdlov and then Stalin to St Petersburg to put matters right, but Malinovsky tipped off the Okhrana, and both of these leading Bolsheviks were exiled to Siberia, where they remained until 1917.

Malinovsky's career as deputy ended abruptly in May 1914, when he resigned from the Duma on the orders of the Ministry of the Interior—since it was feared that his activities might come to light and provoke a damaging scandal. By now some revolutionaries suspected that Malinovsky was not what he seemed, but Lenin repeatedly pronounced him guiltless. Only when the Okhrana files were scrutinised in 1917 was it no longer possible for him to doubt the outstanding worker-leader's treachery. Daring to the end, Malinovsky took the reckless step of returning to Petrograd from abroad in November 1918, a year after the Bolshevik seizure of power. He was arrested, tried, sentenced to death and immediately shot without obtaining the personal interview with Lenin which he vainly demanded. Nor can the possibility be discounted that the Bolshevik leader had known Malinovsky for a spy all along, but had been adroitly using his services. After all, as Lenin himself informed the Extraordinary Investigating Commission of the Provisional Government in June 1917, his party had stood to gain far more than the police force from the activities of Malinovsky, *provocateur* or no *provocateur*.[2]

Malinovsky, incidentally, was only the most influential among many police spies lodged in the various Bolshevik organisations. But though the planting of this super-agent was the Okhrana's most brilliant single feat of political espionage, its ultimate utility was nil. Informed in the minutest detail on Lenin's doings and plans, the Okhrana yet failed to avert the triumph of Bolshevism —and the consequent execution by the new government of many officials of the Imperial political police which had for years kept Lenin and his colleagues under a surveillance so benevolent.

Among Lenin's younger revolutionary colleagues was the Georgian Joseph Dzhugashvili, later known as Stalin, whose relations with the Okhrana pose an intriguing problem which may never receive its final solution.

To ask whether Stalin was ever an Okhrana agent would be to phrase the question crudely, since so many gradations were found between out-and-out police spy and revolutionary unsullied by taint of official contact. Devoted more to self-advancement and self-protection than to any outside cause, Stalin was to show himself a skilful and unscrupulous tactician in the years of his power —and one outstandingly vindictive in his treatment of individuals and social groups. These features clearly emerge from the period 1917–53, when Stalin lived in the public eye—which, however, could observe him only through the distorting prism interposed by the public relations men whom he periodically slaughtered. There is evidence that Stalin was already behaving with similar vengefulness and unscrupulousness, if on an inevitably smaller scale, during the obscure period of his young manhood, when he took part in the political underground as a Bolshevik—at first in his native Caucasus and then on a nationwide and international scale.

The wholesale rewriting of history, sponsored by Stalin as Soviet dictator, involved the obliteration of evidence on his early career and the substitution of material more ennobling. As a recent biographer states, 'most of the people who had personal knowledge about Stalin's first thirty-seven years were executed after being forced to write adulatory and falsified accounts of that knowledge'.[3] The same biographer, Edward Ellis Smith, considers it likely that Stalin was an Okhrana agent, having possibly been recruited by the Tiflis Gendarme Administration as early as 1899.[4] There is nothing intrinsically implausible in this suggestion. On the contrary, it would be downright astonishing if an ambitious conspirator of young Dzhugashvili's stamp had entirely refrained from denouncing his revolutionary rivals. Owing to the Okhrana's skill in securing promotion for its spies, by conveniently arresting their main competitors within the revolutionary parties, some degree of service with the police was almost unavoidable for an ambitious revolutionary—even if he meant to jettison the polluting contact later. Nothing in Stalin's known character suggests that he would have been deterred from availing himself of such facilities by moral scruple. That he may indeed have co-operated with the Okhrana seems indicated by many pointers. During his frequent travels on revolutionary errands Stalin blandly passed innumerable police check-points at times when he was supposedly a wanted man. Sentences of prison and exile, imposed on him on various occasions, were remarkably mild, and he seemed able to elude custody at will—the practice of staging mock arrests and mock escapes of their spies being a common Okhrana procedure and a necessary contribution to maintaining their cover as revolutionaries. To such indications may be added individual episodes in Stalin's conspiratorial history which remain puzzling on any assumption other than that of co-operation between him and the police. These episodes add weight to the supposition of collusion. However, despite Smith's patent determination to establish such collusion, and persistence in sifting evidence, he has produced no clinching documentary proof—a tribute, perhaps, to Stalinist refashioners of history and to their competence in destroying the true record of the dictator's early years.

On this obscure matter perhaps only one statement can be made with certainty: for the Okhrana and Stalin not to have made use of each other's services would have been as much out of character for the organisation as for the man.

Within the Russian armed forces the Okhrana had established a network of police spies: military personnel paid to furnish secret reports on the political reliability of their comrades in arms. In early 1914, however, General V. F. Dzhunkovsky—Deputy Minister of the Interior—issued a circular expressly forbidding such espionage, which was prejudicial to military honour, morale and discipline. Though credit is due to the Deputy Minister for thus purging the army of police spies, it must be noted that this prohibition deprived the Okhrana of its most effective weapon against subversion in the very area which was to have most impact on the collapse of autocracy in 1917. Other, no less dubious, Okhrana procedures, were also curbed by Dzhunkovsky, who banned the recruiting of police spies among schoolchildren—enlisted, as he discovered, to operate as junior Okhranniks among their classmates. It was Dzhunkovsky, too, who insisted that Roman Malinovsky, the notorious police spy and pseudo-Bolshevik, should resign from the Duma in 1914.

In August 1914 war with Germany brought many changes to the Okhrana. At first the great conflict seemed to help security work by stimulating Russian patriotic fervour—and hence a lull in revolutionary activity. The centre of gravity therefore shifted to combating espionage on behalf of Germany and her allies.

This operation was complicated by the presence on Russian soil of many German-speaking citizens, including residents of the Baltic provinces and 'colonist' farmers long settled in areas of rural Russia. There were also numerous native Russian-speakers whose German surnames made them potential suspects.

After the early surge of patriotic zeal the further progress of the war brought disillusionment and a renewed impetus to the Russian revolutionary movement—which began to receive from the German enemy clandestine subsidies calculated to weaken the Empire internally. The Okhrana accordingly swung back towards the campaign against internal subversion—a task now closely interwoven with the problem of military counter-espionage. Nor was all harmony between the Okhrana and the military—for example, friction occurred between these competing authorities after the army had received exclusive powers to expel political suspects, of whom there were many, from the zone behind the Russian western front.

Dzhunkovsky's attempts to purge the Imperial system of disreputable features led to his dismissal from the Ministry of the Interior in August 1915 through involvement in the Rasputin Affair. Even in an empire so dogged by public improprieties that stupendous scandal became a *cause célèbre* beyond compare, owing to the domination over the imperial household, and particularly over the Empress Alexandra, exercised by a coarse, drunken Siberian peasant credited with hypnotic powers, and reputedly the only person able to save the haemophiliac Tsarevich Alexis. Rasputin was notorious for acts of rampant bad taste. Now it was averred that this monster of misplaced virility was conducting a liaison with the First Lady of the Empire, now that he was intriguing for the Germans. In the latter's interest he was allegedly responsible for influencing the Tsar to appoint new and grotesquely incompetent Ministers at a time when otherwise inexplicable appointments and dismissals leapfrogged so swiftly that they seemed designed to undermine Russian resistance. Though rumours attributing significant direct political influence to Rasputin—especially those claiming both him and the Empress as German agents—are discounted by responsible historians, it is generally agreed that incalculable damage was done, indirectly, to public confidence in the declining Imperial system, by the presence near the throne of this preposterous, piercing-eyed, roistering, fornicating muzhik.

Rasputin's rise inevitably brought him under police surveillance. The Okhrana maintained spies among his servants, receiving daily reports on his comings and goings, and also on the many petitioners and intriguers who visited him. Then, when passing through Moscow in April 1915, Rasputin created at the fashionable Yar Restaurant a particularly ripe scandal of which several accounts exist.[5] One version alleges that he publicly exposed himself and boasted of his sexual relations with the Empress. Another speaks of his attempt to seduce 'a pretty maid-servant'— not, one would have thought, an event to arouse great interest in a biography so replete with similar exploits.[6] In any case Dzhunkovsky was ill-advisedly public-spirited enough to submit to the Emperor a report on Rasputin's latest indiscretions.[7] This reached the Empress's ears, and caused Dzhunkovsky's transfer to an army command—just as an earlier police chief, Peter Rachkovsky, had also fallen from imperial favour after criticising the French charlatan Philippe, a previous domestic guru of the Tsar's household.

The more outrageously Rasputin behaved, the more gratified were discerning enemies of the Imperial system, owing to the mounting discredit which so degrading an association brought on the Tsar. It is, therefore, understandable that the assassination of the healer-buffoon, accomplished on 18 December 1916, should have been the work of monarchists and extreme rightists. In the investigation of Rasputin's murder the Police Department was heavily involved. It was conducted by A. T. Vasilyev, the last Director, who traced the deed to Prince Felix Yusupov and his associates. Hastening to search Rasputin's quarters, Vasilyev was prepared to impound any compromising correspondence from Empress to seer, but found none.[8]

From other major scandals of the late Empire the Rasputin Affair differs in that the central figure was not a police spy. The Okhrana was indeed closely concerned, but this was not essentially a police scandal—rather a case in which the Okhrana to some extent diminished scandal. However, at least one senior police official—S. P. Beletsky—was alleged to have supported Rasputin in order to further his own career.[9] In any case Rasputin's contribution to the fall of the monarchy was surely greater than that of Azef, Bogrov and Malinovsky combined.

Long awaited, heralded in advance for many decades, desired by many sections of the community, feared by a minority of

Imperial administrators and Court hangers-on—the first successful Russian revolution took the nation by surprise. On 2 March
1917, the Emperor Nicholas II abdicated after ten days' confused
rioting in Petrograd, as St Petersburg had been renamed in 1914.
The term 'spontaneous', often applied to the February Revolution, is unhelpful, but the events of February 24 to 2 March 1917
were not directly organised by the revolutionary parties, whose
main leaders were absent from the capital at the time.

For eight months after the abdication some semblance of power
was uneasily wielded by a Provisional Government of newly-
appointed Ministers—chiefly liberals formerly prominent in the
Duma. Meanwhile much of the complex structure of Imperial
administration had collapsed along with the monarchy. The old
police, 'higher' and 'lower' alike, disappeared almost overnight in
the capital on the insistence of the Petrograd Soviet, acting as a
rival centre of power to the Provisional Government. Telegrams
announced the abolition of the police to the provinces, and
declarations to the same effect appeared in the press. 'In the end
the State's seemingly solid administrative apparatus, backed by
what was then the most extensively organised police system in the
world, collapsed virtually without a fight.'[10] Together with the
Okhrana and the Corps of Gendarmes, the very word police
(politsiya) disappeared, ordinary civil police duties being carried
out henceforward by a so-called militia. This motley body elected
its own officers and included many common criminals such as had
been released from the Petrograd jails in their thousands by the
rampaging mobs.[11] In the liberating spasm of early 1917 many
Russians thought that they were creating a heaven on earth—a
society in which all authority had been forever overthrown. One
early symptom of this blissful dawn was an increase in armed
robbery and assault in the streets—often the work of petty crooks
calling themselves Anarchists and equipped with a smattering of
modish political catch-phrases.

Despite such dangers few citizens hankered for a return to
discipline as once imposed by the Imperial police. How intensely
that body had been detested by the population at large was shown
by the events of 1917. During the February riots uniformed men
hastily changed into civilian clothes and went into hiding to
escape lynching by inflamed mobs incorrectly informed that
police had set up roof-top machine-gun nests and intended to
massacre the rioting population. Former gendarmes and secret
agents tried to conceal their careers, and many prominent

Okhranniks went underground or were arrested. A. T. Vasilyev, last Director of the Police Department, has described how he reported to the Taurid Palace, seat of the Provisional Government, during the February Revolution, in case he could be useful in some capacity—only to be seized and consigned to the Peter and Paul Fortress for six months.[12] Many Okhranniks were later shot by the Bolshevik Cheka, but many others escaped abroad—in some cases after fighting for the Whites in the Civil War of 1918–21. In emigration certain of them—including Gerasimov, Kurlov and Vasilyev—produced memoirs containing valuable material on the later Okhrana.

Vasilyev's adventures on foreign soil included an attempt to recruit him to the Cheka. Approached in Berlin by an envoy of this, the first Soviet political police force, and offered a large bribe, the last Police Department Director reacted vigorously: 'I have seldom in my life experienced such satisfaction as I felt at the moment when I had the privilege of throwing that gentleman downstairs.'[13] Couched in the courtly idiom pioneered by Benckendorff's Third Section, the remark makes a suitable *envoi* to an age of political police activity now terminated.

Later Okhrana history was scrutinised in detail by the Extraordinary Investigating Commission of the Provisional Government. The Commissioners interrogated such former officials of the disbanded Okhrana as seemed best able to illuminate the dark corners of pre-revolutionary administration. Witnesses included one-time Ministers and Deputy Ministers of the Interior, Police Department Directors and Vice-Directors, and Heads of the St Petersburg (Petrograd) Okhrana Section. Themselves schooled in squeezing reluctant suspects, these *ci-devant* interrogators were on the alert for traps set by the Commission, and their evidence was evasive in the extreme. But though they regularly 'forgot' details of past activity, or glibly shifted responsibility for police malpractices on to colleagues, these interrogations throw considerable light on Imperial political police activity in the years of its decline and collapse.

Again and again the commissioners probed major scandals described above—particularly the Azef, Bogrov and Malinovsky cases, the last item representing a startling revelation sprung by the opening of surviving Okhrana files in early 1917. Many lesser scandals also figured. They included the murder of Colonel S.G. Karpov, a successor of Gerasimov as head of the St Petersburg

Okhrana—blown up in a 'safe' apartment by explosive planted in a table leg and detonated by one Alexander Petrov, whose 'escape' from prison Karpov had himself arranged in the mistaken belief that he was recruiting a valuable police spy. Of such tales police history of the late Empire contains far more than can be catalogued in the present account.

The Commission was interested above all in general policy—notably in police use of *agents provocateurs*, on which many an intricate argument developed. The Okhrana bosses protested that they had never countenanced 'provocation', and that what the Commission called *agents provocateurs* were merely 'secret collaborators'. The police chiefs insisted that these operatives had been used exclusively as collectors of political intelligence, and had not been instructed to take active part in revolutionary work. Former Okhranniks were, however, forced to admit that it had been difficult for any secret collaborator long to maintain a completely passive posture within his revolutionary group, owing to the need to preserve cover by making at least some show of activity. For many years, accordingly, Okhrana agents had organised assassinations, fomented strikes and printed stirring calls to bloody revolution. Moreover, since a bonus was paid to Okhranniks who unearthed illegal printing presses, it was not uncommon for a police official to found such a press himself—and on police money —as a preliminary to 'detecting' it and claiming the customary reward, also from police funds. In these and other ways the Okhrana had systematically undermined the very legality which it was charged to uphold—as the Commissioners lost no opportunity of pointing out. Some former Okhrana chiefs asked in reply what effective means were available of combating clandestine political groups other than that of penetration by secret police agents. That no convincing answer could be given to this question was a measure of the impasse in which the late Okhrana found itself. Another point is perhaps worth adding. Fantastic as were the absurdities promoted during the Empire's dying spasms by political police provocation run riot, the Okhrana was in essence merely using a routine technique of detection as employed all over the world by civil police forces in the investigation of common crime. To state this is not to deny, but to set in context, such an apparently extravagant but well-justified claim as Bertram Wolfe's: 'There was something in the Russian temperament and scene that engendered these men of ambivalent spirit and double role, these Gapons, Azefs . . . Bogrovs and Malinovskys—these figures without parallel in the police and revolutionary movements of other lands.'[14]

Besides probing provocation, the Extraordinary Commission also investigated the practice of intercepting mail. This was an extensive activity of the late Okhrana, which maintained 'Black Cabinets' for the purpose, with special apparatus for steaming open envelopes, replacing seals and photographically 'raising' secret-ink palimpsests lurking between the lines of inoffensive-seeming letters. Since revolutionaries made frequent use of codes and cyphers, a skilled cryptographer, Ivan Zybin, was employed by the Police Department to work on intercepted mail. One of his assignments was the encyphered correspondence of an Archbishop of Irkutsk. The cypher turned out to be based on a passage of the Scriptures, but the text yielded scant intelligence, either political or ecclesiastical, consisting as it did of love letters addressed to an abbess.[15]

Whether postal interception or *agents provocateurs* were the subject, the arguments on both sides were essentially sterile, for there seems little to choose between the squirming self-justification of many ex-Okhrana chiefs and the pedantic fencing of their interrogators. Such legalistic hair-splitting appears all the more futile when one remembers the dubious basis of legality on which the Commission rested, being the creation of a Provisional Government itself possessing only flimsy entitlement in law.[16] Furthermore, while this illegal, or semi-legal, Commission was impugning former policemen for upholding Imperial law by unlawful means, Lenin and his associates were pursuing on the streets outside a campaign destined to provoke a further change of government which would entail the impartial liquidation both of the interrogated Okhrana chiefs and of their high-minded inquisitors. In this context the commissioners' obsession with legal niceties becomes more excusable, if only as an attempt to defend the rule of law by a last-ditch stand. Such an obsession by individual officials with legal correctness runs through later Imperial history—a lost cause, yet one which deserves more honour than it has sometimes received.

Persistent probing by the Commissioners signally failed to reveal the former Okhrana chiefs as fiends in human shape. Many indeed were the gross defects of character and organisation laid bare, including rivalries between individuals, self-seeking, anti-Semitism, attempts to shift responsibility by implicating others, as also sterile inter-office, inter-departmental and interministerial feuds. Again and again an endemic flaw in police organisation—the lack of any clear-cut chain of command—was thrown into relief. Confessions of weakness by the fallen mighty lent occasional variety to the depositions, as when Beletsky (generally regarded as more of a scoundrel than most other police officials of the period) kept harping on the plight of his wife and small children while he languished in jail—for, like several others among the interrogated, he was held in custody at the time. Beletsky tried to claim a fee for describing his experiences to the Commission, though stories of his extortionist practices in office suggest that he must already have been a rouble millionaire several times over. As for Gerasimov, that rugged Okhrana chief had retired from the service several years before facing the Commission, and had taken to playing the stock exchange—thus faithfully following an Okhrannik's rake's progress as conceived in folk myth. Yet even this stalwart figure was now sufficiently demoralised to inform the Commission that 'when I left the service I changed completely and saw that in serving the system I had committed a crime. . . . I am ashamed at having worked there and recently I've almost become a revolutionary myself.'[17] In emigration later Gerasimov recovered his morale—to judge from his forthright memoirs, which reveal no such infirmity of purpose.

Between the February and October Revolutions of 1917 Russia lacked any formally constituted political police organisation. Political police functions were, however, discharged by the Counter-Espionage Bureau of the Petrograd Military District under Colonel B. V. Nikitin—another valuable memoirist of the period. He has described his appointment to this office, much against his will, by General Kornilov, G.O.C. of Petrograd Military District. Nikitin was at first unable to pay the salary of his newly-recruited staff, but had to borrow the money privately. So discredited were the former authorities that he could not even consider recruiting any individual tainted with Imperial police associations. 'My assistants were at great pains to make it clear to all and sundry that the personnel of the Counter-Espionage Bureau did not include a single gendarme.'[18]

Nikitin's Bureau was charged to confine itself strictly to military counter-espionage, eschewing the discredited activity of political security work. As 1917 proceeded, however, Nikitin found it increasingly difficult to draw any hard and fast line between German spies and Russian revolutionaries, owing to the widespread scale on which (according to his findings) the German government was now subsidising subversive forces within Russia.[19] The situation was complicated by the uneasy status of the Provisional Government as a mere caretaker administration intended to hold office only until a properly elected Constituent Assembly should meet. The Provisional Government was also increasingly hampered by the Petrograd Soviet, the unruly competing authority which claimed to speak for the workers, soldiers and peasants—besides which, of course, Russia was still engaged in fighting a major war during the whole of 1917.

In these chaotic conditions Nikitin's Bureau managed to uncover some German agents operating in Petrograd—but often enough only to see them 'sprung' from jail by a revolutionary mob. Nikitin became more and more convinced that the movement to overthrow the Provisional Government was largely under German control, consisting of agents in the pay of Berlin. As head of counter-espionage, he therefore found himself usurping the functions of a political police chief. 'My friends in the Public Prosecutor's Department [he explains in his memoirs] pointed out to me that, notwithstanding my previously expressed determination to keep the Counter-Espionage Bureau clear of politics, the wheels of fate had, nevertheless, turned it into a political police instrument.'[20] Political police or not, the Bureau became increasingly impotent, all the more so when the Provisional Government failed to crush the Bolsheviks after their abortive, and perhaps unintentional, attempt to stage an insurrection in July 1917. By the time of Lenin's successful and almost bloodless *coup* in October 1917, when the Bolsheviks made themselves masters of a Petrograd utterly demoralised and chaotic, no effective political police or other authority remained in Russia.

The year 1917, accordingly, saw the end of the Okhrana, and also the beginning and end of such shadowy political police activity as was conducted under the Provisional Government. The remainder of the present study must be devoted to the more formidable organisations developed under Lenin and his successors to perform the task in which the Okhrana and Colonel Nikitin had so signally failed—that of protecting the rulers of Russia and their political system.

7
The Cheka
1917–1922

On 25 October (7 November) 1917 the Bolsheviks seized power in Petrograd by an almost bloodless *coup*, while Moscow saw a week's hard fighting before Lenin's adherents made themselves masters of the city. In most other parts of the former Empire their revolution was something of which people read in the press or learnt by word of mouth, rather than an event which found its immediate expression in fighting. Bloodshed was to come in time, but not on any extensive scale until the Bolsheviks had been in power for a few months.

The leading organ of the new government—a cabinet, in effect —was the Council of People's Commissars, who performed the function of Ministers, a term which was now discarded. They were fifteen in number at the outset, all Bolsheviks, and worked under Lenin's chairmanship. Their hold on the country was precarious in the extreme, however, and for a time Lenin's administration wore as temporary an air as had the supplanted Provisional Government. The Bolsheviks had seized power at a time of acute weariness with the war against Germany and her allies, which had now dragged on for more than three years, and had included many serious Russian military defeats. Nor did the Russian home front offer the new rulers an encouraging spectacle. Late 1917 was a period of serious food shortages, of soaring prices, of increasing robbery with violence on the streets and of general indiscipline and demoralisation which had been useful as a lever to overthrow the Provisional Government, but urgently required a controlling hand now that the Bolsheviks themselves were in power. However, Lenin did not command anything approaching majority support throughout the country at large, for the number of Bolshevik Party members was tiny—only about a quarter of a million in a nation of about 140 million[1]—though it is also true that enthusiasm for Bolshevism was widespread among people, particularly factory workers and soldiers garrisoned in Petrograd, who were not necessarily Party members. Meanwhile the bulk of the population, consisting of peasants or peasant soldiers, still owed allegiance to the party of the peasantry—that of the Socialist Revolutionaries. In November 1917 this party further complicated the political picture by splitting into two wings—left and right. The Left Socialist Revolutionaries allied themselves with the Bolsheviks, and for a few months—between December 1917 and March 1918—leading Left Socialist Revolutionaries held posts as People's Commissars in Lenin's government.

As this temporary collaboration illustrates, the early months of the new Soviet Government were not marred by the brutal repression of all political rivals which later became so characteristic of Bolshevik methods. One of the first acts of Lenin's administration was to repeal the death penalty (restored in September 1917 by Kerensky, then Prime Minister of the Provisional Government). Lenin himself opposed the repeal, which he called madness.[2] However, on 5 (18) November 1917 Lenin was able to assert that 'we are not using the kind of terror used by the French revolutionaries who guillotined defenceless people, and I hope we will not, for we have strength with us.'[3] At the time when Lenin made this remark his revolution was not yet two weeks old, and the first signs of a harsher approach were not long in appearing. The non-Bolshevik press was suppressed—first right-wing publications and then liberal—though it was some time before all rival Socialist and Anarchist publications disappeared entirely. On 28 November (11 December) 1917 Lenin decreed that leading members of the Kadet (liberal) party should be arrested and tried by revolutionary tribunals.[4] However, it was civil rather than political crime which chiefly exercised the new authorities—in particular the frequent 'drink pogroms' which occurred when looters broke open and ransacked the spirit stores of the capital, loosing off firearms at random as they waded through streams of wine released from staved-in barrels—often to fall unconscious or even dead as the result of these orgies. Measures to curb such practices were taken by the Military Revolutionary Committee, the temporary organisation which had planned the Bolshevik rising, and orders were issued to shoot the drunken looters.

On 7 (20) December 1917 the suppression of political offences against the new order was put on a more regular basis when the Council of People's Commissars established the Cheka—the All-Russian Extraordinary Commission for Combating Counter-Revolution and Sabotage, which remained the official Bolshevik political police organ until it was reorganised as the GPU in February 1922. The name Cheka under which the new organisation is best known, derives from the Russian initials of its abbreviated title. The Cheka's functions were later semi-officially defined as 'hunting out and liquidating all counter-revolution and sabotage . . . handing over all saboteurs and counter-revolutionaries to a Revolutionary Tribunal . . . carrying out preliminary investigations only'.[5] In other words, the Cheka was designed to be, like the Okhrana before it, an investigatory rather than a punitive body, though it was entitled to impose such penalties as confiscation of property, deprivation of ration cards, publication of lists of enemies of the people and so on. The Cheka was evidently not at first envisaged as the organ of ultra-severe repression into which it later developed.

Opinions differ as to whether the original project for the Cheka was essentially the brain-child of Lenin himself, as Soviet spokesmen maintain, or of Felix Dzerzhinsky, its first head.[6] Dzerzhinsky came from a genteel Polish family of moderate means, and had been well equipped for his new role as chief of political police by two decades of intense struggle against the Okhrana, during which he had been many times arrested and had also effected frequent escapes. As an adolescent he had planned to become a Catholic priest until revolution provided a more attractive channel for his enthusiasms.[7] However, this ascetic, monk-like, cold-blooded and incorruptible figure always remained something of a Grand Inquisitor. In October 1917 he had joined the Military Revolutionary Committee which staged the Bolshevik *coup*, and had become Commandant of the Smolny Institute—the Bolshevik headquarters—with personal responsibility for the safety of the main party leaders. It was from this position that he graduated to head the Cheka and its successors, the GPU and OGPU.

The year 1918 saw Lenin's government harassed by many preoccupations transcending the sphere of political police activities. Peace must, at all costs, be made with Germany and her allies, as was done at Brest-Litovsk on 3 March 1918 on terms highly unfavourable to Soviet Russia. This was followed by the development of Civil War between the Reds (supporters of the Soviet Government) and their opponents, known as Whites or White Guards, a further complication being the military intervention of foreign powers on the White side. During this period acts of extreme violence were confined neither to military campaigns nor to any one of the competing factions.

As if to emphasise the need for an efficient political police on the Red side, the year 1918 had begun with an unsuccessful attempt to kill Lenin undertaken on 1 (14) January by assassins who eluded capture after firing through the windscreen of his car in Petrograd. A few days later Lenin's troops used violence in the opposite direction to disperse the Constituent Assembly, the body elected in the previous November to provide Russia with a new and permanent form of government. The Bolsheviks held only a minority of seats, being greatly outnumbered by Socialist Revolutionaries, and it was therefore necessary for Lenin to destroy the Assembly by force unless he was prepared to renounce his rule. Early 1918 also saw sporadic outbreaks of mob violence, often the work of sailors—notoriously the most unruly element in the population. On 5 (18) January revolutionary sailors murdered two former Kadet Ministers, Shingaryov and Kokoshkin, in a Petrograd hospital, and in the following month sailors of the Black Sea Fleet conducted a three-day massacre of the *bourgeoisie* in the Crimean port of Sevastopol.[8] February 1918 also witnessed a particularly momentous event when, on the 25th of the month, the Cheka shot a criminal who called himself Prince Eboli, and was said to have posed as a Chekist in order to practise extortion. Otherwise undistinguished, Eboli made history as the first recorded example among many victims executed without trial by the Cheka, which was soon to assume the combined functions of policeman, judge and executioner on a nationwide scale. For the moment, however, the number of its officials was fairly small— about 120 all told in the central Cheka at the time when, in March 1918, the new government transferred its capital to Moscow.[9] In the same month the Bolsheviks adopted the title 'All-Russian Communist Party (of Bolsheviks)'.

The central Cheka accompanied the government to the new capital, occupying the headquarters of a former insurance company in the Lubyanka, and eventually transforming this area of central Moscow into a network of Cheka prisons and offices. This transfer of the political police headquarters to Moscow was unpopular in the city, as the Cheka boss Peters has recorded. One reason was a shooting affray which occurred in a Moscow café between Cheka agents and customers whom Peters describes as drunken bandit-hooligans. Another was the extraordinarily dramatic arrest, during a circus performance, of the clown Bim-Bom as he was making fun of the Soviet Government under the big top. An armed detachment of Chekists invaded the ring, their attempts to arrest Bim-Bom being interpreted by the delighted audience as all part of the act until their favourite clown fled—pursued, not by custard pies, but by real bullets, as general panic broke out.[10]

As 1918 proceeded it became increasingly difficult to discover where political activity ended and gangsterism began. This was true of the Cheka itself, and also of many of the Cheka's opponents, among whom the Anarchists were prominent—including in their ranks both political idealists and out-and-out criminals. Anarchists terming themselves a Black Guard had set up house in some twenty-five Moscow villas, formerly the property of wealthy citizens, and had turned them into fortified gang strongholds, the scene of unspeakable orgies from which they issued to rob and murder on the streets. On the night of 11–12 April 1918 the Cheka made a concerted attack on these strong points, mounting a military operation which involved the use of artillery on both sides, for the Black Guard had set up a mountain gun in the gateway of its chief headquarters—the former Merchant's Club on Malaya Dmitrovka Street, while Anarchist machine-gunners manned the windows. Twelve Chekists were killed in this engagement, and there were some thirty casualties among the Anarchists.[11] Mass arrests of Anarchists followed in Moscow and other parts of the country.

Meanwhile the Soviet political police was rapidly expanding throughout Red Russia, and a recent Soviet authority claims that over four hundred provincial Cheka organisations were set up in the first half of 1918.[12] This territorial expansion was accompanied by the formation of specialised Cheka units operating in such fields as transport, frontier defence and the armed forces. By mid-1918, moreover, the Soviet authorities were giving open encouragement to political terror—a tactic which Lenin had firmly opposed in the Imperial period, when it had been employed unsuccessfully by the Socialist Revolutionaries as a means of seizing power. As a technique of preserving power once seized, however, Lenin was willing, not to say eager, to use a very different kind of terror—that which involved the arrest, imprisonment and shooting of large numbers of people on the grounds, not of any specific political activity, but of the social class to which they had once belonged ... or of political offences which they might conceivably have committed one day had they not been arrested in good time. The excuse for such a tactic was found in the increasingly violent methods employed by opponents of the régime with the backing of foreign capitalists, diplomats and spies.

Though political terrorism was not adopted on an intensive scale until September 1918, it was heralded by lesser violence, by official threats and by ferocious declarations of intent. At a press interview in early June, Dzerzhinsky expressed his policy in especially ominous terms:

> 'We stand for organised terror. . . . Terror is an absolute necessity during times of revolution. . . . The Cheka is obliged to defend the revolution and conquer the enemy even if its sword does by chance sometimes fall upon the heads of the innocent.'[13]

The same month saw an important further measure against political opponents when Mensheviks and Right Socialist Revolutionaries were expelled from the Central Executive Committee of the Soviets. Then a Socialist Revolutionary assassinated Volodarsky, a Bolshevik official, on 20 June, after which, on the day following, sentence of death was pronounced on an Admiral Shchastny by a Revolutionary Tribunal and carried out shortly afterwards. This was important as the first death sentence pronounced by a judicial body since the October Revolution, and followed hard upon the official readoption of capital punishment, abolished immediately after the Bolshevik seizure of power. However, such legalistic niceties exercised little influence on the practice of the Cheka, which had been executing its victims unofficially ever since the shooting of Prince Eboli in February, though the number of such killings still remained relatively modest, so far as can be established, for by June 1918 they probably totalled only dozens or scores.[14]

In July 1918 the Left Socialist Revolutionaries were the only non-Bolsheviks to retain an officially tolerated political organisation, but their relations with their dominant Bolshevik allies were steadily deteriorating. The Peace of Brest-Litovsk had caused their leaders to resign from the Council of People's Commissars in protest. However, Left Socialist Revolutionaries remained prominent on the Cheka, where one of their number, Aleksandro-vich, served as Deputy Chairman to Dzerzhinsky, while others were members of the Collegium. In view of their bad relations with the Bolsheviks, their continued presence in the highest echelons of the political police was becoming increasingly anoma-lous and was soon to end under dramatic circumstances.

Objecting as they did to the peace treaty with Germany, the Left Socialist Revolutionaries protested against the presence in Moscow of the newly arrived German Ambassador Count Mirbach, whose assassination they proceeded to organise as a means of stirring up conflict between Soviet Russia and Germany. On 6 July 1918 two Left Socialist Revolutionaries who were also members of the Cheka, Blyumkin and Andreyev, gained access to the German Embassy in Moscow by means of a forged letter purportedly signed by Dzerzhinsky. Obtaining audience with the Ambassador, they shot him dead, threw two hand grenades, and escaped in the confusion. The episode did not, however, lead to a serious breach between Germany and the Bolsheviks. Nor can another possible interpretation of this affair be discounted—that Blyumkin and Andreyev were, in effect, Bolshevik agents engaged in discrediting the Left Socialist Revolutionaries and providing an excuse to liquidate them.[15] Such, at all events, was the sequel to the episode of Mirbach's assassination, which coincided with an ill-organised armed revolt launched by the Left Socialist Revolutionaries in Moscow, a prominent part being played by those members of the party who held office in the Cheka. Captur-ing the very headquarters of the Cheka in the Lubyanka, they arrested Dzerzhinsky and his Latvian henchman Latsis. They also seized the main telegraph office on Myasnitsky Street and sent telegrams all over Russia announcing the overthrow of the Bolsheviks. This news soon turned out to be premature, for the revolt was quickly suppressed. It was, moreover, so poorly co-ordinated that Chekists loyal to Bolshevism were able to arrest some four hundred Left Socialist Revolutionaries in the Bolshoy Theatre where they sat as delegates to the Fifth All-Russian Congress of Soviets, apparently unaware that their party was in process of staging a minor revolution all around them. The Left Socialist Revolutionary Party was now suppressed, though not officially declared illegal, and the Cheka was reconstituted with a Collegium consisting exclusively of Bolsheviks.[16] From now on Lenin could rule unallied with any rival political party, though it was not until 1921 that open activity by rival Socialist factions was finally brought to an end after some four years of severe but fluctuating persecution.

Mirbach's assassination and the Moscow uprising chanced to coincide with the outbreak, on the same day, of anti-Bolshevik risings organised by the former Socialist Revolutionary terrorist Boris Savinkov in various provincial towns north and east of Moscow. The most serious of these revolts occurred at Yaroslavl on the Volga, which was not recaptured by Soviet forces until 19 July. Reprisals followed the retaking of the town, including the shooting of 350 persons in Yaroslavl itself and of smaller batches of victims in other localities.[17] Meanwhile, on the night of 16–17 July, the deposed Tsar Nicholas II, together with his wife, children and certain servants, had been shot and bayoneted in the cellar of a house in Yekaterinburg (now Sverdlovsk) in the Urals, by order of Lenin. The chief executioner was Jacob Yurovsky, a member of the Ural Regional Soviet, who was assisted by Latvian guards and Cheka agents. All other members of the Imperial Family who fell into Communist hands were also put to death, and though there had been no significant movement to restore the House of Romanov, these murders were of immense symbolic importance as a landmark on the road to ever greater terror.

A yet more significant date in the evolution of mass terror was 30 August 1918, when attempts—the one unsuccessful, the other successful—were made to assassinate two leading Communists. It was on this fateful day that Fanya (or Dora) Kaplan, who claimed herself a Socialist Revolutionary and had been a political prisoner under the Tsar, ambushed Lenin as he was leaving a workers' meeting and fired a revolver, twice wounding him—seriously, but not fatally. On the same day—by coincidence and not, it appears, as part of a concerted plot—another Socialist Revolutionary, Kannegiesser, fatally shot Uritsky, the head of the Petrograd Cheka. To these events the authorities at once reacted with un-exampled fury. On 3 September *Izvestiya* announced that over five hundred people had been shot in Petrograd as a reprisal for the death of Uritsky. On the following day the Commissar of the Interior circularised all Soviets, instructing them to proceed with a campaign of 'mass terror', and on the day after that (5 September) the Council of People's Commissars issued a decree on terror. This stated that class enemies must be isolated in concentration camps, and that all persons connected with counter-revolutionary organisations must be shot, their names and the reasons for their execution being published.[18] The Petrograd shootings were accordingly followed by other massacres in Moscow and provincial Russia. Despite the fact that the attacks on Lenin and Uritsky had been the work of dissident Socialists, the Red Terror of autumn 1918 was chiefly directed against members of the non-Socialist former middle class, consisting of one-time landlords, capitalists, ministers under the Tsar, professional persons, officers, businessmen and factory owners. Not that non-Bolshevik Socialists by any means remained immune, besides which many peasants fell victims to the Cheka when they resisted attempts to confiscate their stocks of grain.

One episode in the Red Terror was the arrest of R. H. Bruce Lockhart, whom the British government had sent to Russia in early 1918, vaguely briefed to establish unofficial relations with the Bolsheviks.[19] Shortly after his arrival the British had landed troops in Murmansk, joining with their allies in a policy of armed intervention on Russian territory which seriously embarrassed Lockhart's attempts to negotiate with the Bolsheviks in Moscow. To a Cheka increasingly obsessed with the plots, real or imaginary, of foreign spies, he soon began to appeal as the most sinister among various suspicious diplomats—British, American and French—now active on Soviet territory. Steps were accordingly taken to set a trap through an *agent provocateur*, the Latvian army officer E. P. Berzin, who proceeded to contact Lockhart on the instructions of the Cheka.[20] Speaking to this brief, Berzin informed the British representative that Latvian units of the Soviet armed forces were politically disaffected and wished to surrender to the British forces now embarked at Arkhangel under General Poole. Lockhart took this story at face value, and supplied Berzin with a letter to enable a Latvian emissary to pass through British lines and make contact with Poole.[21] Other, more far-reaching plans were also attributed to Lockhart by the Soviet authorities. He was astonished to read in the Bolshevik press a 'fantastic account of a so-called Lockhart Plot. We were accused of having conspired to murder Lenin and Trotsky, to set up a military dictatorship in Moscow, and by blowing up all the railway bridges to reduce the populations of Moscow and St Petersburg to starvation.'[22] The ramifications of this affair included an armed attack by the Cheka on the former British Embassy in Petrograd, which led to the shooting of the British Naval Attaché Captain Cromie and also (according to Soviet sources) to the arrest of some forty White supporters found on the premises.[23]

Granted favourable treatment under arrest, Lockhart was

taken to the Kremlin, where he was assigned quarters conveniently vacated by S. P. Beletsky, once a Director of the Police Department under the Tsar, who had been shot on the same afternoon.[24]
In the course of his imprisonment, Lockhart had interviews with
various Soviet notabilities, including the Latvian Cheka boss
Peters, who appeared in customary Cheka garb—in a leather
jacket with a Mauser pistol strapped to his side. After a month in
custody, Lockhart was released in exchange for the future Soviet
Commissar for Foreign Affairs Litvinov, who had been arrested in
London. Less fortunate than their alleged leader, several of
Lockhart's supposed accomplices—Soviet citizens or lacking
diplomatic immunity—received prison sentences, and two were
sentenced to death.

The Red Terror sets the Cheka apart from all preceding
Russian political police forces since it was responsible for far more
political arrests and executions in some five years of activity than
had occurred during the entire sway of the Okhrana, the Third
Section and all their predecessors put together—with the possible
exception of Ivan the Terrible's Oprichnina, which has only
flimsy claims to be regarded as a true police authority. As with the
Oprichnina, the number of the Cheka's victims defies exact com-
putation. The Cheka boss Latsis gives a surprisingly precise figure
for the number of individuals shot in the first three years of operations—12,733—but there are reasons for regarding this as a gross
underestimate.[25] By contrast, the figure of victims quoted by the
White Russian General Denikin for the years 1918–19 is 1,700,000,
which appears to be a considerable exaggeration.[26] W. H. Chamberlin's rough estimate of fifty thousand executed by the Cheka
during the Civil War must be nearer the true mark.[27]
The Cheka did not execute its victims in public, but published
lists of victims. Though this practice later lapsed, the executions
lost nothing in terror-inspiring quality through greater secrecy.
Hangings, drownings and various other forms of death are liberally
recorded in the literature of the subject, and in horrific wealth of
detail, but execution by shooting formed the standard practice
wherever the Cheka held sway, whether in Moscow, Petrograd,
Odessa, Astrakhan, Tiflis, Central Asia, Siberia or elsewhere.
The normal procedure was as follows. While lice-infested prisoners
lie, immured with their huge latrine pail in their filthy, over-
crowded, stinking, bug-ridden cell, frozen or stifling according to

the time of year, steps resound ominously in the corridor, a key turns in the lock, an armed guard enters and reads off certain names from a list, roughly ordering the designated victims to accompany him 'with things'—that is, with their personal belongings. These trappings are a traditional perquisite of the Chekist executioners, as is also the outer clothing of the condemned, for they are generally required to strip off before shooting, which usually takes place in some suitable cellar, garage or yard. Clad in his leather jacket, holding a Colt revolver and often festooned with a whole armoury of daggers, cutlasses, Mauser pistols and the like, the executioner dispatches each in turn by shooting through the back of the head—a procedure calculated to make the victim's face unrecognisable. Following old-established Imperial tradition, the executioner is usually drunk when performing his duties—so much so that the delivery of liquor in quantity to the Cheka office may well be interpreted on the prison 'grape-vine' as a sign that executions are impending.[28] An additional variant is the lavish use of cocaine to overcome any lingering vestige of squeamishness. During executions the engines of stationary lorries are revved up in order to drown the shots, the screams of the victims and—in the case of dissident Socialists—the revolutionary songs with which the more heroic meet their doom.

Of these terrible occasions innumerable accounts have been given. One Chekist executioner used to shoot each victim piecemeal, beginning with a wrist, continuing with an elbow and so on —all this between sniffs of cocaine.[29] In Moscow the notorious headsman Maga once shot a batch of fifteen or twenty . . . and then suddenly pounced, in a frenzy of blood lust, on the very Commandant of the central Cheka prison, Popov, who chanced to have been witnessing the butchery, and screamed 'get your clothes off, you bastard!' With bloodshot eyes, ghastly, bespattered with gore and fragments of brain, the berserk killer would certainly have slaughtered his terrified superior officer had not some humbler Chekists rushed to the rescue in time.[30]

Besides these cellar shootings, numerous mass executions also took place in convenient waste areas outside the towns, where the condemned were dispatched by revolver, machine-gun and bayonet after being forced to dig communal graves. Another method was to fill old barges with condemned prisoners, tow them out to the middle of a river and machine-gun them from the banks. Though Cheka executions tended to follow a uniform drill throughout the country, albeit with many variations, the same is not true of torture, which was widespread indeed, but was applied according to individual discretion. Many are the reports of savage beatings and mutilations administered to prisoners to extract information or provide amusement, and many too are the accounts of such practices as the insertion of needles under fingernails, besides innumerable other bestialities which need not be catalogued here. Moral torments were also used, including threats to close relatives and mock executions, as when a Cheka official would fire a revolver but miss, apparently by accident—which was found a valuable adjunct to more conventional forms of interrogation.

Such were the methods adopted throughout the Civil War of 1918–21 by the Cheka in those fluctuating areas of Russia which were under Red control. The Whites employed similar techniques in the areas controlled by them, and since both sides were accustomed to massacre prisoners, the distinction between military and political atrocities was apt to become blurred. Soviet setbacks on the Civil War fronts provoked widespread executions of the Cheka's jailed captives, but so too did Soviet successes. Moreover, by one of those many paradoxes which distinguish Russian police history, the very prison amnesties periodically declared by the authorities themselves frequently served as the impulse for a new wave of executions. When, for example, the death penalty was once again formally abolished, on 14 January 1920, the Moscow Cheka celebrated by hurriedly shooting 160 persons in their yard.[31]

From the beginning, arbitrariness was the hallmark of the Cheka's operations. Punishment was meted out according to the whim of the local police chief, and the nature of the victim's offence might remain a mystery to all concerned, not necessarily deriving even from anything as solid as an anonymous denunciation. It frequently happened that an individual was shot because his surname happened to coincide with that of someone else who figured on a list of condemned persons. In prison agonising uncertainty about the future could be the severest ordeal of all, for it was Chekist practice to give prisoners no information either on the cause of their arrest or on their prospects. Some spent years in jail simply because the Cheka had mislaid a file. Protests and appeals might be accepted by a stolid official, but usually went unanswered, while prisoners remained at the mercy of Chekists and warders who were little better than, and in many cases actually were, common thieves. Food parcels from outside—of crucial importance at a time of general shortage—were regularly confiscated or pilfered by the Cheka.

Against these manifold abuses the prisoners had only the drastic redress of hunger strikes. As the outcome of such a strike the Left Socialist Revolutionary leader Maria Spiridonov secured release from prison in September 1921, while others obtained relaxations in the prison régime. Spiridonov was only one among many Socialists of non-Bolshevik persuasion imprisoned for long periods by the Cheka, which made use of surviving Okhrana records to track down these opponents of successive Russian governments.[32] Many of the Socialist Revolutionaries, Mensheviks or Anarchists in question had suffered long terms of imprisonment and exile under the Tsars. Since those days, as such prisoners have reported, prison conditions had greatly deteriorated.[33] More numerous arrests and executions, with even less process of law behind them, desperate overcrowding, worse food and the total ineffectiveness of official regulations—such as, however illiberal, had controlled the operations of the Imperial penal system—these were among the points of comparison made to the discredit of the new social system by witnesses who had experience of the old.

One outstanding difference between political police practice in Imperial and Soviet times lay in an increase in social discrimination. Despite the wide gulf separating privileged and under-privileged in Imperial Russia, social origin in itself had never been a political crime. Under the Cheka, however, many were imprisoned and executed because they had once been landowners, officers, or were simply educated people—perhaps possessed of some such sinister skill as knowledge of a foreign language. Not that these guide-lines were followed with full consistency—otherwise Lenin himself, as a former member of the gentry class, son of a senior Tsarist official and a tolerable linguist, would have made an ideal political hostage. Another new feature of Leninism was the concept of the 'revolutionary conscience', deemed to qualify Chekists to decide matters of life and death by instinct, since proletarian origin combined with proper political convictions supposedly guaranteed a sense of justice superior to that embodied in any code of law.

In defence of the Cheka it has been argued that the Imperial practice of fettering with foot-irons had lapsed. Prisoners no longer wore coats with diamond-shaped patches on the back. They now had the whole of the head shaved instead of only half of it and they did not have to jump to attention when addressed by a prison officer or visiting notability. It must also be conceded that the Cheka operated during a ferocious civil war when comparable treatment of political opponents was common in the areas under White rule, not to mention the unspeakable atrocities committed by various private armies owing allegiance to neither side. However, these considerations help to explain rather than justify the excesses of the Cheka—excesses later dwarfed by the mass atrocities of the Stalin period. Since Stalin's repressions were yet more widespread, the Cheka and the main sponsor of the Red Terror, Lenin, havè tended to be overshadowed, acquiring a wholly undeserved reputation for following relatively humane and civilised policies. It is therefore worth stressing that the true author of Soviet police terror was not Stalin, but Lenin.[34] Lenin's great achievements as a pioneer of totalitarian terror have unfortunately been belittled by recent attempts in the Soviet Union to emasculate the Cheka in retrospect and smear it with a reputation for benevolence. Lenin's political police was not, as is now suggested by its Soviet historians, a band of scrupulously 'correct' public-spirited officials sternly but regretfully chastising political error in a spirit more of sorrow than of anger under the inspiration of the saintly Dzerzhinsky: a picture which reminds one of the public 'image' of Benckendorff's gendarmes as cultivated—absurdly, if somewhat less so—in official propaganda from 1826 onwards.

In November 1920 the defeat of General Wrangel in the south assured the Reds of victory in the Civil War by destroying their most formidable remaining enemy. The time had clearly come to reconsider the methods of the Cheka, so far essentially a war-time organisation and now grown from small beginnings to a total of 31,000 members, according to Latsis.[35] Dzerzhinsky accordingly issued an order designed to curb the worst excesses of the terror. Persons accused of minor offences were distinguished from major political criminals, and orders were given for their release. The automatic oppression of 'class enemies' was to end, kulaks, ex-officers, former gentlemen and such being from now on liable to punishment only for specific offences and not solely on the basis of social origin.[36] With the coming of peace the Cheka also began to divert more of its energies into the economic field, this change of emphasis being designed to assist the reconstruction of Russia's devastated industries, set the shattered transport system to rights and improve the desperate fuel situation.

Lenin introduced two especially important changes of policy at the Tenth Party Congress in March 1921. Firstly, he brought in the New Economic Policy (NEP), which permitted a degree of private trade such as had been banned as 'speculation' during the Civil War. Secondly, Lenin prohibited oppositionist activity within the Communist party itself, which had begun to throw up important groups hostile to the policies of the top leadership now that all effective opposition from outside the Party had been totally crushed. Henceforward dissident Party members were to be denied freedom of speech such as they had retained after helping to gag non-Communist members of the community.

The Tenth Party Congress coincided with revolt against Communist rule by the sailors of Kronstadt, once famous as a leading Bolshevik stronghold. This was a rebellion against Lenin by the very revolutionaries who had once been the bulwark of his movement. Now utterly disillusioned, the Kronstadt rebels accused the Bolsheviks of 'having brought the workers, instead of freedom, an ever present fear of being dragged into the torture chambers of the Cheka, which exceeds by many times in its horrors the gendarmerie administration of the Tsarist régime'.[37] A recent Soviet historian of the Cheka blames the Petrograd branch of that organisation for permitting such a dangerous armed revolt to break out near the city without taking steps to isolate the leaders in advance.[38] As it was, the insurgents had to be crushed by military force, after which survivors fell into the clutches of the Cheka and were either shot or put into concentration camps.[39] To the same period belongs the peasant revolt which had flared up in the Tambov Province in August of the previous year under the guerrilla leader Antonov. Eventually developing into a widespread but irregular military campaign against Red Army forces under Tukhachevsky, the Tambov affair saw Chekist military units in action against the rebels. The Cheka also used the technique of infiltrating its agents into Antonov's guerrilla units in the guise of pretended sympathisers—a practice termed provocation when adopted by enemies of Bolshevism. Among these infiltrators a certain Belugin received the Order of the Red Banner for his skill in luring one of Antonov's local commanders to a secret 'conference', where he was ambushed by a unit of Red cavalry.[40]

Many other Chekist exploits relating to this and other partisan actions of the period are also on record, for Kronstadt and Tambov were only two among many local revolts which blazed up at the end of the Civil War. Others included the rebellion of the Basmachi in Central Asia and the activities of anti-Soviet forces operating near the Polish and Finnish borders. It was Communist practice to term members of such forces bandits and to emphasise or invent links between them and foreign capitalists and spies, as well as to associate such uprisings with the banned native Menshevik and Socialist Revolutionary Parties. In combating these affairs the Cheka remained active, the number of military units of the organisation having been greatly increased over the years. Internal Cheka troops numbered nearly 70,000 by December 1920, and at the beginning of the following year they became entirely independent of regular army control, being directly subordinated to the central Cheka in Moscow.[41] Moreover, now that the fighting had ceased on the Civil War fronts, a vast borderland required supervision and patrolling, and units of the Chekist frontier guard were expanded accordingly. Amongst other difficulties of the period was the problem posed by destitute children orphaned in the Civil War, of whom there were believed to be some four million in all. Many roamed the country in murderous packs, adding yet another to the hazards of existence in the young Soviet republic. The control of these delinquent juveniles was given to the Cheka, and according to Sofinov numerous children's homes were built on the proceeds of voluntary deductions from the salary of Cheka agents[42] —a story which reminds one of the famous handkerchief with which Nicholas I had once told the chief of his Third Section to wipe away orphans' tears.

In 1921 a disastrous harvest created terrible famine in the area of the Volga and elsewhere, with the result that several millions perished from starvation. Amongst other bodies, native and foreign, engaged on feeding the starving, the American Relief Administration under Herbert Hoover was prominent, its assistance being received grudgingly by a Soviet Government which felt that it had good reason for treating all foreigners as potential spies. The Administration was subjected to harassment by the Cheka, while many Russians active in famine relief were first condemned to execution by a Cheka tribunal, but then released and deported from the country in response to protests from abroad.[43]

By the end of 1921 Lenin was emphasising the importance of preserving a greater measure of legality in political police operations. A decree of 6 February 1922 accordingly abolished the Cheka, its functions being taken over by a newly created branch of the People's Commissariat of the Interior—the General Political Administration (GPU). Once again a Russian political police force had apparently disappeared, only to resurface immediately under a new name.

8

The GPU/OGPU

1922–1934

In May and December 1922, and again in March 1923, Lenin suffered the three major cerebral strokes which increasingly incapacitated him until he died on 21 January 1924, having almost entirely withdrawn from the conduct of affairs during the last twenty months of his life except for brief periods in late 1922 and early 1923. Exercising enormous natural authority over his political colleagues, he had never acquired or needed the status of a fully fledged totalitarian dictator. His illness and death therefore left a power vacuum—one which was cautiously and skilfully filled by Stalin, whose rise to ascendancy over all rivals was the most important political development of the 1920s.

In its early stages Stalin's rise owed much to his ability to play a waiting game. Parading as a comparative nonentity, he diverted the fears of two rival contenders, Zinovyev and Kamenev, towards a third—Trotsky—whose record as a flamboyant revolutionary leader made him the most obvious choice as Lenin's successor. Trotsky, however, remained mysteriously inactive, refraining from mobilising his immense potential support. Meanwhile Stalin was discreetly establishing a remorseless grip on various key bodies in the Party organisation while his rivals tended to look down on such humdrum bureaucratic activity as beneath their notice. By the time of Lenin's death Stalin already held, or had held, a great variety of influential posts. He was a member of the Politburo, the small policy-making body which came to dominate and overrule the larger Party Central Committee to which it was nominally subordinated. Stalin was also a member of the Party's Organisation Bureau, and dominated another important body, the Central Control Commission. Above all, Stalin was Secretary-General of the Party's Central Committee, a post and title conferred on him in April 1922. From this vantage-point he built up the Party Secretariat as a rival centre of power to the Politburo. On the governmental side Stalin was, until 1923, People's Commissar for the Worker-Peasant Inspectorate as well as for Nationalities—posts which conferred wide powers to intervene in administration throughout the length and breadth of the country.

Though all Party and governmental bodies had overlapping membership, no one managed to compete with Stalin in belonging to so many powerful interlocking committees. Nor did his rivals at first notice the unremitting care with which the Secretary-General was infiltrating his personal supporters into key positions throughout the country until he could eventually control decisions at all levels of the Party, from the large—theoretically annual and theoretically sovereign—Party Congresses down to sessions of the Central Committee, also packed with his nominees, and the several smaller and still more influential bodies mentioned above. While building up his political apparatus in this way, Stalin manoeuvred between the left opposition (Trotsky, Zinovyev and Kamenev), who pinned their hopes for Russia's future on the outbreak of world revolution, and the right opposition (Bukharin, Rykov and Tomsky), who advocated a more cautious and conservative approach. Himself promoting the policy of socialism in one country, Stalin contrived to tack between these competing factions, setting one against the other or posing as a benevolent intermediary, while destroying first the leftists and then the rightists.

Though the political police was only one of many organisations adroitly manipulated by Stalin during his rise to power, its role was inevitably vital to the budding totalitarian dictator, who had himself been a member of the Cheka collegium.[1] The organisation underwent important changes during the period. After the abolition of the Cheka in early 1922, the successor body operated under the title GPU for nearly two years before suffering a further, minor, change of title on 15 November 1923 when the initial O (standing for Russian *obyedinyonnoye*, 'united') was prefixed to the three original syllables denoting State Political Administration. Thus the GPU re-emerged as the OGPU. This change of name occurred in conjunction with the adoption of a new name for the country as a whole—the Union of Soviet Socialist Republics (USSR)—to signalise the fusion in a single political entity of four territorial units hitherto nominally independent of each other: the

RSFSR (Russian Soviet Federative Socialist Republic) and the Ukrainian, Belorussian and Transcaucasian Republics. In fact all four republics were already ruled from Moscow, the capital of the RSFSR, which was overwhelmingly the largest of the four units, stretching from the western frontier to Vladivostok in eastern Siberia. Other republics were to be added in due course, making the present total of fifteen.

Administratively speaking, the transformation of the Cheka into the GPU, and then into the OGPU, left many aspects of political police work unchanged. The organisation not only retained Dzerzhinsky as its titular head, but also kept substantially the same personnel, while continuing to operate from its old head-quarters in the Lubyanka. The methods of the GPU/OGPU did, however, differ greatly from those of the Cheka at the height of its atrocities, since the extremes of police terrorism, as it had flourished during the Civil War, now became the exception rather than the rule. In particular, the practice of shooting victims *en masse*, or by relays in cellars, underwent a decline and the new organisation was subjected to various formal restrictions designed to present it as the adjunct of a properly constituted legal system. Now explicitly deprived of the right to shoot its victims, except when these might be looters caught red-handed, the police was to confine its activities to investigations and preliminary proceedings, turning over all offenders to regularly constituted courts. It re-tained the power to arrest suspects, but was under an obligation to release them after two months' detention if by the end of that time no specific charge had been preferred. Similar restrictions had from time to time been placed on the Cheka without seriously curbing its arbitrary powers, and it must be admitted that in the case of the GPU/OGPU such regulations were never fully effective. The detention of suspects, for example, could be pro-longed indefinitely by obtaining the sanction of the Central Executive Committee of the Soviets, which was a mere formality, and the new security organisation remained essentially outside and above the law despite all formal restrictions placed upon it. The GPU was, accordingly, left (as E. H. Carr states) with 'more arbitrary powers to deal with . . . [political] offences than the defunct Cheka had ever claimed or exercised'.[2] The remark should, however, be qualified to this extent—that the wide use of these powers on a scale amounting to mass terrorism belongs, strictly speaking, to the history of the OGPU rather than of the GPU, and then to the period from 1928 onwards. Without yet employing mass terror, the early OGPU did, however, enjoy a superior status to the Cheka in the sense that it was a regular (no longer an 'extraordinary') office of the State, and one for which provision was specifically made in the Constitution of the USSR adopted in July 1923. Members of the organisation were granted increased privileges, receiving higher pay, access to special provision stores and other concessions. This was, accordingly, a period of build-up during which the political police played a relatively unobtrusive role behind the scenes. Meanwhile general living conditions were modestly improving under an economic system, NEP, which permitted small-scale private trade to operate, and under a political dispensation which severely punished overt opposition, but did not yet seek to impose universal thought control. Freedom was severely curtailed, but not yet crushed, and while harsh authoritarian rule remained, fully developed totalitarianism lay in the future.

In place of execution the characteristic method of repression by the political police now became imprisonment in concentration camps, to which the OGPU had the power to consign its victims without trial. Concentration camps had not, however, acquired the evil repute which they were to receive in the days of Hitlerite and Stalinist totalitarianism. In the 1920s Soviet camps were organised on a comparatively modest scale, the prisoners being numbered in tens of thousands rather than in the millions of the developed Stalinist period.

Concentration camps of a sort had already been established in a small way in the first year of Soviet rule, what is probably the first recorded reference to them being found in a telegram of August 1918 sent by Lenin instructing the local authorities of Penza to employ 'merciless mass terror' against enemies of his régime and to confine suspects in concentration camps outside the city.[3] The Cheka had maintained its own network of concentration camps, as did the GPU/OGPU after it, the original purpose being preventive rather than punitive and directed to the isolation of political opponents or potential opponents—not yet to the exploitation of their labour as a major element in building up the economy. In these early days the kernel of the OGPU system of concentration camps was found in the extreme north of European Russia on the Solovetsky Islands in the White Sea, where a notorious network of monastery dungeons had for many centuries served the rulers of Moscow as a place of confinement for their political enemies, a few dozen at a time. In 1923 the Solovetsky

Monastery was established as the GPU's main concentration camp, at which time the number of prisoners was calculated at four thousand, increasing to over twenty thousand some four or five years later—and to over a hundred thousand by the end of the 1920s.[4] These establishments housed individuals categorised as opponents of the régime, who fell into two main classes—representatives of classes privileged before the Revolution and members of non-Communist Socialist parties. The latter were still treated with a certain revolutionary camaraderie in the 1920s, having been old allies and associates of the Bolsheviks in the assault on Tsarism, but this period of sentimentality was doomed to end. Meanwhile when political prisoners staged a demonstration of protest at the Solovetsky camp in December 1923, and drew shots from the panicky or over-cautious camp administration (five or more being killed), the episode led to an international scandal and to the appointment of an official commission of inquiry to look into the affair, which was even publicly ventilated in the Soviet press.[5] So much fuss over so few killings—it is an eloquent comment on the decline of the political police since the great days of the Cheka when far bloodier episodes were a daily occurrence and passed unnoticed.

Despite the relative mildness of early OGPU procedures, particular interest attaches to certain practices which arose in experimental and embryonic form, and which were later to flourish as characteristic features of unbridled police terror. One such episode was the staging in Moscow of the first great Communist political show trial, in June–July 1922. An attempt was made to saddle thirty-four Socialist Revolutionaries, some of whom had been in the hands of the Cheka/GPU for long periods, with responsibility for terrorist conspiracy against the Soviet Government and for co-operating with the White General Denikin in the Civil War. As a pageant this, the only notable example of a Leninist show trial, seems an amateurish affair by comparison with the great classical frame-ups of the Stalin period. The faulty stage-management of 1922 became apparent even before the accused had been brought into the dock. In order to placate western European Socialists, now increasingly troubled by the rapid development of political repression in the Soviet Union, two Soviet representatives (Bukharin and Radek) gave an assurance that no death sentences would be imposed—for which they were in turn publicly reprimanded by Lenin. The trial proceedings were marred by various indecorous occurrences such as the intrusion of demonstrating workers, who broke into the courtroom and demanded death sentences for the traitors. Nor were the latter allowed to produce witnesses and evidence in their own defence. The chief counsel for the defence, the Belgian Socialist Vandervelde and the Russian Muravyov—walked out in protest. Finally (most unseemly detail of all) the accused were not prepared to confess their guilt—not, at least, to the more far-fetched charges such as that of collaborating with Denikin. In the end sentences of imprisonment and (in twelve instances) death were pronounced on all except for certain of the accused who had been acting in collusion with the prosecution all along. Though the death sentences were duly suspended, as had been promised, it appears that none of the condemned was ever released from confinement.[6] The affair suggests that Leninist justice, given time to develop, might eventually have rivalled its Stalinist successor as an exercise in the creative use of the imagination. In 1922, however, milder procedures were still possible. By contrast with the framing of the Socialist Revolutionaries at this show trial, a group of Menshevik political prisoners managed to effect their release in the same year by conducting a hunger strike. About ten of them were permitted to emigrate from the Soviet Union, including Boris Nikolayevsky whose later contributions to the understanding of Russian political police procedures have been particularly valuable.

While feeling his way from relative obscurity to total supremacy, Stalin was especially fortunate or skilful in making a close ally of the successive head of the Cheka/GPU/OGPU, Felix Dzerzhinsky. In cementing this alliance developments in Stalin's native Georgia played an important part. After invasion and conquest by the Red Army in 1921, Georgia had been placed under the rule of local Communist bosses. These, however, soon showed themselves unwilling to take orders from Moscow—in practice from Stalin, since he held general responsibility for affairs in the outposts of the Soviet Empire, being Commissar for Nationalities at the time. In particular the Georgian men on the spot, headed by Mdivani and Makharadze, attempted to resist Stalin's decision to combine Georgia with Armenia and Azerbaydzhan in a single Transcaucasian Republic which, in turn, was to become a component unit of the USSR. Stalin sent Ordzhonikidze, a fellow-Georgian and his own close ally, to impose his wishes in Tiflis. When Ordzhonikidze asserted himself with considerable tactlessness the local Georgian Communists appealed to

Lenin, who regarded Stalin's policy towards the minority nationalities as over-dictatorial, but was hampered by illness in attempts to overrule his domineering Commissar for Nationalities. Stalin now risked his career by defying the incapacitated leader's wishes and imposing his will on the dissident Georgian Communists. Then, in November 1922, Lenin sent Dzerzhinsky to Georgia to report on Stalin's and Ordzhonikidze's misdemeanours, but Dzerzhinsky gave his full support to these overweening proconsuls. Thus the Georgian future dictator and the Polish founder of the political police combined to thwart the wishes of the dying Russian leader by coercing a minority Communist Party in the interests of domination from Moscow.[7]

As the Georgian episode illustrates, Party members still retained considerable freedom to oppose decisions made by the top leadership. Such opposition within the Party was becoming an increasing preoccupation of Stalin's, and presented a particularly intractable problem owing to the immunity from arrest enjoyed by Party members. Only by breaking this immunity could Stalin obtain unrestricted control over policy, and though many years were to elapse before he achieved that goal, he can already be observed in 1923 combining with the GPU to repress a leading Party member. The victim was the prominent Tatar Communist Sultan-Galiyev, who championed the interests of Communists from Muslim areas against the demands of Moscow. He adopted, in other words, an attitude similar to that of the dissident Georgians, as was confirmed by a letter written by him and intercepted by the GPU.[8] However, the importance of the episode lies less in the views put forward by Sultan-Galiyev than in Stalin's success in ordering the arrest of a leading Party member by the political police. This was an unheard-of event—so much so that it was debated at an expanded session of the Party Central Committee in June 1923, when Stalin's action was upheld. Later in the same year the Party Central Committee approved the GPU's action in liquidating two Communist underground movements—the Workers' Group and Workers' Truth, which had helped to foment strikes in the summer.[9] At the same time a sub-committee on internal Party problems under Dzerzhinsky's chairmanship came out with a recommendation that members should be obliged to report all dissident political activity by fellow-Communists to the GPU—an attempt to accelerate the subjection of the Party to the political police for which the Party was not yet prepared.

The mysterious death of Michael Frunze was another episode

of the period foreshadowing acts of violence perpetrated a decade later. When Trotsky was ousted from his post as Commissar for War in 1925, Frunze succeeded him, but became unacceptable to Stalin by opposing him in his struggle against Zinovyev and Kamenev. Frunze also went too far, according to Trotsky, in protecting the army from interference by the OGPU.[10] In any event the new Commissar died in November 1925 most conveniently for Stalin, and while undergoing a surgical operation for the treatment of an ulcerated stomach. The interest of the affair lies in the allegation, commonly made at the time, that this represented a form of medical murder committed on Stalin's instructions. Frunze's personal physicians had advised him against submitting to a general anaesthetic on the grounds of his heart condition, whereupon Stalin convoked a panel of pliant medicos, who recommended that the operation should go ahead all the same. This ruling was confirmed by a Politburo empowered to enforce decisions in matters affecting an important Party member's health ever since the days of Lenin, who had himself been subjected, much against his will, to a strict medical regimen during the last twenty months of his life.[11] All doctors treating members of the Central Committee, were, incidentally, themselves on the staff of the political police.[12] This circumstance lent colour to the accusations of medical murder put forward at the Bukharin trial in 1938 and in the notorious Doctors' Plot fabricated by the political police in 1953.

The political activities of Russian émigrés were a major concern of the Soviet security machine from the end of the Civil War onwards—and naturally so. Emigré conspirators had, after all, done much to accomplish the downfall of the Russian government in 1917, and the OGPU was anxious to ensure that anti-Soviet plotters should be in no position to repeat the performance in the following decade. The Soviet political police could, therefore, congratulate itself on an important *coup* when the leading living Russian terrorist Boris Savinkov—one-time colleague of Azef as an organiser of Socialist Revolutionary assassinations, and later (in 1918) a fomenter of anti-Soviet rebellion on the Volga— returned to Russia in August 1924 from his last spell of foreign exile. He wore a disguise and carried false papers which deceived nobody, the probability being that he had been tricked into entering the country by the OGPU.[13] Arrested in Minsk, he was arraigned at a semi-public trial in Moscow, receiving a death sentence which was commuted to ten years' imprisonment, whereupon he reputedly committed suicide in prison. At his trial he had publicly renounced his anti-Soviet views in a long speech which represented a considerable propaganda success for the Soviet government. Moreover, Savinkov was the last White of any importance to challenge Soviet rule on Soviet territory, and his death accordingly marks the end of a chapter in the activities of the OGPU.

If the OGPU had indeed lured Savinkov back over the Soviet frontier, as seems probable, this was far from the last occasion on which the Soviet political police performed such an operation on a Russian émigré. A particularly notorious episode occurred in the winter of 1925–6 after the leading right-wing émigré politician Vasily Shulgin, a former Duma deputy, had been gulled into undertaking a supposedly secret journey through Soviet Russia. His mission was to make contact on Soviet soil with the Trust, a powerful underground right-wing anti-Soviet resistance network operating on a wide scale throughout the USSR—or so he had been convincingly assured before departing on his travels by representatives of this wholly bogus organisation, which was in fact a concoction of the OGPU. Suspecting nothing of this, Shulgin crossed the Soviet frontier—by a special Trust route, wearing a beard expressly grown for the occasion—and embarked on a four-month conducted tour of an unusual type. He visited Kiev, Moscow and Leningrad (as Petrograd had been renamed after Lenin's death), all the time unaware that every courier who accompanied him was an OGPU agent, as were the numerous volubly anti-Soviet individuals to whom he was introduced *en route*. According to one improbable story, Shulgin even attended a church service specially celebrated for him in a Moscow cellar, kissing the hands of an officiating 'Orthodox priest' whose robes in fact concealed the disguised OGPU deputy chief Menzhinsky.[14] Eventually Shulgin left the country as illegally as he had entered it, for the OGPU's purpose was not to trap him in the Soviet Union, but to manipulate him into making a fool of himself outside it. He obliged by publishing, in Berlin, a book about his adventures under the title *Three Capitals*, having even sent the manuscript back to Moscow for vetting by one of his Trust contacts there.[15] After Shulgin had so co-operatively disclosed the existence of a mighty political underground which was in fact entirely spurious, the truth about his mission was leaked. This neatly destroyed his authority as a politician, and assisted in the general process of demoralising politically active Russian émigrés.

The Trust was only one among a number of similar front organisations of the OGPU. Others specialised in penetrating émigré Liberal, Socialist and Anarchist circles, and they were also active in planting misleading information about Soviet intentions and conditions on foreign intelligence services. Though the Trust itself was wound up shortly after provoking the Shulgin fiasco, similar activities have continued under the OGPU's successors.[16]

Another significant episode in the developing foreign relations of the OGPU occurred when two German students, Wolscht and Kindermann, were arrested in Moscow. On being searched, one of them was found in possession of a particularly damning piece of evidence—the visiting card of an official of his own embassy. Both were accordingly charged with espionage, and with plans to assassinate Stalin and Trotsky, for which offences they were sentenced to death on 3 July 1925. The purpose of this trial was not, of course, to establish the guilt or innocence of the accused. It was, in fact, designed—and effectively so—to persuade the German authorities not to execute death sentences pronounced in Leipzig earlier in the year in the case of one Skoblevsky and certain other alleged OGPU agents found guilty of political assassination and terrorism in Germany.[17] This was, accordingly, an early example of a procedure commonly followed under the OGPU's successors, that of protecting Soviet agents by enforcing an exchange with some suitable foreigner arrested in the Soviet Union. The Wolscht-Kindermann affair appears, however, to have been a purer example of 'framing' than were the cases of Gary Powers, Greville Wynne and Gerald Brooke—all exchanged for Soviet agents in the 1960s, but all to some extent avowedly guilty of the offences with which they were charged. Be this as it may, it seems evident that the Soviet political police was already cultivating a reputation for 'looking after its own' as early as 1925.

On 20 July 1926 Dzerzhinsky died, an event which had little influence on the immediate future of the political police, for while remaining nominal head of the organisation until the end he had been mainly concerned with economic problems for at least two years. He was succeeded as head of the OGPU by Vyacheslav Menzhinsky—also of genteel Polish origin, but a milder personality with more scholarly inclinations and a knack of picking up foreign languages. The suggestion has been made that Stalin fostered the appointment of a weakling so that he could convert the political police into a more obedient instrument for quelling oppositionist Party members.[18] Stalin also relied increasingly on the aid of the deputy head of the OGPU, Henry Yagoda.

In suppressing the last spasms of open resistance to Stalin within the Communist Party the OGPU proved fully effective in 1927. By this time oppositionists headed by Trotsky, Zinovyev and Kamenev had belatedly joined forces against Stalin's dictatorship. However, the OGPU penetrated their organisation, and their attempt to print their programme on an illegal press resulted in the seizure of the plant and the arrest of its operators. On 7 November 1927, the tenth anniversary of the Bolshevik Revolution, a futile attempt was made to carry the conflict into the streets of Moscow and Leningrad, where the opposition leaders staged demonstrations—only to have them broken up by the OGPU. Meanwhile the opposition leaders were being progressively ousted, first from the Politburo, then from the Central Committee, and finally from the Party itself. In January 1928 about thirty leading oppositionists were sent into exile within the Soviet Union, Trotsky himself being consigned to Alma Ata in Central Asia.

In 1928 the OGPU entered a new phase of activity characterised by a considerable expansion in the organisation and by the adoption of far harsher methods of repression. The change was an inevitable result of Stalin's success in replacing the relatively mild political and economic dispensation of the NEP years (1921–8) with policies drastic in the extreme. These included the expropriation of virtually all privately owned farms, of which there were some twenty million in 1928, the peasant owners—whose way of life had changed surprisingly little since the days of the last Tsar—being compelled to enter collective or State farms. In this way a form of serfdom was revived nearly seven decades after its abolition in 1861. At the same time Stalin launched the First Five Year Plan, and with it an intensive drive to expand industry. He thus plunged the Soviet Union into headlong collectivisation and headlong industrialisation, twin processes which totally disrupted every aspect of the country's life, bringing about a social transformation in many ways more far-reaching than that which had occurred in 1917. Violent as this change of policy was, the Secretary-General introduced it with his usual caution and skill over the two years 1928–9, incidentally using the establishment of the new line as an occasion to oust his right-wing rivals Bukharin, Rykov and Tomsky.

It was now that Stalin first revealed the awesome dimensions of his personality and a genius, perhaps unparalleled in the annals of tyranny, for manipulating large sections of a potentially harmonious community into a frenzy of mutual slaughter. Collectivisation in particular displayed to the full a capacity for conceiving and carrying through policies such as lesser men would have dismissed as wildly impossible. That Stalin's prime motive in collectivising the peasantry was political seems abundantly clear. Even after a decade of Bolshevik rule the peasants retained a spirit of independence which challenged the Secretary-General's drive towards total imposed conformity. They must be crushed. As for his other motives in ordaining collectivisation, these were clearly secondary, but were not without importance, including as they did the need to increase grain deliveries to the State in the short term and to improve the long-term efficiency of agriculture by creating large mechanised units in place of small farms tilled by primitive means.

Stalin's main implement in imposing collectivisation was the OGPU, backed on occasion by units of the Red Army as a supplementary enforcement agency. In the first instance, however, he relied on causing dissension within individual village communities by exploiting the official division of the peasants into three categories: poor, middle and kulak. This last, highly opprobrious term was applied to the least indigent members of the community, few of whom would have been recognised as prosperous by non-Soviet standards, but who did enjoy some economic advantages over their still poorer neighbours. They were also the most efficient producers in the village, and as such a natural target for envy. The tactic of collectivisation was, accordingly, to incite the poor and middle peasants against the kulaks. The kulaks were expelled from their farms, which were then turned over to the new collectives along with the owners' implements, livestock and other property. At the same time the kulaks themselves were divided into categories according to the degree of political criminality ascribed to each. Those rated as serious counter-revolutionaries were shot, while others—in descending order of political guilt— were sent to concentration camps, exiled to distant regions of the Soviet Union, or assigned to land of poor quality within their original provinces. In any event all classed as kulaks were turned out of their homes, together with their wives and children. It must be added that the category of kulak, as applied in practice, was highly flexible. Any peasant, whatever his economic situation, could conveniently be labelled as a kulak if he was unwise enough to express opposition to authority. Thus the liquidation of the kulaks as a class, as decreed by Stalin on 27 December 1929, became a formula for persecuting the peasantry at large.

In considering the number of peasants 'liquidated' one enters, for the first time in Russian political police history, the area of really high statistics. Discussing collectivisation with Winston Churchill in Moscow in August 1942, Stalin himself put the figure of peasants with whom he had been 'dealing' at ten million.[19] A more scholarly authority on the economics of the concentration camp system, S. Swianiewicz, finds Stalin's figure in accordance with the available evidence, claiming a total of 'about 10-11 million persons forcibly removed from the villages through de-kulakisation'. He breaks this total down into about one third concentration camp inmates, one third deportees to forced exile without imprisonment and one third deaths from execution and sundry causes.[20] The practice of conveying prisoners to the camps in railway goods wagons—locked in for weeks on end, shunted from siding to siding, often without water and food, often without heat in the depths of the arctic winter—led to extensive deterioration of goods in transit. Many of the freighted slaves were dead on arrival from freezing, asphyxiation, starvation, dysentery and other causes—a squandering of natural resources which would have involved the OGPU in charges of sabotage had cattle or machinery been similarly neglected, as of course they often were.

For the mechanics of dispossessing kulak families an exact ritual was prescribed, but the rude peasantry was ill equipped to appreciate such bureaucratic niceties. In practice unruly villagers, inflamed by the prospect of despoiling their fellows with official sanction, were liable to descend in a mob on the home of any neighbour less poor—or simply less popular—than the rest. An orgy of looting would ensue, the first object being any store of hard liquor which the victim happened to possess. There were, accordingly, occasions when OGPU units (whose prime function was to supervise the enforcement of official regulations) intervened against irregular 'dekulakisation' and ensured that the victims were driven into death or exile according to the exact letter of the law. Stalin himself denounced the excesses of dekulakisation from on high, thus dissociating himself from a campaign which he had personally ordained and had no intention of countermanding.

To judge from the Smolensk Archives—the best detailed evidence available on the day-to-day processes of collectivisation—

many villagers rejected the role of poor peasant, middle peasant or kulak to which official doctrine assigned each individual, showing instead a strong solidarity within their village as a whole and refusing to dispossess any of their number.[21] Such an attitude laid them open to wholesale reprisals as part of a sporadic but savage civil war which broke out in thousands of different localities. On occasions whole villages were surrounded and their inhabitants wiped out by the machine-guns of the OGPU, and there were even times when artillery and aircraft were employed against the reluctant muzhik. Besides assassinating many Communist officials, whom they identified as their main enemy, the peasants also took to slaughtering their farm beasts rather than see them communised—and this on such a scale that in 1933, after some five years of collectivisation, the agricultural livestock of the country had been depleted by roughly fifty per cent. Having gorged themselves on their horses, sheep and cattle rather than hand them over to a collective, the peasants suffered in the winter of 1932–3 a famine during which some $5\frac{1}{2}$ million died of starvation, over half of them in the Ukraine. This has been called 'perhaps the only case in history of a purely man-made famine'.[22] It did not occur at a time of acute food shortage, but was brought about by the enforced collection of the peasants' last food stocks, since Stalin insisted on maintaining the export of grain to foreign countries. For a country to export $1\frac{3}{4}$ million tons of grain in a famine year, as Stalinist Russia did in 1932–3,[23] is another example of the grandiose sweep of the Secretary-General's imagination. That the existence of this great famine could be officially denied, and so effectively as to convince a sizeable section of foreign public opinion, is an index of the mastery now achieved by the Stalin machine over the control of communications inside and outside his dominions.

In addition to other organs of control drafted into the village— the army, the Party, industrial workers commissioned to supervise collectivisation—Machine Tractor Stations performed an important disciplinary role. Serving a large clutch of collective farms, spread over a sizeable area, each station held a pool of agricultural machinery for communal use, and also contained a Political Section with responsibility for making the farms responsive to the will of the Party. Since few peasants were Party members, or wished to become such, the task presented many difficulties. Nor was the detailed organisation of the Machine Tractor Stations such as to smooth the path for the officials concerned. As his deputy the head of the Political Section had an OGPU officer who kept himself informed through a network of secret agents on such matters as counter-revolutionary activity, sabotage, speculation and anti-Soviet talk among the muzhiks. An agent subject to control through OGPU channels, the OGPU man on the spot was in certain matters independent of his nominal superior—who was in turn by no means totally subordinated to his own nominal superior, the overall Director of the Machine Tractor Station. Constant friction occurred between these three officials, as also between them and Party District Headquarters. Thus the conflict of powers, an endemic defect of Russian political police organisation since Imperial times, was imported into the terrorised countryside.[24] However, despite such minor disadvantages as bureaucratic feuding, and despite the continuing failure of collectivisation, up to the present day, to effect any increase in agricultural productivity remotely proportionate to the sacrifices exacted, Stalin's war against the peasantry had resulted by 1933 in total political victory for the dictator and his police.

To the collectivisation of agriculture the intensive industrialisation of the economy under the First Five Year Plan formed a parallel. This was more successful than collectivisation in attaining its economic aims, and aroused a measure of genuine enthusiasm among those on whom it was imposed. However, though industrial workers were not made the target for any frontal assault comparable to that launched on the countryside, they nevertheless found themselves severely regimented and rendered increasingly subject to harsh labour legislation. This came to include instant dismissal for a single day's absence and the introduction of the piece rate system once denounced by Marx as a feature of capitalist exploitation.[25] Never notably independent at any period of Soviet rule, the trade unions were now converted into a factory police in all but name, and thus a useful adjunct to the OGPU. The workers were also affected by the introduction in December 1932 of the internal passport system obliging all citizens to carry an identity card—a measure which had once been in force under the Tsars, when it had been widely decried as an instance of police control run riot.

From 1930 onwards concentration camps were the most characteristic feature of the Stalinist state—the basic implement of repression operated by the OGPU and its successors. Operated by GULAG (the Main Administration of Camps), the new establishments differed from those of the previous decade in three major respects. Firstly, the number of inmates swelled about a hundredfold until they totalled millions rather than tens of thousands. Secondly, their general character changed, the typical camp slave of the early 1930s being an illiterate 'dekulakised' muzhik, whereas the typical inmate of the earlier decade had been an opponent of official attitudes—cultural, religious or political— possessed of a certain level of education. Thirdly, a policy was adopted of exploiting concentration camp labour as a major element in the task of building up the economy.

The political police now controlled, and continued to control throughout the Stalin era, a huge slave empire containing networks of camps set up in extensive areas of the USSR, vast, remote areas being colonised with freshly enslaved peasants. From the original nucleus on the Solovetsky Islands in the White Sea, the camp network of northern European Russia fanned out far to south and east. Lumbering was the chief enterprise in these parts, and the OGPU now came to control virtually the entire output of Soviet timber—especially important as a major export and source of foreign currency. Another important northern slave enterprise was coal-mining in Vorkuta, while further OGPU coal-mines were set up in Karaganda in Uzbekistan and elsewhere.

Officially known as corrective labour camps, these immense pools of slave labour were theoretically dedicated to the reclamation of political and other criminals through honest toil, and were widely celebrated as such in official Soviet publications. The canal joining the White Sea with the Baltic was the most renowned among these early massive public works. Begun in November 1931 and completed in August 1933, it came under the personal direction of Yagoda, who drafted nearly 300,000 convicts to the task. They toiled with primitive implements, and under climatic and general living conditions so severe that perhaps as many as a third of the workers died on the job, casualty figures comparable to those imposed by Peter the Great during the building of St Petersburg at the beginning of the eighteenth century.[26] Of those who survived the building of the White Sea Canal some seventy thousand were amnestied while the remainder were drafted to constructing the Baikal-Amur Railroad in the far east and to other forced labour projects. Meanwhile a large volume containing enthusiastic descriptions of this murderous affair was collectively compiled by the great Soviet writer and humanist Maxim Gorky and thirty-six other authors.[27] Illustrations show workers queuing up for hot pies, and stress such cultural amenities as libraries and brass bands. ('Music Speeds the Men on the Sluice.')

As this publication reminds one, the activities of Gorky, Bernard Shaw and like-minded celebrities constituted a major hazard to the OGPU's prisoners during this period, owing to the practice of shepherding such persons through slave labour sites, while striving to present the institution as an essentially civilising concern.[28] The rumoured arrival of these credulous verbalisers in any of the great slave provinces was a signal for feverish preparations designed to convert camps into uncamps. Watch-towers were speedily demolished, barbed wire was taken down and inmates were hurriedly driven out into the forests. Especial care was necessary on such occasions to keep convicts out of sight of the railway lines, lest a travelling dupe chance to look up from his vodka and *zakuski*, glimpse the haggard scarecrows and draw 'incorrect conclusions'.[29] The dismantling of camps in honour of some benevolent busybody reputedly led to much loss of life above the customary high norm.[30]

Though the main brunt of OGPU oppression fell on the peasantry during the early 1930s, other classes of the community by no means remained immune. As part of a general policy of inflaming social antagonisms throughout his dominions, Stalin now sought to disrupt a working alliance, which had existed since the days of Lenin, between the Soviet authorities and those members of the pre-revolutionary middle class who had shown themselves prepared to serve the revolutionary State in a professional capacity without necessarily regarding themselves as potential Communists. In the assault on these non-Party professional men an important role was assigned to the first Stalinist show trials, at which specially selected victims, arrested and carefully groomed by the OGPU, were publicly condemned for wrecking and sabotaging the industries in which they were employed. The only previous Soviet show trial of any note had been the case of the thirty-four Socialist Revolutionaries arraigned in 1922 under Lenin. Not until May 1928 did this find its sequel in the first Stalinist show trial, that of fifty-two technicians and engineers who had been employed in the coal industry at Shakhty in the Donbass. Like all the other show trials, the Shakhty affair was a frame-up concocted by the political police on Stalin's orders. Most of the accused had been arrested some months previously on the denunciation of an OGPU official of middle rank, Ye. G. Yevdokimov, who was head of the political police in the North Caucasus, but also happened to be a drinking companion of Stalin's.[31] When Menzhinsky rejected Yevdokimov's denunciation, offering to prosecute him for sabotage on his own account—since his intrigue threatened to deprive the coal industry of many leading engineers—Yevdokimov appealed directly to Stalin, at whose bidding he may well have instigated this affair in the first place.[32] On Stalin's insistence the Politburo agreed to proceed with the case, which received extensive publicity—partly because the accused made convenient scapegoats for the many shortcomings of Soviet industry.

The Shakhty affair shows the Soviet show trial still in its infancy. Only sixteen of the fifty-two defendants were prepared to confess their guilt, and then several of them later attempted to retract their confessions in open court—a grave reflexion on the OGPU production team. That the prisoners were physically tortured by the OGPU, as an encouragement to adhere to the agreed script and refrain from ad-libbing, was the conclusion of Eugene Lyons, and seems an inescapable deduction from his eye-witness account of the court proceedings.[33] These took place before a host of high officials, foreign diplomats and press representatives in the House of Trade Unions in Moscow, the décor being enlivened by white pillars, crystal chandeliers, red bunting, inflammatory inscriptions and a squad of OGPU soldiers who stood at attention with their fixed bayonets glinting in the floodlights. This great pageant was dominated by the Public Prosecutor Krylenko, a squat, shaven-headed figure in hunting jacket and riding breeches who was himself to ripen for liquidation twelve years later. The presiding judge was A. Ya. Vyshinsky. A former Menshevik lawyer of exceptional survival potential, he was later to conduct the prosecution at all the great show trials of the 1930s and even to outlive Stalin himself.

The Shakhty trial provided a grim and varied spectacle, some of the accused grovelling as they begged for their lives or promised, amid laughter in court, to atone for their previous misdeeds by honest hard work. Others bore themselves with impressive dignity. They included the seventy-year-old Rabinovich, for years the country's leading coal-mining engineer, who firmly denied the charges against him, even managing to discomfit the prosecutor and one of the hostile witnesses. Grossly miscast for a star role in this expensive gala performance, he should have been decently shot off stage. Other minor details showed a surer touch by the production team as the Stalinist style of management at last began to emerge. Andrew Kolodub, thirteen-year-old son of one of the accused, wrote (or was 'persuaded' to write) a letter, published in *Pravda* during the trial, in which he called for his father's execution as an enemy of the working class, and demonstratively renounced his surname in favour of Shakhtin. This helped to set the pattern for the many denunciations of framed parents by loyalist children so characteristic of the fully developed Stalinist era. Aided by Kolodub Junior, and by a sustained press and radio campaign vilifying the accused, the court pronounced sentence after a six-week hearing. Three German defendants were released, while of the forty-nine Russians implicated, thirty-eight received prison sentences, the remaining eleven being condemned to death. Only five of them were executed, however, the other six being reprieved in return for help given in stage-managing the trial.

Three other notable show trials followed in the period before the great terror of 1934. The first was that of the Industrial Party, which took place in November–December 1930, and has been claimed by one observer as the most sensational of all Stalinist show trials, not excluding even those of the late 1930s.[34] Among the features of this lavish pantomime was a parade of half a million workers screaming 'Death to the Wreckers' as they marched past in the streets outside the courtroom for hours. Inside eight men of scholarly appearance were charged with plotting the sabotage of industry and the overthrow of the government in collusion with two prominent Russian émigrés who had in fact both died several years earlier. Though found guilty, the Industrial Party prisoners were treated leniently. Five received death sentences, but these were all commuted to ten years' imprisonment, while Professor Ramzin (alleged leader of the conspiracy) was freed and restored to his former post a few years later.

In March 1931 fourteen Mensheviks suffered public trial for allegedly plotting to restore capitalism in Russia in collusion with the émigré Menshevik leader Raphael Abramovich who had secretly visited Russia to direct the conspiracy. So at least the prosecution contended, but ascribed Abramovich's presence on Soviet soil to a period when he had in fact been attending a Socialist conference in Brussels.[35] Once again the OGPU had helped to prepare a faulty script, but that did not save the accused Mensheviks, for none of them emerged from prison, so far as is known.[36]

April 1933 saw the trial of the Metro-Vickers engineers, in

which six British citizens figured among those accused of wrecking and sabotage. Once again, however, the OGPU had failed to groom its victims with sufficient care, for though some of the British engineers had signed false confessions under duress, they insisted on retracting them in court. They received only short prison sentences, or were expelled from the country, while their Russian 'accomplices' were treated more severely—though none received the death penalty.

Thus the Metro-Vickers case was another bungled affair, but by now constant repetition was slowly perfecting the technique of the show trial. It had been found advisable to make the material of the trials as complex and technical as possible, thus dazzling the gullible with a welter of confusing detail. But was deception really Stalin's sole aim? So grotesque were some of the features of these and later frame-ups that an alternative explanation suggests itself. No fully developed despot, it may be surmised, can content himself with compelling his subjects' assent to policies exclusively rational. Only then may he regard his people as fully subject to his will when he can compel their assent to procedures palpably outrageous and absurd. That injustice should be done was clearly a major purpose of the show trials, but a no less important aim, perhaps, was that injustice should manifestly be seen to be done. Thus the OGPU's very lapses in introducing impossible details into the prosecution's case, though no doubt originally due to incompetence or carelessness, had a positive part to play. The purpose was, after all, not merely to obtain the applause of Bernard Shaw and similar mischievous notabilities, but also to extract the plaudits of Soviet citizens less easily deceived—yet dragooned by total terror into postures of affirmation.

Show trials were merely a minor element in the oppressions of 1928–34, since many other trials were also held in secret during the same period, apart from which the OGPU was now increasingly shooting its victims without trial in the manner of the old Cheka. Among those secretly tried or executed without trial during the period were bacteriologists charged with having caused a horse epidemic, officials of the food industry shot for sabotaging food supplies, as well as sundry agricultural experts, various officials of State Farms and a batch of academic historians.[37]

Another characteristic theme in the crescendo of OGPU oppression was the extortion of gold, jewellery and foreign currency from members of the former *bourgeoisie* or anyone else unfortunate enough to be suspected of hoarding such valuables. The standard torture, as applied by a special division of the OGPU, was to confine several hundred of such persons in a small, overheated, virtually airless room. Compelled to remain standing for days on end, infested by lice, with swollen legs and in imminent danger of asphyxiation, individual victims were occasionally removed from these 'louse-pits' (or 'steam-houses') for brutal interrogation on the 'conveyor' where a series of tables was manned by a relay of screaming interrogators, the victim being compelled to run from one to the other, a target for unremitting blows and abuse. Many of the victims of this form of extortion were reputedly Jews. Thus the OGPU is found once again contributing is own peculiar skills to the stabilisation of Soviet finances.[38]

Despite the general progress of his policies in the early 1920s, one achievement continued to elude Stalin. While procuring the massacre, imprisonment and starvation of millions of peasants, he was still not free to order the execution of a single leading Party member. Nor were Communists yet considered suitable material for the show trials which they greeted with such frenzied displays of enthusiasm, unaware as yet that their own turn would come. Behind the scenes, however, the great dictator was grappling with the problem of liquidating recalcitrant Party members, while still compelled to use relatively mild methods. Trotsky, expelled from the Party in 1927 and exiled to Alma Ata in 1928, was banished from Soviet territory in February 1929. That Stalin found it politic to deal so gently with his arch-enemy is an indication of how carefully he still had to tread. That he need not always feel so restricted was, however, shown by another event which occurred later in the same year when the OGPU agent Jacob Blyumkin was shot—for making contact with Trotsky during a visit to Turkey. This was the same Blyumkin whose chequered career had begun with the assassination of the German ambassador to Moscow in 1918. His death made history as the first occasion on which a Party member (and Cheka/OGPU agent of some standing) was simply executed, as opposed to being expelled from the Party as a prelude to imprisonment or exile.

Blyumkin's liquidation was something of a special case and further attempts by Stalin to extend the principle of executing erring Party members foundered—for the time being—on stubborn resistance within the Politburo from political associates who owed their own careers to the Secretary-General, but now opposed him to the extent of rejecting the principle that leading

Party members might be handed over to the OGPU for execution. Among several instances when Stalin unsuccessfully urged the death penalty for erring Party members, the Ryutin case rankled most. In summer 1932 this minor Party official disseminated a document of two hundred pages in which he called for the removal of Stalin from the leadership. The Secretary-General probably hoped that the OGPU would shoot Ryutin without more ado. As it turned out, however, the OGPU referred the case to the Party's Central Control Commission, which referred it to the Politburo, where Stalin was outvoted—with the result that Ryutin merely suffered expulsion from the Party and exile.[39] Four years were still to pass before Stalin could unleash his political police on Party members.

9
The NKVD under Yagoda and Yezhov
1934–1938

The year 1934—more precisely, its first eleven months—witnessed a temporary check to the development of the Soviet political police as an instrument of terror. By now Stalin's Russia seemed to have weathered the worst storms. Collectivisation of agriculture had been carried through, the OGPU was no longer arresting and shooting peasants in bulk, the great famine was over and adequate food stocks were to hand. Though the industrial aims of the First Five Year Plan had not all been attained, a comparatively modest second plan now held out the promise of a less hectic future. Meanwhile Hitler's rise to power in Germany was no hopeful sign for the Soviet Union, yet at least fostered a sense of solidarity among her citizens.

Meeting in Moscow from 26 January to 10 February 1934, the Seventeenth Party Congress emphasised the themes of unity, relaxation and hope. In many ways this 'Congress of Victors' seemed to set the seal on Stalin's establishment as supreme ruler. His vanquished rivals (Zinovyev, Kamenev, Pyatakov, Bukharin, Rykov and others) were permitted to take part, and to pay their master fulsome tributes which received a respectful hearing—no *claque* of Stalinists howled them down, as formerly. Now, it appeared, the Secretary-General could at last afford to be generous to his enemies. In his own report to the Congress he encouraged this impression, remarking that it had been necessary to finish off the remnants of opposition within the Party at the previous, Sixteenth Congress, but that 'at the present Congress there is nothing [left] to prove'.[1] Adding his impression that there was 'nobody left to beat', Stalin was perhaps exercising his grim sense of humour, if—as seems likely—he had already marked down his own colleagues, followers and sycophants for extermination. From among 1,966 congressmen who now basked in the sunshine of their genial leader's smile, 1,108 were to be arrested and charged with counter-revolutionary crimes within the next few years.[2]

Meanwhile, however, Stalin still seemed far from achieving unquestioned power of life and death over Party members. On this issue he still had opponents in the Central Committee, while the Politburo itself contained three such comparative moderates in Kirov, Ordzhonikidze and Kuybyshev. Kirov was now the Party's rising star. He led its Leningrad branch, and thus possessed his own power base. He was also young, eloquent, good-looking and Russian—enjoying in all these respects an advantage over his pock-marked Georgian senior. At the Seventeenth Congress, moreover, Kirov received applause rivalling that accorded to Stalin himself. There was even a movement—how influential can only be guessed—to remove Stalin and make Kirov leader in his place.[3] In the elections to highest Party office held after the Congress, Kirov greatly strengthened his position when he was appointed to the powerful Central Committee Secretariat alongside Stalin, Kaganovich and Zhdanov. Stalin, on the other hand, suffered a rebuff, being re-elected as a mere 'Secretary', instead of 'Secretary-General', as hitherto. Though no one could doubt his continuing pre-eminence, this change of title certainly represented an attempt to curb his powers, for such variations of protocol are least of all accidental in a Soviet context. Stalin, accordingly, began 1934 with his thrust for absolute supremacy thwarted and his position vulnerable to pressure behind the scenes.

When faced with obstacles, Stalin often adopted a yielding posture, while secretly conspiring to destroy those who stood in his way. Such were his tactics between the Seventeenth Congress and December 1934, during which months several notable concessions were made, including a suspension of the indiscriminate prosecution of engineers and managers,[4] an easing of the peasants' position and a relaxation of political controls within the army. Most significant of all, a decree of 10 July 1934 abolished the OGPU. Its functions were transferred to a newly created organ, the Main Administration of State Security (GUGB), which was in turn subordinated to a reconstituted People's Commissariat for Internal Affairs (NKVD). From now on, and until the People's Commissariats were renamed Ministries in 1946, the Soviet political police was most commonly referred to as the NKVD, though the NKVD also controlled the militia (ordinary police), fire services, registry offices and various other departments not directly concerned with State security. As with earlier changes of name, an apparent concession turned out to be the opposite. It was as the NKVD that the Russian political police operated the most oppressive campaign in its history—the great terror of 1937–8. Sometimes known as the great purge, this episode also became notorious in Russia as the *Yezhovshchina* from the name of Nicholas Yezhov, head of the NKVD during the two peak years. The true architect of the terror was Stalin himself, however, Yezhov being merely his tool.

In 1934 Yezhov's hour had not yet struck. Menzhinsky, the preceding head of the political police, had died in May, and Stalin appointed as first People's Commissar of the new NKVD Henry Yagoda, an ally of long standing. Of Polish origin, like his two predecessors, he had been high up in the Cheka/GPU/OGPU machine since 1920, and had shown great ruthlessness when responsible, as head of GULAG, for building the White Sea Canal by slave labour. Another key appointment (made in 1933), was that of Andrew Vyshinsky, later one of the chief actors in the great Moscow trials, to head the newly established Procurator-Generalship of the USSR. Stalin also secured the promotion of Yezhov to the Party's Organisation Bureau in February 1934, having perhaps already selected this evil dwarf as first reserve for Yagoda. Finally, Stalin was further developing a body about which little is known, but which is agreed to have played a crucial part in orchestrating the terror—the Special Branch of the Party Central Committee. Charged with surveillance over the political police itself, this organ was headed by Alexander Poskryobyshev, also head of the dictator's personal secretariat. He thereby came to function as chief custodian of Stalin's custodians.[5]

Thus, by the end of 1934, four of Stalin's future terror-masters were already taking up their positions in the shadows against the day when he would be free to strike—Yagoda, Vyshinsky, Yezhov and Poskryobyshev.

The turning point between relaxation and intensified—but still far from total—terror, came in the afternoon of 1 December 1934, when a gunman shot Sergey Kirov in the back in the corridor outside his office on the third floor of the Smolny building, headquarters of the Leningrad Communist Party. The killer was immediately arrested. He was Leonid Nikolayev, a thirty-year-old Communist who had recently been expelled from the Party and then reinstated, but retained a grudge against the leadership, and saw himself in a romantic light as heir to the political assassins of Imperial Russia. It seems likely that Zaporozhets, second-in-command of the Leningrad NKVD, encouraged and helped Nikolayev to shoot Kirov on the instructions of Yagoda—who, in turn, was acting on Stalin's instructions. The security precautions surrounding Party leaders were extremely stringent, and it is almost inconceivable that Nikolayev could have penetrated the closely guarded Smolny building without the connivance of the local NKVD. That the clues ultimately led back to Stalin himself was strongly suggested, though not explicitly asserted, in Khrushchev's 'secret speech', delivered over twenty years later at the Twentieth Party Congress in 1956, the theme being further expanded in a second speech by Khrushchev, given at the Twenty-Second Party Congress in 1961. Whatever the degree of Stalin's involvement, the murder played into his hands by removing a rival, and also by furnishing a pretext to launch the first stage in his terror campaign. It was the first murder of any prominent Party figure since Uritsky's assassination had unleashed the Cheka's Red Terror in 1918. Now the new killing might stampede the moderates in the Politburo and Central Committee into approving the terrorist measures which Stalin had so far urged in vain—and against Kirov's own opposition.

On hearing of Kirov's death, Stalin at once went to Leningrad with Yagoda and other police chiefs to take personal charge of the investigation. He also ordered the issue of a decree requiring the speedier prosecution of political offenders and providing for the immediate execution of the condemned without right of appeal. Large-scale, unpublicised shootings followed in Leningrad, and thousands or tens of thousands were privily deported from the city to concentration camps and exile, while publicly acknowledged reprisals struck down four groups within a few weeks. Firstly, over a hundred White Guards (alleged anti-Communists and supporters of the old régime) were shot in Moscow, Leningrad and other cities on vague charges of terrorism. Secondly, the assassin Nikolayev was put on secret trial, together with thirteen alleged associates. They were all shot on 29 December—and Nikolayev therefore took with him to the grave any material implicating Stalin of which he may have been aware. Thirdly,

Zaporozhets—Nikolayev's probable accomplice in the Leningrad NKVD—was also arrested, together with his superior officer Medved, and other local NKVD officers. All were sentenced to concentration camps, but the sentences were surprisingly mild considered as punishment for negligence ending in the death of a prominent leader. It was also noted within the NKVD that Zaporozhets, Medved and their colleagues received preferential treatment in camp, though when the affair had blown over, they were all shot—in 1937, when a few extra shootings were least of all likely to attract attention.[6]

Finally and most importantly, Stalin sought to implicate Zinovyev, Kamenev and their supporters in the Kirov assassination. They were tried *in camera* in January 1935, but turned out to have been inadequately processed for confession at this stage, and denied direct complicity, though allowing that their policies might have encouraged the assassin. Zinovyev and Kamenev received only prison sentences, of ten and five years respectively. Undeterred by this failure, Stalin sustained pressure for several months, seeking to convert the law into a more effective instrument of terror. In April 1935 he secured the introduction of an infamous new provision extending all legal penalties, including execution, to children down to the age of twelve. The purpose was to supply the NKVD with a new form of pressure for use against fathers of families under interrogation, since they might now find their own children framed alongside them—in the same dock, on the same faked charges. Other new laws prescribed execution for those seeking refuge abroad, and prison sentences for members of a military deserter's family—even those who had been unaware of his original intention to defect. With all this went clamorous public demands for intensified vigilance and the issue of secret official circulars calling for the purge of persons hostile to the Party.

Stalin still continued to shift the key figures whom he was already grooming as his instruments of terror. Yezhov replaced Kirov on the Secretariat in February 1935, and became head of the Party Control Commission later in the same month, while Zhdanov took over Kirov's post as Party First Secretary in Leningrad. Khrushchev, hitherto a minor figure, became First Secretary of the Moscow Party, and Vyshinsky was promoted from deputy to full Procurator-General. Meanwhile influential opponents of terror were killed or otherwise discouraged. January 1935 saw the announcement of the death through heart disease of

Valerian Kuybyshev, believed to have combined with his Polit-buro colleagues Ordzhonikidze and Kirov in opposing the extension of the death penalty to Party leaders. In 1938 Yagoda was to stand accused of procuring Kuybyshev's murder by medical means, but how he in fact perished remains a mystery. In any case yet another death convenient to Stalin had occurred. Shortly afterwards a second moderate, Abel Yenukidze, lost his post as Secretary of the Central Executive Committee of the Congress of Soviets, and with it his responsibility for the supervision of the Kremlin, all this as a prelude to his arrest and execution. Other supporters of moderation were threatened or abused —notably Lenin's widow Nadezhda Krupsky and the 'humanist' writer Maxim Gorky who was now losing his earlier enthusiasm for Yagoda's style of work. Stalin also closed down two influential political societies, both of them opposed to the extension of the death penalty: the Society of Old Bolsheviks and the Society of Former Political Prisoners and Exiles. They were dissolved in May and June 1935 respectively, whereupon Stalin's minions Yezhov and Shkiryatov seized their records—a useful weapon in the impending campaign to exterminate Party members of pre-revolutionary standing.[7]

Once again, in July 1935, Stalin secured Kamenev's trial *in camera* and once again the attempt to obtain the death penalty collapsed, the defendant receiving only a ten-year prison sentence in place of the shorter sentence already imposed on him in January. After this second failure Stalin seems to have decided to feign retreat, and accordingly relaxed overt pressure during a period of over twelve months, while continuing to prosecute his plans behind the scenes.

Between July 1935 and August 1936 Stalin was secretly forging a new instrument, or rather reforging an old one—that of the show trial, to which purpose he harnessed Yagoda and the NKVD. The basic techniques had already been evolved in proceedings against the Shakhty engineers and other non-Party defendants in 1928–33. They were now to be switched against Communists of the first magnitude, beginning with Zinovyev and Kamenev—so far tried only in secret. Now Stalin planned to parade before the world these bedraggled titans of early Bolshevism and to make them confess abjectly to a series of horrific crimes, after which they were to be sentenced to death and shot in the cellars of the NKVD. If Stalin could bring off so neat a *coup*, no individual would be safe from him.

The three major show trials of 1936–8 involved the indictment of fifty-four carefully selected individuals. Besides political leaders of the front rank, they also included some petty criminals and NKVD 'stooges' working for the prosecution. Though other publicised trials took place in the provinces, including Georgia and Siberia, during the same period, the number of those prosecuted in public or publicised trials was insignificant compared with the total of millions unavowedly liquidated during the great terror. Nevertheless the show trials played a crucial part in making the terror possible, while also supplying its rationale and barbaric ritual backcloth. Nor must Stalin's success in impressing foreign observers be forgotten. Faced with the alternative of believing the charges or dismissing the head of a great State as an unusually effective gangster, many non-Soviet verbalisers of the period opted for the former, less unnerving, alternative.

The first of the great trials began on 19 August 1936. Sixteen persons, Zinovyev and Kamenev being the most notable, faced the court indicted as members of a Trotskyite-Zinovyevite Terrorist Centre. They were tried, as were the defendants in the two later Moscow trials, by the Military Collegium of the Supreme Court in the small October Hall of the Trade Union House. The trials were public in the sense of receiving worldwide coverage, but not in that of admitting a large audience of uncommitted spectators. At the Zinovyev trial, for example, the audience consisted of a *claque* of drafted NKVD clerks and typists, who were under instructions to create a disturbance if any of the accused should depart significantly from the prearranged script.[8] Some thirty foreign journalists were also present as an escort of NKVD soldiers, bearing rifles with bayonets fixed, marched in the accused to face a tribunal of three judges. The president was Ulrich, himself a former Cheka official, while Vyshinsky conducted the prosecution—a team already proven as producers of previous, less momentous, judicial pageants. Under Vyshinsky's guidance the accused, with two exceptions, pleaded guilty to the charges. These were all based on terrorism. They included organising the murder of Kirov, and planning to murder Stalin, Kaganovich, Voroshilov, Zhdanov and other leaders. In conformity with previous show trials the performance was accompanied by a nationwide press campaign calling for the death penalty. This was indeed pronounced, and carried out within twenty-four hours. Arranging for the trial to be held in the height of summer, when he himself was absent on the Black Sea coast, Stalin had taken the country and most of the Party leadership completely unawares—as also by the death sentences, and by the speed with which they were carried out.

It soon became clear that to execute leaders of the standing of Zinovyev and Kamenev was indeed to create a precedent permitting Stalin to exterminate former Party members. Within a week he had ordered Yagoda and Yezhov to arrange the secret shooting of five thousand 'oppositionists' now in exile or concentration camps—the first instance in the history of the USSR when a mass execution was applied to Communists without even the formality of bringing charges against them.[9]

One feature of the show trials was the failure to offer evidence against the accused apart from their own statements extorted under preliminary investigation by the NKVD. The extraction of these confessions during months of interrogation was the business of Yagoda and his senior subordinates, acting under Stalin's direct personal control. If it is still asked why leading members of the Party—some of them courageous men with records of resistance to the Imperial Russian police and of brave action in the Civil War—should have collaborated in these degrading judicial farces, the answer can easily be given. It does not lie only in physical torture, deprivation of sleep, glaring lights and rubber truncheons, nor in threats of suffering and death to the prisoner, his wife, children, associates and followers. Nor does it lie in the promise of their lives to those who should prove co-operative in court, nor yet in undertakings to refrain from killing members of a co-operative defendant's family. Still less does the explanation lie solely in appeals to Party loyalty whereby the doomed men were persuaded that collaboration with the trial-fakers was one last service which they could still render to the cause which had claimed their lifelong devotion. Confessions were extracted by none of the above means exclusively, but rather by the determined application to each defendant of whatever combination of such pressures seemed most promising in his case. There was also the practice of confronting the stubborn non-confessor with the signed confessions of others—friends, relatives or colleagues who had already been broken and forced to implicate others. Yet another device was the use of minor NKVD officials as *agents provocateurs*. Lined up in dock as accused persons, these were apt to give their evidence confidently, having been promised their lives in return for speaking their lines accurately. In the event, of course, such witnesses were simply sentenced and shot along with the weightier figures whom they had so jauntily betrayed.

Despite all these techniques several of the accused at the show trials withdrew or modified their original confessions in court, while many other individuals chosen for confession may well have been rejected after resisting pressure, in which case it was easy to shoot them in secret without trial. The defendants paraded at the trials represented only such victims as had broken, and they had been selected from a vast reservoir of potential defendants precisely because of their pliability and histrionic potential. This was very largely a casting problem. Indeed, the entire spectacle of the show trials may best be understood as a theatrical performance of an unusual type, for which the NKVD supplied script-writers, producers, scene-shifters, stage-managers and prompters.[10] Not least dramatic was an element often overlooked—even as he struggled to extort the required co-operation each NKVD inquisitor knew himself to be fighting for his own life, since failure or suspected lack of vigilance on his part might drag him down with his victim. This kept the torturers on their toes.

One function of the Zinovyev trial was to compromise Party leaders still at liberty, thus preparing for their appearance at later show trials. Among those so implicated were Bukharin and Rykov, whose cases (Vyshinsky announced at the Zinovyev trial) were already under investigation. On 10 September, however, it was stated in *Pravda* that the charges against Bukharin and Rykov had been dropped under pressure of some members of the Politburo. Evidently there were elements in that supreme policy-making body still capable of rallying resistance to Stalin, even after the Zinovyev trial. Such opposition could no longer deter the dictator, however. He retaliated, as was his wont, with yet another baffling move—the dismissal of Yagoda and his replacement as People's Commissar of the NKVD by Yezhov. Stalin issued this instruction in a notable document of the terror, the telegram of 25 September 1936 sent from Sochi to the Politburo:

> We deem it absolutely necessary and urgent that Comrade Yezhov be nominated to the post of People's Commissar of the NKVD. Yagoda has definitely proved himself to be incapable of unmasking the Trotskyite-Zinovyevite bloc. The OGPU is four years behind in this matter.[11]

As mentioned above, the reference to 'four years behind' alludes to the OGPU's failure, in 1932, to execute Ryutin, after he had called for Stalin's removal.

Yagoda was not shot at once but put into cold storage, being transferred to the post of People's Commissar of Communications, where he languished for some six months before his arrest in April 1937. Stalin's motives for liquidating his chief liquidator at this stage remain obscure. One reason may have been Yagoda's guilty knowledge that the true author of Kirov's murder had been Stalin himself, if indeed this was the case. There is also the more general point that even the most abjectly sycophantic political police chief always represents a potential threat to his master. The wise despot refreshes his police from time to time by spilling old blood and bringing in new.

Two minor episodes of late 1936 well illustrate the style of police rule as it was now developing. The first was the approval, in December 1936, of a new Constitution guaranteeing freedom of speech, freedom of assembly, a free press, inviolability of correspondence, protection against arbitrary arrest and other civil liberties. This was proclaimed with superb timing—on the eve of the terrible year when its provisions were to be trampled underfoot as never before. In the very months when they were moulding the edifying periods of the text, its two main drafters Bukharin and Radek had already been marked down for show trial and the executioner's bullet. Yet even the supposedly astute Bukharin had mesmerised himself into believing that the Constitution would usher in a new era of tolerance.[12]

The same period also witnessed an instructive domestic scene. On 20 December 1936 Stalin celebrated the nineteenth anniversary of the Cheka's foundation by carousing with a group of favoured political policemen. Yezhov himself was there, and so was the Hungarian K. V. Pauker, who had risen from the office of valet-barber with the pre-1914 Budapest opera to become head of the Operations Department of the NKVD, and as such responsible for the personal safety of Soviet Party leaders. Celebrated as a court buffoon and reputedly the first individual ever permitted to shave Stalin,[13] Pauker now regaled the tipsy dictator by enacting the scene of Zinovyev's last moments as he was dragged from his cell to be shot, supported by two 'warders' (other NKVD officers). Moaning, rolling his eyes in fear and dragging his feet, Pauker-Zinovyev fell on his knees, embraced the boot of a warder and cried out: 'For God's sake, Comrade, call up Joseph Vissarionovich.' When the drunken guests asked for a repeat performance, the demon barber introduced a new variant, raising his hands aloft and screaming: 'Hear, Israel, our God is the only God!' Joseph Vissarionovich Stalin was rendered so helpless with laughter at this mockery of his ethnically Jewish, but ideologically atheist victim that he bent down and clutched his belly in both hands, and had to sign to Pauker to stop.[14] That Pauker, himself a Jew, and many of the other guests at this ghoulish feast should have been liquidated in turn before long is yet another demonstration of the anti-Semitic Stalin's love of order and symmetry.

The second great Moscow show trial took place between 23 and 30 January 1937. Among seventeen persons arraigned as members of an imaginary Anti-Soviet Trotskyite Centre the most noteworthy were Pyatakov (Deputy People's Commissar for Heavy Industry) and the prominent publicist Radek. Once again terrorism by attempted assassination figured in the indictment together with extensive charges such as had not appeared at the Zinovyev trial. The new theme was sabotage on the grand scale—by deliberately introducing gas into coal pits, wrecking trains and the like—as part of a plot hatched by the exiled Trotsky to undo industrialisation and collectivisation and to cede parts of the USSR to Germany and Japan. The defendants were found guilty, and most of them were shot. While the court was still in session Yezhov received a new title: General Commissar of State Security. By inserting the word General in the official designation of his chief executioner—and at such a moment—Stalin must surely have been reminding colleagues of their folly in robbing him of that honorific in 1934, when he had become a mere Secretary instead of Secretary-General.

A few weeks after the trial Pyatakov's main protector, Ordzhonikidze, met his death in suspicious circumstances. According to Khrushchev this was a case of suicide, Stalin having brought Ordzhonikidze 'to such a state that he was forced to shoot himself'.[15] At the time, however, a verdict of heart failure was pronounced in a bulletin signed by leading doctors, of whom the first signatory (the People's Commissar for Health, G. Kaminsky) was himself shot later in the same year, while two others were enmeshed in the medical conspiracies later concocted by the NKVD on Stalin's instructions. Their bulletin accordingly commands little respect, and a third possibility—that the NKVD murdered Ordzhonikidze—cannot be discounted.

The last attempt to halt the terror took place at a plenum of the Party Central Committee in February–March, 1937. Though no official transcript exists, accounts of the proceedings have filtered through. One minor episode was the attack launched by Stalin on the disgraced Yagoda, who was present at the deliberations—still hovering in the limbo between high office and liquidation. It was on this or some similar occasion that Yagoda rounded on Stalin's jeering supporters and shouted that six months earlier he could have put them all under arrest.[16] Stalin's chief concern at the plenum was to obtain the Central Committee's approval for the expulsion and arrest of Bukharin and Rykov. Already selected as the main defendants in the third show trial of the period, these rightist leaders had been implicated some six months earlier at the Zinovyev trial. Now, at the plenum, the Politburo candidate-member Postyshev headed a concerted attempt to rally support for the victims. He began with a general denunciation of the framing of Stalin's political opponents—but then withdrew this charge, according to one version.[17] It is also reported that Bukharin and Rykov, who were present at the meeting, vigorously defended themselves—but in vain, for they were arrested on the spot and taken off to the Lubyanka. This was the last occasion on which the expulsion and arrest of Central Committee members were sanctioned by the Central Committee itself, as Party statutes required. From now on Stalin could dispense with such formalities —to such an extent that, of 139 members and candidate members of this, the last Central Committee to make any show of independence during his lifetime, 98 (some 70 per cent), were arrested and shot, mostly in 1937–8.[18]

The first important repression to follow the Pyatakov trial occurred within the NKVD itself as Yezhov proceeded to liquidate Yagoda's senior subordinates, many of whom traced their careers back to the Cheka. Planned by Stalin and Yezhov, the main assault was launched in March 1937. Yezhov barricaded himself in a separate wing of the Lubyanka, turning it into an impregnable fort, and then ordered certain heads of NKVD departments out of Moscow to conduct inspections in different parts of the country. They left by various trains, but at the first stop down the line each was arrested and brought back to the cells by car. Owing to their supposed absence on detachment their disappearance attracted no attention for some time, and two days later the same trick was played on their unsuspecting deputies, to be followed by a general purge of the NKVD. Over three thousand officers were executed in 1937 alone. There were also many NKVD suicides. The notoriously cruel, aptly named interrogator Chertok (Little Devil), flung himself from the balcony of his twelfth-floor flat to death in the street below, while other minor demons defenestrated themselves from their Lubyanka offices in full view of the populace, a source of scandal to the terrorised capital.[19]

Now the great terror was in full career, reaching a particularly savage climax between May and September 1937. It was a period of nationwide arrests affecting all sections of the population, but bearing with especial severity on Stalin's own supporters—the élite in every branch of Soviet life. It accordingly took a particularly high proportion of victims from Party members, though the absolute number of non-Party repressions was considerably greater.

During 1933-7 inclusive the total number of Party members (including candidate members) fell drastically, from 3,555,338 to 1,920,002.[20] That the drop was largely due to the purges which continued throughout this period is clear enough, but certain additional points must also be borne in mind if the impact of the terror on the Party is to be understood. Firstly, all recruitment of new members was suspended between January 1933 and November 1936.[21] Secondly, there was a significant difference between being purged in 1933-6 and in 1937-8. During the earlier period purging generally involved no more than expulsion from the Party, while in the latter phase it carried certain further implications— slow death by concentration camp or quick death by shooting. Finally, one must bear in mind that Party members fell into two distinct classes. The majority had their principal employment outside the field of Party work—in government, administration, industrial management, the armed forces and so on. Virtually all influential members of such groups were Party members. So too, of course, were NKVD officers. With all such Party members in the broader sense must be contrasted members of the Apparatus, which consisted of full-time Party functionaries. Such *apparatchiki* comprised only a small proportion of the total. The terror consisted basically in unleashing the NKVD (itself consisting of Party members in the broader sense) on the community at large, but with a special brief to attack other Party members—in government, industrial management, the armed forces, the Comintern and so on . . . but above all in the Apparatus. Yet the aggressive role of the political police was only the most obvious feature in a campaign orchestrated by Stalin with exceptional ingenuity. As

already described, the purging NKVD was itself an early object
for attacks which continued in fits and starts throughout the
terror. Moreover, though Stalin did indeed use the NKVD to
destroy the Apparatus, he was also using the Apparatus to destroy
the NKVD. The arch-purger Yezhov himself was, after all, foisted
on the NKVD by Stalin. An *apparatchik* through and through and
lacking any known Cheka/OGPU background, he brought a
staff of *apparatchiki* with him when he took over and purged the
Yagoda machine. Thus Stalin turned these two great organisations, political police and Party Apparatus, against each other in
an orgy of mutual destruction. It was the NKVD, however, which
held the whip hand, disposing as it did of the organs of repression
—the prisons, the camps, the interrogation system and the execution cellars. The Party as such could impose no sanction more
severe than expulsion, after which the victim was handed over for
inquisition to the secular arm of the NKVD. Now, at the height of
the terror, the NKVD itself seized the initiative in persecutions of
Party members, the victim being informed of his secret expulsion
only at the moment of his arrest, if at all. The habit of undermin-
ing important figures by first seizing their subordinates was common, as was that already mentioned of proceeding gradually—
first demoting a high official to some relatively unimportant post,
as happened to Yagoda, then leaving him to simmer in the knowledge that liquidation was sure to follow. Another practice
characteristic of Stalin's twisted mind, or simply of administrative
inefficiency, was the timing of high honours to coincide with
disaster, for the award of an Order of Lenin in the morning was
no guarantee of immunity from arrest in the afternoon.

Launching full-scale terror on the Party Apparatus throughout
the USSR in the early summer of 1937, Stalin relied on trusted
satraps prepared to purge without limit in three areas. These were
Khrushchev, Zhdanov and Beria, the First Party Secretaries in
Moscow, Leningrad and Transcaucasia respectively—of whom,
incidentally, only Beria was a policeman by career. To other
regions, where no leader of adequate ruthlessness was in power,
Stalin dispatched peripatetic liquidators of proven mettle. The
dreaded Kaganovich descended on Smolensk to denounce the
Party leadership in that province,[22] while Mikoyan helped Beria
to crush the Armenian Apparatus.[23] Similar purges were con-
ducted in every part of the Soviet Union—in Belorussia and
Bashkiria, in Uzbekia, Kirgizia, Kazakhstan and the rest of
Central Asia, and in all provinces of the RSFSR, including,

eventually, far eastern Siberia. In the Ukraine local leaders resisted self-destruction until Molotov, Khrushchev and Yezhov arrived with NKVD Special Troops and imposed full-scale terror in Kiev. In January 1938 Khrushchev was foisted on the Ukraine as First Secretary. The normal process in all areas was to arrest virtually all high Party and government officials, replacing them with junior figures who would be replaced in turn within a month or two—and so on, while the terror lasted. Destroying the top Party Apparatus throughout the Soviet Union, the top purgers themselves survived—Khrushchev, Zhdanov, Beria, Kaganovich, Molotov.

Stalin also required the slaughter of foreign Communists resident in the USSR, both members of fraternal Communist parties and Comintern officials. This onslaught left British and American Communists alone, but raged among parties banned in their home country, especially the Polish and German. Many of these foreign comrades resided in the delightfully-named Hotel Luxe in Moscow, where the special amenities came to include nocturnal raids by the NKVD. The Hungarian Communist Bela Kun, himself no mean terror-master in the past, was denounced at an executive committee meeting of the Comintern in May 1937 by Stalin's hatchet-man Manuilsky, removed to the Lefort Prison, tortured and executed as a spy. Almost all Polish Communists in Soviet clutches were liquidated, including one who resisted arrest in the Hotel Luxe by shooting it out with the police. The German Communists too suffered terrible losses.

Besides the liquidation of foreign Communists, Stalin also enforced a purge of domestic Communists polluted by contact with other countries. This involved an assault on the large espionage establishments maintained by the NKVD on foreign territory—a difficult operation, since foreign-based spy-masters could not be arrested by Soviet police on the streets of Paris or Berlin. Steps were therefore taken to lure them back to Moscow, while the liquidation of home-based officials of the controlling Foreign Department of the NKVD was postponed in order not to arouse undue suspicion in the field. Some of the proposed victims refused to walk into the trap, and claimed asylum in the West. Yezhov accordingly established mobile squads for the assassination of such undesirables on foreign territory. Victims included non-returning espionage chiefs of the Foreign Department, among whom was Ignace Reiss, an NKVD Resident in Switzerland—his bullet-riddled body was found on the highway near Lausanne on

4 September 1937.[24] A victim of different political colouring fell to the NKVD when General Miller, head of the Union of Tsarist Veterans, was kidnapped in Paris on 22 September, and never heard of again.[25]

In addition to the NKVD's espionage establishment, the Red Army maintained its own entirely separate network of spies on foreign territory. Friction developed between the two organisations, reaching a climax in Spain, where Yan Berzin—for many years head of army intelligence—was attached to the Spanish Republican forces during the Civil War. After protesting against NKVD activities in Spain, Berzin was recalled to Russia and shot. His successor as head of military intelligence was also shot. As Berzin's fate reminds one, the numerous Soviet citizens serving on the Republican side in the Spanish Civil War all became prime objects of suspicion to Stalin, whatever their individual military or diplomatic record might be. In Spain the NKVD operated almost as freely as on home territory, liquidating non-approved persons and groups, and by no means confining its repressions to Soviet citizens, for Spaniards—including many Anarchists and individual prominent politicians—were also done to death. On return to Russia the executioners themselves faced execution in accordance with Stalin's new style of leadership.

Besides embracing all other power complexes, the terror also took in the home-based army. On 11 and 12 July 1937 the great military purge exploded with the announcement that eight high-ranking officers had been executed for treason after secret trial. The most prominent was Marshal Tukhachevsky, recently Deputy People's Commissar of Defence. His execution represented no impulse killing by the dictator, but had ripened in secret for years —Tukhachevsky and Stalin had clashed over Stalin's disastrous attempt to impose his own strategy during the Soviet invasion of Poland in 1920. A more recent contribution to the Marshal's downfall in 1937 was damning documentary evidence in the form of treasonable correspondence between him and members of the German High Command—in fact forged for the German *Sicherheitsdienst* on Heydrich's instructions and skilfully planted on Stalin's intelligence service by the Nazis.

Tukhachevsky's execution was only the beginning of a general slaughter of Red Army officers reaching its peak in 1937-8 and involving about 35,000 victims—that is, about half the Soviet officer corps, the navy also being attacked. The casualty rate rose with the rank of the victims to take in 90 per cent of Generals and

80 per cent of Colonels.[26] Thus the Soviet High Command was all but destroyed.

A study of the military purge involves considering the complex interrelations now existing between Stalin's three main organs of control—NKVD, Party and army. Though it is usual to refer to individual actors in the drama as 'belonging' to one or other of these bodies, this was true only in the sense that a given military individual had his main employment with one or other of them. Whichever of the three it might be, he could not escape close involvement with the other two. The great majority of officers, especially in the senior ranks, consisted of card-holding Communists. As such they attended Party meetings and were subject to Party discipline. To be an army officer was, therefore, by no means to be independent of the Party. In addition to this arrangement, however, there also existed a special Party organisation within the army—the Political Administration. This supplied the Political Commissars who at various times acted as joint commanders of units and formations. The Political Administration had its own hierarchy independent of the military chain of command, but this proved no protection against the tornado. On 1 June 1937 the suicide of Yan Gamarnik, head of the Political Administration since 1929, was reported, and an official statement implicated him in the military conspiracy. L. Z. Mekhlis, a minion of Stalin's, replaced him and purged his new subordinates, himself proving one of the rare breed of senior purgers to survive the terror.

In studying the impact of the political police on the dual mechanism of army and Political Administration, one must distinguish between the military organisation of the NKVD outside the army and that within it. Outside the army the NKVD maintained its own private forces consisting exclusively of NKVD personnel. The history of this organisation goes back to the early days of the Cheka, when Special Purpose Units were first formed, afterwards re-emerging as the OGPU Troops which helped to impose collectivisation. By 1936 NKVD Special Purpose Troops numbered over 150,000,[27] and included infantry, cavalry, tanks and aircraft. Besides this *corps d'élite*, which was used to repress internal disorders generally, the NKVD also maintained other specialised forces—Frontier Troops, Railway Troops, Convoy Troops for escorting slave labourers to concentration camps and GULAG Troops to ensure that they did not escape after they had arrived.

In addition to these establishments, the NKVD also maintained Special Branches in all army units above battalion level and in military schools and installations generally. These branches censored mail, regulated the issue of ammunition, and, above all, recruited secret informers to spy on their comrades in arms—an arrangement such as General Dzhunkovsky had discontinued back in 1914 as detrimental to the morale and honour of the Imperial Russian army. The Special Branches of the NKVD within the army had their own separate hierarchy, independent both of the regular army and of the Political Administration. But separate as the three bodies were organisationally, their members were closely interconnected in their professional activities. A Special Branch officer of the NKVD within the army himself held military rank and wore military uniform, but earned a higher salary than regular officers of the same rank and was a Party member.[28] Furthermore, regular army officers, themselves usually Party members, were also liable to recruitment by the Special Branches as secret informers on their brother officers. Even if they were not so formally recruited, thus becoming in a sense unofficial members of the NKVD, they were no doubt all aware of Lenin's dictum that 'every Communist must be a Chekist'.[29] Ensnared in these meshes, the armed forces were helpless before the dictator—bound hand and foot, one is tempted to say, with red tape in triplicate.

By such means Stalin had put the army in a position where a military plot to assassinate him and overthrow his government could have little hope of success. Nor has evidence for the existence of such a plot ever materialised, either during the military purge or as the result of later disclosures. It is also noteworthy that Stalin destroyed the flower of his military command at the very time when Hitler threatened his western frontiers. Moreover, at the time of Tukhachevsky's execution for allegedly negotiating with the German authorities, the Soviet dictator had himself been engaged for about six months in promoting precisely such negotiations behind the scenes through his private agent David Kandelaki.[30] To this as to so much else he imparted his own special brand of perverted symmetry.

The terror took a heavy toll in cultural and intellectual life. Writers were victimised, at least six hundred being sent to concentration camps, according to one statement.[31] Among novelists Boris Pilnyak had been expelled from the Union of Writers for bringing out his short novel *Mahogany* in Berlin in 1929, and rewrote it under another title to conform with official requirements. By some grotesque coincidence, Yezhov himself (while still a comparative unknown) was assigned to help Pilnyak revise the work, and listed no less than fifty passages requiring to be changed outright. 'They'll end up by throwing me in jail,' Pilnyak predicted.[32] They did—he is reported shot as a Japanese spy in 1937 or 1938. The short-story writer Isaac Babel was arrested in the writers' colony at Peredelkino, eventually perishing in prison or camp in 1941.[33] The same fate might have overtaken Pasternak too, since he was required to sign a document approving the execution of the military leaders, but refused, escaping arrest only because no one dared to report this misdemeanour to higher authority.[34] Another outstanding poet, Osip Mandelshtam, died in December 1938 at Vladivostok in transit for Kolyma, probably insane, and believing that the camp authorities were trying to poison him.[35]

The terror also raged in the academic world, where there were few branches of knowledge so recondite as to provide a safe haven. Historians, ancient and modern, were commonly arrested for terrorism. One professor of history fell into disgrace for ill-chosen remarks about topics as various as Joan of Arc, the legend of Midas and the Donatist movement in North Africa. Through some chain of thought characteristic of the NKVD, he was forced to confess that he had plotted the murder of the Ukrainian Party leader Kosior. Then Kosior happened to fall into disfavour, and the charge of espionage on behalf of Japan was hurriedly substituted.[36] In certain branches of knowledge charlatans obtained official backing, which was followed by the arrest and liquidation of serious workers in the same field. The most notorious was the spurious geneticist Trofim Lysenko, whose sway ebbed and flowed into the Khrushchev era and led to the repression of numerous authentic biologists and geneticists. In linguistics the nonsensical theories of N. Ya. Marr gained acceptance with similarly drastic results until Stalin personally denounced them in 1950, long after Marr's death.

The above were merely some prominent episodes in a campaign of terror which took its victims from every walk of life. Adequate statistics on the toll in death and suffering are not available. It may, however, be asserted with complete certainty that the victims were numbered in millions, not in any smaller unit. A conservative estimate for the arrests effected during 1937–8 is seven million, and on the assumption that five million were already in custody at the beginning of 1937, that would give a grand total of twelve million by the end of 1938, were it not for extensive seepage caused by executions, starvation and exhaustion. Some two million probably perished in custody during the two years, apart from which about ten per cent of those arrested were shot—to the tune of about a million in 1937–8. Thus the overall number in custody at the end of 1938 may have been about nine million, some eight million of them in concentration camps and about a million in prisons.[37]

Like the gendarmes of Imperial Russia, NKVD operatives often effected arrests in the small hours, when resistance is low and all is dark outside. Arrest usually involved painstaking search of the victim's belongings and person on the spot, followed by his removal to prison. Here the typical captive first spent several months in the cells, from which he was periodically summoned for interrogation designed to extract confession of complicity under some provision of Article 58 of the Criminal Code—that covering political offences. Most prisoners believed themselves innocent, and would protest vehemently when required to simulate guilt. Nor were the NKVD interrogators always helpful in indicating what kind of confession would be acceptable, but often required the prisoner to invent his own crime. Long subjected to bullying, blows, threats, blackmail, torture and expressions of sympathy, many victims yearned to sign any statement which might end an ordeal so terrible. Finally the interrogator, himself exhausted, might relent and suggest a suitable admission, or more experienced prisoners would help a cell-mate by analysing the formulae currently in vogue. Although such confessions—to terrorism, sabotage, wrecking, espionage, Trotskyism and the like—were almost all works of fiction, it occasionally happened that a genuine foreign spy fell into the NKVD's clutches, causing consternation in a system geared to operate only on the plane of fantasy.

Interrogators usually insisted on detailed answers to two key questions: 'Who recruited you?' and 'Whom did you recruit?' Thus a single arrest could lead to hundreds more, especially as certain prisoners conceived it their civic duty to clog the machinery of terror by informing against every individual whom they could name—once everyone in the country had been denounced, it was felt, the nightmare must end. Individuals still at liberty also supplied denunciations lest they incur the charge of defective vigilance, for silence was a sure way of drawing suspicion on oneself. To rational motives for betraying one's associates must be added the activity of hysterical, neurotic persons, as of the compulsive busybodies, fanatics and lunatics who flourished under these conditions, with the result that the NKVD eventually came to hold a dossier on almost every town-dweller in the country.

Despite the fanciful charges to which an individual might confess, some genuine though trifling occurrence had not uncommonly provoked his original arrest. This might be telling an anecdote about a Party leader, or failing to adopt the correct facial expression during a collective hate session. Gustav Herling fell under suspicion because his name bore a vague resemblance to that of Herman Goering.[38] Another prisoner was convicted of murder . . . but murder of himself. Attempts to prove his innocence by demonstrating that he was still alive led nowhere.[39] As this extreme instance shows, it was virtually impossible for any arrested person to secure his acquittal, since that would be to cast doubt on the efficiency of an organisation officially deemed flawless. Yet all must undergo the agonising ritual of interrogation and enforced confession before being sentenced perfunctorily or *in absentia* to execution, or to a term of between five and twenty-five years in the camps. The term mattered little since few inmates survived it, and these were often reimprisoned on some trumped-up charge just as their sentence was about to expire.

As the terror progressed, political prisoners were more and more victimised as a matter of official policy. NKVD guards were sent on brutalisation courses, privileges were curtailed, and all shreds of preferential treatment for political detainees vanished. It was now *urki* (ordinary criminals) who received privileges. For years these had benefited from amnesties which did not apply to politicals. Now they received responsible posts as 'trusties' within the prison and camp administrations, being permitted to beat up, rob, murder and rape politicals while NKVD guards looked on impassively. *Urki* would play cards for the possessions, and even for the lives, of the 'white-handed ones', as they termed politicals, the loser being obliged to remove the selected stake by force or intimidation—or else, depending on the conditions of the game, to slit a throat. To some *urki* political prisoners seemed fair game, since these were all (wrongly) considered to be Communist Party members, and as such were held responsible for the general woe.[40]

Summer 1937 saw the official sanction of physical torture as a staple feature of interrogations, and from now on prisons echoed all night with the victims' screams. They would return bloody, wounded, often with ribs or limbs broken—an example to their cell-mates of the importance of co-operation. Torture was generally employed on an improvised basis, without the use of special instruments—except possibly in the dreaded Lefort Prison in Moscow.[41] The NKVD interrogator would reach for whatever weapon came to hand. Beating with a chair-leg or rubber truncheon is commonly mentioned in accounts of these affairs, as is the slamming of fingers in a door. Beatings not uncommonly crippled the victim for life, inflicting permanent deafness or other still more serious injury, besides which an unknown number died under interrogation. One seemingly gentler technique was to require the victim to remain standing—but for many days on end. This involved another common form of pressure, deprivation of sleep, as also did continued use of the 'conveyor' system of non-stop interrogation by a team working in relays. Further, more refined, devices included plunging the victim's head in a full spittoon, and making him kneel while the inquisitor urinated on his head.[42]

With or without torture, jail conditions constituted a severe ordeal in themselves, prisoners being jammed into cells intended for one quarter or one tenth of the number. By long-standing convention, the latest arrival received a place by the *parasha* (latrine pail) near the door, working his way gradually through accumulated seniority towards the window, which was usually white-washed and boarded on the outside, with only a small pane for ventilation purposes. Food, consisting of bread, skilly and obscurely flavoured hot water, was minimal. So too were facilities for exercise and correspondence with the outside world. Such privileges could be withdrawn on the whim of the administration, as could the right to use the prison shop from which food and clothing could be bought on a limited scale. Though visits to bathhouse and barber might vary the monotony, frequent body searches were carried out with extreme thoroughness at irregular intervals. The eminent literary critic Ivanov-Razumnik received the order to bend down and display his anal passage for inspection fifty times in three years.[43]

Once sentenced, enemies of the people faced new ordeals by rail transit to a concentration camp under conditions described above. In the early 1930s the horrors of bulk freighting increased with the establishment of the vast new slave empire of Dalstroy around the basin of the River Kolyma. This involved a journey of several months to the far north-east of Siberia where the new GULAG colony sprawled over an area four times the size of France—a vast gold-mining enterprise. Deportees were first transported by goods wagon to transit camp in Vladivostok, and then shipped across the Sea of Okhotsk, a passage of eight or nine days. Between Vladivostok and Dalstroy slave hulks plied, among which the *Dzhurma* acquired especially evil repute. On this and other slavers the cargo of up to twelve thousand souls was battened down below decks, being distributed in cages to frustrate mutiny in transit. No guard dared descend, for the holds were infested with *urki*, but machine-gun nests and powerful hoses were placed at strategic points in case of trouble. One deportee, Yevgeniya Ginsburg, describes how prisoners started rioting when fire once broke out in the hold and the hoses were used, boiling some of the cargo in the process and filling the *Dzhurma* with the stench of burnt flesh.[44] In the winter of 1933–4 the *Dzhurma* was converted into a refrigeration ship of an unusual kind—it became icebound in arctic waters for months and the entire slave shipment perished while many of the crew became insane on deck.[45] A reconstituted log of the *Dzhurma* would also include the occasion when *urki* used a needle to put out the eyes of someone who had raped a female political earmarked by his gang boss.[46]

The Kolyma gold-fields were situated in an area of permanent frost with a climate severe even by Siberian standards. At any given time the total convict population of about half a million was less than that held in the north of European Russia—the original area of Soviet concentration camps, which continued to expand during the terror. The death rate was still higher on the Kolyma, however, and has been put at thirty per cent per annum among the miners.[47] There were also many frost-bite cripples—inevitably so when convicts were driven to work at temperatures of 50 degrees below zero centigrade and worse in inadequate clothing and footwear. For the severely maimed special death camps were established in the deep northern hinterland. A Polish prisoner gave General Anders an account of the arrival at the port of Nakhodka of 7,000 such cripples of the Kolyma—convicts who had lost feet, hands, ears or noses in various combinations, while some were blind or mad.[48]

Being so far from Moscow, the Kolyma became something of an independent satrapy under its first head, Reinhold Berzin—until, in mid-1937, a special squad of NKVD mobile purgers suddenly flew into Magadan with instructions to depose this emperor of Dalstroy. To lull any possible suspicion, they had brought with them a fake copy of the newspaper *Izvestiya*, specially printed for Berzin's eyes only and announcing that he had been awarded the Order of Lenin. He was invited to Moscow to receive this honour in person, but held a farewell party in Magadan before proceeding in triumph to the airport—which had been quietly seized by the visitors while he was celebrating his good luck. Arrested and flown to the capital, Berzin and his associates were duly shot. Meanwhile the newly arrived liquidators took control of his former fief, embarking on a general purge of the Kolyma.[49]

Wherever individual concentration camp networks might be, GULAG's regimen remained fairly uniform, and was based on the extraction of effort by the calculated withholding of food. Those who fulfilled the severe work norms received just enough nourishment to sustain life for a time, while the many who missed their target were put, literally, on a starvation diet. For the recalcitrant, punishment cells and special penal camps, with even worse conditions, were available. The convicts' day began with reveille— the banging of a hammer on an iron rail—and the routine continued with roll-calls, food queues and searches. Most of the day, twelve hours or more, was spent on a work site outside the camp zone, the slaves being marched there five abreast by armed escorts and Alsatian dogs which received a meat ration denied to their charges. Anyone falling out of line was shot. Such details abound in the numerous accounts of concentration camp life now long available and remarkable for the consistent picture which they draw. During Stalin's lifetime, by contrast, the very existence of concentration camps was officially denied as an invention of hostile propaganda. According to Soviet spokesmen of the period and their foreign dupes, Stalin's rule was characterised by a uniquely tender and humane care for the welfare of his subjects. Here once again one recognises the signature of the great dictator who, as his daughter Svetlana has explained, 'couldn't stand the sound of a child crying or screaming'[50]—though it must be added, as a natural corollary to this, that minors too were taken into the slave camps, including the children of 'enemies of the people'.

As this reminds one, the fate of convicts' wives and children was unenviable. Families lost their homes, the children were derided as outcasts at school, while the wives were officially encouraged to renounce and divorce condemned husbands. Many women were also sent to the camps owing to guilt by association with husbands and lovers previously framed, and GULAG kept a special section in Potma for 7,000 wives and sisters of 'enemies of the people'.[51]

Women were also freighted to other slave camp empires further afield, including the Kolyma, besides which they could of course also qualify as spies, saboteurs, wreckers or Trotskyites in their own right. They totalled only about ten per cent of the whole concentration camp intake—which means, however, that GULAG must have held nearly a million women by the end of 1938.

A female convict could sometimes improve her situation by forming a liaison with an officer of the camp administration, doctor or other privileged person, but she also faced hazards to which men were less exposed, in mass rape and consequent infection with venereal disease. Gangs of *urki* would ambush young girls among new arrivals, one grotesque collective ravishing being described particularly well by Herling.[52] For the children of those who became pregnant the NKVD maintained special homes in its camp empires with facilities for occasional visits by surviving mothers, and women prisoners often courted pregnancy, since it entailed release from work for a period. That men could also be objects for collective sexual attack is illustrated by Raphael Rupert's horrific account of the good-looking, blond German prisoner who was violated by a succession of sex-crazed camp nurses, using a device of which the less said the better, after which he had to be carried back to his barracks on a stretcher.[53] The same witness (a post-war Hungarian prisoner) also recounts what is perhaps the most gruesome of all camp stories—how a gang of famished *urki* caught, ravished, cooked and ate a fat, free, female Russian doctor.[54]

In this context it is perhaps worth recalling the formula with which kindly old lags would greet newly arrived prisoners: these comforting words, *zhit budesh, no yebat ne zakhochesh,* may be delicately translated as 'You'll live but you won't want any sex'. As some of the above accounts suggest, the prophecy tended to prove inaccurate in both its particulars. However, it must be added that, despite some of the lurid episodes mentioned, strict segregation of men and women was the normal drill in the camps. In any detailed treatise on sexual practices behind the wire the homosexual theme would, accordingly, loom large.

The last Moscow show trial to be staged during the great terror opened on 2 March 1938. Bukharin, Rykov and Yagoda were chief defendants among the twenty-one members of a Bloc of Rightists and Trotskyites indicted in proceedings outstandingly spurious even by show-trial standards. More than Zinovyev's and Pyatakov's trials—which were functional in the sense that they helped to extend the terror—the Bukharin affair was a work of art for art's sake. It fused together all themes previously mooted—wrecking, sabotage, spying for Britain, Germany, Poland and Japan, a plot to provoke foreign attack on the Soviet Union, conspiracies to assassinate Stalin, Molotov and Kaganovich, causing the death of Kirov and the failing to sanction the death of Ryutin. As at the Pyatakov trial, an incidental aim was to find scapegoats for the many economic shortages of the period, and the charges therefore included depriving the Soviet consumer of eggs and tobacco, putting nails and glass in butter, wantonly withholding serum from horses threatened with anthrax in Siberia and deliberately infecting the pigs of Leningrad Province with erysipelas.

Yagoda's was the most exotic charge sheet. He was accused of accepting Yenukidze's instructions to kill Kirov and of ordering the NKVD officer Zaporozhets to arrange the murder. This accusation may have been true, except that Stalin's name should perhaps have figured in place of Yenukidze's. Yagoda was also charged with several more murders or attempted murders, all harmonising with his pre-revolutionary profession of pharmacist. He had allegedly tried to kill Yezhov by ordering subordinates to spray his office with a solution of mercury and some other unnamed poison, and he was also accused of maintaining his own poison laboratory. He was further charged with organising assassinations by medical means, acting through several doctors. One of these, Dr Levin, had been on the Cheka/OGPU/NKVD medical staff since 1920, while another, Professor Pletnyov, was the most distinguished Soviet physician of the day, but had lacked any political police connexions until these had been conveniently supplied in the previous year. A female NKVD agent had framed him and brought him to trial for biting her on the breast during a medical consultation, after which his arrest gave the NKVD a chance to break him at leisure and teach him his lines for the Bukharin trial. According to the testimony now produced, Yagoda had arranged four medical murders in all—of Menzhinsky (his own predecessor as head of the OGPU), of Kuybyshev, of Maxim Gorky and of Gorky's son Maxim Peshkov. Yagoda's medical minions had reputedly killed Kuybyshev by giving him incorrect treatment for heart trouble. They had weakened Gorky's tubercular lungs by encouraging him to stand near bonfires, of which he was inordinately fond, whereupon they had infected him with a cold by bringing him into contact with his snuffling grandchildren. They had overdosed Menzhinsky with some quack nostrum, and had given Peshkov a chill by leaving him untended on a garden bench when dead drunk.

The Bukharin trial proved less successful than the Zinovyev and Pyatakov affairs in that more of the charges were denied in court. Yagoda rejected accusations of espionage, showing the defiance of a cornered rat, but reappeared crushed and listless after a night in the cells where torture was probably applied. A co-defendant, the former Politburo-member Krestinsky, had gone further—flatly pleading not guilty at the opening of the trial, and thus withdrawing the confession extorted from him under preliminary investigation. During the adjournment he was reputedly tortured by the dislocation of his shoulder,[55] and he reappeared in court on the following day to reaffirm his original testimony. The star defendant, Nicholas Bukharin, sustained a more determined attempt to frustrate the trial. Roundly denying charges of espion-age, and of attempting to assassinate Lenin in 1918, he would accept responsibility for other crimes only in vague terms, such as cast doubt on the very existence of the Rightist-Trotskyite Bloc which he had allegedly headed—a counter-attack too ingenious to be widely understood at the time.

This was the last show trial of Soviet citizens to be staged in Moscow, but the terror continued to rage after Bukharin and most of his co-defendants had been shot. Stalin assaulted the Komsomol (Communist Youth) organisation—unaccountably neglected until so late a stage. He also ordered a belated purge in the far east, where Russian troops under Marshal Blyukher were caught be-tween the NKVD and Japanese forces engaged in probing Soviet defences by local military action. In May 1938 the NKVD chief Frinovsky arrived in the far east with Mekhlis, head of the army's Political Administration. They shot all the leading far eastern NKVD officers and arrested Blyukher's regular army subordinates in quantity. However, General Lyushkov, commander of the NKVD Frontier Troops in the far east, escaped by slipping over the Manchurian border on 13 June 1938 and surrendering to the Japanese Kwantung army. Under Japanese and German interro-gation he supplied valuable intelligence on Soviet military and political dispositions. Details of the details disclosed by Lyushkov were in turn fed back to Moscow by Richard Sorge, the outstand-ing agent of Soviet military intelligence who operated in Tokyo under the cover of journalism.[56]

In autumn 1938 Marshal Blyukher at last fell, being removed to Moscow, arrested on 22 October, flung into the Lefort Prison, tortured and killed. Meanwhile Yezhov too was slipping from power, and like Yagoda he went to his doom gradually. On 20 July 1938 Lavrenty Beria, whose main career had been in Transcaucasia, was transferred to the central NKVD as its deputy head. About a month later Yezhov became People's Commissar for Inland Water Transport, while still retaining nominal control over the NKVD, but his dismissal was announced on 8 December, and Beria became People's Commissar in his place. Yezhov's later fate is shrouded in mystery, and though concentration camp rumour has spoken of him hanging himself on a tree in a lunatic asylum, it seems probable that he was secretly executed.

The terror spread mutual distrust throughout the Soviet Union, breaking the spirit of the nation and turning it into the docile instrument of the supreme manipulator. Unable to trust wife, children, parents, superiors, subordinates, friends, acquaintances or associates, an individual could hope to preserve his own position only by a combination of fawning, treachery, ruthlessness and luck. It would be rash to assume that even Hitlerite Germany or Maoist China have outdone Stalin's achievement in the systematic degrading of human beings to lower than animal level, though it must also be admitted that precise criteria for measuring success in this process have not yet been evolved. Stalin's motives for mounting the *Yezhovshchina* may never be plumbed, and it is not surprising if there has been a tendency to describe him as a lunatic whose actions defy rational explanation. Nor can one wonder that an authoritative work on the terror offers no less than seventeen theories to explain the phenomenon, including one ascribing it to the influence of sunspots.[57] It seems more plausible, however, to assume that Stalin knew what he was about, pursuing specific aims among which the extension of his own power and the preservation of his personal safety loomed large. These aims were pursued with persistence, nerve, uncanny skill, an acute sense of timing, a total absence of moral restraint and a certain perverse humour, the political police being the dictator's prime instrument but also one of his prime victims.

Beria and the NKVD/NKGB
1938–1945

Assuming full command of the NKVD in December 1938, the Georgian Lavrenty Beria replaced Yezhov, whose two-year stint thus represents the only period between 1917 and 1953 during which a Russian occupied the post of Soviet political police chief. Beria's career had begun with ten years in the Transcaucasian Cheka/GPU machine. By 1931 he was head of the entire Transcaucasian GPU, but was then transferred to high Party office as Georgian and later Transcaucasian First Secretary. Both as Chekist and boss *apparatchik* he had shown himself a ruthless purger, and one less averse to the humbler duties of the profession than his compatriot Stalin—it is reported, for instance, that Beria personally, in his own office, shot Khandzhyan, the Armenian First Secretary, on 11 August 1936.[1] In 1937 Beria had the privilege of staging his own publicised, though by no means public, trials in Georgia. By methods of this kind Beria earned the highest political distinction which Stalin could bestow: being mentioned in a Moscow show trial (that of Pyatakov) as a target for an unsuccessful assassination attempt.

Beria must have possessed some special ability to worm his way into Stalin's confidence. According to Stalin's daughter Svetlana Alliluyev, Beria 'succeeded in confounding . . . my father' by 'Oriental perfidy, flattery and hypocrisy'.[2] An example of this had occurred in July 1935, when Beria published a history of prerevolutionary Bolshevism in the Caucasus—faked to an extent exceeding even the norm at that time established, and grossly exaggerating the contribution made to the Party's first struggles by the young Dzhugashvili (Stalin).

As will be remembered, Beria had succeeded a head of political police—Yezhov—who had mysteriously vanished, certainly disgraced and probably secretly executed, having himself allegedly been the object of an unsuccessful poisoning plot organised by his own immediate predecessor—Yagoda—while Yagoda in his turn had publicly confessed to the murder of *his* predecessor, Menzhinsky. These were not traditions of service calculated to encourage any new incumbent, but Beria was made of tenacious material, and clung to high office for a further decade and a half, surviving Stalin himself. Only some months after Stalin's death was Beria finally 'unmasked' as one who had allegedly been an agent of foreign powers during the whole of his Cheka/GPU/Party Apparatus/NKVD/MVD career.

Taking over the NKVD, Beria followed Yezhov's example by importing his own cronies to fill key positions, while discreetly exterminating the ousted departmental chiefs. The new team consisted largely of Georgians or other Caucasians with names as outlandish (to a Russian ear) as Goglidze, Gvishiani and Tsanava besides the more innocent-sounding Merkulovs, Kobulovs and Dekanozovs. Blooded in the purges of their native mountains, these functionaries were later to become infamous as the Beria gang and were to share their master's eventual fate. Meanwhile they were already demoralising such Cheka and OGPU veterans as still survived in the top echelons of the NKVD by jabbering away like conspirators in incomprehensible Georgian or issuing orders in broken Russian with a sinister guttural burr.[3]

Under new management the concentration camps did not disgorge their victims, nor were political arrests halted. Far from renouncing terror, the NKVD streamlined, controlled and institutionalised it. Though the average Soviet citizen was somewhat safer under Beria than he had been under Yezhov, the full terror machine was switched against the many millions of new citizens acquired by the USSR in 1939–40.

In September 1939 the USSR annexed eastern Poland, the country as a whole being partitioned between Hitler and Stalin, and thus falling a prey to both Gestapo and NKVD. Then, in the following year, the USSR annexed the three Baltic countries (Estonia, Latvia and Lithuania), while Rumania was forced to cede Bessarabia and northern Bukovina. All these territories were incorporated in the USSR, besides which certain areas of Finland were annexed through the Soviet-Finnish Winter War of 1939–40. The total population accruing to the USSR in 1939–40 amounted to some 23 million.[4] Thus the NKVD acquired responsibility for new human material sufficient or probably sufficient to replace the tally of lives cut short by execution, starvation and imprisonment during the preceding dozen years.

The peoples of the newly acquired territories had not been regimented by years of totalitarian terror, and confronted the NKVD with the problem of telescoping into a few months processes which had occupied decades within the USSR. Protracted intimidation by extortion of spurious confessions was therefore neglected in favour of mass arrests effected without warning, and followed by deportation to concentration camp or exile in the remote hinterland of the USSR.

Eastern Poland, the most populous of the new areas, was also the first to suffer—to the total, according to one estimate, of about 1,200,000 deported, in addition to which some 250,000 Polish soldiers and officers, largely captured in eastern Poland during military operations, were also taken.[5] About 200,000 persons were also deported from Bessarabia in 1941, as were a similar number from the Baltic countries. Here mass arrests began on 6 June 1941, within less than three weeks of Hitler's invasion of the USSR, and could not be completed.

Despite its relatively modest scale, the Baltic deportation is particularly instructive to the student of NKVD/NKGB methods, since many of the relevant secret operation orders have become available to Western scholars.[6] Directed by Ivan Serov, Deputy Commissar of the security police and the great Soviet expert in deportation, the round-up was systematically planned in all its details. The lists of those selected for removal were drawn up in secret beforehand, being based on reports by spies, and individuals were included on the basis of the social and economic category to which they belonged—not of any hostility to Soviet rule which they might have expressed in deed or word. They included bankers, businessmen, hotel proprietors, titled persons, restaurateurs and shopkeepers as well as intellectuals and professional persons generally, members of all political parties other than the Communist, persons expelled from the Communist Party and the Komsomol, officials, policemen, gendarmes, prison warders, clergymen together with other religious activists, smugglers, Red Cross staff, immigrants and natives polluted by foreign contact whether through travel, stamp-collecting or the study of Esperanto. On the appointed night the dwellings of these undesirables were suddenly raided by armed squads including Party and NKVD representatives. Allowed two hours to pack and assemble up to one hundred kilograms of baggage, the deportees were driven to the nearest railway station, where sealed cattle trucks waited to receive them, fathers of families being separated from their dependants at this stage. An incalculable number, especially among the very old and very young, died from starvation and disease on the long journey eastward. Of those who reached their destination about a quarter were put in concentration camps, while the remainder were assigned to places of exile, mostly in remote areas of Siberia and the east. High mortality continued in both categories, amounting to 270,000 deaths within two years among deported Poles alone, according to one figure.[7]

Of the Polish prisoners of war captured in September 1939 about 15,000, over half being officers, were held in three concentration camps at Kozelsk, Starobelsk and Ostashkov in the west and centre of European Russia. In April 1940 the inmates of Kozelsk, over four thousand in number, were taken by the NKVD to the forest at Katyn ten miles west of Smolensk and killed, being shot one by one in the back of the head and buried in a mass grave. Three years later the Germans, then in military occupation of the area, found the grave and published details of the shootings in order to cause dissension between the Soviet government and the Polish government-in-exile. The Soviet authorities retorted by accusing the Germans of perpetrating the massacre themselves, and the charge was not *prima facie* implausible in view of the Nazi record of mass slaughter of helpless victims on a far larger scale than the Katyn affair. That the NKVD was in fact responsible has, however, been established beyond shadow of doubt.[8] It has been possible to reconstruct details of the victims' life in camp before execution, when they were subjected to intensive agitation by the NKVD in order to subvert them to the Soviet service. This was successful only in a small minority of instances.[9] The unconverted majority had proved incorrigible social enemies, and as such became liable to execution according to NKVD logic. The order for the shootings certainly came from Moscow and possibly from Stalin himself, or Beria.[10] It seems certain that a similar fate overtook the inmates of the Starobelsk and Ostashkov camps. An unconfirmed rumour, that some of the Polish officers involved were towed out into the White Sea in barges and sunk by artillery fire,[11] suggests a reversion to techniques used by the Cheka during the

Civil War. After Katyn, however, the mass shooting of prisoners of war does not appear to have been practised by the NKVD, though countless numbers of such prisoners perished from overwork and malnutrition in the camps.

The numerous civilians deported from Soviet-occupied Poland included Henryk Erlich and Viktor Alter, prominent leaders of the Jewish Socialist Bund. Their fate in Soviet hands included imprisonment, interrogation by Beria in person and a sentence of ten years' imprisonment on charges of sabotage. After the diplomatic agreement signed between the Soviet and Polish governments on 30 July 1941 in response to Hitler's attack on the USSR, Erlich and Alter were released and received encouragement from Beria to found a Jewish Anti-Fascist Committee. In December of the same year, however, they disappeared in Kuybyshev. Only in 1943, after an international campaign to discover their whereabouts, did the Soviet authorities reveal that the two men had been executed on the grotesque charge of pro-Hitler agitation among Soviet troops.

During the period of the Hitler-Stalin Pact the NKVD handed over several hundred German citizens, including Communists and Jews, to the German Gestapo, as the result of which some unfortunate individuals were enabled to compare at first hand the practices of the two most formidable political police forces of the day. One such victim, Margarete Buber-Neumann, has described how she was transferred at the bridge over the Bug at Brest-Litovsk, a combined operation of the NKVD and the German SS.[12] There were also instances of traffic in the opposite direction, including the episode of the Viennese Jew imprisoned first in Dachau and then in a Soviet concentration camp, where he hanged himself from his bunk.[13]

The Soviet-Finnish Winter War of 1939-40 enabled the NKVD to pioneer a practice which was to be developed on a larger scale during the Soviet-German conflict. Not only were Finnish prisoners assigned to GULAG, but so also—more surprisingly—were Red Army soldiers who had been taken prisoner in action against the Finns. Temporarily liberated by Soviet victory, these former captives marched into Leningrad under a triumphal arch, with bands playing martial music and streamers proclaiming 'The Fatherland Greets its Heroes'. This function ended, they were marched straight to a railway siding beyond the city, where cattle trucks were waiting to take them to the camps.[14]

Under Beria's jurisdiction the NKVD's mobile murder squad

continued to liquidate political undesirables on foreign soil. Among their probable victims was the great Communist propagandist Willi Münzenberg, who had not been so bemused by his own publicity material as to obey a summons to Moscow in 1938. Two years later he was found hanging in a forest near Grenoble under circumstances pointing to murder.[15] Walter Krivitsky, former chief of Soviet Military Intelligence in Western Europe, claimed asylum in the West and published one of the most reliable inside stories of the purge a year before assassination overtook him too—he was found shot in a Washington hotel room in February 1941. Trotsky's was, however, the outstanding assassination of the period, a large NKVD staff having been mobilised for this purpose, according to reports. After several failures the plan eventually succeeded on 20 August 1940 when Ramon Mercader gained access to Trotsky's household by posing as a political sympathiser and struck him down with an ice-axe. Mercader served a twenty-year sentence for the murder, never admitting the complicity of Stalin and the NKVD in organising the affair.

On a less spectacular level the Soviet political police suffered yet another change, or partial change, of name on 3 February 1941 when the NKVD was split into two separate commissariats, one of which retained the title NKVD and remained under Beria, being responsible for internal affairs generally. The other, new, commissariat was the NKGB (People's Commissariat for State Security) and was to specialise in political police affairs in the narrower sense, being commanded by Beria's close associate, V. N. Merkulov. Thus the political security organisation reverted nominally to the status which it had enjoyed as the OGPU—that of an independent organ directly subordinated only to the highest leadership. The new arrangement lasted only six months, the outbreak of war with Germany being followed, on 20 July 1941, by the re-establishment of a single police commissariat—the NKVD under Beria. April 1943 saw the re-emergence of a separate NKGB, once more under Merkulov, and it continued to operate alongside the NKVD as an independent commissariat until the end of the war and after. To avoid unnecessary confusion the term NKVD will generally be used here to denote the political police organisation as a whole. No diminution of Beria's status seems implied by these administrative shifts, since he bore overall responsibility for political police affairs throughout, while a series of honours and further promotions awarded during and after the war continued to improve his position.

During the Soviet-German War of 1941–5 the NKVD maintained the basic *modus operandi* evolved in peace time, but faced a large variety of new tasks and adapted its ways accordingly.

Ample warnings of impending German invasion had reached Moscow in the first half of 1941 from sources which included Winston Churchill. In April 1941 Richard Sorge, Moscow's agent in Tokyo, supplied detailed information on Hitler's intentions and his invasion timetable.[16] NKVD intelligence conveyed numerous other warnings of German preparations to Moscow, as described in an anonymous article published in the Soviet *Voprosy istorii* for May 1965 as part of a general campaign mounted in the 1960s to glorify the Soviet political police. As the author complains, all warnings were lost on Stalin. Up to the last moment the Soviet dictator seems to have placed boundless confidence in his many measures to appease Hitler, perhaps the only individual whom he ever fully trusted. That Beria was comparably lacking in vigilance is indicated by his refusal to heed reports reaching him of the German military buildup on the Western Bug.[17] Thus the top Soviet leadership was caught unawares by the German *Blitzkrieg* launched along some 1,500 miles of the Soviet western frontier at 4 a.m. on 22 June 1941. Of the lack of initiative, absence of firm contingency orders and general helplessness on the Soviet side at this time one famous exchange of messages between front and rear gives a vivid picture:

'We are being fired on, what shall we do?'

'You must be insane, and why is your signal not in code?'[18]

While the German invaders swept on, encircling, destroying and capturing entire Soviet armies and wrecking Soviet aircraft on the ground, Stalin himself betrayed no obvious signs of activity for twelve days. Then, on 3 July, the author of the great terror emerged to broadcast to the nation, unexpectedly addressing his subjects as his brothers and sisters, and also as his friends,[19] for all the world as if he had suddenly embraced a combination of Quaker and Baptist beliefs.

The NKVD, operating as Stalin's instrument, must be held partly responsible for the rout of the Soviet forces in the early weeks of the war, for the military purge had deprived the Red Army of almost all its experienced commanders. To this must be added the general demoralisation which police terror had caused in the USSR as a whole, with the result that some Soviet units had no heart for combat and surrendered voluntarily, while in certain areas the Germans were welcomed as liberators by the civilian population. The most common reaction, however, was one of apathy.[20] Then, as the war proceeded, the Gestapo and SS committed so many atrocities in Soviet territory, that even the OGPU/NKVD record was rivalled or eclipsed by the mass shootings of hostages, deportation of slave labourers to Germany, slaughter of Jews and Communists, and starvation of prisoners of war. A desire for revenge now helped to inspire patriotic fervour among the Soviet peoples. This in turn was fostered at the Centre by a change in policy whereby patriotism, and particularly Russian patriotism, replaced Marxism-Leninism as the *leit-motiv* of official verbalisers, while persecution of the Russian Orthodox Church ceased, the Church itself being mobilised to lend supernatural support to Soviet arms. The Communist Party accordingly came to play a less obtrusive role during the war years, and though it greatly increased its membership—largely by intensive recruiting among front-line troops—this very fact tended to diminish its influence.

The political police, by contrast, only enhanced its role in wartime conditions. When a five-man (later expanded) State Committee of Defence with overriding powers was set up on 30 June 1941 under Stalin's chairmanship, Beria became a member alongside Stalin, Molotov, Voroshilov and Malenkov—which meant that Beria now received precedence over Kaganovich, Mikoyan and Zhdanov, though all three were his political seniors. Meanwhile, on 29 June, the Party Central Committee and Council of People's Commissars had addressed to the political security forces a joint directive ordering them to concentrate on giving support to the Red Army, and on defending the Soviet rear areas against attack by German spies, diversionaries and parachutists. A merciless struggle was also to be conducted against Soviet deserters, panic-mongers and spreaders of rumour.[21] Thus high authority outlined the tasks of the NKVD as they were to be carried out in the first, defensive phase of the war, which lasted from its outbreak until the Germans cracked at Stalingrad in the winter of 1942–3.

During the defensive phase of hostilities the NKVD adopted a number of characteristic procedures. Immediately on the outbreak of war political undesirables still remaining at liberty were rounded up and put in prisons and concentration camps, a process accompanied by widespread executions of the imprisoned. Orders were given to evacuate prisoners held in the line of the enemy advance, but such was the momentum of the German onslaught that this was not always possible, in which event the procedure was to release the ordinary criminals and kill the politicals. This occurred on a considerable scale, chiefly in the Baltic States, Belorussia and the western Ukraine. One authority gives a detailed account of the horrors enacted at Minsk, where a small prison—intended for one thousand inmates only—was packed with ten times that number shortly after the outbreak of war. Then, as German tanks were about to enter the city, two lorry-loads of NKVD Special Purpose Troops arrived and machine-gunned the inmates of the crowded cells through the judas windows, finishing them off with grenades before spreading petrol through the building and setting fire to it.[22] Similar horrors are reported from Lwow by Borys Lewytzkyj as occurring between 22 and 28 June 1941,[23] while other mass killings of prisoners took place in Smolensk, Kiev, Kharkov, Dnepropetrovsk and Zaporozhye.[24] With the further eastwards advance of the German invaders such episodes were reported as far inland as Nalchik in the Caucasus—the NKVD head of the Kabardino-Balkar Autonomous Republic organised the machine-gunning of several hundred slave-labourers at a molybdenum *kombinat* when they could not be evacuated in time.[25] Working in an opposite direction, the NKVD also permitted some recruiting of combat troops from volunteers among concentration camp inmates. Certain victims of the military purge were liberated, in particular Generals Rokossovsky and Gorbatov, who were set free as early as 1940. Yet the shooting of high-ranking officers in custody continued during the war.[26] As a further boost to military morale, Soviet high commanders were also shot after suffering defeat in the field.

Such measures did nothing to halt the victorious German advance, which came near to engulfing both Moscow and Leningrad in late 1941. Government offices and diplomatic missions were evacuated from Moscow to Kuybyshev, while the capital was given over to panic. Aware of the German practice of shooting captured Communists, Party members hurriedly destroyed their membership cards while the famished population ransacked food stores undeterred by NKVD shootings. Meanwhile, on the fronts, the ill-equipped and ill-led Red Army continued to sustain enormous casualties—yet held the line until the onset of winter caught the Germans themselves ill-prepared for the Russian will to resist and for the rigours of a climate which had vanquished Napoleon.

On the front the NKVD exercised a variety of functions, including activities directed against the Red Army. Blocking battalions, consisting of NKVD troops armed with automatic weapons, were set up in areas behind the fighting line to shoot down military units which might desert or be thrown back in action. The NKVD also operated against Red Army personnel who chanced to escape from encirclement by German forces, since the very fact that they had been surrounded brought them under suspicion as deserters. In addition the NKVD also played a leading role in the development of the partisan troops which operated over wide areas of German-occupied Russia and came to number several hundred thousand. Individual partisan units had their own Special Branches of NKVD corresponding to the Special Branches which operated in formations of the regular Red Army, as mentioned above.[27] The NKVD was also used against the Germans in several important roles. It helped to organise bands of Soviet saboteurs and diversionaries for action in areas held by the Germans, and established Destruction Battalions to combat the activities of German parachutists, saboteurs and diversionaries in the Soviet rear. It was also actively engaged against German agents, a pursuit for which extensive peacetime experience in inventing imaginary German spies was not the ideal preparation. In 1937–8 only one or two genuine foreign agents had been caught trying to cross the western frontier, but with the approach and onset of hostilities the number grew to hundreds as special schools were set up in Germany to train them.[28] The USSR also possessed, and had inherited from Imperial Russia, a sizeable community of its own German citizens, the majority of them belonging to the Volga German Autonomous Republic. The inhabitants of the Republic numbered about 600,000 souls in all, of whom some two-thirds were Germans. These were earmarked for transportation to distant parts of the USSR in a Supreme Soviet decree of 28 August 1941, and the operation was controlled by the master-deporter Ivan Serov, who had already supervised the removal of so many selected deportees from the Baltic republics. A characteristic twist was given to this affair when the NKVD parachuted a battalion of its own agents, dressed in German uniform, on the Republic and massacred such Volga Germans as betrayed sympathy for these supposed deliverers.[29] Despite this ploy, the deportation of the Volga Germans proved a comparatively humane affair by Serov's standards.[30]

Of the extent to which the NKVD dominated all fields of Soviet life, both military and civilian, in the early months of the war, a vivid impression is given in the memoirs of the Polish General Wladyslaw Anders, who was unusually well placed to gauge the organisation's influence. He had been wounded and captured during the Soviet invasion of Poland in September 1939, but had escaped the fate of his brother officers at Katyn and elsewhere because he happened to be in hospital at the time when they were corralled for extermination.[31] After twenty months in Soviet prisons, Anders figured in a dramatic change of fortune. Summoned from his crowded cell in the Lubyanka on 4 August 1941, he was surprised to be marched along the corridors without the usual arm-twisting and blows, and to find himself in a luxurious office facing two officials in civilian dress who stood up when he came through the door. They turned out to be Beria and Merkulov, the two senior political police functionaries of the USSR, from whom Anders, on learning that he was now a prisoner no longer, accepted an offer of tea and cigarettes. He had, it turned out, been selected as commander-in-chief of the as yet non-existent army which was to be recruited among Polish concentration camp inmates in the USSR, and which eventually went to the Middle East to fight against the Germans. After his release from the Lubyanka, Anders acquired extensive experience of the Soviet power structure as it operated in the first months of the war, and has recorded the superior position occupied by the NKVD over the army. 'The military elements had no say. In all fields of civilian and military life the all-powerful NKVD reigned.'[32] Anders, incidentally, met Serov as well as Beria and Merkulov, and noted the hatred and rage expressed by the great deporter against the Nazi leaders, of whom he remarked:

'I've only one wish in life—to conduct the interrogation of Hitler and Goering.'[33]

The comment is a revealing reflection on the attitude to interrogation at the highest NKVD level.

The war progressed over the hump of the Stalingrad battle in the winter of 1942–3, while Soviet forces drove through from the Caucasus to Berlin and the NKVD continued to extend its sphere of operations. Its armed formations saw action alongside the Red Army against the retreating *Wehrmacht*—for instance, under General I. I. Maslennikov, whose NKVD Army of Special Purpose helped to smash the German defences in the Kuban and on the

Taman Peninsular in 1943.[34] The NKVD also turned its forces against various minority Soviet nationalities in the same general area, transporting six entire peoples from their homes in the south of the USSR to scattered areas in the wastes of Siberia and Central Asia between October 1943 and June 1944. These were all communities which had been overrun or partly overrun by the retreating German invader. Four of the peoples involved occupied lands on the northern slopes of the Caucasus—the Chechens, the Ingushes, the Karachays, the Balkars. The Kalmyks, who lived in the steppeland north-west of the Caspian, were also deported, as were the Crimean Tatars from the Crimea. The total number of individuals exiled was probably just under a million, the Chechens with over four hundred thousand being the most numerous single people involved and the Balkars the smallest, with about forty thousand.[35] Big or small, they were rounded up by the NKVD and deported, becoming 'unnations'—just as individuals liquidated in the great terror became 'unpersons' in George Orwell's memorable phrase for those expunged from historical record. This silence was briefly broken in June 1946 with the publication in *Izvestiya* of a decree abolishing the Chechen-Ingush and Crimean Republics, and since Stalin's death the remnants of the Caucasian peoples involved, and also the Kalmyks, have been permitted to return to their old homes.

More information is available on the Chechen deportation than on any other, partly through the testimony of Lt Col Burlitsky, a defecting NKVD/MVD officer.[36] During the period preceding the swoop, NKVD forces, including Special Purpose, Frontier and Convoy Troops, quietly infiltrated the area, posing as regular army units engaged on military manoeuvres. Then, during celebrations held on 23 February 1944 in honour of Red Army Day, they surrounded the jubilant hillsmen, read out the decree of deportation, shot those who protested and removed the rest in lend-lease Studebaker trucks for further delivery eastwards by goods wagon. At Grozny, capital of the Chechen-Ingush Republic, a special meeting of the Republic's Party and government officials was organised and these functionaries were arrested *en bloc*. Once again General Serov, the NKVD's chief deporter, had supplied the well-lubricated mass delivery service for which he was noted. The Karachays, Balkars, Kalmyks and Crimean Tatars were similarly deported, the last-mentioned (numbering about a quarter of a million) only a few weeks after the German invader had been driven from their territory in April 1944.

The dictator's motives for deporting the six peoples remain inscrutable. They admittedly had some record of sympathy for the Germans, who had recruited military units among the Chechens and others. These were, however, by no means the only minority peoples of the USSR to have provided Hitler with recruits, apart from which defecting Russians themselves furnished the Vlasov Army in support of the Germans. Whatever influence their war record may have had, it is perhaps relevant that some of the six peoples concerned, especially those of the Caucasus, had a history of armed opposition to Russian rule going back through the centuries and including local revolts which had continued to flare up in the Soviet period. Alleged collaboration with the Germans may have been partly an excuse to liquidate nations already earmarked as obstreperous. The relatively small numbers involved may also have been a consideration, since Stalin would really have liked to deport the Ukrainians in their entirety according to Khrushchev, had there not been too many of them.[37]

To the offensive period of the war also belong certain measures of a gentler kind designed to regulate religious life in the USSR. This had long been the concern of the Cheka and OGPU which had set themselves, unsuccessfully, to eradicate religion from Soviet life. Then, during the war, religion received official encouragement, being tolerated as a means of boosting national morale. However, since religious activities could not be allowed to run riot, even in war-time, the authorities set up two lay organisations to control them—the Council for the Affairs of the Russian Orthodox Church and the Council for the Affairs of Religious Cults (to handle all religious persuasions other than the Orthodox). These were established in September 1943 and May 1944 respectively, and it is significant that a political police functionary, G. G. Karpov, was put in charge of the first-named body, while I. V. Polyansky, who headed the second, may also have had an OGPU background.[38]

Besides the Chechens and other deported peoples mentioned above, all Soviet citizens who had been in contact with the German occupiers became special objects for the attention of the NKVD during the last years of the war and afterwards. The suspects ranged from recruits of the defecting Soviet Lieutenant-General Vlasov and other Soviet subjects who had enlisted on the German side, to all Soviet prisoners of war released from German custody by the Red Army's advance. This vast reservoir of undesirables further included those who had been deported by the

Germans as forced labourers *(Ostarbeiter)*. On liberation by the Red Army members of all these categories were automatically herded into camps and subjected to intensive individual screening by the Soviet political police, after which all those found to have fought with the Germans (except for some leaders who were hanged), and a high but unknown proportion of former prisoners of war and *Ostarbeiter*, were sent to Soviet concentration camps, exchanging one form of slavery for another. A similar but inevitably less thorough screening was applied to the many millions of Soviet citizens who had lived under German occupation, and who were also assumed guilty of collaboration with the enemy unless proved innocent. Official suspicion also extended to the hundreds of thousands of Soviet citizens who had taken an active part in partisan warfare in German-occupied Soviet territory. These had, after all, shown themselves capable of resisting authority—and totalitarian authority at that. They were therefore automatically objects for suspicion, and many of them ended their military careers in the labour camps.

Besides processing Soviet citizens, the political police also took overall responsibility for controlling the entire human content, military and non-military, of the vast areas overrun by the Red Army. This involved handling prisoners of war taken from the enemy, among whom were Germans, Austrians, Italians, Rumanians, Hungarians and eventually, in the far east, Japanese. Now long experienced in netting, caging, crating, freighting and dumping humanity in the mass, the NKVD was an ideally equipped carrier. Prisoners of war were delivered to GULAG and maintained in camps under conditions of controlled undernourishment geared to labour norms and similar to those applied to enslaved Soviet citizens. In occupied Germany the Soviet authorities at once set up eleven internment camps, three of them being Nazi concentration camps which were simply taken over and used for their original purpose—Neubrandenburg, Buchenwald and Sachsenhausen.[39] In Poland the notorious Auschwitz camp was diverted from its original purpose of gassing Jews, becoming a concentration camp for Soviet citizens facing the further ordeal of repatriation.[40]

The camps played a vital role in the Soviet war economy, as GULAG's hordes slaved on strategic railroads and highways, building aerodromes and ammunition dumps above and below ground, while not neglecting the more traditional pursuits of lumbering and gold-mining. A lower standard of discipline and food rationing on a level still less adequate than before were found in the camps in the war years. Continuing high mortality among the inmates was, however, offset by the millions streaming in from an ever-widening catchment area in eastern Europe as the Red Army's advance first took in Soviet areas of long standing, followed by the territories, including eastern Poland, which had been incorporated in the USSR in 1939–40 and then temporarily lost to the Germans, after which lands which had never belonged to the USSR also fell.

Whether on recovered Soviet territory or on Soviet-occupied foreign territory, political security operations during the second half of the war were very largely carried out by a body established in late 1942 or 1943 and attached to the Red Army to supersede the old Special Branches already mentioned as responsible for political security within the army. The new organisation was called Smersh, a contraction of Russian *smert shpionam*, 'death to spies'. This body has since acquired a vogue among readers of light fiction owing to the part which it plays in Ian Fleming's James Bond novels—where, however, its term of life has been extended by poetic licence beyond the actual period of its opertion, which ended in 1946 when the Special Branches were restored. A more authentic account of Smersh's activity from the inside is given by Nicholas Sinevirsky, who spent seven months in the organisation as an interpreter with the rank of Junior Lieutenant between December 1944 and August 1945. Sinevirsky's diary of these events was published by an émigré Russian press in 1948. He writes as a native of Transcarpathian Russia, the small area of under a million inhabitants which formed the extreme eastern tip of Czechoslovakia until 1939. Considering himself a Russian in the full sense of the word and not merely a Transcarpathian, Sinevirsky was a strong opponent of Bolshevism. He was naturally careful to conceal this fact from his new employers, but must have been in extreme danger during the whole of his seven months' service with the Smersh unit attached to the Fourth Ukrainian Front.

Sinevirsky's diary followed the westward advance of the Red Army, tracing the activity of Smersh in Poland and Czechoslovakia, and then going back to Transcarpathia itself. The Smersh unit for which he worked came under Lieutenant-General Kovalchuk, whom Sinevirsky describes as exercising control even over the commander-in-chief of the whole army group, General Yeremenko. Sinevirsky himself served with the Second or Operat-

ive Department which was concerned with the local population
—the First Department dealt with political security within the
army itself, while Departments Three, Four and Five were concerned with liaison with Moscow, investigation and trial respectively. Directed against all enemies or potential enemies of the
Soviet system among the local populations, Sinevirsky's branch
was concerned to arrest members of all non-Communist political
parties and associations, including the German Nazi Party, but
also the Polish Home Army, the Slovak Hlinka Guard, the
Hungarian Nilos Party and the separatist movement in his native
Transcarpathia.[41] A further concern were German prisoners of
war, and also all the numerous former Russian or Soviet citizens
found on the territory. These included 'old émigrés', who had fled
from Bolshevism in the early years, *Ostarbeiter* deported from
Soviet territory during World War II, Soviet prisoners of war
found in German custody and members of the Vlasov Army recruited among Soviet defectors to fight for the Germans. With this
last group Smersh was not greatly concerned, Sinevirsky reports,
since all Vlasovites were destined for long terms in the camps.
Vlasov himself, however, and eleven leading associates were
executed by hanging in accordance with a new form of execution
for which provision was made in a law of 19 April 1943.

Among the other groups typical Stalinist techniques were used.
They were herded in camps or prisons with intolerable living conditions, great stress being laid on recruiting informers among
prisoners who could be frightened or bribed into betraying the
true identity and political activities of their camp-mates. These
were then hauled out individually for screening and the brutal
extortion of confessions in which fantasy heavily predominated.
Sinevirsky describes in detail the beatings which accompanied
this process, but also sheds light on the spare-time activities of his
brother officers. Though they were kept busy by the demands of
the service, they nevertheless found scope for the pursuit of alcohol,
girls and wrist-watches throughout Soviet-occupied Europe.

Finding themselves in territory occupied by allies of the USSR,
many former Soviet citizens were reluctant to return to a homeland where prison camps or execution awaited them. Soviet
authority applied great persistence and resourcefulness to the
recovery of such recalcitrants, obtaining at the Yalta conference
of 1945 a repatriation agreement with Britain and the United
States, which was kept secret until March 1947. Under the terms
of this agreement the British and American military authorities

handed over many non-returners to the Soviet authorities by force. This procedure led to attempts at resistance by these unarmed captives, and also to numerous suicides—a process no doubt gratifying to Soviet authority, which had now manoeuvred non-Soviet authority into behaving with comparable brutality. Forcible repatriation with accompanying suicides occurred from the United States itself as well as from occupied Europe. The Soviet authorities also put pressure on France which resulted in the establishment of an NKVD concentration camp at Beauregard near Paris.[42] NKVD men, both uniformed and in plain clothes, were permitted to operate on French soil, seizing non-returners and taking them to Beauregard, whence they were forcibly repatriated to the Soviet Union. Sweden also agreed to the forcible return of over one hundred and fifty Baltic citizens demanded by the Soviet authorities, apart from which one prominent Swedish citizen himself fell foul of the NKVD. This was the diplomat Raul Wallenberg, who worked in Hungary during the war to save Hungarian Jews from extermination by the Germans. His office was in Pest, occupied by the Red Army on 15 January 1944, after which Wallenberg was never traced again, despite persistent enquiries extending until after Stalin's death.[43]

The allied victory over Hitler was followed by a Moscow show trial such as had not been staged in the Soviet capital since the Bukharin trial of 1938. On this latest occasion the sixteen defendants were all Poles, and the object of the demonstration was to further Soviet domination of Poland as a satellite state by discrediting the Polish underground government and army—thus putting pressure on the London-based government-in-exile to join a coalition with the Soviet-backed Lublin Committee now governing Poland. The defendants were accused of sabotaging the Red Army's advance across Poland in the later stages of the war, and all but one pleaded guilty. As the solitary exception, Zbigniew Stypulkowski—a leader of the Polish National Democratic Party—became the only person so far to undergo public trial in Moscow without having pleaded guilty at any stage of the interrogation.[44] His memoirs are a valuable source on NKVD practices in Poland and Russia from 1939 onwards, and give a particularly vivid account of his arrest in March 1945, as also of the grooming process designed to prepare him for confession. The NKVD revealed its usual sense of the dramatic from the outset. Stypulkowski and the other Polish leaders were invited to meet the Soviet Marshal Zhukov for political discussions over lunch, but when they reached the appointed local rendezvous, neither lunch nor Marshal was forthcoming. Instead they were kidnapped by aeroplane and flown hundreds of miles east to the dungeons of the Lubyanka. Here Stypulkowski's fifteen colleagues all cracked under interrogation, confessing to various fabricated charges, but he himself resisted with rare stubbornness. The main pressure consisted of carefully calculated discomfort applied over some seventy days—an ordeal by cold, bright lights, minimal food and sleep systematically frustrated, the whole programme punctuated by prolonged interrogations staged at irregular intervals and amounting to a hundred and forty-one in all. By contrast with the practice of Smersh, as described by Sinevirsky and others, the treatment was 'correct' to the extent that physical torture in the strict sense was not applied. However, Stypulkowski clearly revealed exceptional reserves of physical and moral stamina in wearing out an interrogator who was not himself deprived of food and sleep, while using the intervals between sessions to learn Russian in his cell and prepare his own defence. He escaped with a four-month prison term, and was later able to emigrate to the West. With this and other comparatively lenient sentences, the last of the Moscow show trials ended.

Occurring in 1944–5, two spectacular defections from Soviet diplomatic posts substantially increased western knowledge of the workings of the NKVD, even though neither of the defectors concerned happened to be an officer of political police. The first case was that of Victor Kravchenko, who escaped from the Soviet Purchasing Commission in Washington and shortly afterwards began work on his revealing autobiography, *I Chose Freedom*. His defection was announced in the New York press late on the night of 3 April 1944, being timed to break before the Soviet Embassy in Washington could learn what was in the wind. Otherwise, Kravchenko claims, he would certainly have been denounced to the American State Department, perhaps as a German agent, and might have been deported to the USSR.[45] Kravchenko's evidence on Soviet police methodology includes a graphic description of the elaborate precautions taken by the war-time NKVD to safeguard Stalin and other Soviet leaders from assassination as they commuted each day along the Mozhaysk Highway between the Kremlin and their heavily-guarded suburban villas. They would sweep past to the wail of sirens in green-windowed, bullet-proof Packards, preceded and followed by armed, plain-clothes NKVD guards in Lincolns, down a route densely policed by thousands of uniformed police and detectives, their right hands on their revolvers ready for the draw, 'for they know that their own lives will be forfeit if anything should happen to the Beloved Leaders behind the bullet-proof glass'.[46]

The second notable diplomatic defector of the period was Igor Guzenko, a cypher clerk who walked out of the Soviet Embassy in Ottawa on the evening of 5 October 1945 with more than a hundred secret documents stuffed inside his shirt. Over a nightmare period of nearly two days he trudged round the city seeking in vain to interest Canadian editors or government officials in this sensational archive and in his personal predicament, while the danger to himself, his wife and small son mounted with every hour. His *bona fides* was finally confirmed in dramatic fashion by the Soviet secret police itself, when Vitaly Pavlov, NKVD chief for the whole of Canada, was caught by two constables of the Royal Canadian Mounted Police in the act of burgling Guzenko's deserted flat, having gained access with a jemmy.[47] Though less informative than Kravchenko on the workings of the NKVD on home territory, Guzenko's revelations of Soviet espionage activities led to the arrest and conviction of Dr Allan Nunn May and other western citizens in the service of Soviet atomic intelligence. Investigated by Royal Commission, his disclosures helped— as did also those of Kravchenko—to erode western optimism on the possibilities of post-war co-operation with the Soviet Union and to usher in the period of the Cold War. In their memoirs Kravchenko and Guzenko both stress the danger to defecting Soviet officials of assassination by their own political police, for which reason both took the precaution of going into hiding and living in emigration under assumed names.

Beria and the MVD/MGB
1945–1953

Stalin's post-war years, 1945–53, represent the most obscure period in the history of the Soviet security apparatus. During this phase one is dealing more than ever with a *secret* police, the development of which must be chronicled in terms of strong, or less strong, presumption rather than on the basis of hard facts such as are often simply not available. With this reservation, which must be understood as underlying much of the account given below, the saga falls into four main phases in accordance with the wavering fortunes of the police overlord Lavrenty Beria. These phases are: Beria in decline (1946–8); Beria resurgent (1949–50); Beria in danger (1951 to 5 March 1953); Beria triumphant (6 March 1953 to 26 June 1953).

In recognition of the important part played by the NKVD/ NKGB during the war, the use of military ranks for political police chiefs was extended in July 1945, Beria himself becoming a Marshal of the Soviet Union. The next year saw the following changes in the organisation's top leadership. In January Beria lost his post as head of the NKVD to Colonel-General S. N. Kruglov, a deputy head of Smersh—this great military security machine ceased to exist in the same year, its responsibilities reverting to Special Branches of the political police within the army, as in pre-Smersh days. Then, in March 1946, all the people's commissariats were renamed ministries, and the NKVD and NKGB were consequently re-entitled MVD and MGB (Ministries of the Interior and of State Security) respectively. Thus Kruglov automatically became Minister for the MVD, while his opposite number in the NKGB, Colonel-General Merkulov became Minister for the

MGB. In October, however, Merkulov was replaced by Army General Victor Abakumov, previously Kruglov's superior as the overall head of Smersh. By the end of 1946, accordingly, chiefs of the defunct Smersh had taken over the entire MVD/MGB machine, while Beria had already ceased to exercise formal control over any part of the police complex in January of that year. That Beria continued to maintain general supervision over the police ministries is considered probable by several authorities,[1] and is *prima facie* likely in view of his unique experience in these matters, continued direct access to Stalin and close personal ties with Merkulov and Abakumov—though not with Kruglov. However, if Beria himself was functioning as unofficial police overlord, he was not the only one in the field. According to Khrushchev's evidence, Stalin entrusted 'supervision of the state security organs' to A. A. Kuznetsov, a rising Party *apparatchik* who was a Secretary of the Party Central Committee from 1945 to 1949, and also an ally of Beria's rival Zhdanov.[2]

Whether or not Beria's influence over the police was in decline at this time, it is clear that his general political fortunes were flourishing. In 1946 he received an important promotion within the Politburo—to full from candidate membership, and also became Deputy Chairman of the Council of Ministers, as the Council of People's Commissars was now re-named. Beria is also reported as taking charge in the vital sphere of Soviet nuclear development, which incidentally involved responsibility for atomic espionage directed against the United States and Britain.

Whatever Beria's precise status may have been at any given time, one may safely assume that the changes in police organisation of 1946-8, like those of other periods, owed much to Stalin's recurring need to insure himself against the possibility of attack from the institution best of all adapted to mount a *coup d'état*. Hence the need to divide security responsibilities among two ministries, to shunt individual police branches between one ministry and another, and to keep the security bosses on the move lest the organisation as a whole ever attain sufficient equilibrium to be turned against its supreme master.

The early post-war years saw the extension of Soviet domination over eastern European territories containing nearly a hundred million people and belonging to eight States—Albania, Bulgaria, Czechoslovakia, Hungary, Poland, Rumania, Yugoslavia and East Germany. The USSR did not formally annex these countries, apart from certain areas of some of them, but gradually or suddenly subjected them, between 1945 and 1948, to control from Moscow, through skilfully prefabricated revolutions adjusted to local conditions and supported on the spot by the ever-active Soviet political police. Under MVD/MGB guidance the satellite states were soon well on their way to becoming small-scale totalitarian societies on the Stalinist model, though Yugoslavia was to break its Soviet associations in 1948, followed by Albania in 1961. It must be stressed that each satellite political police force came to take its orders direct from Soviet police officials, thus becoming more or less an agency of the MVD/MGB and remaining independent of its own Party and government to a greater extent than could be claimed for the MVD/MGB itself.[3]

Stalin's decision to extend the Soviet police state to so many nominally independent countries has been explained by the need to defend the USSR against the aggressive designs of a resurgent western Germany supported by the USA and the Soviet Union's other war-time allies. That such considerations indeed helped to inspire the take-over of eastern Europe is indeed likely, especially in view of the ageing despot's growing paranoid tendencies, now feeding on dread of western nuclear superiority. However, another fear was probably more prominent in Stalin's mind—that of the political contamination which inevitably radiated from western societies free of police rule, a danger especially acute at the end of a war which had brought so many Soviet citizens into contact with the West. Nor can Russian empire-building be ruled out as an impulse to exploit the defeat of the Axis powers by drawing the bounds of Moscow's sway ever wider. The USSR had inherited the expansionist drive of Imperial Russia, pursuing under the hammer and sickle policies similar to those which had once raised the two-headed eagle over the heads of so many lesser breeds originally independent of Russian rule. For many years the Georgian dictator had shown himself a Russian chauvinist by adoption, and he was concerned to suppress strivings for independence among all his subject peoples, whether these belonged to the satellite group or to the USSR proper.

In the early post-war years Soviet rule was particularly resented by the inhabitants of territories annexed by the USSR in 1939–40, lost to Germany in 1941 and recovered with victory. These areas —the Baltic Republics and former Polish lands (now western Belorussia and the western Ukraine)—were reincorporated in the Soviet Union at the end of the war and extensive deportations of their political undesirables were resumed. Meanwhile disaffected persons remaining at liberty in the same territories continued to conduct sporadic guerrilla warfare from secret forest bases against the Soviet authorities. In the struggle against these 'bandits', which continued into the early 1950s, the MVD/MGB was heavily involved, and made wide use of a technique pioneered by the Cheka in the Civil War—that of infiltrating such partisan groups with bogus partisans who were in fact disguised MVD/MGB personnel. Both sides sustained considerable casualties in the struggle.

The days when any rival leader could hope to replace a living Stalin had long passed, but competition continued among the dictator's subordinates for influence over him while he lived and also—increasingly—for the opportunity to succeed him when he should eventually die. In these jockeyings for position two younger men, Zhdanov and Malenkov, were especially active. Zhdanov took the lead first until he became buried in the war-time defence of Leningrad while Malenkov made headway at the centre, but the position was reversed after Zhdanov had returned to Moscow in 1945 as a Secretary of the Central Committee. He arrived as a missionary of Communist ideology, which had suffered temporary neglect during the war, but was now to be re-established in its former dominant position.

Literature became the first object for Zhdanov's attention with the notorious Party decree of 14 August 1946 condemning the magazines *Zvezda* and *Leningrad* for opening their columns to works which displayed inadequate political zeal. Two writers were singled out for special attention—the poetess Anna Akhmatov and Zoshchenko, the author of humorous fiction. They were charged with pessimism, frivolity and a lack of ideological fervour, as also (by implication) with failure to supply advertising copy in the interests of the Party. Commonly termed the *Zhdanovshchina*, the crusade also involved attacks on the theatre for not showing Soviet plays on contemporary themes, on composers (for not writing hummable tunes) and on philosophers—for showing undue respect to western authority. Also known as kow-towing to the West, the last-mentioned offence bulked prominently, and as the witch-hunt gained momentum those who displayed deference to foreign cultural influence found themselves pilloried as rootless cosmopolitans. There was a growing tendency to emphasise the Jewish nationality of such heretics, and eventually the campaign acquired a distinct anti-Semitic complexion. It is, however, also true that some of the leading heresy-hunters were themselves

Jews, and that the *Zhdanovshchina* was directed not against Jews as such, but against representatives of any minority group to show undue local patriotism. Thus representatives of Tatar, Ukrainian and other cultures also found themselves stigmatised as *bourgeois* nationalists.

One minor detail of Zhdanov's cultural pogrom had implications uniting the political police of the sixteenth and twentieth centuries. This was the attack on Part Two of Eisenstein's film *Ivan the Terrible* for portraying the first Tsar's 'progressive army of the Oprichniki as a band of degenerates, similar to the American Ku Klux Klan'. Notorious oppressors, the Oprichniki had been condemned as such in a Soviet reference work as late as 1939, but they had been fully rehabilitated as a progressive phenomenon by 1946.[4] This was, however, only a natural development, since among all pre-revolutionary Russian institutions the Oprichnina was that which most closely anticipated the MVD/MGB in its methods.

Savage as the Zhdanovite atmosphere was, Zhdanov himself did not operate as a political policeman. He was a Party spokesman, not an exterminator. Erring scholars, writers and other cultural figures were verbally castigated, lost their jobs and were compelled to make abject public recantation of their errors—a degrading and farcical spectacle. They were not, however, subjected to arrest, concentration camp and execution—not, at least, on the same scale as formerly. A far noisier operation than the *Yezhovshchina*, the *Zhdanovshchina* was therefore considerably less inhumane.

Zhdanov's evangelism also extended to the satellite states when he became the moving spirit behind the Cominform. This new association of Communist parties was established in 1947 and replaced the Comintern (abolished in 1943), but with a membership confined to the parties of Eastern Europe, France and Italy. The Cominform soon struck disaster when, in 1948, the Yugoslavs under Tito's leadership refused to accept continued subjection to Moscow. At about the same time signs began to appear that Zhdanov was in decline. In particular, his great rival Malenkov returned to prominence in the Central Committee Secretariat in July 1948. Then, on 31 August, Zhdanov suddenly died, with his ideological crusade still in mid-career. That he had been in poor health for some time is well attested,[5] but was his illness natural? Nearly five years later his doctors were to be accused of hastening his death by incorrect medical treatment, this being part of the build-up in the notorious Doctors' Plot Affair, to be described below. Later on this same accusation was to be officially disavowed. Whatever the truth about Zhdanov's death may be, a Communist leader had once again perished at a time highly convenient to his rivals and under circumstances which still remain obscure.

With Zhdanov's death a new phase begins in the development of the security police, that of a Beria resurgent in alliance with Malenkov. However, though Zhdanov was dead, he had not suffered official disgrace and his domestic ideological witch-hunt continued—perhaps because the practical-minded Malenkov was not sufficiently interested in ideology to think the *Zhdanovshchina* even worth countermanding. In any case one must not forget that final policy decisions on such matters rested with Stalin, who was still active, continuing to hold the whip hand while realignments took place among his subordinates.

Though the *Zhdanovshchina* went marching on, Zhdanov's death had violent repercussions in the savage purge of his minions conducted by Malenkov, Beria and Abakumov in 1949–50. This was the so-called Leningrad Affair, in which the most eminent victim was N. A. Voznesensky, a full Politburo member since 1947, who was shot—reputedly on 30 September 1950.[6] Though Voznesensky was indeed a Zhdanov man, his fate was further complicated by a divergence between his views on economics and those of Stalin. Other, earlier, victims of the Affair were Popkov, the First Secretary of the Leningrad Party, and also his predecessor in that office, A. A. Kuznetsov—an especially significant figure, for this was the same Kuznetsov who had also been entrusted by Stalin with general supervision over the security organs. To some extent, therefore, his execution may represent a revenge killing by Beria and Abakumov. There were also extensive repressions of minor Party officials in Leningrad,[7] though the scope and nature of these remains obscure. Nor was the new purge confined to Leningrad. It also removed from office G. M. Popov, Party First Secretary in Moscow, who was succeeded in that office by Khrushchev in December 1949. Not until December 1954 was official mention first made of the Leningrad Affair, in reports of the trial of Abakumov (the MGB boss at the time) who was shot for his part in fabricating the case, in association with Beria. Only in 1957 was Malenkov charged, by Khrushchev, with prime responsibility.

When Tito successfully threw off Soviet control in mid-1948, the enraged Stalin decided to block further defections by tightening his grip on the remaining satellites. By Soviet standards these countries had so far been ruled fairly leniently on the whole, albeit more severely than under the illiberal régimes of Pilsudski, Horthy and others, which had operated before or during the war. Now, after Tito's defection, the residual puppets were to be subjected to a fuller measure of Stalinism. The instrument of their further subjugation was to be a characteristically Stalinist device—show trials of Party leaders staged in each satellite by other Party leaders.

The first round of these trials occurred in 1949. Albania took the lead when Koci Xoxe, Vice-Premier and Minister of the Interior, was tried in May, confessing to collaborating with Tito, and was shot on 11 June. In the same month Laszlo Rajk, Hungarian Minister of the Interior, was arrested. Tried in September, he too confessed to plotting with Tito, on behalf of the USA, and to having been an agent of Horthy's political police before the war. He was hanged, with three others, in October. In December Traicho Kostov, Vice-Premier of Bulgaria, was hanged after a trial badly botched, for he stubbornly refused to confess his guilt to charges which included that of working for the British Secret Service. In these and other prosecutions of the period the defendants tended to be spokesmen of local national interests against the demands of the Kremlin. They also tended to have records of service on the Republican side in the Spanish Civil War and of resistance to the Germans during World War II. Their persecutors, by contrast, were 'Muscovites', that is, they had spent periods of exile in the USSR.

These judicial spectacles would fall outside the subject-matter of the present study were it not for the crucial role played by the Soviet political police in staging them. Of the strenuous efforts made by the NKVD/NKGB/MVD/MGB to recruit agents in the satellites the evolution of Yugoslavia during the years before the break with Moscow provides evidence. One of the many causes of the quarrel had been precisely this—that the Soviet political police insisted, despite Yugoslav protests, on recruiting its own agents in Tito's camp. Such spies were liberally enlisted in the Yugoslav army, for example, among them being Tito's chief of staff during the partisan campaign against the Germans.[8] Soviet missions to Titoist Yugoslavia recruited 'in all quarters, from members of the Central Committee to cypher clerks in the Party and State machine'.[9] Among those enlisted was Andrija Hebrang, a member of the Yugoslav Politburo.

In 1946 the antagonism, not yet overt, between the Yugoslav and Soviet political police establishments, was stressed in one of Stalin's characteristic teasing quips on the occasion when Beria and his Yugoslav opposite number, Aleksandar Rankovic (Minister of the Interior), were guests at one of the notorious midnight feasts which the Soviet dictator liked to improvise for important guests. On this occasion Stalin 'turned suddenly to Rankovic, advising him to be careful of Beria, and then to Beria, asking him: "And you two? Which of you will trap the other?" '[10] As Rankovic must have been aware, the likely winner in such a contest was Beria, and it is highly probable that only the Yugoslav breach with Moscow saved Tito's police chief from sharing the fate of Xoxe, Rajk and Kostov.

On Soviet police control over the satellites useful evidence is supplied by Lieutenant-Colonel Jozef Swiatlo of the Polish Bezpieka (security police), who escaped to the West in 1953. As Swiatlo explains, a General Lalin had been chief Soviet adviser to the Bezpieka, besides which most of that extensive organisation's seventeen departments had their individual junior Soviet advisers or heads. 'These advisers receive their instructions directly from Moscow and personally control on Moscow's behalf the carrying out of the political and economic tasks assigned to Warsaw.'[11]

Particularly valuable evidence also comes from the archives of the Czechoslovak Communist Party's Central Committee as investigated during the Czechoslovak 'thaw' of 1968. The Czechoslovak leaders had shown a decent reluctance to persecute each other, and they had not contributed their share to the first round of satellite show trials, which ended in late 1949. However, as is now revealed, pacemakers in the other satellites (notably the Hungarian leader Rakosi) put pressure on the laggard Klement Gottwald, President of Czechoslovakia, to regain lost ground. After the Rajk trial the Hungarian and Polish security services proposed that the Czechoslovaks should ask for Soviet security advisers. The Soviet adviser in Hungary, Belkin, also pressed this view on the Czechoslovak authorities. 'Thus it came about that the first Soviet advisers, Makarov and Lichacev [Likhachov] came to Czechoslovakia in October 1949 at Klement Gottwald's request. . . . Upon their arrival they expressed great surprise that no enemies had as yet been discovered in the Party.'[12] The search began for a 'Czechoslovak Rajk'—a political leader of sufficient stature to figure as main defendant in a show trial. First choice fell upon the Foreign Minister, Vlado Clementis, who had adopted a critical attitude to the Soviet Union in 1939 and rated as suitable for trial as a national Communist and sympathiser of Tito. It is an index of Czechoslovak sluggishness, however, that, by the time when Clementis's arrest was announced, in February 1951, this charge was already out of fashion. The time had now come to purge the purgers, as had once happened to Yagoda in Moscow. So far, however, the Czechs had no purgers available to purge, and the search for a new victim therefore continued feverishly after the arrest of Clementis.

Meanwhile certain changes were occurring in the fortunes of the millions imprisoned on Soviet territory. From 1948 onwards the lot of concentration camp victims was somewhat alleviated, medical facilities and hygiene being marginally improved and rations becoming slightly less inadequate. This was the result, apparently, of explicit instructions to reduce mortality among slaves no longer regarded as expendable[13]—for the general level of mass arrests had now been reduced and the dying were not being immediately replaced, as previously, by relays of the partly living. Not that wholesale deportations ceased entirely—for instance, some 40,000 Greek residents of the Caucasus were rounded up in June 1949 and sent to Central Asia, besides which a great number of Jews were arrested and sent to the camps in the last years of Stalin's reign. The influx of new slaves was, however, less than the torrent of previous years.

One new relaxation in camp procedure was especially welcome to those enslaved on political grounds—the segregation of many of the *urki* in special, comparatively privileged camps, so that these common criminals were no longer in a position to maintain their reign of terror behind the barbed wire on the same scale as formerly. Among the politicals, hitherto beaten and listless, signs of solidarity and of a will to resist began to be felt as they took to protecting themselves by counter-terrorising the *urki* remaining among them. There were also many murders of *stukachi*—the stool-pigeons among the slaves, who, in return for certain privileges, undertook to furnish the security authorities with reports on the conduct and conversation of their fellow-prisoners. This sporadic anti-*stukach* terror reduced to some extent the value of the elaborate informer networks set up by the security machine in all the concentration camps, as in all other walks of Soviet life.

Widespread camp strikes did not break out until after Stalin's death, but in 1948 a remarkable, though isolated, mutiny occurred in the Vorkuta complex. Led by a Colonel Mekhteyev, a posse of imprisoned ex-officers seized arms, took over the camp in which they were held, freed the inmates and led this ragged army against Vorkuta itself, with the aim of liberating the entire camp empire centred on that slave metropolis of the north. Thrown back from the town, the insurgents embarked on a trek towards the Urals, intending to hide out in the forests as anti-Soviet partisans. Most were massacred from the air, and a few wounded were caught and brought back to face increased sentences.[14]

Amongst other post-war preoccupations of the Soviet security forces were the activities of anti-Soviet émigrés parachuted or otherwise introduced into Soviet and satellite territory by western intelligence services. Though the scale of such operations cannot be established, it seems likely that many of them were effectively thwarted by the MVD/MGB. For instance, in the early summer of 1951 the British dropped three six-man parachute teams in the Ukraine and eastern Poland. The operation had, however, been betrayed in advance by the formerly English agent of Soviet intelligence Philby—or so he leaves it to be understood in his account of these proceedings.[15] It seems clear, incidentally, that Philby was also engaged in betraying an extensive and prolonged attempt to raise a revolt in the Soviet satellite Albania from 1946 onwards, by gradually infiltrating some three hundred anti-Communist Albanian émigrés, who were all captured on or shortly after entering the country at points already communicated to Soviet intelligence.[16] An occasional echo of such activities is to be found in Soviet published sources, as when *Pravda* of 19 December 1951 announced that the two diversionaries Osmanov and Sarantsev had been sentenced to death—these being former members of Vlasov's army parachuted by the Americans into the Moldavian Republic. Though information, both Soviet and non-Soviet, on such matters is naturally scant, it seems likely that few attempts to infiltrate agents into the Soviet Empire can have escaped betrayal during the period up to mid-1951, when the flight of two English spies in Soviet service, Burgess and Maclean, cast sufficient suspicion on the Third Man Philby to cause his removal from the central counsels of British and American intelligence.

In or about 1950 a change occurred in the balance of the Soviet political police when certain important branches, hitherto part of the MVD, were transferred to the MGB. These included the Militia (ordinary police), the Frontier Troops, and probably the Special Purpose Troops, and possibly also the Railway Troops.[17] The effect was to leave the MVD as a more exclusively economic agency, since its main residual concern was with GULAG, the slave camp empire—still of vital importance as a vast pool of labour employed in many branches of industry and construction. Meanwhile the striking arm of the police had been switched to the MGB, and one can only speculate about the motive behind the move. It may have been inspired by Beria in order to strengthen his close associate Abakumov (Minister of the MGB) at the expense of the more alien Kruglov (Minister of the MVD). If this was indeed the motive for the regrouping, Beria found that he had miscalculated disastrously when, probably in November 1951,[18] Abakumov was dismissed as MGB head. His successor, Simon Ignatyev, was a Party *apparatchik*, lacking political police experience and in no way a Beria associate.[19] This was only one among several blows struck by Stalin against Beria in late 1951—part of a campaign designed to culminate in a new great terror. Like the *Yezhovshchina* before it, the new campaign was intended to strike down the Soviet élite as a whole, Beria himself being merely the earliest prominent victim-designate among a whole crop of high-ranking leaders scheduled for elimination in a new show trial or series of trials. Such, at least, seems the only possible interpretation of events occurring in the months between Abakumov's dismissal and Stalin's death in March 1953.

That Stalin had long mistrusted Beria has been widely and plausibly assumed—for whom, apart from Hitler, did Stalin ever trust? Now this mistrust can be documented from the revelations of his daughter Svetlana Alliluyev. Still a schoolgirl at the outbreak of war, she chanced to be staying at that time with Beria's wife Nina in the police chief's country villa. When Stalin realised that his only daughter was in Beria's clutches at such a crisis point, he telephoned her in great alarm and swore at her, telling her to come home at once because 'I don't trust Beria'.[20] It seems therefore that Stalin could imagine Beria kidnapping his daughter and using her as a hostage, and in view of Beria's record such an apprehension cannot be dismissed as far-fetched.

Stalin's daughter has also supplied valuable details on Beria's role in the unsavoury nocturnal orgies whereat, as already indicated, her father would regale high-ranking guests (including

Politburo members) with hard swearing, scabrous anecdotes, crude practical jokes and compulsory heavy drinking while the host himself exercised restraint in his consumption of alcohol. On these indecorous occasions it was customary to lace the wine with liberal infusions of salt or vodka. Often a ripe tomato would be slipped on someone's chair as he was about to sit down—to a chorus of tipsy guffaws all the more uproarious in a context where only a hair's breadth might be said to separate the tomato on the seat of the pants from the bullet in the back of the neck. This was all very much in the spirit of Peter the Great's banquets. More-over, Stalin—like Peter before him—had his own favourite butts, the principal two being Mikoyan and—more surprisingly—the sinister Poskryobyshev, often described as Stalin's chief agent in mounting the purges. Be that as it may, Poskryobyshev was generally carried home dead drunk from these carousals, after lurching about the bathroom vomiting. Beria's role was to egg the dictator on, for none dared mock the chief of political police—excepting only Stalin himself, who was fond of relating one par-ticular anecdote aimed against his security overlord. According to this well-worn legend a certain professor once quarrelled with his neighbour, an uneducated boor who also happened to be an NKVD officer. The Professor accused him of 'not even knowing who wrote *Yevgeny Onegin*'—a deadly insult, implying as it did ignorance of Russia's greatest poet Pushkin, and hence the feared charge of lack of culture. It is not surprising that the imprudent scholar found himself placed under arrest. Before long, however, the insulted and puzzled NKVD officer was able to boast to his friends that he had now established the authorship of *Yevgeny Onegin*, for the Professor had confessed—presumably under tor-ture—that it was he. Even though the raconteur was Stalin him-self, this somewhat ponderous tale rarely raised the intended laugh at Beria's expense, which is hardly remarkable in such an assembly of killers great and small.[21]

In addition to Abakumov's dismissal and Ignatyev's appoint-ment to head the MGB, the anti-Beria campaign of the early 1950s included an attack on the MVD/MGB in general, both in the Soviet Union and in the satellites. These interlinked motifs appear in four particularly important episodes, all intimately in-volving the Soviet political police, and often as victim as well as oppressor: the Mingrelian Affair, the Crimean Affair, the Slansky trial and the Doctors' Plot Affair.

Since 1938 Beria's chief service had been at the Centre, but he still retained close ties with his native Georgia, as also did Stalin himself, the greatest Georgian of all. As a natural result of concern on so high a level, Georgian events, and Caucasian happenings generally, have tended to mirror or anticipate events in the Centre. So it was with the Mingrelian Affair—the purging, personally ordered by Stalin, of Beria's associates in the Georgian Party, government and police, many of whom, like Beria himself, happened to hail from the Georgian province of Mingrelia. The Mingrelian Affair began in November 1951 with the denunciation by the Georgian Party's Central Committee of Baramiya, Rapava and Shoniya, respectively Second Secretary, Minister of Justice and Prosecutor of the Georgian Republic. In March 1952 the Georgian First Party Secretary, Charkviani, fell and was replaced by Beria's enemy Mgeladze, while the purge fanned out to embrace the Georgian élite as a whole. It involved dismissals and arrests rather than executions, and was almost certainly a pilot scheme for Beria's elimination.

Among other items prominent in the development of late Stalinism was an intensified persecution of Soviet Jews which never remotely approached Hitler's Final Solution in severity, but seems harsh enough if judged by non-totalitarian standards. This campaign, too, contributed to the orchestration of the abortive new *Yezhovshchina* abandoned on Stalin's death, while also constituting an indirect threat to Beria.

During the war Jewish religion and culture had enjoyed a measure of official toleration in the Soviet Union, and Soviet Jews had been allowed to form a Jewish Anti-Fascist Committee, two members of which—the leading actor Salomon Mikhoels and the writer Itzik Fefer—visited the USA in 1943 to collect donations towards the Soviet war effort, thus laying themselves open to later charges of espionage. It was not until 1948 that official discrimination against Soviet Jews became notably intensive, especially after the foundation of Israel in May of that year. In the autumn Golda Meir (then Israel's Foreign Secretary) visited Moscow, and thousands of Soviet Jews gathered to express their enthusiasm. This was an example of something not seen on the streets of the Soviet capital for many years—a mass demonstration neither organised nor sanctioned by the Party/police complex. Foreign connexions and spontaneous political initiative—the two ingredients most calculated to inflame Stalin's suspicions—were both present, besides which he had in any case long nourished a strong prejudice against the race represented by Trotsky, Zinovyev and Kamenev.

Some months before the Jewish demonstrations in Moscow, Mikhoels had suddenly died in Minsk—assassinated by the MGB on Stalin's orders, according to widespread rumour. Stalin's daughter Svetlana has recorded her own conviction that he was responsible for this murder, and it even happens that she heard him give instructions over the telephone to ascribe Mikhoels's death to a car accident.[22] Further repressions followed in November 1948, when the Jewish Anti-Fascist Committee was dissolved, Yiddish publications were suppressed and there were mass arrests of Jewish intellectuals throughout the Soviet Union. Among those seized were the five most distinguished writers in Yiddish, and also Lozovsky, a Jewish member of the Party Central Committee. On 12 August 1952 members of this group were secretly shot, accused of planning to detach the Crimea from the USSR. Only in 1956, as the result of persistent enquiry from outside the Soviet Union, did this 'Crimean Affair' come to light.

Though Beria was never formally implicated in the political and cultural offences of Soviet Jews, he could easily have been drawn in at any time owing to his sponsorship of Jewish interests in the past. So sympathetic had he shown himself that he was widely rumoured to be a Jew himself.[23] He had been a personal friend of Mikhoels and other leaders of the Jewish Anti-Fascist Committee. It was at Beria's suggestion that Mikhoels and Fefer had undertaken their fatal war-time journey to the USA which later gave rise to charges of espionage.[24]

Attacks on satellite Jews helped to swell the crescendo, the arrest of the Czechoslovak leaders Slansky and Geminder being an especially ominous portent, for both were Jews and both were thought to be associates of Beria. Thus the Czechs had at last found two new-style trial victims qualified alike by their racial origin and international police links to steal the limelight from the *bourgeois* nationalist Clementis, the first leading Czechoslovak Communist to suffer arrest. Not that the effort expended on Clementis was wasted, for he eventually appeared in dock alongside Slansky, Geminder and others—but with Slansky cast in the starring role. Fourteen persons in all (eleven of them Jews) were publicly tried in November 1952 and eleven were hanged. Thus ended another dress rehearsal for Beria's own trial.

Between 5 and 14 October 1952 a Party Congress, the Nineteenth, met in Moscow after a lapse of thirteen years (ten more than the rules prescribed) since the previous Congress. The new meeting was memorable for an emphasis on vigilance, the standard alarm note sounded in times of impending terror. Though the main report was made by Malenkov, an unusually prominent part was assigned to Poskryobyshev, who normally operated off stage. Amongst other changes the Congress decreed the abolition of the Politburo and the establishment in its place of a new policy-making organ—the Party Presidium. When elected, this turned out to include nine of the eleven full members of the defunct Politburo, but also incorporated a majority of relatively junior figures, which made it a much larger body, with twenty-five full members. By bringing in so much new blood alongside the old guard (Molotov, Malenkov, Beria, Voroshilov, Kaganovich, Mikoyan, Khrushchev and Bulganin) Stalin was putting himself in a position to destroy some or all of these stalwarts of Bolshevism.

That Stalin indeed planned to finish off the old members of the Politburo was directly confirmed by Khrushchev in 1956. At the Central Committee plenum held after the Nineteenth Congress the ageing dictator had spoken of Molotov's and Mikoyan's guilt on some baseless charge. Voroshilov too was in bad odour, as Khrushchev also explained, for Stalin suspected him of being an English agent, forbade him to attend Politburo meetings and had his room 'bugged' with a listening device.[25] Whether other Polit-buro members—for instance Malenkov and Khrushchev himself —had yet been assigned a role in the new terror, as purgers, victims or both in succession, cannot be reliably deduced from the material. That Beria remained Stalin's principal target the Congress gave further evidence by failing to re-elect his close associates, Dekanozov and Gvishiani, to the Central Committee and by reducing Merkulov from full to candidate member. November 7 saw a further tightening of the noose when Beria was demoted from fourth to sixth position in the order of precedence assigned to Party leaders on the anniversary of the Bolshevik Revolution.[26] Then a new group of Jews was tried and shot in the Ukraine—on this occasion for economic crimes. November was also the month when Slanksy, Beria's probable protégé, was put on trial in Czechoslovakia.

On 13 January 1953 *Pravda* at last sprang the Doctors' Plot on a stunned USSR, proclaiming the arrest of a terrorist group of Kremlin physicians who had confessed to the murder or attempted murder of leading Soviet figures through incorrect medical treatment. They had already killed Colonel-General Shcherbakov (once head of the army's Political Administration) in 1945, and Zhdanov in 1948. They had also sought to put out of action three

Marshals, one General and one Admiral, but these had all survived. Three of the doctors had proved to be British and five to be American spies, the latter group being 'connected with the international Jewish bourgeois nationalist organisation "Joint" established by American intelligence'.[27] Of the nine doctors arrested, several bore apparently Jewish surnames and between four and seven, according to varying reckonings, actually were of Jewish origin.[28] It is clear, however, that Stalin designed the new great terror to embrace the Soviet élite as a whole, not merely Jewish citizens.

As Khrushchev later revealed, the Doctors' Plot was true show trial material. It was entirely fabricated, according to him, on the flimsy basis of a letter sent to Stalin by a Lydia Timashuk, a woman doctor who was also an unofficial agent of the organs of state security, and had probably been 'influenced or ordered by someone' to make her denunciation. Khrushchev further reveals the close personal and even technical interest taken by Stalin in the breaking of the doctors for confession and trial. He gave orders for one of them, Academician Vinogradov, to be put in chains, issued general instructions to 'beat, beat and once again beat' (with such effect that two doctors may have died under interrogation), and threatened the MGB chief Ignatyev that if the required confessions were not forthcoming 'we will shorten you by a head'.[29] As later transpired, Ignatyev's deputy Ryumin was the real processer of the doctors, he and Poskryobyshev probably being Stalin's two chief assistants in rigging the affair, while Ignatyev was more of a figurehead.

The announcement of the doctors' arrest sparked off something virtually unknown in the Soviet press—a direct attack on the security organs for failing to detect the plot. This attack was not aimed at the Ignatyev-Ryumin team, recently established at the top of the MGB, but at the earlier security chiefs—at Beria especially, but also at Merkulov and Abakumov, for it was they who had headed the NKGB/MGB at the time of Shcherbakov's and Zhdanov's deaths in 1945 and 1948 respectively.

Late January 1953 proceeded in an atmosphere of mass hysteria stimulated by every possible means—the vigilance campaign in the press, the award of an Order of Lenin to the informer Timashuk, and even the staging in Moscow of a play by one Kubaryov resurrecting the memory of the sinister Pavlik Morozov. This was the fourteen-year-old peasant boy who had become an official folk hero back in 1932 for denouncing his father as a grain-hoarder, the father being duly shot, after which Pavlik was lynched in revenge by kulaks and canonised as a Soviet martyr. According to *Pravda*, wild applause greeted the scene in Kubaryov's play where this juvenile nark is found unmasking his father.[30] Early February saw no letup in the witch-hunt hysteria, and a particularly chilling episode occurred on the seventeenth of the month. It was then that Stalin's last known interview took place, with the Indian ambassador K. P. S. Menon. During their conversation Stalin was noticed to be doodling—a favourite habit of his. On this occasion he was drawing wolves in various poses, and made a comment on the ability of wolves to thwart attempts made to destroy them.[31] Though the remark seems highly sinister in the context of Stalin's obsession with his domestic enemies, and of his current moves to destroy them through the Doctors' Plot, Menon's narrative makes it clear that the wolves were chiefly symbols for Americans in the doodler's mind at the time when he made this remark.

On the day of the Menon interview a new note is heard, and one at variance with the mounting frenzy of the Doctors' Plot— *Izvestiya* announced that a Major-General Kosynkin of the Kremlin guard had 'died prematurely'. This might signify that some individual or group menaced by Stalin (as who indeed was not?) had found means to undermine his personal security. The wolves, perhaps, were biting back. Then again, and no less mysteriously, the vigilance campaign was quietly dropped from the press on 22 February, which strongly suggests that Stalin may have become incapacitated as early as that date. Not until 4 March, however, was an official announcement made to the effect that the dictator had suffered a severe, but not yet fatal, stroke. This was reported as occurring on the night of 1–2 March, so that well over two days had elapsed before the announcement was made. Finally, on the morning of Friday 6 March, Moscow Radio solemnly proclaimed that the despot's death had occurred on the previous evening.

As with so many of his own victims or rumoured victims, the possibility that Stalin was discreetly assassinated cannot be entirely discounted. All that can be said with certainty is that a convenient death had once again occurred—and this time a death more convenient than any other which could have been conceived.

On 7 March 1953, two days after Stalin's reported death, the

Moscow press announced sweeping Party and governmental changes. The MVD and MGB were now fused into a single ministry—an enlarged MVD, of which Beria became Minister. He thus acquired a position similar to that which he had held up to 1943—as head of the NKVD before the NKGB received the status of a separate commissariat. Now that no Stalin stood over him, Beria's position was far more powerful than before, and one can only wonder by what process he had so swiftly ousted the two sitting police Ministers Kruglov and Ignatyev at the time of Stalin's death. Until more information is forthcoming, the details of this *coup* must be added to the many unknowns of this crucial period.

Another mystery concerns the part played by the Special Purpose and Frontier Troops, the chief striking arm of the political police, which had been decanted from the MVD to the MGB several years earlier, as already mentioned. In 1953, and possibly as early as January, they reappear under MVD control.[32] On the night of 6–7 March, that following Stalin's reported death, MVD troops, which can only have been acting on Beria's orders, surrounded Moscow and proceeded to block off all streets leading to the centre. This was a wise precaution, since who could prophesy how a population so long cowed would react to the tyrant's death? Crowds did indeed gather in the centre of Moscow, but the city remained fairly quiet, obeying a request to avoid confusion and panic which had followed the official radio announcement of Stalin's death. It is unlikely, however, that Beria moved his troops into Moscow purely as a measure of crowd control. More probably they were the instrument which forced or persuaded his colleagues to grant him, overnight, the second place in the newly established hierarchy of leaders as it emerged on 7 March.

In this reshuffle the top position went to Malenkov, who immediately inherited the two key posts held by Stalin—those of leading Secretary of the Party Central Committee and Chairman of the Council of Ministers. Though the name Presidium was retained, its full membership was reduced from twenty-five to ten. Of the new men recently brought in only two (Pervukhin and Saburov) retained full membership, the remaining eight places going to the old guard of former Politburo members (Malenkov, Beria, Molotov, Voroshilov, Khrushchev, Bulganin, Kaganovich, Mikoyan). A week later Malenkov lost his secretaryship of the Central Committee, which went to Khrushchev, but retained his chairmanship of the Council of Ministers. Though reduced in status by this change, Malenkov still remained the most powerful figure, but had submitted to the new principle of collective leadership, proclaimed in a *Pravda* leading article of 27 March and intended to supplant the principle of one-man rule.

One early concern of the new leadership was to relax the purge hysteria whipped up during Stalin's last months. Articles accordingly appeared in the press stressing the need for Socialist legality, as opposed to the arbitrary police rule with which all were so familiar. The most dramatic symbol of the new relaxation was the public unscrambling of the Doctors' Plot. On 4 April Beria's MVD issued an official communiqué stating that the accused physicians had already been set free without a stain on their characters, since their confessions had been extorted by 'impermissible means'. Curiously enough, the published list of thirteen doctors now rehabilitated by no means corresponded exactly with the list originally given of those arrested, of whom there had been only nine. Moreover, two of the original batch—Etinger and M. B. Kogan—were not mentioned at all in the new list (perhaps because they had died under interrogation), besides which six entirely new names now appeared. These were perhaps doctors seized and earmarked for confession along with the others, but not broken by the time when the Doctors' Plot was first announced.

Among Stalin's chief assistants in concocting the Doctors' Plot, Poskryobyshev immediately vanished under circumstances which remain obscure. He has been variously reported as killed on the spot or surviving to write what might yet prove the most sensational memoirs ever penned, for many indications suggest that, as head of Stalin's personal secretariat, he may have been for years the second most powerful figure in the country.[33] Incidentally, this secretariat too disappeared from the scene along with Poskryobyshev. As for Ignatyev, the MGB minister whom Stalin had once threatened with beheading should he fail to extract the required medical confessions, he lost his ministry to Beria's MVD, but received astonishingly lenient treatment—moving back to humbler offices outside the police machine. It was on Ignatyev's deputy, Ryumin, that the main odium for rigging the Doctors' Plot fell. Arrested after Stalin's death, he was to suffer trial and execution in the following year.

On the day when the doctors' rehabilitation was announced, it was also revealed that the nark who had originally denounced them, Dr Lydia Timashuk, had been deprived of the Order of Lenin awarded to her for performing that public disservice.

Beria's sway as Number Two in the Soviet hierarchy lasted some three and a half months only, ending with his sudden disgrace and arrest, which took place, according to official statements, on 26 June 1953. In any case Beria's downfall was not made public until a fortnight later, on 10 July, when it became the occasion for a press campaign against the deposed police chief, now unmasked as an enemy of the people and hireling of the imperialist secret services. Beria eventually underwent a secret, but well-publicised, trial in December 1953, and was condemned to be executed. On one prominent charge, that he had been a foreign agent since the Civil War, it is not necessary to comment. Other accusations involved exercising a malign influence on the development of Soviet agriculture, lapsing into *bourgeois* nationalism, attempting to set the MVD above Party and government, and infringing the principles of Socialist legality. Some of these charges seem to derive from policies actually pursued by Beria. In the sphere of agriculture he may have annoyed Khrushchev, who regarded this as his special preserve, by proposing a radical relaxation of the collective farm system.[34] Such an intention would be in keeping with Beria's general policies during his months as head of the MVD, for it was now that this veteran assassin emerged as a reforming liberal—not, surely, from inner conviction but as a bid for the popularity which he sorely needed if he was to maintain or improve his position. Though already endangered by his pro-Jewish postures in the past, he now championed the interests of the minority peoples in general, working against the enforced russification of the periphery of the USSR. He also promoted a relaxation of Soviet control over the satellite countries, especially in the Soviet zone of Germany. Hence the charges of *bourgeois* nationalism.

Like Stalin before him, Beria had also sought to place his minions in influential positions throughout the Soviet Empire. He had descended on Georgia in person to purge those Georgians who had purged his own followers during the Mingrelian Affair, and appointed a particularly close associate, Dekanozov, to be head of the Georgian MVD. He had also replaced the political police chiefs in the Baltic countries and the Ukraine. According to evidence from a Polish source, a secret Party circular was sent to the satellites listing certain additional charges against Beria otherwise not yet publicised. In this document Beria was blamed for the

Leningrad Affair, for bringing the Kremlin guard under his personal control, for obtaining reports on his Presidium colleagues' conversation and for having one of them shadowed by his agents when travelling to Lwow. Hence, no doubt, the accusations of ignoring Socialist legality and attempting to set the MVD over Party and government. Svetlana Alliluyev refers to yet another secret indictment of Beria, which was read out at Party meetings, taking over three hours in the recitation. More than half of this tirade was devoted to a high-minded denunciation of Beria's unsavoury sexual habits[35]—a reminder that the police overlord was reputedly accustomed to undertake raping expeditions by prowl car in the streets of the capital. To this habit the Soviet poet Yevgeny Yevtushenko refers in his memoirs: 'I saw the vulture face of Beria, half hidden by a muffler, glued to the window of his limousine as he drove slowly by the kerb hunting down a woman for the night.[36]

Such frivolities apart, Beria's aim as post-Stalin police overlord was probably to tune up the MVD until it was powerful enough to protect him against his colleagues, while simultaneously building support by championing local interests away from the centre. Thus he sought to escape from the essentially unstable position of police overlord combined with Number Two in the hierarchy—a position from which he could only advance or retreat. To the other leaders the political police posed completely different problems. They wished to keep the security machine sufficiently disarmed to remove the threat which had hung over all of them since 1934, yet in doing so they must be careful not to weaken it to the point where it could no longer defend the Soviet system. For Beria, however, such a compromise was impossible—he must either become a second Stalin or preside over the liquidation of the Soviet Empire, and his colleagues were prepared to tolerate neither alternative.

Beria was shot on 23 December 1953—immediately after sentence had been pronounced at his trial, according to an announcement published in *Pravda* on the following day. Nearly three years later, however, a different and far livelier account of his death was given by Khrushchev in conversation with a leading Italian Communist. This version has Beria using his control of the police to grasp for supreme power, but lured by his threatened colleagues to a special combined meeting of the Presidium and Party Secretariat with certain army leaders, where he is denounced by Malenkov and informed that he is to stand trial there and then. Separated from his bodyguard, and realising too late that he has been tricked, Beria reaches for a gun, but is tackled and strangled by Malenkov, Mikoyan, Marshal Konev and Marshal Moshkalenko. Another version of the story, given by Khrushchev at about the same time to a French Senator, is substantially the same—but has Beria shot, not strangled.[37]

On a less gruesome level Beria's downfall caused grave embarrassment to the editors of the *Great Soviet Encyclopedia*, which had recently put out a lavish eulogy of the defunct police minister now suddenly become an 'unperson'. Subscribers were circulated and told to cut out with scissors or razor blade certain pages containing Beria's picture and the offending article. These were to be replaced by other pages specially supplied and including material on the German diarist Friedrich Berkholtz, together with photographs of the Bering Sea, showing a whaler towing two dead whales and several dead walruses on an ice floe.[38]

The KGB under Khrushchev
1954–1964

Beria's fall in June 1953 marks a turning point in the history of the Soviet political police, now effectively subordinated to the top Party leadership. The deposed overlord's first four successors as heads of security—Kruglov, Serov, Shelepin and Semichastny—were, accordingly, denied top power-status (that is, membership of the Party Presidium/Politburo or Central Committee Secretariat), while the fifth, Andropov, was made only a candidate, not a full, Politburo-member.

The disgrace of Beria heralded numerous measures designed to weaken the police apparatus. S. N. Kruglov, a secondary figure, resumed office as Minister in charge of the MVD, the post which he had held from 1946 until Beria superseded him after Stalin's death. As a sign of the new subordination local MVD offices were obliged to inform local Party Secretaries of proposed arrests.[1] Meanwhile the MVD was losing various responsibilities to other ministries. For a time the Internal and Frontier Police Troops were probably subordinated to the Ministry of Defence, the concentration camp system came under the Ministry of Justice, and Dalstroy went to the Ministry of Metallurgy. The supra-judicial powers of the political police were also reduced—notably with the abolition of the Special Conference, a body set up by Stalin in 1934 and empowered to sentence individuals without legal formality. The Procurator-Generalship received powers, such as it had not possessed under Stalin, to exercise supervision over the security machine. Then came the announcement, on 24 December 1953, that Beria and six of his closest police colleagues had been tried and executed—a calculated blow against the old political police, and one clearly designed by the top leaders to reassure both themselves and the population at large that the bad old days would never return. Behind the scenes numerous veteran security men ('Beriaites') were dismissed from the MVD and replaced by figures from the Party Apparatus and the army. This reassertion of Party authority over the police was associated with the rise of Khrushchev, as advertised when he acquired the title *first* secretary (as opposed to secretary unadorned) of the Party Central Committee in September 1953.

For twelve months the MVD exercised political police authority, first under Beria and then under Kruglov. Then, by a decree of 13 March 1954, yet another specialist organisation was set up, while the MVD still continued in being—its responsibilities henceforward confined to home affairs outside the political security sphere. The new body was the KGB (Committee of State Security), which remains the Soviet security organisation at the time of writing, having lasted longer than any previous Soviet political police force. Humble though the designation committee may sound, the KGB is not inferior to any ministry, and has been described as a Super-Ministry of State Security.[2] The KGB Chairman is, incidentally, *ex officio* member of the Council of Ministers, and the first to hold the office was Ivan Serov. This notorious mass deporter of the Stalin era was a former subordinate of Khrushchev in the Ukraine—as also was the Procurator-General R. A. Rudenko, now charged with supervising the security machine.

On the vital part played by the police apparatus in advancing Khrushchev's career the defecting Soviet military intelligence officer Oleg Penkovsky is extremely forthright. He claims that Khrushchev could never have risen to supreme power had it not been for the KGB and Serov.[3] Penkovsky also confirms a close tie-up between Chairman Serov and Procurator-General Rudenko, who happened to live next door to each other in Granovsky Street. Serov arrested people, and Rudenko signed the death sentences. 'One would drop into the other's flat in the evening for a drink, and together they would decide who should be put in jail and who should be shot. Very convenient.'[4]

This is not the place to detail the process whereby Khrushchev, fifth-ranking leader at the time of Stalin's death, gradually outwitted his rivals. Beria's downfall was followed by the disgrace of Malenkov—compelled, in February 1955, to resign the premiership (that is, the chairmanship of the Council of Ministers) to

Khrushchev's temporary ally Bulganin. In June 1957 the Central Committee dismissed the 'Anti-Party Group' (Molotov, Kaganovich, Malenkov and Shepilov) from the top leadership, their disgrace being followed by Bulganin's in March 1958. Succeeding Bulganin as Premier, while remaining leading secretary of the Party Central Committee, Khrushchev now at last held both of the two great offices jointly filled by Stalin in his last years. Not that Khrushchev came to enjoy Stalinist powers, for he remained a dictator only in so far as he could dominate the Presidium, his ability to do this being subject to an erratic ebb and flow. The Soviet government of his time was, accordingly, one-man rule subject to varying control by a powerful oligarchy washed by submerged currents of intrigue against, by and for the podgy but mentally nimble First Secretary.

Khrushchev's rise and fall followed the conventions of Soviet (and Imperial Russian) public life in that a façade of outward harmony was periodically disrupted by sudden, dramatic scandals. These included the successive downfall of Beria, Malenkov, Molotov, Kaganovich, Shepilov, Bulganin and Voroshilov—and finally of Khrushchev himself. That the mirror-like surface shattered by such commotions was the cover for swirling undercurrents has been demonstrated by the techniques of kremlinology applied, in the works of Rush, Leonhard and Tatu listed in the Bibliography, below. As they have shown, the top leadership has regularly spoken to the Party, governmental and managerial élite through esoteric code signals slipped into *Pravda* and other vehicles of communication. The varying order in which leaders' names are listed is one pointer, and may be reinforced by a study of who appears how prominently in what press photograph, who attends what ballet or opera, who greets whom at what airport—and so on. There is also the significance of typography—as when Khrushchev's own title of First Secretary was successively listed as *pervy sekretar*, *Pervy Sekretar*, and finally, by a working compromise, as *Pervy sekretar*, the ennobling capital letters being awarded and withdrawn in accordance with his vacillating status.[5]

Indispensable as kremlinology is to an understanding of the power struggle in general, it reveals surprisingly little trace of the part played by the KGB in Khrushchev's rise to supremacy. The only period when he appears to have exploited the security machine as a direct threat came before and during the political crisis of June 1957 which ended with the dismissal of the Anti-Party Group. The frontier and possibly also the internal police troops, hitherto under MVD control (after their brief spell, already mentioned, under the Ministry of Defence), were transferred to the KGB between late March and early June. Thus the cutting edge of police power was brought under Khrushchev's minion Serov at a particularly sensitive moment. Soon afterwards, during the June plenum of the Central Committee, a coded threat was conveyed to the army: the Ministry of Defence journal *Red Star* gave Serov, a mere General of the Army in military rank, precedence over his nominal seniors by listing him ahead of nine Marshals of the Soviet Union. The probable purpose of this esoteric signal was to remind 'members of the defence establishment that they are answerable to the political police for actions which might be deemed politically suspicious'.[6]

This deeply buried signal is the only known instance of a positive use made of the political police by one leader to threaten others during the period of Khrushchev's rise. A more important element in the power struggle was the negative exploitation of the police through attacks on its murky Stalinist record. These were launched in order to invest the assailant (usually Khrushchev himself) with an aura of historically unjustified integrity by besmirching rivals with the taint of Yezhov's and Beria's crimes.

It is in this context that the five police trials of 1953–6 should be understood. These affairs saw twenty-eight former police officials tried and condemned in Moscow, Leningrad, Tbilisi and Baku, twenty-two being shot and six sentenced to imprisonment. The first police trial—that of Beria and six others in December 1953—has already been mentioned, and presents no particular problems, reflecting as it surely must a decision by the top leaders to dissociate themselves collectively from Stalinist malpractices which they had all vigorously promoted at the time. But what of Ryumin's trial and execution in July 1954? Ryumin had originally been arrested by Beria, and is believed to have been responsible under Poskryobyshev and Stalin for rigging the abortive Doctors' Plot, as already stated. Why, though, a delay of fifteen months between his arrest and trial? And why was he charged under Section 7 of Article 58 of the Penal Code—that covering *economic* crimes—when his only known offence was the torturing of elderly physicians? One theory is that Ryumin had secretly been instructed to proceed from extorting doctors' confessions to framing the top economic managers—Malenkov's particular allies.[7] Occurring in July 1954, when Malenkov was briefly reascendant after his decline of the previous winter, the Ryumin trial may conceivably have been intended to discredit Khrushchev. This suggestion would, however, involve an assumption which can neither be confirmed nor disproved—that Khrushchev had been allied with Ryumin as a secret sponsor and scheduled beneficiary of the Doctors' Plot in the days when Stalin was hatching up that nefarious scheme.[8]

Be this as it may, the police trial immediately following Ryumin's—that of the former MGB Minister Abakumov and five associates in December 1954—almost certainly represents an offensive by Khrushchev, who was now making up ground lost a few months earlier. The main charge against Abakumov—of fabricating the Leningrad Case in 1949—was aimed against Malenkov as chief instigator of that murderous onslaught on the entourage of his deceased rival Zhdanov. Malenkov was not mentioned in the indictment, but the trial was understood by those in the know as a blow against his position, though it was not until July 1957 that he was finally named as responsible for the Leningrad Affair.

The Tbilisi trial (of Rapava and seven other Georgian police chiefs in September 1955) and the Baku trial (of Bagirov and five Azerbaydzhani security potentates in April 1956) were obscure affairs reported only by local press and radio. In each case the charges included persecution of the Georgian leader Ordzhonikidze—murdered or driven to suicide back in 1937, as described above—and it seems likely that some hitherto unrevealed scandal involved some enemy of Khrushchev (Malenkov, Molotov, Kaganovich?) in responsibility for Ordzhonikidze's death.[9] It is clear in any case that none of the five police trials of 1953–6 derived from a passion for abstract justice. All were political moves, and all except the Ryumin trial probably had the backing of Khrushchev, most skilful among the top leaders in exploiting bygone misdeeds to promote his own career. Though Khrushchev himself may well have been no less deeply implicated in Stalin's crimes than his defeated rivals, he seemed partly exonerated by one lucky circumstance—only in 1939, when the main repressions were over, had he become a full member of Stalin's Politburo.

On 25 February 1956 Khrushchev delivered to the Twentieth Party Congress the celebrated 'secret' speech which has never been officially published in the Soviet Union, but has been issued by the American State Department in an English version accepted as genuine by all students of the period.[10] It was in this speech, to which frequent reference is made above, that Khrushchev attacked Stalin's reputation with a vehemence then unparalleled on any official occasion. The speech was an important turning point in Khrushchev's own career. Since Stalin's death he had, on the whole, built his rise to power on the championship of hard-line Stalinist principles—notably the primacy of heavy industry—as opposed to the milder policies advocated by Beria and Malenkov. Now that Beria had been removed, and Malenkov half removed, Khrushchev suddenly switched course in mid-congress, assuming leadership of the destalinisation lobby, which had wide appeal both inside the Party and among the population at large. Thus Khrushchev swerved to attack the main residual hard-liners Molotov and Kaganovich. Working from a central position to destroy first one wing and then another, he was repeating Stalin's technique of tacking between leftists and rightists in the middle 1920s.

The assault on Stalin inevitably involved Stalin's political police, and Khrushchev's secret speech deals at length with the policies implemented by Yezhov and Beria. He depicts the former as a tool of the dictator, while the crafty Beria is shown (as also by Stalin's daughter) influencing his master through low cunning. Khrushchev deals with the Kirov Case, the Leningrad Affair, the Mingrelian Affair, the Doctors' Plot and many another police scandal. He describes the extraction of false confessions by torture, supplying valuable detail which might otherwise have remained buried in the archives of the NKVD. In assessing Khrushchev's evidence it must, of course, be remembered that he was a verbally incontinent individual less concerned to establish historical truth than to outwit political rivals. Not that there is reason to doubt the details of police procedure which he supplies, much of his information being supported by independent sources. The general balance of his speech is, however, another matter altogether. Remarkable as Khrushchev's statements are in the context of official mendacity and reticence about Stalin, they leave more unsaid than at first seemed apparent. In particular, Khrushchev devotes himself almost exclusively to police repressions of Communist Party members—who, if anyone, deserved their fate, having so enthusiastically approved or administered the massacre of others during collectivisation. As for Stalin's non-Party victims, Khrushchev ignores them almost entirely, besides which he denounces only the post-1934 repressions, explicitly exempting Stalin the liquidator of peasants from his strictures.

At certain points of his speech Khrushchev was careful to hint that his three current rivals, Malenkov, Molotov and Kaganovich, were all implicated in the crimes or follies of the Stalin era. In June 1957 he was able to go further and destroy them politically as members of an 'Anti-Party Group'. That they were not put on trial or physically suppressed, but shunted into minor offices, shows that Stalin's methods had indeed been modified. It is, however, unlikely that such delicacy derived from any reluctance on Khrushchev's part to throw his defeated rivals to the KGB—most probably he was prevented from doing so by powerful colleagues no less immune to sentimental promptings than he, but anxious not to help him dig for others a pit into which they themselves might in turn be pushed.

After Stalin's death the concentration camp system underwent continuing reform along lines already pioneered in the dictator's last years—besides which the population of the camps was considerably reduced between 1953 and 1956, as all authorities agree. However, reliable figures on the number detained, whether on political or criminal charges, are available neither for the period before, nor for the period after, what are sometimes described as mass releases. At no time has the concentration camp system been abandoned.

Some releases were effected through post-Stalin amnesties. The first was that of 27 March 1953, from which political prisoners were virtually excluded, those freed being chiefly *urki*. Restored to freedom, this army of petty crooks embarked on a renewed career of crime which put many of them back behind barbed wire. Among other amnesties was that of 17 September 1955, releasing prisoners sentenced for collaborating with the Germans as members of the German police or armed forces during the war. Such positive treason accordingly received more favourable treatment than the crime—not subject to the same amnesty—of living passively under foreign occupation, which had brought many unfortunates into the camps since the German retreat.[11] Surprising though such discrimination might seem, it was perhaps logical for the Soviet security authorities to indulge those who had shown the greater initiative in co-operating with a totalitarian system.

Despite a tendency to persist with large-scale releases in the early post-Stalin period, political arrests continued, and included a contingent of former security policemen reported in Vorkuta in

August 1955.[12] The period also saw a new category of political detainee: that of pro-Stalinist Georgian students and others who had taken part in demonstrations against Khrushchev's denunciation of their national hero—popular in his homeland as a mass liquidator of Russians, if for no other reason. The camps also took in new prisoners among young people who had participated in the campaign launched by Khrushchev to open up the Virgin Lands of Central Asia for cultivation, but had expressed dissatisfaction with the primitive conditions encountered on the spot.

Besides a reduction in numbers, the early post-Stalin years also saw further relaxations in the régime of the camps, partly achieved through a wave of prisoners' strikes and demonstrations which swept the slave empire between 1952 and 1954, hitting networks as far apart as those of Vorkuta in the north, Karaganda and Kingir in Central Asia, and Norilsk in far eastern Siberia. Many such risings were brutally repressed—for example, seventy-six slaves are reported massacred at Kingir on 17 May 1954, when drunken soldiers broke into the barracks to bayonet women prisoners.[13] Despite such horrors, the central authorities paid considerable attention to demands formulated with remarkable unanimity by clandestine prisoners' organisations throughout the far-flung slave empire. As the result of these representations, amnesties and other privileges restricted to *urki* were extended to politicals, slaves were relieved of the obligation to display numbers on their clothing, grilles were removed from barrack windows, and barracks were no longer locked at night. There was also some improvement in rationing, while correspondence with the outside world and visits from relatives became less exceptional, and remission of part of a sentence could be earned by those who maintained or over-fulfilled the severe work norms still enforced throughout the system. There was, however, also some reversion to the practice of using *urki* to police the politicals.

In May 1957, in one of the few official statements ever made on camp statistics, P. I. Kudryavtsev (Assistant Prosecutor-General of the USSR) gave Professor H. Berman of the Harvard Law School certain information suggesting that there had been some three million camp prisoners, almost half of them politicals, at the time of Stalin's death. Of these between eight and nine hundred thousand remained in detention in 1957, less than 18,000 of them being politicals.[14] This information appears highly suspect. While Kudryavtsev was thus maintaining two per cent to be the proportion of politicals, an official of the MVD informed Berman at about the same time that the true figure was less than one per cent. Then, in January 1959, Khrushchev himself explicitly stated at the Twenty-First Party Congress that 'there are no political prisoners in the prisons of our country at present'.[15]

This claim represents an attempt to absolve the Soviet system from responsibility for a widely execrated practice by juggling with terminology. Though a new and somewhat more liberal penal code, introduced in December 1958, made no provision for offences explicitly defined by the adjective political, it did list numerous crimes against the State. Besides espionage, terrorism and sabotage, these also included 'anti-Soviet agitation and propaganda', this last being a vague concept which the KGB and the courts could twist as they wished. Detention of up to seven years was established as the penalty for slandering the Soviet State and social order—another concept open to abuse since it made complaints about living conditions a possible ground for prosecution. The scope for disguised political oppression was further widened from May 1957 onwards, when various republics of the USSR began to enact laws providing sentences of two to five years' exile for 'anti-social parasitical elements'. This provision could be stretched to embrace almost any so-called idler deemed politically undesirable. Newly-instituted comrades' courts, factory meetings, and other popular assemblages lacking judicial status, were empowered to pronounce such sentences by simple majority vote— a process which could easily be exploited by officious busybodies to persecute anyone against whom they chanced to nurture a grudge. In this context a decision of 1956 to abolish Corrective Labour Camps in name, by calling them Corrective Labour Colonies (thus adding them to an existing category of places of detention where a milder régime was practised) was of little significance. It made small difference to the prisoners whether the authority under which they served was called GULAG (as formerly) or GUITK (as henceforward). Furthermore, though the security police had now relinquished overall control of places of detention to the MVD and local republican authorities, it still maintained supervision over prisons and camps (as over all other Soviet institutions) through KGB officers operating networks of secret informers.

On the continued success of the security forces in combating the penetration of the Soviet Union by anti-Soviet émigrés or foreign spies, occasional officially released details were forthcoming in the early post-Stalin period. For instance, *Pravda* of 27 May 1953 announced the execution of four Russian émigrés who had parachuted into Soviet territory from a Munich base. On 19 May of the following year Radio Kiev proclaimed the execution of another Munich-based anti-Soviet émigré infiltrator called Okhrymovich. These were, however, bare announcements such as had also been made during the Stalin period. From 1956 onwards a new policy was followed—that of giving greater publicity to success achieved by the KGB in thwarting such enterprises. Among the episodes thus advertised was that of Square B–52, code name for a four-man team of Belorussian émigrés parachuted into their homeland from a Frankfurt-based aircraft. Apprised of their arrival and whereabouts, the security police reacted in traditional manner by creating its own spurious band of anti-Soviet Belorussian partisans (in fact KGB agents) picturesquely decked out with rusty machine-guns and carbines borrowed from a local museum. These bogus diversionists duly made contact with Square B–52, fully exploiting the intelligence potentialities of the liaison before arresting the four duped parachutists. In 1956 the Soviet publishing house *Molodaya gvardiya* issued a detailed account of this affair, complete with photographs.[16] Even wider publicity was given to another case dating from December 1956, when a Swedish spy, Endel Mumm, was reported as arrested in the Estonian Republic while seeking radio contact with his Stockholm base. In the same operation thirteen other Swedish or American agents were also seized, as was an assortment of transmitters, cyphers, codes, secret inks, automatic weapons, cameras, maps, false documents, roubles, watches and jewellery.[17] In 1960 a Soviet documentary film was devoted to this affair—a landmark in the campaign to glorify security activities such as had previously been ignored.

Stalin's death by no means ended the policy of kidnapping or assassinating political undesirables on foreign territory. In 1954 two notorious attacks were mounted against NTS (National Labour Union), the émigré Russian anti-Soviet organisation. On April 13 Alexander Trushnovich, a prominent NTS member, disappeared in Berlin, presumably kidnapped by the KGB.[18] The second attack failed because the officer charged with its execution, Captain Nicholas Khokhlov, abandoned his mission and defected to the West. His instructions were to assassinate Georgy Okolovich, described as head of NTS clandestine operations.[19] For this purpose Khokhlov controlled two junior assassins, and also special weapons constructed in the laboratories of the MVD—soundless pistols firing poisoned bullets and disguised as cigarette cases. However, instead of using these weapons when he presented himself at Okolovich's flat in Frankfurt on 18 February, Khokhlov confronted his scheduled victim with a confession: 'Georgy Sergeyevich . . . I've come to you from Moscow. The Central Committee of the Communist Party of the Soviet Union ordered your liquidation. The murder is entrusted to my group.'[20] Khokhlov's further adventures in emigration included his attempted poisoning at the annual conference organised by the Russian émigré journal *Posev* in September 1957. After drinking half, and fortunately no more, of a cup of coffee on the terrace of the Frankfurt Palmengarten, he contracted appalling symptoms which defied diagnosis until it eventually emerged that he had been fed a hitherto unknown poison—the metal thallium in specially radioactivated form. That this represented an attempt by the KGB to assassinate its own unwilling assassin, Khokhlov clearly implies. If he is right, the attempt was consistent with various assassinations previously carried out by the Soviet political police on foreign territory, as also with Penkovsky's statement: 'One of the tasks of the [Soviet] intelligence service is to remove agents who are not needed any more by murdering them, either by poisoning them or by some other means.'[21]

April 1954, the month when Khokhlov's defection from Soviet service was announced, also saw another much publicised defection—that of Vladimir Petrov, Colonel of the MVD and head of the Soviet espionage organisation in Australia. After he had taken refuge with the Australian security authorities, his wife Yevdokiya, a Captain in the same service, was held incommunicado in the Soviet Embassy in Canberra as a prelude to being forcibly repatriated to the Soviet Union. Minus one shoe, she was manhandled beneath floodlights through an excited crowd on to a plane at Mascot Airport by armed Soviet couriers under conditions resembling a public kidnapping combined with a deliberate challenge to Australian sovereignty—and indeed to Australian virility. The plane took off, and it was only at the very last moment—during a refuelling stop at Darwin—that Mrs Petrov, bewildered by these proceedings, at last made up her mind to refuse repatriation. Helped by an Australian official, she escaped from her escort and was reunited with her husband.[22] This incident was attended by the widest publicity throughout, and well illustrates the lengths to which the Soviet authorities may go in policing would-be police defectors, undeterred even by ridicule on a global scale. That there was good reason to keep the Petrovs under cover is shown in their book *Empire of Fear*, as also by their evidence before the Australian Royal Commission on Espionage, which has enriched the dossier on the Soviet political police with valuable information based on over forty years' joint experience of OGPU, NKVD, MVD and KGB.

Other foreign activities of the KGB during this period proved more expensive in human life than those of Khokhlov and the Petrovs. In 1957 and 1959 respectively the émigré Ukrainian leaders Lev Rebet and Stepan Bandera were killed with a special gas pistol by one Bohdan Stashynsky, as admitted by him at his trial in Karlsruhe in October 1962, when he described these as tasks assigned to him as an agent of the KGB.[23]

In December 1958 an important change occurred in the KGB when Serov gave way to a new Chairman, Alexander Shelepin. By no means disgraced, Serov was transferred to a far less important post as head of the GRU, the army's main intelligence administration. On the reasons for this downgrading one of his new subordinates, Colonel Penkovsky, has supplied a valuable clue, describing Serov as 'not the most brilliant of men. He knows how to interrogate people, imprison them and shoot them. In more sophisticated intelligence work he is not so skilful.'[24]

Chairman Shelepin possessed the greater subtlety needed for the Khrushchev era—one of growing flexibility in the exercise of political control. Considerable freedom to express individual viewpoints, and to indulge in controversy touching on politics, was now allowed to imaginative writers, whose fluctuating status had become a barometer for Soviet intellectual controls in general. By contrast with the unrelieved deep freeze of Stalin's time, periods of thaw now alternated with periods of frozen slush, such as that introduced by the Hungarian Rising of October 1956. This new and more flexible method of control had the advantage of confusing gullible foreign observers of the Soviet scene. Eternally optimistic about the prospects for an abandonment of Soviet police rule, these alien intellects seemed to discern among Moscow's meanderings a general trend towards ever greater liberalisation. Foreign belief in this fancied trend in turn helped to lull suspicions of Soviet aggressive intent, and thus to create a climate favourable to the development of Soviet foreign policy.

It was part of Shelepin's task to foster such illusions. Aged only forty at the time of his translation to the KGB, he had so far lacked any openly acknowledged political police connexion, having served in the Komsomol during most of his career. His transfer to the police followed a brief period in the apparatus of the Party Central Committee, and thus harmonises with the general pattern followed since Beria's death whereby the security police has remained strictly subservient to the Party. In keeping with this policy Khrushchev himself worked closely with his new KGB Chairman, as with Serov before him. It has been reported that 'Shelepin spends more time in Khrushchev's office than in his own office on Dzerzhinsky Square', as the result of Khrushchev's decision to control his political police directly, a matter in which he—wisely—would trust no one else.[25]

As KGB Chairman, Shelepin had obtained an important promotion, but one liable to prove a diminishing asset, since the days had passed when direct control of the political police could be combined with the very highest office. His departure from the KGB, on 14 November 1961, accordingly marked a further advancement, coinciding as it did with a far more influential appointment—as a Secretary of the Party Central Committee.

Shelepin's successor as KGB head was a Ukrainian six years his junior, Vladimir Semichastny, who had trodden in Shelepin's footsteps as First Secretary of the Komsomol and in the Central Committee apparatus. Semichastny had become notorious for a speech delivered during the politico-literary crisis following the offer of the Nobel Prize for Literature to Pasternak in autumn 1958, when he contrasted Pasternak's domestic habits with those of the supposedly cleaner pig. Despite the versatility displayed in this shaft of literary criticism, Semichastny was a less enterprising manoeuvrer than Shelepin. As head of the KGB he seems to have acted largely as the agent of Shelepin, who probably continued to count security among his responsibilities as Central Committee Secretary. The policy of close co-operation between Khrushchev and KGB continued under both men. However, as will be shown below, the Shelepin-Semichastny team had reservations in its attitude towards the First Secretary, and eventually helped to bring him down.

The Twenty-Second Party Congress of October 1961 saw a

determined attempt by Khrushchev to impose a new phase of more intense destalinisation. On the 27th of the month he addressed the Congress with what was, in effect, an officially acknowledged potted version of his secret speech of 1956. Calling for the fullest inquiry into Kirov's murder and the mass repressions of the Stalin era, he also proposed the erection of a monument in Moscow 'to the memory of the comrades who fell victim to arbitrary rule'.[26] Three days later the Congress took an important symbolic decision, immediately carried out, to remove Stalin's embalmed corpse from the Red Square Mausoleum, where it had rested alongside Lenin's since 1953, and to bury it in comparative obscurity.

In pressing for further destalinisation at this stage, Khrushchev was himself seeking Stalinist powers—and by using methods reminiscent of Stalin's in that he sought the support of his allies within the top leadership for a campaign to discredit further, expel from the Party, and possibly put on trial, the members of the Anti-Party Group—Malenkov, Molotov and Kaganovich—to whom Voroshilov was now belatedly added. In this context it is particularly significant that the outgoing KGB Chairman Shelepin denounced the Anti-Party Group more vehemently than any other speaker at the Congress. However, Shelepin was not yet a Presidium member, and Khrushchev's allies within the Presidium had the precedent of Stalin to show them that their acquiescence in police measures against discredited leaders must eventually endanger themselves. They were therefore by no means eager to see prosecution of the Anti-Party Group, just as some of Stalin's allies had once attempted, though in vain, to halt the great terror in its early stages. Hence Khrushchev's attempt to seek support below Presidium level by exploiting once again the popular appeal of destalinisation. Where Stalin had succeeded, however, Khrushchev failed, for the removal of Stalin's body from the mausoleum was the only item in the new programme of destalinisation to be implemented. As for the monument to Stalin's victims, the further investigation of Stalin's crimes and severer sanctions against the Anti-Party Group—Khrushchev had to jettison all these schemes, excepting only that members of the Group eventually suffered the mild penalty of expulsion from the Party. Thus frustrated after the Twentieth Congress, Khrushchev continued in uneasy balance with the other Presidium members, unable to destroy the ultimate authority of the oligarchy, while yet retaining powers within and over it which may reasonably be described as dictatorial.

Some details on the KGB's style of work during the second half of the Khrushchev era are available through certain cases which might have remained buried in obscurity had not information about them chanced to reach the West. Two politico-literary trials of the period—those of Olga Ivinsky and Joseph Brodsky— were especially remarkable for an element of personal spite which appears to have been present in the police conduct of these cases.

Olga Ivinsky was the close friend and literary executor of the poet and novelist Boris Pasternak. In August 1960, a few weeks after his death, she was seized by the KGB, the arrest of her daughter Irina Yemelyanov following shortly afterwards. In December mother and daughter received sentences of eight and three years' imprisonment respectively for committing alleged currency offences. The KGB had contrived to exploit the provisions made by Pasternak—for the two women to receive certain sums of money accruing from foreign royalties on his works—and to make these innocent but complex financial ramifications into the basis of a judicial frame-up sprung at a secret trial.[27] Thus the police pursued, after the poet's death, a vendetta already aimed at him through Olga Ivinsky during his lifetime. A further motive for this miscarriage of justice was the wish to explain away Pasternak's hostility to the Soviet system, expressed in his later work, as due to influence exercised over him by one now pilloried as an unscrupulous adventuress.

An element of personal vendetta was also apparent in February–March 1964 at the trial, in Leningrad, of the poet Joseph Brodsky under the anti-parasite laws. The young man was already a distinguished translator and poet, but these are not disciplines in which norm-fulfilment can easily be measured, and it was therefore possible to present him as an anti-social idler. As has so often happened with Soviet trials, the issue was prejudged in various ways long before the court sat. An abusive article attacking Brodsky had appeared in the newspaper *Evening Leningrad* in November of the previous year, being partly the work of a dismissed captain of the political police called Lerner, who appears to have been the poet's main persecutor. A large notice, *Trial of Parasite Brodsky*, displayed in the courtroom before proceedings had even begun, would have led to charges of contempt under a less flexible judicial system. This farcical affair might never have come to light had not a transcript been smuggled out and conveyed to the West. As it reveals, various self-righteous Soviet *bourgeois* were ready to stand up in court and condemn Brodsky's way of life on the basis of hearsay—a parade of anti-intellectual prejudice which ended with the poet's sentence to five years' forced labour on a remote state farm in northern Russia.

In addition to anti-intellectual bias, Brodsky's trial also struck an occasional anti-Semitic note—a reminder that anti-Semitism had been a common seasoning to political persecutions during Stalin's last years. There were many other indications of the same trend in the Khrushchev era. In October 1961, for example, a certain Peshersky, a leader of the Leningrad Jewish community, was put on trial with two associates. Since Stalin's death he had been pressing for concessions to the Leningrad Jewish community, such as permission to reopen the Leningrad synagogue and to maintain kosher butcher shops. He was sentenced to twelve years' imprisonment as an agent of a foreign power.[28]

In the late Khrushchev era the KGB's activities increased after the death penalty had been extended to cover a wide range of crimes, by no means all political, which had hitherto incurred lesser punishments. After a three-year period of suspension, capital punishment had been reintroduced in 1950 for treason and espionage, and had then been extended, in 1954, to cover murder under aggravating circumstances. The new legal code of 1958 prescribed the death penalty for sabotage and acts of terrorism in addition to the above, and a further extension occurred in 1961, when large-scale embezzlement of State or public property, forgery and counterfeiting of currency, and also currency speculation, became capital crimes. In 1962 attempted murder of a militiaman (ordinary, non-political policeman) or member of the newly founded corps of vigilantes *(druzhinniki)* was added, as was rape under aggravating circumstances and the acceptance of bribes by officials. That death sentences were widely imposed for economic crimes was revealed by brief announcements in the press listing those shot for committing these offences—over 300 in all up to October 1964. Even the illegal manufacture of such fripperies as hair-ribbons and lipstick brought certain offenders before the firing squad, and a study of the surnames of those executed for misdeeds of this kind shows some thirty per cent of them as apparently Jewish, whereas the proportion of Jews within the Soviet population as a whole is only one-and-a-half per cent.[29] Despite the non-political character of these economic offences, the KGB was employed to investigate them, perhaps in order to increase the deterrent effect.

In one or two especially notorious cases individuals accused of economic offences received short prison sentences, but were later brought back to court, retried and shot. One Yan Rokotov was fetched out of prison where he was serving a sentence for currency offences, retried and executed for acts which he had committed before the extension of the death penalty to cover his crime. In another, equally unsavoury case—that of Shakerman and Roifman, sentenced to short prison terms for bribing officials in 1963—a retrial was also ordered, and they too were shot. This affair reveals keen rivalry between the KGB, exclusively authorised to investigate economic crime in 1961, and the newly established MOOP (Ministry for the Protection of Public Order, successor to the now —temporarily—disbanded MVD), which was granted parallel powers of investigation in the same field by a decree of April 1963. The point here is that the original investigation of Shakerman and Roifman had been conducted by MOOP, whereupon the ruffled KGB intervened with a further investigation, established a higher degree of guilt, and enforced the death sentence on the accused, who thus fell victims to a bureaucratic feud.[30]

Certain cases involving foreign citizens form a particularly fascinating aspect of KGB work during the Shelepin-Semichastny period, not least because of the occasional use made of the security machine at home to thwart Khrushchev's initiatives on foreign soil. On at least three occasions the First Secretary's policy of seeking a *détente* with the USA was attacked by or through his police. In autumn 1959, when Khrushchev was fraternising with President Eisenhower at Camp David, Shelepin's men arrested and expelled Mr Russell A. Langelle, a member of the American embassy in Moscow, the calls for vigilance sounded in the press being 'so out of keeping with the diplomatic atmosphere of the moment that the timing cannot be regarded as accidental'.[31] A similar episode occurred in October 1963, when a well-known American specialist in Soviet affairs, Professor F. C. Barghoorn of Yale University, was arrested and held on charges of espionage, as was announced on 12 November. The affair seemed destined to wreck Soviet-American cultural intercourse, but suddenly collapsed a few days later when Mr Barghoorn was released and expelled from the USSR after strong personal intervention by President Kennedy (who was assassinated shortly afterwards). Similarly, on· 28 September 1964, fifteen plain-clothes agents burst into a hotel room in Khabarovsk occupied by three American military attachés and a British colleague, searched their baggage and confiscated their travel notes—probably one more attempt to disrupt the American-Soviet relationship fostered by Khrushchev. Yet again, in September 1964, a bizarre attempt was made to disrupt a *rapprochement* with Bonn now sought by Khrushchev. Herr Schwirkmann, a West German diplomat, was attacked with some toxic gas while attending a church service at Zagorsk near Moscow. For this episode, presumably staged by a KGB operative, the Khrushchev government offered profuse apology to the West Germans—somewhat late in the day, for by now Khrushchev himself had only a few weeks of power to run.

Two earlier and better-known affairs, each involving the trial of a foreigner, had already seriously damaged Khrushchev's vacillating prestige. Neither case had been originally provoked by the KGB, but the KGB managed to exploit both in order to rescue a Soviet spy imprisoned abroad by effecting an exchange. Thus the KGB of Shelepin and Semichastny re-established a reputation for 'looking after its own' which reminds one of the OGPU's handling of the Wolscht-Kindermann affair of 1925 and foreshadowed other exchanges, including the Brooke-Krogers barter of 1969.

The first of these episodes began on 1 May 1960, when Francis Gary Powers, pilot of an American U2 reconnaissance plane, was shot down over Soviet territory near Sverdlovsk. Tried in Moscow and sentenced to ten years' imprisonment, he was held in the notorious prison at Vladimir about a hundred miles east of the capital. A detailed report on his conditions of detention has recently been furnished by a more obscure fellow-prisoner of the period, Anatoly Marchenko. According to Marchenko, basing himself on the prison 'grape-vine', the American pilot was accorded exceptional privileges at Vladimir, being exempted from the usual head-shaving and permitted to wear his own clothes. Powers was confined with a certain specially trained English-speaking stool-pigeon—a Balt whose name was not known and who had been promised (probably falsely, as it turned out) his own liberty immediately after his cell-mate's release if he should succeed in fostering Powers's ignorance of the appalling conditions obtaining in the Vladimir jail, as also in the USSR as a whole.[32] Powers was later exchanged for the Soviet Colonel Rudolf Abel—a more dangerous and experienced, albeit earthbound, intelligence operative serving a prison sentence in the USA. On the special treatment sometimes accorded to foreign nationals under Soviet detention, Mr Gerald Brooke provides confirmation. He writes that throughout his own imprisonment in Vladimir and Mordovia he was shielded by his British citizenship and restricted in his contacts with Soviet prisoners.[33]

In late 1962 Khrushchev's prestige suffered a further blow with the arrest by the KGB of Oleg Penkovsky, Colonel in the rival GRU, who had for nearly two years been secretly supplying the West with valuable and detailed information on Soviet military and political affairs. Mr Greville Wynne, Penkovsky's English contact and courier, was arrested in Budapest shortly afterwards and taken to the Lubyanka in Moscow. The posthumously published *Penkovsky Papers* are a most important source on KGB procedures in general, while Wynne's book, *The Man from Moscow*, is revealing on the technique employed in this particular case. Perhaps because a rival Soviet intelligence outfit was involved, the KGB handled the affair with especial venom. While Wynne enjoyed few of the privileges accorded to Powers, being beaten, starved and otherwise terrorised in order to extract confessions both before and after his trial, Penkovsky as chief accused suffered far more severely. But though he was reduced to making abject confession in court, he yet contrived to hold back certain information implicating Wynne, and it is difficult to read Wynne's book without feeling that both men showed a high degree of physical and moral courage throughout their ordeal. On the trial itself, which began on 7 May 1963, Wynne provides fascinating detail. His account is particularly valuable since it confirms the use on such occasions of a detailed word-for-word text—a bulky typescript prepared in advance of the court hearing and frequently rehearsed until the authorities were satisfied that it could be performed without hitch.[34] Unable to learn the whole of his extensive lines by heart, Wynne was permitted to read out his answers, but his libretto was placed on a concealed ledge in front of him and he had to wear a headphone with specially shortened leads which prevented him from raising his head. These arrangements obliged him to intone his recitative in such a way that none of the mixed public (who included Mrs Wynne and some journalists besides a *claque* of 'Moscow workers' representatives')[35] could tell that every word had been scripted in advance. When sentence was pronounced Wynne received a term of eight years' imprisonment, while Penkovsky was condemned to death. They were not the only victims, for the affair ended the career of the intelligence and security veteran Serov. He was dismissed as head of GRU in February or March 1964—as is hardly surprising, for Penkovsky had been to some extent his personal protégé. Certain military dimissals also occurred. From the general débâcle the KGB extracted one small advantage when arrangements were made with the British authorities to exchange Wynne for the imprisoned Soviet spy known as Gordon Lonsdale on 22 April 1964.

After the Twenty-Second Party Congress of 1961 Khrushchev persisted throughout the following year with attempts to compromise rival leaders as neo-Stalinists and thereby improve his own position. On 4 April 1962 a decree cancelled decorations granted to 700 NKVD officers and dating back to March 1944, the likelihood being that these were honours bestowed for participation in the mass deportation of Chechens, Crimean Tatars and other uprooted peoples. Among those now disgraced was the prime deporter (and also recent head of the KGB) Ivan Serov. In autumn of the same year Khrushchev received Bukharin's widow and told her that her husband had been exonerated from the charges which had led to his execution in 1938—a sign that extensive rehabilitations of Stalin's leading victims were now contemplated. Then, in late November 1962, the monthly literary magazine *Novy mir*, celebrated as the organ of liberal-minded writers, brought out Alexander Solzhenitsyn's short novel *One Day in the Life of Ivan Denisovich*, which vividly describes everyday existence in a Stalinist concentration camp. The novel caused a tremendous shock, for though the facts which it 'revealed' were a matter of common knowledge and experience, this was the first occasion on which any legally permitted Soviet publication had set them down in black and white. The open secret betrayed by Solzhenitsyn was simply that Stalin's terror had encompassed the Soviet population as a whole—and not merely (as Khrushchev and others had previously implied) Communist Party members. Nor was Solzhenitsyn's the only literary barb now aimed at Khrushchev's hard-line enemies. 21 October 1962 also saw the publication in *Pravda* of Yevtushenko's poem *Stalin's Heirs*, in which the suggestion was made that powerful residual neo-Stalinists were now biding their time until they could assert themselves once again. Incidental hints—references to the 'pruning of rosebushes' and to 'heart attacks'—show that the poem was aimed at two particular objects of Khrushchev's hostility: the disgraced Bulganin and the Leningrad First Secretary Frol Kozlov (a hard-liner, and for a time Khrushchev's heir-apparent).

Both Yevtushenko's poem and Solzhenitsyn's novel had been

published on Khrushchev's strong personal insistence.[36] For their part, liberal-minded writers and editors were glad to profit from his pseudo-liberal manoeuvres, though there was of course nothing which most of these temporary allies less desired than to assist Khrushchev's assumption of Stalinist powers by abetting him in his attempts to simulate anti-Stalinist postures. As the campaign proceeded, Solzhenitsyn became an ever more potent symbol of opposition to police rule. He was permitted to bring out one or two politically innocent stories after *One Day*, but such major works as his novels *The First Circle* and *Cancer Ward* were blocked, though they were eventually published abroad. In 1964 an attempt to have the Lenin Prize for Literature awarded to Solzhenitsyn was also frustrated. However, these various manoeuvres had at least brought from obscurity one of the most noteworthy Soviet prose writers since the Revolution, who is also the most effective fictional chronicler of the horrors of the Soviet police State—above all in *The First Circle*. This describes a peculiar kind of privileged Stalinist prison. A research establishment devoted to improving police techniques, it is engaged on investigating voice peculiarities to enable the MGB to trace wanted political criminals through records of their personal speech-prints as made on 'bugged' telephone calls. The novel also gives a panorama of Stalinist police procedures in general. Among its most revealing episodes is the induction of an arrested diplomat into the Lubyanka, as also an imaginary interview between Stalin and the MGB Minister (later executed) Abakumov, and an imaginary visit by Mrs Eleanor Roosevelt to the Butyrki prison—specially spruced up and given a wholly spurious air of decorum for the occasion.

Perhaps Khrushchev would have liked to see this powerful novel published by *Novy mir*, in which case it might possibly have assisted him to put down Suslov and other remaining rivals—the dangerous Kozlov having been removed as a power-contender in April 1963 by a further heart attack. However, this was not to be. On 13 October 1964 Khrushchev's political career was suddenly destroyed at a session of the Party Presidium followed by a hastily convened Central Committee meeting on the following day at which he 'asked to be relieved' of his highest offices—those of First Party Secretary, Presidium-member and Premier—on grounds of advanced age and poor health. He was succeeded as First Party Secretary by Brezhnev, and as Premier by Kosygin. Though many details remain obscure, the development of the *coup* has been convincingly reconstructed by M. Michel Tatu, correspondent of the Paris newspaper *Le Monde*. From this and other accounts it appears that the volatile First Secretary had shown himself increasingly brash and light-headed during 1964. Carelessly absenting himself from the seat of power on various travels during a great part of the year, he had also contrived to antagonise a wide variety of pressure groups within the Soviet establishment—the planners, the heavy industry lobby, the agricultural experts, the diplomats. Above all, he was alarming his fellow Presidium-members by seeking to initiate measures not previously cleared by that supreme policy-making body, and there were indications that he still sought to establish himself as absolute dictator with Stalinist powers. It was under these circumstances that Michael Suslov, Presidium-member and leading Party ideologist, mounted the plot to oust Khrushchev while he was on holiday in Sochi. On 13 October Khrushchev flew or was flown back to Moscow under heavy police escort, and was reputedly met at the airport by Shelepin and Semichastny. To what extent the present and the former KGB Chairman were now openly operating as Khrushchev's jailers, or masquerading as his protectors, remains obscure. It was in the evening that the key meeting of the Presidium took place, and Suslov violently denounced the First Secretary. Meanwhile arrangements had been made to prevent Khrushchev from repeating his performance of June 1957—when he had successfully appealed to the Central Committee over the heads of a hostile majority in the Presidium. The Central Committee of 14 October 1964 proved solidly opposed to Khrushchev, who became a political corpse on that day. The *coup* can only have been accomplished with the connivance, if not the active help, of Semichastny's KGB—an assumption confirmed by the ensuing promotion of Semichastny to the Central Committee and of Shelepin to the Presidium.

13
The KGB after Khrushchev
1964–1970

During more than half a decade since Khrushchev's fall the partnership of Brezhnev and Kosygin, as respective heads of Party and government, proved stable, thus confounding prophets who had foretold upheavals in the leadership comparable to those which followed the deaths of Lenin and Stalin. From the beginning Khrushchev's heirs cultivated a style of rule less flamboyant, to put it mildly, than that of their immediate precursor. Khrushchev had been, in theatrical terms, a music-hall comic to whom all his colleagues, great and small, were a succession of 'straight-feed men'. Brezhnev, by contrast, was a natural heavy—and yet revealed considerable flexibility behind the scenes, effectively asserting his authority without causing major upsets. During the eighteen months following his appointment as First Secretary of the Party Central Committee he advanced from the apparent status of a stop-gap or caretaker number one until, at the Twenty-Third Party Congress of March–April 1966, he received the official title of Secretary-General, which superseded his previous title of First Secretary. Since the only previous holder of the Secretary-Generalship had been Stalin, this personal success also signalised a triumph for the policy identified with Brezhnev—that of cautious restalinisation. At the same Party Congress, incidentally, the Presidium of the Central Committee readopted the earlier title of Politburo, thus reverting to the practice of Lenin's and most of Stalin's reign.

By this time Brezhnev had firmly relegated Kosygin to second place in public standing, while preventing either Podgorny or Suslov, two other strong potential rivals, from emerging as heir apparent. Meanwhile the ambition and keen political instincts of the *jeune premier*, Shelepin made him a potentially greater danger, and correspondingly greater effort was accordingly made to put him in his place. Shelepin's rise and decline represented the nearest approach to any dramatic peripeteia among the top leaders during the immediate post-Khrushchev years.

As already indicated, Khrushchev's fall brought an immediate major gain to Shelepin, who was promoted full Presidium-member (without any interval as candidate) in November 1964, while his protégé as head of the KGB, Chairman Semichastny, sprang to full membership of the Party Central Committee. Shelepin also retained the secretaryship of the Party Central Committee (but as one of Brezhnev's juniors) to which he had been appointed on relinquishing titular control of the KGB to Semichastny in 1961. He held the post of Deputy Premier too, and was Chairman of the Party-State Control Committee, a vast body called into being by Khrushchev in 1962 in order to watch over all Party and government agencies, though these were already subject to intensive supervision of various kinds. An extreme instance of a superimposed and interlaced Soviet control nexus, Shelepin's new bureaucratic structure came to include some five million voluntary 'snoopers', and was slotted into a machine in which all important government officials were already Party members, while both Party and government were covertly watched by a KGB itself subject to Party and State supervision. At no time did Shelepin fully exploit the virtually unlimited powers of interference theoretically vested in him as head of the new Control Committee, but there was no telling when he might begin to do so. Moreover, there were those who remembered the early Soviet period, when the closest parallel to Shelepin's Committee had been the Workers' and Peasants' Inspection *(Rabkrin)*. Dissolved in 1934, this had been headed in the early 1920s by Stalin and adroitly levered by him during his rise to supreme power.

The combination of Shelepin's many offices with youth and ingenuity seemed to mark him out as the coming man, perhaps even the coming Stalin, and he was widely tipped as a successor to Brezhnev both in Moscow and abroad. No doubt the seeming pachyderm Brezhnev was well aware of such dangers, but in any case the years 1964–7 saw the gradual disarming of Shelepin and the removal of the Shelepin-Semichastny team from control of the KGB. The erosion of Shelepin's position began at the very moment of his greatest triumph when, in the announcement of his appointment to the Party Presidium in November 1964, another newly appointed Presidium-member, Shelest, received preferential listing out of alphabetical order. There was also, at this time, an ostentatious absence of appropriately senior colleagues among those who saw Shelepin off at airports and welcomed him on his return from official missions. In April 1965 Shelepin presided at a police and judicial conference, which indicates that he still retained security responsibilities, but it was the last occasion on which such a sign was forthcoming. In December of the same year his Party-State Control Committee went the way of various other typically Khrushchevite institutions, being disbanded in effect. At the same time Shelepin also lost his deputy premiership, though still combining the extensive powers of Presidium-member and Central Committee Secretary. At the Twenty-Third Party Congress of March–April 1966, Shelepin was listed only seventh among Politburo-members, besides which he was now charged with duties in the sphere of light industry and trade—no proper field of operation for an aspiring autocrat. A further set-back occurred in June of the following year, when he was appointed Chairman of the Central Trade Union Council, a deadly backwater to any power-seeker of his seniority, apart from which it also involved him in the loss of his Central Committee secretaryship. On 18 May 1967, the final disappearance of Shelepin's influence over the political police had been signalised by the transfer of his protégé Semichastny to the ludicrous post of First Deputy Premier of the Ukraine, the KGB chairmanship being taken over by Yury Andropov.

Once again the political police had been disarmed by the appointment of an official with no known police background to head its organisation. Andropov was ten years older than Semichastny. He had been Soviet ambassador to Hungary at the time of the Hungarian uprising of 1956, after which his work had been within the central Party apparatus. In 1962 he had been appointed a Central Committee Secretary, taking charge of relations between the Soviet Party and Communist Parties of the Eastern Bloc. On appointment to the KGB in 1967 Andropov lost his secretaryship of the Party Central Committee. He was compensated by elevation to membership, but only candidate membership, of the Politburo, thus becoming the first head of political police to sit on the Presidium/Politburo since Beria.

Late 1964 saw an important change in the public posture of the KGB as the organisation embarked on an intensified publicity campaign designed to glorify exploits hitherto shrouded in secrecy. This involved advertising the deeds of Soviet spies who had so far rated as unspies—as when, for instance, the British defectors Burgess and Maclean had been paraded (in 1956) to proclaim in all solemnity that they had never engaged in espionage.[1] Now, twenty years after his execution by the Japanese, the Soviet master-spy Richard Sorge had his cover blown by the Soviet advertising machine and was posthumously created a Hero of the Soviet Union for his wartime and pre-war spying exploits. He also had a tanker and a Moscow street named after him, and appeared full-face on a new four-copeck stamp specially designed in his honour.[2] Thus, from having no spies at all, the Soviet Union suddenly turned out to have the best spies in the world, no doubt as part of a campaign to encourage Soviet agents still in the field after their morale had been shattered by the revelation of Penkovsky's revelations, as also by the arrest of their colleagues George Blake and Gordon Lonsdale in England, and of Stif Wennerström in Sweden. Another Soviet hero-spy was acknowledged when Chairman Semichastny wrote in honour of Colonel Rudolf Abel in *Pravda* of 7 May 1965—the first occasion on which Abel was officially honoured, an exchange having been effected between him and the American U2 pilot Gary Powers in 1961.

Another exchanged Soviet spy, Colonel Konon Molody alias Gordon Lonsdale, published a book in English, *Spy*, about his professional activities after an unsuccessful attempt had allegedly been made to trade two British-held Soviet spies, the Krogers, for a promise to withhold these inflammatory memoirs from publication.[3] Lonsdale's crudely propagandistic saga has a certain importance as the first example of such material emanating from an avowed Soviet agent. That the entire text has been KGB-vetted may be inferred, and it need hardly be said that the material must be treated with caution. The same is true of *My Silent War*, the more polished memoirs of the formerly English Soviet intelligence agent Kim Philby. These received publication in 1968, five years after the author had obtained political asylum in the USSR and Soviet citizenship, as announced in *Izvestiya* on 31 July 1963. On 19 December 1967 the same newspaper published an article 'Hello, Comrade Philby', quoting the veteran master-spy in praise of Dzerzhinsky as a 'great humanist'—the formula commonly applied in Soviet parlance to successful sponsors of mass killings.

Philby's views on his own former chiefs Menzhinsky, Yagoda, Yezhov and Beria are unfortunately not available. They would have been particularly valuable in the light of certain circumstances outlined in earlier chapters, for it was at about the time of Philby's original recruitment that his ultimate superior Yagoda was, according to official Soviet record, engaged in murdering or attempting to murder Menzhinsky and Yezhov, his immediate precursor and follower as security police overlords. Meanwhile the future police chief Beria was (again according to official doctrine) secretly in league with Britain—the very country which his underling, the still youthful Philby, had so blithely congratulated himself on betraying. In this context Philby's comment on his reason for enlisting as a Soviet intelligence agent ('One does not look twice at an offer of enrolment in an élite force') [4] seems to carry a certain pungency all of its own.

Be that as it may, the main purpose of the new publicity given to Philby and to the KGB in general was to demoralise and intimidate the non-Communist world by creating the impression of an 'ubiquitous KGB man . . . dedicated servant of an international government', who 'moves like a superior being, irresistible, among the ill-guarded, guilty secrets of the divided West'. [5] In this campaign by the KGB various 'capitalist' newspapers showed an eagerness to co-operate which appeared to confirm Soviet claims of western decadence in an alarming degree.

The *Izvestiya* interview with Philby formed only a small part of elaborate celebrations staged on and about 20 December 1967 in honour of the Soviet security machine's fiftieth birthday. Along with eminent spies, domestic agents too were honoured, including four elderly Chekists—survivors of the anti-Leninist White Terror, as also of the Stalinist great terror in which so many of their colleagues had fallen. Probably selected for their benevolent facial expressions, these former hunters of Bruce Lockhart and Boris Savinkov beam down like elderly uncles from the pages of *Pravda* as if in assurance that all is for the best in the best of all possible worlds. So much for the small fry. On a more august level the crowning point of the KGB's jubilee was a speech by Chairman Andropov in the presence of Politburo-members, including Shelepin and other notabilities. Shelepin received no personal tribute in Andropov's speech. Nor was any other head of the security machine so honoured, excepting only the organisation's first two chiefs: Dzerzhinsky and Menzhinsky, the saintly and the unobtrusive Pole. Thus Yagoda, Yezhov and Beria were passed over in silence apart from an oracular reference to political adventurers in the NKVD who had once committed unlawful acts, attempting to remove the State security agencies from the Party's control. In stressing the primacy of Party over police, Andropov's statement was especially typical of post-Beria etiquette for KGB Chairmen. Characteristic too was the devotional language in which Andropov referred to the typical Chekist as 'a man of pure honesty and enormous personal courage, implacable in the struggle against enemies, stern in the name of duty, humane and prepared to sacrifice himself for the people's cause'.[6] Such was the post-Stalinist projection of the KGB officer—that of a jovial padre with a core of steel, an image reinforced by the numerous hagiographies of the butcher Dzerzhinsky which began to flood the presses.

On 10–14 February 1966 two young writers, Yuly Daniel and Andrew Sinyavsky, stood trial in Moscow—an important landmark in the evolution of the post-Khrushchevite police. Despite manifold persecutions inflicted on hundreds of Soviet authors in the past, particularly during the *Yezhovshchina*, this affair broke new ground as 'the first time in the history of the Soviet Union [when] writers had been put on trial *for what they had written*'.[7] The works concerned had been smuggled abroad from 1956 onwards, being published in Russian, English and other languages under the pseudonyms Nikolai Arzhak (Daniel) and Abram Tertz (Sinyavsky). To bring out a work under a pseudonym, or in a foreign country, is not an offence in Soviet law, for which reason no charge could be brought on such grounds. It was, however, possible to build a sort of case against the two authors under Article 70 of the Criminal Code of the RSFSR, which covers 'agitation or propaganda carried out with the purpose of subverting or weakening the Soviet regime', and also 'the dissemination ... of slanderous inventions defamatory to the Soviet political and social system'.

In cases held to involve national security, of which the Daniel-Sinyavsky affair was one, preliminary investigation is conducted by the KGB—and not, as in other cases, by the Procurator-Generalship. Thus it came about that the defendants, arrested in mid-September 1965, were processed by the security police for five months before a trial camouflaged as public. It was regularly reported in the Moscow press, but in heavily slanted form. All foreign observers, even non-Soviet Communists, were excluded from a courtroom packed with the usual *claque* of conformists, though the defendants' wives were also present. The arrangements were botched to the extent that demonstrations against the trial smouldered outside the building, while inside some unknown person was contriving to take a detailed transcript of the proceedings. This, in turn, was leaked abroad in the wake of Tertz's and Arzhak's own stories.[8] As the document reveals, both defendants refused to plead guilty. They thus presented the producers with the problem of a trial unscripted and unrehearsed—all the more embarrassing since the accused had already suffered trial and sentence in the national press, where they had been condemned as imperialist agents and the like. In these articles, as in the courtroom proceedings which followed, odd sentences torn out of context from imaginative writings were quoted as evidence for the prosecution, the assumption being made that any remark put into the mouth of a fictional character could legitimately be taken as an expression of the author's own views. In the case of ironic fantasists, such as Daniel and Sinyavsky, this led to particularly grotesque results, and an additional ironical twist was supplied by Sinyavsky's authorship of *The Trial Begins*, which had predicted, in effect, his own appearance in court some ten years previously.

The Sinyavsky-Daniel trial provoked a storm of protest in non-Communist countries, where prominent Party members, John Gollan, Louis Aragon and others, contributed denunciations of an ill-managed spectacle which had publicised indecorous features of Soviet police and judicial practice to the world. Both Soviet law and the methods of its enforcement seemed equally discredited, and the question arises as to how far the prosecution was inspired by official vindictiveness. Certainly neither author had spared the organisation which forms the subject of the present study. Sinyavsky's *The Trial Begins* is an ironical portrayal of the late Stalinist police state, allusions to which had become tactless in the early Brezhnevite era. Daniel's story *Hands* portrays a veteran Chekist afflicted with uncontrollable trembling ever since he had once attempted to shoot a group of priests in the Civil War—only to witness their apparently miraculous survival, in fact due to the action of his own fellow-policemen in secretly loading his gun with blank ammunition by way of a joke. To Daniel's pen also belongs the fantasy *This is Moscow Speaking*, which propounds the theme of an official Murder Day when Soviet citizens are encouraged to kill each other. By presenting this as a call to mass political terrorism, and by other, similar superimposed courtroom fantasies the prosecution secured severe sentences of imprisonment (seven for Sinyavsky, five for Daniel) and the condemned men were removed to the Potma concentration camp empire two hundred miles south-east of Moscow.

This trial of two authors deemed illicit itself produced a spate of further illicit literature, less in the form of fiction than of documents protesting against and arising from the Daniel-Sinyavsky case. Then these documents provoked further cases, and thus further protest documents, in a chain reaction which continued for several years. Much of this material consisted of unanswered open letters addressed to the various Soviet legal, governmental, Party and police authorities. In detailed argument the protesters listed again and again the many headings under which Soviet authority had infringed its own legal code, as also the Constitution of the USSR and the United Nations' Declaration of Human Rights. Widely duplicated and circulated, these protest documents found their way abroad in large quantity. Among them were contributions from Yuly Daniel's wife Larisa, and also from Mrs Maya Sinyavsky. They described how their apartments were searched, their friends harassed, their conversations 'bugged', and their letters opened by the KGB, while KGB officers also intimidated them in personal confrontations.

After pronouncement of sentence on Daniel and Sinyavsky a group of sixty-three Moscow writers addressed a petition for the release of the two men to the Presidiums of the Twenty-Third Party Congress and of the USSR and RSFSR Supreme Soviets. Telegrams and petitions on their behalf were also signed by various senior members of Moscow University and of the Soviet Institute of Linguistics. On a more general topic twenty-seven writers, scientists and artists signed a petition to the Party Central Committee on the eve of the Twenty-Third Party Congress (of 29 March to 8 April 1966), warning against the danger of any further rehabilitation of Stalin. A leading Soviet scientist, Academician Andrew Sakharov (sometimes called 'father of the Soviet H-bomb'), circulated a document attacking the techniques of police dictatorship and other features of Soviet rule.

Thus a Soviet protest industry was born out of the Sinyavsky-Daniel trial, and the KGB found itself obliged to deal with an embryonic civil rights movement. Though authority appeared to hold all the weapons in this struggle, steps were taken to strengthen its hand still further by enacting certain additions to Article 190 of the RSFSR Criminal Code, which serves as a pattern for legislation in the other republics. From September 1966 onwards penalties of up to three years' imprisonment could be imposed for disseminating 'fabrications discrediting the Soviet State and social order', and for the organisation of 'group activities which violate public order'. Petition-writers, authors of illicit documents, street demonstrators—all were further menaced by this new law.

January 1967 saw the arrest of Alexander Ginsburg, compiler of a *White Book* on the Daniel-Sinyavsky trial, and also of Yury Galanskov and others who had helped to publish the clandestine journal *Phoenix-66*. The arrest provoked a public demonstration by some fifty young people in Moscow. This was broken up by the police, and various participants were tried during the following months, including V. Khaustov and V. Bukovsky, who each received three years' hard labour under the September 1966 amendment quoted above. On 8–12 January 1968 the trial of Ginsburg and Galanskov was at last held, after they had been kept in custody for twelve months. Accused of contacts with the NTS, Galanskov was condemned to seven years' hard labour, while Ginsburg received a five year sentence, but the chain reaction of protests still continued and further illicit documents continued to flow across the Soviet frontier. The Ginsburg-Galanskov trial evoked a protesting manifesto signed by Larisa Daniel, and also by Paul Litvinov—grandson of the former Commissar for Foreign Affairs Maxim Litvinov. They complained that defence counsel had been officially hampered, and that witnesses for the defence had been ejected from court unheard, to the laughs, jeers and howls of 'specially selected people—officials of the KGB and volunteer militia' who had been charged with creating the simulacrum of an open public trial.[9] In accordance with the developing relay system whereby the protestors against one trial become the defendants at a later trial, Paul Litvinov and Larisa Daniel found themselves in the dock, as reported by *Tass* on 9 October 1968—for making public protest in Moscow's Red Square against the Soviet invasion of Czechoslovakia by 'shouting and other actions insulting to the dignity of the Soviet people'. They were sentenced to five and four years' exile respectively.

The above-mentioned trials of Russian intellectuals were the outcome of agitation in favour of intellectual, legal and political freedoms. Meanwhile other, parallel campaigns were also being waged as growing resentment of religious persecution took in masses of comparatively uneducated people, while on the periphery of the Soviet Empire resistance to Russian cultural and political domination also found an outlet in demonstrations, petitions and agitation. Against these religious and national movements the KGB used weapons similar to those employed against dissident intellectuals. Wavering protesters were discouraged by threats and persuasion, a process which slowly winnowed out the hard-core dissidents, who were then prosecuted in carefully rigged, allegedly public trials. There was, however, little evidence of any serious attempt by the KGB to stem the flow of protest literature entirely, for it continued to reach the West in quantity, with the result that extensive information on current police practices became available. The material contained repeated references to the threatening of witnesses by the KGB, to the packing of courts with pre-selected stooges, to the 'bugging' of private apartments, to secret searches of personal belongings and to the surveillance of individuals—sometimes clandestine and sometimes openly conducted as a means of intimidation. The KGB also made a practice of securing the dismissal of undesirables from their place of work by bringing pressure on employers, besides which it was able to imprison dissidents without trial in mental hospitals manned by demon doctors such as have been a useful adjunct to the political police ever since the days of Frunze's death in 1925.

The Serbsky Institute of Forensic Psychiatry in Moscow appears to be a favourite place of detention, and the later trial-victims Bukovsky, Galanskov and Ginsburg are among those who have passed through its portals. There is also evidence suggesting that certain mental hospitals may contain special police wings outside the control of the Ministry of Health.[10] This practice of branding literary-political deviants as lunatics goes back at least as far as Tsar Nicholas I and Peter Chaadayev. In Soviet times it had already flourished during the Khrushchev era, when a number of disaffected writers were so treated. They included Alexander Yesenin-Volpin (son of the poet Sergey Yesenin and himself both a poet and a mathematician) and Michael Naritsa, author of a little-known, thinly fictionalised account, smuggled abroad, of his sufferings under Soviet rule. Another reluctant mental patient was the critic and novelist Valery Tarsis—immured in a Moscow psychiatric ward in August 1962 just before his book *The Bluebottle* was published abroad in English translation under the pseudonym Ivan Valeriy. Released in March 1963, he proceeded to compound his indiscipline still further by exporting another novel, *Ward 7*, in which he describes his own experiences under psychiatric detention. According to suggestions put forward in what is admittedly an imaginative work, the number of sane persons thus detained may have been fairly large—Tarsis speaks of only one genuine madman in a section containing 150 men.[11] A non-fictionalised report on the imprisonment of political offenders in mental hospitals, written by Tarsis in emigration and at the request of Amnesty, had unfortunately not been published at the time of writing.[12]

As the result of a surprise decision made or implemented by the KGB in early 1966, Mr Tarsis received permission to leave the Soviet Union at the very time when his colleagues Daniel and Sinyavsky were undergoing trial and sentence for implying criticism of authority comparatively restrained by the standards of *Ward 7*. Deprived of his Soviet citizenship, Tarsis appears to have flourished in exile, and the question arises as to why so outspoken a dissenter should have been treated so leniently. Possibly the KGB aimed at a liberal gesture calculated to distract attention from the Daniel-Sinyavsky trial and thus further bemuse the credulous foreigner. Alternatively, the security authorities may possibly have miscalculated, wrongly believing Tarsis to be in a condition of mental disequilibrium likely to discredit him, and all other Soviet intellectual dissidents, by provoking over-excitable behaviour on foreign soil.

Whatever the reason for expelling Tarsis may have been, the episode illustrates a fairly prevalent feature of recent KGB procedure—a tendency to postpone extreme measures of repression. This may be illustrated from the case of Larisa Daniel. Threatened by the KGB at the time of her husband's arrest, she persisted in her open attempts to influence Soviet authority over a period of nearly three years before her own arrest and trial in autumn 1968. Other notable long-term KGB-baiters have been Paul Litvinov, mentioned above and Major-General Grigorenko. Both were allowed an extended run of protest before their eventual arrest—Litvinov's coinciding with Larisa Daniel's, while Grigorenko's occurred in May 1969 after a long record of activity on behalf of victims of Soviet oppression of many different brands, including the Czechoslovaks invaded in August 1968, and the Crimean Tatars still (at the time of writing) exiled to Central Asia.

That these and other protesters have shown extreme courage and persistence under pressure hardly needs emphasising, but one must also remember that to the KGB they are obstinate trouble-makers who could easily have been put down earlier. Why this apparent lack of initiative on the part of the security police? One among various possible explanations—a desire to avoid unpopularity at home—is unlikely to have been a major factor. It is more probable that the KGB has been practising the traditional police device of leaving known offenders at large until a sizeable number of sympathisers have identified themselves. The question of foreign public opinion also arises. To claim that KGB policymakers respect public opinion, whether foreign or domestic, might be to mis-state their attitude. It remains true, however, that Soviet authority continues to cultivate on alien soil the myth that the Soviet Union is constantly moving in the direction of ever greater liberalisation. To this fantasy the western brain seems hopelessly prone in any case, even in the teeth of all evidence—how much the more so, therefore, when the illusion is deliberately fostered by permitting a semblance of give and take in the struggle between Soviet intellectuals and police. The staging of this peep-show costs little, and presents few real dangers to Soviet authority. This consideration may therefore be the prime cause of the relatively gentle treatment meted out to dissident intellectuals—but only until the time at last comes to spring the trap.

Meanwhile there are indications that the KGB may well have felt free to deal more peremptorily with non-intellectual malcontents, whose misfortunes possess limited publicity appeal for such western readers as cultivate an interest in Soviet affairs. Nothing, in any case, is known of the ultimate fate of the obscure citizens, including workers, who rioted at Temir Tau in Kazakhstan in 1959, at Kemerovo in Siberia in 1960 and at Novocherkassk near Rostov-on-Don in 1962. On the ill-treatment and torture of provincial religious practitioners evidence has, however, filtered through.[13] One of Grigorenko's manifestos contains horrific details on the suppression, with clubs and cannon firing some toxic fluid, of an assemblage of exiled Crimean Tatars at Chirchik in the Uzbek Republic in April 1968. This was followed by widespread arrests.[14]

Among Soviet dissidents of the Brezhnev period one in particular, Alexander Solzhenitsyn, may well have been protected at home by his reputation in foreign countries, as happened to Leo Tolstoy and Pasternak in their time. Be this as it may, the stubborn Solzhenitsyn remains a key figure on the Soviet horizon at the time of writing, having even become a 'leader of the political opposition in our country', according to one hostile fellow-scribe.[15]

On 16 May 1967 Solzhenitsyn wrote an open letter to the Fourth All-Union Writers' Congress, calling for the abolition of censorship, and also bewailing the fate of his own manuscripts on Soviet and foreign soil. He accused the KGB of stealing the text of his major novel, *The First Circle*, and of 'publishing' it themselves without his permission in a limited edition for the consumption of literary bureaucrats. According to Solzhenitsyn, the KGB also removed other literary papers dating back 15–20 years and including items not intended for publication, having traced these hidden documents by the use of bugging devices, wire-tapping and surveillance. From this archive tendentious excerpts were also published and circulated, by the police, while the early verse play, *Feast of the Conquerors*, now spurned by Solzhenitsyn himself, was paraded as his 'latest work'. Other items which he *did* hope to bring out in Soviet journals (notably his other major novel, *Cancer Ward*) continued to rate as unpublishable. According to information reaching Solzhenitsyn by telegram from the émigré Russian magazine *Grani*, the KGB itself sent a copy of *Cancer Ward* to the West in order to prevent the possibility of its publication in Russia. Solzhenitsyn has also stated that he had never sent a foreign publisher a copy of the novel. He had neither authorised its publication as legal nor granted anyone the copyright.[16] A similar case of interference is recorded by Stalin's daughter Svetlana Alliluyev. She describes how the KGB contrived to disrupt the publication of her first book, *Twenty Letters to a Friend*, after her defection to the West. Foreign publishers were flooded with copies of a variant version seized in her Moscow apartment. Certain family photographs were also stolen and released for publication abroad under the title *Stalin's Secret Albums*.[17]

From such evidence it seems that the KGB, far from combating the widespread smuggling of illicit manuscripts over the Soviet frontier, may itself have promoted or connived at this traffic. If so no student of the organisation need be unduly surprised. Ever since the days of the Okhrana the Russian political police has been accustomed to attack its opponents by joining them. In Solzhenitsyn's case the KGB's motive in disseminating his unpublished manuscripts may indeed have been a wish to compromise the author with the taint of anti-Soviet activity, thus hampering his chances of publication in a Soviet journal. Such a practice would also help to demoralise and confuse those engaged on the *bona fide* export and publication of illicit manuscripts, apart from which the possibility cannot be entirely discounted that the KGB itself may contain an element which does not entirely support the official hard line, and is prepared to turn a blind eye to the traffic in such material. Whatever the reason may be, the flow of illicit documents could presumably never have reached such dimensions in the late 1960s if the Soviet security authorities had not decided to tolerate it, and even participate in it, to a limited extent.

Among the flood of 'smuggled' documents one recurring item acquired especial significance from mid-1968 onwards: the *Chronicle of Current Events*. Successive issues of this illicit bi-monthly serial publication found their way to the West, appearing with a regularity which some legally permitted Soviet magazines might envy. The *Chronicle* supplied a detailed catalogue of police repression as it developed over the months—listing arrests and prosecutions, providing much general information on KGB methodology, and giving the full text of the various current open letters and other protest documents. One striking feature is the neutral, business-like, professional tone of the editing. Running to some 10,000 words per issue, and of progressively increasing length, the publication must surely be unique as an unofficial political police dossier—it may, indeed, be useful to the central KGB in keeping its own files up to date. One impressive feature of the *Chronicle* is the amount of devoted and skilled organisational effort evidently expended by its clandestine compilers. More, perhaps, than any other illicit publication, it helped to substantiate the thesis that the civil rights movement, as developed in the Soviet Union of the late 1960s, represented a viable and broadly based trend with good prospects for extensive future development—a point of view which the author of the present study regards with continued scepticism. Be that as it may, there can be few items in the mass of smuggled literature which a 'hard-line' KGB officer would rather liquidate than the *Chronicle of Current Events*.

Despite the KGB's apparent reluctance to undertake mass arrests and repressions in the early Brezhnev period, and despite its campaign to deflect political dissidents by threats, fatherly warnings, dismissals from jobs and the like, the contest remains a grim and humourless affair, since those who persist in protest risk a fate scarcely more enviable than that of Stalin's concentration camp victims. According to the most valuable recent evidence, today's Soviet camps for political prisoners show no improvement on those of Stalin's day—a few things are better, a few worse, and that is all.[18] This is the verdict of Anatoly Marchenko, author of *My Testimony* (1969), one of the most important illicit documents to have come out of the Soviet Union, being an account of recent concentration camp and prison conditions. The author was himself a political prisoner in 1960-6, and was rearrested on 29 July 1968. He has reputedly been retried since then on some charge arising from the publication of his book abroad.[19] In his account, as in other available descriptions, one particular abuse looms larger than all others—the continued use of semi-controlled starvation as a means of keeping the prisoners submissive and depressed. From this and other evidence it appears that the maximum daily food issue for a political prisoner contains no more than 2,400 calories, the quantity established as adequate only for a ten-year-old child, besides being deficient in vitamins and fats. For those who fail to meet the severe production norms still enforced, or who infringe prison discipline, the ration may be cut to 1,300 calories. Though rations can occasionally be supplemented by black-market trafficking with free workers possessing access to the camp, and by purchases from the camp shop, the last privilege is strictly limited and liable to withdrawal on the whim of an administration containing many old Stalinist screws and professionally vindictive in its attitude to its captives. Prisoners can win certain concessions for good conduct. Only one kind of good conduct enjoys practical recognition, however—membership of the huge secret staff of *stukachi*: informers maintained by the KGB among concentration camp prisoners, administrators and guards, as also in every other walk of Soviet life.

In their despair prisoners have resorted to fantastic procedures of self-mutilation, swallowing items of cutlery and glass, tattooing themselves with inscriptions such as 'Slave of the Communist Party of the Soviet Union' and 'Slave of Khrushchev' on forehead and cheeks and in certain cases all over the body. One man tattooed 'a present to the 23rd Congress of the CPSU' on his ear, cut it off and flung it at a warder. Another nailed himself to a stool by his scrotum. Such indiscipline only led to further repressions. Nor did the overthrow and official criticism of Khrushchev in 1964 bring the release of those who had been imprisoned for anticipating such criticism in conversations which they had believed private. Attempts to escape resulted in the prisoner being savaged by the fierce guard dogs which enjoyed a meat ration nine times greater than his own, or shot out of hand by guards entitled to a bonus for exercising such vigilance.

In spite of these horrors, Mr Marchenko may be guilty of pardonable exaggeration in equating present conditions with those enforced under Stalin. At least the severest and most lethal forms of hard labour—mining, lumbering, canal construction and the like—have given way to the manufacture of furniture, television sets and chessmen. The overall number of persons imprisoned on political charges is still obscure, though there is general agreement that it has been substantially reduced since Stalin's time. But is the total of political prisoners to be computed in thousands (as some of the illicit documents aver), or in tens, or even hundreds of thousands? One student of the subject has even calculated the 1969 concentration camp population at seven million, though that figure would also include ordinary non-political criminals.[20] Meanwhile the Soviet authorities themselves will provide no statistics and the overall total must remain as much a matter for speculation as it has been for over forty years.

In the summer of 1969 the KGB brought off yet another notable *coup* by prevailing on the British government to exchange the Krogers (Soviet spies who had received long prison sentences in Great Britain in 1961 for their part in the Portland Case) for a British lecturer in Russian, Mr Gerald Brooke, who had been condemned to five years' imprisonment in 1965 by a Moscow court for anti-Soviet agitation and propaganda. Since his release from the Soviet Union Mr Brooke has published newspaper articles describing how his arrest and trial came about.[21] At the behest of NTS, the Russian anti-Soviet organisation of which mention has been made above, he had smuggled into the Soviet Union certain material concealed in a photographic album and dressing-case. He was, accordingly, guilty as charged, though the possibility cannot be discounted that the mysterious 'George' (who had recruited him to carry this compromising material to Russia in the first place) was an *agent provocateur* acting on behalf of the KGB. Be that as it may, the KGB appears to have set itself from the start to use Brooke as a human lever to extort the release of the Krogers. As part of this campaign he was deliberately produced in emaciated condition during one of his wife's visits, and was also prevailed upon by his captors to write to some London newspapers urging the Krogers' release in exchange for his own. When these tactics failed, the prisoner was threatened with a new trial on the more serious charge of espionage. He was informed that this would be backed in court by the evidence of the formerly English KGB spy Philby (now resident in Moscow), who would testify that the NTS was in the pay of British intelligence. These newly concocted espionage activities related to conversations between Brooke and certain other prisoners in a concentration camp sick-bay at Potma. Here he was surrounded by other patients who paraded anti-Soviet views, but who appear from his own description to have been *agents provocateurs*, even though he himself apparently did not recognise them as such. Had the Soviet authorities persisted with the new charge of espionage, Mr Brooke could conceivably have faced a death sentence. In the end, however, the British government capitulated to this long sequence of threats from the KGB by agreeing to release the Krogers. Right or wrong, the decision would appear to put all British visitors to the Soviet Union at hazard during the foreseeable future. So far as the history of the KGB is concerned, the episode is an instructive illustration of the extravagant lengths to which the organisation will go to rescue its agents from foreign imprisonment.

To this and other barter deals across the frontier, as instanced above, further cases may also be added. American citizens were involved in the case of the RB-47 plane, the case of the 'Baltsch' spy ring and the case of the student Marvin W. Makinen. Exchanges involving Germany included the Pripolzev affair, as also the cases of Alfred Frenzel, of Heinz Felfe, of the corpse of Gudrun Heidel and of Wilhelm Lehmann, while other body-swapping deals have involved France and South Africa.[22] A common factor in most of these deals has been the ability of the KGB to impose its will on foreign governments by arresting their nationals during visits to the Soviet Union, trying them on trumped up or artificially inflated charges, ill-treating them in captivity and then offering their release in return for some experienced and highly trained Soviet career spy. As a form of semi-public kidnapping for ransom, the policy has proved its worth again and again.

Valuable further confirmation of certain features in KGB methodology is provided by a recent defector to the West, Anatoly Kuznetsov. On 24 July 1969 this well-known Soviet novelist happened to travel from Moscow to London in the same plane as the released Gerald Brooke. On arrival he eluded the personal escort provided by the Soviet authorities, sought refuge with a leading British daily newspaper, proclaimed his intention of emigrating from the Soviet Union and published articles in the British press describing the particularly close surveillance which the Soviet political police maintains over all Soviet writers. In his own case this had included ostentatious shadowing by agents, the bugging of his flat, the recording of his telephone conversations and sundry attempts at 'provocation'. On one occasion a certain student had sought him out and delivered a tirade against the Soviet Union, describing it as a Fascist country, after which Mr Kuznetsov found himself in trouble for failing to report the incident to the authorities. On another occasion a young woman informed him that she had been instructed to become his mistress, and to report all his activities on pain of expulsion from the institute at which she was studying. Kuznetsov also confirms many accounts by previous Soviet defectors when he speaks of the prolonged and elaborate vetting process to which all Soviet citizens are subjected before receiving the rare and coveted privilege of foreign travel. Out of every fifteen members of one Soviet 'delegation' on which he had travelled, at least five were under KGB instructions to report on the other members' behaviour, apart from which each member of the party was obliged to supply a political report on himself and his fellow-travellers. Kuznetsov also describes how he had compromised himself in various ways in the past by failure to co-operate fully with the KGB, but had then decided to work his passage back by simulating a degree of docility sufficient to qualify him for an exit visa. He had therefore pandered to official conspiracy-mania by inventing an imaginary plot by certain fellow-writers to bring out a new clandestine literary journal, and had then clinched his return to favour by promising to write a novel about Lenin.[23] Such methods finally took him to London and put him in a position to start a new career as an émigré writer.

The tactics employed by Mr Kuznetsov to effect his escape have incurred sporadic criticism from western writers not themselves subject to comparable pressures—an example of self-righteous censoriousness such as is all too easily engendered in societies free from totalitarian police control. So far as the present study is concerned, Mr Kuznetsov can only be saluted for his success in extricating himself from the long line of literary victims of the Russian political police—the list which also includes such illustrious names as Alexander Radishchev, Alexander Pushkin, Nicholas Chernyshevsky, Fyodor Dostoyevsky, Leo Tolstoy, Isaac Babel, Osip Mandelshtam, Boris Pasternak and Alexander Solzhenitsyn.

As is stressed by Vladimir Nabokov, himself in youth a potential victim of Russian police terror, Russian history can be considered from two points of view: 'first, as the evolution of the police . . .

and second, as the development of a marvellous culture.'[24] That these strands are intimately intertwined, and that the second cannot be understood without an appreciation of the first, was one reason for attempting the study now concluded. Though its purpose has been to record the past, one prediction of the future may be risked as a parting word: that between the completion of this book and its appearance in print new scandals will have further enriched the annals of the developing Russian political police.

That the final epitaph of this gigantic and historic organisation will not be written by anyone now living also seems probable.

Conclusion

In the foregoing pages an attempt has been made to describe the operations of Russian political security organisations while quoting sources of information in detail, as is particularly desirable in a field of study so riddled with obscurities and difficulties of various kinds. An attempt will now be made to sum up certain aspects of the material in a manner somewhat more speculative and wide-ranging. This discussion will take the form of a general comparison between the two main historical phases concerned: the Imperial and the Soviet.

To what extent does the post-1917 Russian political police display continuity with its pre-revolutionary forerunner, and in what degree has a break with tradition been involved? One important link between the two periods immediately springs to mind. From the Cheka onwards the various Soviet security police organisations have clearly made it their business never to forget the lessons of the past—lessons to be learnt from the many gross errors committed by their immediate precursor, the Okhrana. It was, accordingly, a wise decision of Lenin's to appoint as head of the Cheka and early OGPU a Bolshevik leader with a prison record as rich and varied as that of Felix Dzerzhinsky—multiple political detainee and escapee under the Imperial régime. Many of Dzerzhinsky's colleagues on the Cheka collegium were also seasoned veterans of the duel between revolutionaries and Okhrana—as were the leading Bolsheviks in general. These men had 'sat' for years in Tsarist jails and exile, and they had escaped from both. They had defied censorship, they had maintained illicit printing presses, they had eluded police surveillance, they had used false names, disguises, codes, secret inks . . . and they were therefore ideally equipped to thwart attempts by any new wave of oppositionists to overthrow their own régime by similar conspiratorial means.

Lenin himself had collected no more than a modest stock of such experiences. Yet no one could be more aware than he of the possibilities for upsetting a great empire by subversion conducted from bases outside its borders. When considering the means of preserving his newly founded government and system he was therefore unlikely to neglect the vital section of frontier control. There had been a time when he and his colleagues could slip, legally or illegally, across the laxly controlled bounds of the Empire, often carrying illicit literature in the false bottoms of their suitcases. So common did such commuting become that an important monograph, Michael Futrell's *Northern Underground*, has been devoted to the traffic in documents, goods and wanted 'politicals' as they came and went by this unofficial trunk line through Scandinavia and Finland in the years 1863–1917. It was in order to halt such traffic across the far-flung periphery of their realm—in the east, south and west as well as through Scandinavia —that the Soviet leaders established, soon after the end of the Civil War, the powerful Frontier Police force which has since generally operated under the overall command of the supreme political police authority. Admittedly Soviet frontier control has been extensively defied in recent times so far as publications are concerned—witness the flood of illicit literature reaching the West in the late 1960s, as described in the text above. At no time, however, have would-be emigrant human bodies enjoyed comparable facilities to cross the Soviet border. Only in highly exceptional circumstances may a Soviet citizen leave the USSR with official permission. As for illegal exits, though the number of defectors to the West may seem impressive, this is partly due to the wide publicity which such activities often receive. Moreover, one constant factor emerges from the many defectors' accounts, culminating in the recent well-publicised case of Anatoly Kuznetsov: to effect a successful escape from the Soviet Union demands courage, persistence, skill and luck—all in extreme degree. The successful defectors must represent only a tiny fraction of those who might choose to emigrate if this were a permitted or less risky process. This situation contrasts vividly with pre-revolutionary days, when political dissidents could generally cross and recross frontiers with such ease, and when—in the late Empire—they were sometimes even permitted to choose permanent foreign exile as an alternative to banishment within the confines of Russia.

When one considers the problem of escaping from Russian prisons, concentration camps or places of exile, a similar contrast emerges. To elude the clutches of the Imperial Russian authorities was relatively easy—as the adventures of Bakunin, Peter Kropotkin, Trotsky, Stalin and many others show. Remembering such escapes—and the deadly blows inflicted on the old régime by the escapees—Dzerzhinsky and his successors tightened Soviet prison and camp security to a point where breaking out became an almost hopeless prospect . . . particularly as effectively guarded frontiers now lay beyond prison wall and camp perimeter. Similarly, effective restrictions were placed on facilities for prisoners to exchange messages illicitly with the outside world, since the greater severity of Soviet procedures, as compared with Imperial times, made it unduly dangerous for any prison guard or warder to act as an unofficial postman. Perhaps this is why the word *golub* (pigeon), used colloquially to describe such helpful bribed intermediaries in Imperial times, now seems to have fallen out of use.

Another eloquent contrast between the two régimes is provided by the latitude allowed to so many political oppositionists of the Imperial period to study, write and publish politically subversive material while in prison or exile. A full bibliography of such pre-revolutionary publications would make an impressive tally. They range from major works, such as Chernyshevsky's *What is to be Done?* and Lenin's *Development of Capitalism in Russia,* to the blood-curdling pamphlet *Young Russia* which P. G. Zaichnevsky smuggled out of a Moscow jail in 1862. It has been the general practice, by contrast, to deny Soviet political prisoners writing materials, except for those occasionally issued under strict control for the specific purpose of recording official complaints such as almost always go unanswered. Rich as descriptions of Soviet penal conditions are, these works have almost invariably had to be composed after release or escape, and often in the safe haven of some foreign country. With a pre-revolutionary Lenin or Trotsky (exiled or imprisoned with no obligation to work, and with access to libraries, bookshops and writing materials) must be contrasted the living—or rather dying—conditions suffered by a Babel, a Pilnyak or a Mandelshtam, each of whom perished inarticulate, among circumstances which remain obscure, after a brief period in the camps.

To suggest that all political prisoners of the Imperial period enjoyed unlimited access to books and writing materials would, however, be to exaggerate. Dostoyevsky, for example, received no such privileges during his four years in the jail at Omsk (1850–4). Even so, the prison conditions so eloquently described in his *Memoirs from the House of the Dead*, published in 1862, were immeasurably less harsh than those no less vividly portrayed in a study of a Stalinist slave camp issued exactly one hundred years later: Alexander Solzhenitsyn's *One Day in the Life of Ivan Denisovich* (1962). As is pointed out in a perceptive comparison between the two works by another notable political prisoner, the Yugoslav critic Mihajlo Mihajlov: 'The penal servitude [which] Dostoyevsky went through was like life in a sanatorium compared with Solzhenitsyn's camp.'[1] And again: 'Compared with twentieth-century conditions, certain scenes from "the worst Siberian prison camp" of the nineteenth century seem idyllic. "At the entrances to the barrack huts", we are told, "the prisoners would sit about with balalaikas." '[2]

One striking difference between the Imperial and Soviet secret police lies in the size of the organisations concerned, in the number of personnel involved, and in the extent of resources allotted to political security operations. During the centuries the Russian secret police has expanded from relatively tiny beginnings until it has come to swamp and penetrate every corner of society—possibly the most impressive example of the working of 'Parkinson's Law' on record. Of all the organisations concerned, Peter the Great's Preobrazhensky Office—perhaps the first true Russian political security force—holds pride of place for the economic and efficient use of resources. As stated above, it conducted political security operations throughout late Muscovy and in the first years of Imperial Russia with a strength of less than a dozen clerks, though admittedly military units—the Preobrazhensky and Semyonovsky Guards—could be co-opted to an unlimited extent to effect arrests and act as couriers. Since then a gradual but inexorably sustained expansion in security personnel has been observed. In the late eighteenth century perhaps only a few dozen or score were so employed, but under Nicholas I the figure soared to some ten thousand, including the Corps of Gendarmes. Further expansion occurred after the foundation of the Okhrana and Police Department in 1880. It becomes increasingly difficult, however, to estimate the precise number of persons working for the secret police at any given moment, since so many gradations of bribed, bullied, blackmailed or terrorised part-time informants were to be found in the middle reaches of police operations—between the inner ring of full-time salaried police officials or agents, and ordinary citizens liable to be summoned for questioning at any time and under an obligation to denounce any manifestation of political opposition which might have come to their notice.

Exact or not, Imperial statistics were soon eclipsed by those of the Cheka. Latsis's figure of 31,000 Chekists employed in 1921 has been quoted above, but this tally was soon to be multiplied many times over as the OGPU and then the NKVD warmed to their work. A further vast increase in overall numbers was effected by the recruitment of various categories of political police troops which came, during most of the period, on the strength of the overall security authority, from Cheka to KGB. The size of these various police forces in the year 1953 has been roughly computed as follows:

Internal troops	150,000
Convoy troops	100–150,000
Railway troops	100,000
Operational troops	100,000
Frontier troops	300,000
Guard troops	150–200,000
Approximate total strength	1,000,000

These forces were thought to include some artillery and tank formations. Between 1953 and 1968, however, their numbers were reduced—perhaps by a half—which is at least an example of Parkinson's Law in reverse.[3]

If one asks how many Soviet—not to mention foreign—citizens arc in some sense working for the Russian secret police at the beginning of the 1970s, it must be answered that the reservoir of potential KGB informants includes practically the entire Soviet population, though dotards, infants and rustics are less likely to be so employed than town-dwellers in the prime of life. Those who encounter Soviet citizens, whether on Soviet or non-Soviet soil, would be well advised to regard all their contacts, however amiable, smiling and sympathetic, as potential KGB informants— not necessarily willing ones—owing to the obligation liable to be placed on all Soviet citizens to furnish detailed political reports on their conversations with foreigners. On this elementary fact of life many western governments now warn businessmen and others travelling to the USSR, apart from which diplomats posted to Moscow necessarily receive detailed and intense briefing on the highly sophisticated and persistent techniques of espionage to which they are certain to be exposed. Owing to the growing refinement of 'bugging' devices, many foreign embassies in Moscow and other Communist countries maintain elaborately constructed safe rooms in which, it is hoped, conversations and transactions of a particularly confidential nature may take place without the danger of eavesdropping by KGB and Soviet military intelligence operatives primed with the latest scientific devices.

So far as the ordinary tourist is concerned, he would be wise to allow for the possibility that any Soviet hotel room, restaurant table, taxi, train or aeroplane which he occupies may be 'bugged' —though of course even the KGB's huge resources, and seemingly unslaked appetite for trivial information, do not extend to the full recording and processing of all remarks uttered by all visitors to the Soviet Union at all times. It is the possibility—not the certainty—of such surveillance which should be allowed for.

Now under-employed since the restrictions on terrorism ordained after Stalin's death, Soviet intelligence by no means confines the collection of information, whether abroad or on home ground, to political, military and economic matters, though these naturally receive high priority. The private lives of individuals also form an object of scrutiny, particularly as such investigation may create an opportunity for recruiting agents through blackmail by threat of exposure. It is also a common KGB practice to compromise potential foreign informants by various techniques—not least by the 'provocation' of individuals earmarked as particularly vulnerable. This has frequently involved the photographing, if necessary through one-way mirrors, of the victim in an embarrassing posture deliberately engineered and implying or recording some combination of drunken, drugged, homosexual or heterosexual misbehaviour.

Certain foreign visitors to the Soviet Union have also been exposed to the additional danger of prosecution for some breach of Soviet law, the long-term purpose of such operations being less the administration of justice than the exchange of these specially selected individuals for Soviet spies serving long prison sentences abroad. As has been indicated above, this danger has been recently much increased, so far as British citizens are concerned, by the decision of the Wilson government to exchange the imprisoned lecturer Gerald Brooke as part of a deal including the release of two Soviet spies serving prison sentences in Great Britain.

For many years Soviet Russian society has been saturated with secret police activity to an extent never remotely attained in Tsarist times—and this despite the fact that Russia has, throughout the ages, been infested with the endemic plague of political denunciation and internal espionage, such as was already prevalent in the early seventeenth century, in the reign of Boris Godunov. Now, in modern times, the Soviet secret police not only constitutes an organisation incomparably larger and more penetrative than its Imperial and Muscovite counterparts, but has also shown itself far more ruthless in its methods than its nineteenth-century and pre-revolutionary twentieth-century predecessors. For example, the number of persons executed for political offences in nineteenth-century Russia was in the region of one hundred altogether—an average of only one per annum. During the last dozen years of the Imperial régime, however, when hundreds or thousands went to the gallows or before the firing squad, this nineteenth-century total was many times exceeded. Then the hangings and shootings of the Age of Assassinations were themselves far outstripped by the excesses of the Cheka and its White counterparts during the Civil War, while these were eclipsed in their own turn by the horrors inflicted by Stalin's NKVD. During the two years 1937–8 the last-named organisation appears to have been responsible for approximately one million executions[4]—a figure which does not take into account additional vast numbers who also perished at the hands of the Stalinist secret police owing to the lethal conditions maintained in the GULAG-operated labour camps. It can therefore be argued that Stalinism at its worst was executing political victims at about five hundred thousand times the rate maintained by the nineteenth-century Imperial authorities so severely castigated by Soviet publicists on the grounds of their inhumanity.

The impression of greatly superior brutality and ruthlessness in Soviet, as opposed to Imperial Russian, police practice is enhanced by certain differences in the distribution of administrative functions, as observed if one compares the two eras. The Okhrana, for example, was both in theory and in practice an investigating, not a punitive, body—for which reason its last head, A. T. Vasilyev, could even claim that his organisation had never had a prisoner executed on its own authority.[5] Nor is this claim easy to refute, despite the thousands of Imperial Russian citizens slaughtered in one way or another on political grounds in the late Empire. The point is that such victims were sentenced, imprisoned and executed by authorities other than the Okhrana, though it was often through Okhrana operations that they had originally come under suspicion. That unspeakable atrocities were committed on each other by Imperial Russian and Muscovite citizens cannot be denied, but at no time since Ivan the Terrible's day did they take a toll (proportionate to the population) in death and suffering comparable to that exacted under Stalin. Moreover, these earlier atrocities were not, generally, committed under police auspices. Some, for example, were the work of landowners who ill-treated their serfs before emancipation in 1861. Others were perpetrated by the military units which crushed such risings as those of Pugachov in 1772–4, of the Novgorod military colonists in 1831, of the villagers of the Chigirin area near Kiev in 1875–7, and of the Tambov peasants quelled by Governor Von der Launitz's Cossacks in 1905. These and other similar episodes were accompanied by widespread savage, and commonly fatal, floggings such as have not been among the most typical features of Soviet repressions.

By contrast with the treatment of political prisoners under the Third Section and Okhrana, the political police of Soviet times has *de facto*, if not *de jure*, generally acted as detecting, arresting, imprisoning, judging and sentencing authority in political cases. These functions are, moreover, retained to a large extent by the present-day KGB, although determined attempts are now made to impart a veneer of legality to political security proceedings by creating the simulacrum of trial by independent courts. Thus the secret police still occupies, at the beginning of the 1970s, a dominant position never held by Third Section or Okhrana—and this despite a significant though by no means total retreat from institutionalised terrorism as practised under Stalin.

A particularly grotesque gloss is imparted to our subject by the many acres of print wherein the horrors of the Imperial Russian Police State have been self-righteously denounced by Soviet publicists and historians themselves subject to the rigours of a Police State far more ruthless and severe. Many of such descriptions were penned in the years of Stalin's worst atrocities, in the light of which the authors' pious indignation, levelled at the abuses of the previous régime, acquires an ironic flavour all its own. It was, for example, in the terrible years 1936–7 that the great historian of Imperial Russian penology, M. N. Gernet, began to devote his full-time energies to his main life's work—*A History of Tsarist Prisons*, the first edition of which appeared in three volumes between 1941 and 1948.[6] Gernet is a considerable scholar whose evidence has been frequently cited in the present study. Yet there is, surely, something downright absurd—and entirely outside normal 'western' experience—about a work in which, for example, the judicial framing of Chernyshevsky (that undeniably shameful event of the early 1860s) could be denounced with such moral fervour at precisely such a nightmare moment in Russian history, and in the following terms. 'The Tsarist system has been swept from the face of the earth. Yet, despite this, it is utterly impossible to preserve one's equanimity when one acquaints oneself through authentic archive material with so odious a concoction of false testimony and forgeries by the very government.'[7] One's own equanimity may, perhaps, be even more severely tested at the thought of so weighty an authority penning these particular lines for publication in a terrorised Moscow at the time of the grandiose frame-up of Bukharin and others indicted as members of a non-existent 'Bloc of Rightists and Trotskyists' concocted for the occasion at the behest of a totalitarian dictator.

By comparison with the Bukharin trial and other Stalinist judicial puppet-shows, the framing of Chernyshevsky was the work of bungling innocents. So too were many of the other excesses and atrocities of the Imperial period described by Gernet. Inexcusable and horrifying as they remain, judged by the standards of non-absolutist and non-totalitarian societies, their scale was after all pitifully small according to Stalinist criteria. With many reservations Gernet's work (now extended to a third edition of five volumes) may even be read as a qualified defence of the Imperial system—so little in the way of full-blooded atrocity material have his researches dredged up, and this despite an evident intention to pillory Tsarist penal and police procedures. It must, however, also be added that this anti-Imperial bias is entirely understandable and excusable in an author who was himself menaced, along with all his fellow-citizens, by the barbed wire and bullets of the Stalinist secret police, and whose choice of research topic made him particularly vulnerable to persecution.

As Gernet many times demonstrates, the Tsar-Emperor's subjects were all too often unjustly condemned—and for crimes which are no crimes in less illiberal societies. Imperial Russian political prisoners were held in dank dungeons where they contracted tuberculosis, scurvy or dysentery and died. Their fate is to be mourned, but their number was at least comparatively small—a few hundred at the best, a few thousand at the worst of times. Moreover, specific attempts by Gernet to document the use of torture by the Third Section and Okhrana have yielded the most meagre results. Nor do tears spring easily to the eyes at the veteran scholar's account (given in the third edition of his monumental treatise) of how, in 1949, he chanced to visit the very cell in the Peter and Paul Fortress where his own father had been held captive back in 1866 at the time of Karakozov's bungled attempt to assassinate the Emperor Alexander II. 'I felt [Gernet writes] a sort of special relationship to the Fortress. My father had fought against the régime of which the Fortress was a bulwark, and the son had lived on to enjoy the happiness of becoming its historian.'[8] By the time when these lines were written the dreaded dungeons of the Peter and Paul Fortress in Leningrad had indeed been turned into a museum exhibit, and were offered to tourists as part of a conducted tour stressing the horrors of the Tsarist régime. It is also true, however, that such tours took place at times when the Kresty Prison, not far away in the same city, held some 30,000 captives under appalling conditions . . . and with sixteen people sharing what had been one-man cells in Imperial times.[9]

As this detail reminds one, the number of persons imprisoned in the worst years of the Stalin period greatly exceeded any figure ever incarcerated under the Tsars, in whose day 'the entire prison population never went much beyond 225,000'.[10] Furthermore, these Tsarist prisoners consisted largely of criminals in the ordinary sense of the word, only a minority of them being political victims —that is, citizens innocent of any crime, including treason as defined by law, but arrested, framed and repressed wholesale for accidental reasons in a context of unbridled political terror.

It is above all in the creation of systematic political terror on a nationwide scale that the Soviet police system may claim to have advanced far beyond its Tsarist prototype. Unless he was extremely lucky, an ordinary unheroic citizen of Imperial Russia could confidently expect to escape persecution on political grounds by keeping his mouth shut, by abstaining from officially disapproved activities—and perhaps by changing his religion. The essence of Stalinism was to destroy such possibilities, leaving no haven of security even for the most timorous and terrorised. In the deliberate intimidation of the entire population, in the wholesale saturation of society with spies and informers, and in the systematic use of pre-emptive arrest to forestall possible trouble by immunising vast sections of potential trouble-makers in advance—in all these techniques the Imperial police lagged far behind the Soviet . . . and this despite the earnest pioneer efforts of certain Tsarist police chiefs born before their time, among whom Actual State Councillor Liprandi and General Strelnikov have been given special mention above.

All improvements and changes in techniques notwithstanding, certain devices have remained common to both phases of the Russian secret police. Prominent among these has been 'provocation'—the procedure of destroying hostile political organisations and individuals by subjecting them to undercover police agents posing as sympathisers. This method, so successfully pioneered by Rachkovsky and Zubatov in the Imperial period, has continued to the present day as a staple feature of Soviet practice. Another endemic feature of the Russian, and perhaps of all political police organisations, has been the inability of the authorities to work out any stable chain of command or system of administration. Repeated switches and changes of balance are, perhaps, an essential when one is administering what is, after all, potentially the most dangerous institution in the State—dangerous to its own masters as well as to its enemies.

Fortunately or unfortunately, the KGB seems, at the moment of writing, to show greater signs of long-term stability than any preceding Russian secret police force. Yet these words could easily be belied by events through sudden unforeseen developments occurring between the preparation of this study and its appearance in print.

Notes

[For fuller details of works to which reference is made, see the Bibliography.]

PREFACE

1. Shilder, *Imperator Nikolay I*, vol. i, pp. 780–1.
2. *Izvestiya* (Moscow), 21 December 1967.

CHAPTER 1: FROM THE OPRICHNINA TO THE DECEMBRISTS

1. Conquest, *The Great Terror*, pp. 75–6.
2. Klyuchevsky, vol. ii, p. 179.
3. Barbour, pp. 63–5.
4. *See Brockhaus-Efron Encyclopedia*, article on 'Samozvantsy'.
5. Solovyov, vol. v, p. 328.
6. Kuznetsov, *see* Bibliography.
7. Kotoshikhin, p. 85.
8. Golikova, *Politicheskiye protsessy pri Petre I*, p. 42.
9. *Ibid.*, pp. 132–3.
10. *Ibid.*, p. 130.
11. Golikova, 'Organy politicheskogo syska', p. 269.
12. Yesipov, pp. 416–44.
13. Solovyov, vol. xi, p. 237.
14. *Ibid.*, vol. xi, p. 124.
15. *Ibid.*, vol. xiii, p. 16.

16. Bilbasov, vol. ii, p. 394.
17. Golikova, 'Organy politicheskogo syska', p. 277.
18. Yevreinov, p. 81.
19. Lang, p. 190.
20. Squire, p. 19.
21. Gernet, vol. i, pp. 206–7.
22. *Ibid.*, vol. i, p. 206.
23. Squire, pp. 21–2.
24. Gernet, vol. i, p. 256.
25. Quoted in Monas, *The Third Section*, p. 37.
26. Squire, pp. 35–6.
27. Monas, *The Third Section*, p. 56.
28. Shilder, *Imperator Aleksandr I*, vol. iv, pp. 203–4.
29. Squire, p. 44.

CHAPTER 2: THE THIRD SECTION UNDER NICHOLAS I

1. Mazour, p. 207.
2. Nechkina, vol. ii, p. 395.
3. *Ibid.*, pp. 408–9.
4. *Ibid.*, p. 394.
5. Mazour, p. 219.
6. Shilder, *Imperator Nikolay I*, vol. i, p. 456.
7. *Ibid.*, pp. 780–1.
8. Squire, pp. 95, 105, 183.
9. Von Vock, quoted in Squire, pp. 66–7.
10. Shilder, *Imperator Nikolay I*, vol. ii, p. 737.
11. I. M. Trotsky, quoted in Squire, p. 129.
12. I. Golovine, quoted in Squire, p. 168.
13. Squire, p. 59.
14. *Ibid.*, p. 216.
15. *Ibid.*, p. 220.
16. *Ibid.*, p. 214.
17. Gernet, vol. ii, pp. 418–23.
18. *Ibid.*, pp. 180–1.
19. Modzelevsky, p. 26.
20. Brodsky, p. 416.
21. Lemke, *Nikolayevskiye zhandarmy*, p. 483.
22. Labedz and Hayward, pp. 42–3.
23. Lemke, *Nikolayevskiye zhandarmy*, p. 494.
24. *Ibid.*, p. 502.

25. *Ibid.*, p. 515.
26. *Ibid.*, p. 524.
27. Monas, *The Third Section*, p. 163.
28. Herzen, vol. i, p. 73.
29. *Ibid.*, pp. 141–2.
30. *Ibid.*, pp. 316–17.
31. *Magarshack*, p. 136.
32. Squire, p. 163.
33. Sablin, p. 6.
34. *Ibid.*, p. 11.
35. Shchogolev, *Petrashevsky v vospominaniyakh sovremennikov*, pp. 165–7.
36. *Ibid.*, p. 97.
37. Sablin, p. 54.

CHAPTER 3: THE THIRD SECTION UNDER ALEXANDER II

1. Seton-Watson, *The Russian Empire*, p. 355.
2. Squire, p. 149.
3. Mikhaylov, pp. 19–20.
4. Kozmin, p. 176.
5. Lampert, p. 120.
6. *Ibid.*, p. 129.
7. Menshchikov, *Okhrana i revolyutsiya*, part ii, p. 12.
8. Gernet, vol. ii, p. 363.
9. *Ibid.*, pp. 363–5.
10. Kropotkin, p. 151.
11. Zayonchkovsky, p. 173.
12. Milyutin, vol. i, pp. 159–60.
13. Feoktistov, p. 312.
14. Valuyev, vol. ii, p. 311.
15. Milyutin, vol. i, p. 158.
16. Schebeko, p. 9.
17. Zayonchkovsky, p. 172.
18. Schebeko, pp. 30–1.
19. Tikhomirov, *Vospominaniya*, p. 118.
20. Zayonchkovsky, p. 81.
21. Feoktistov, pp. 384–7.
22. Footman, *Red Prelude*, p. 105.
23. *Ibid.*, p. 128.
24. Zayonchkovsky, pp. 221–2.

25. *Ibid.*, p. 181.
26. *Ibid.*, p. 207.
27. Footman, *Red Prelude*, p. 135.

CHAPTER 4: THE NINETEENTH-CENTURY OKHRANA

1. Zayonchkovsky, p. 303.
2. *Ibid.*, p. 312.
3. *Ibid.*, p. 379.
4. Yarmolinsky, p. 305.
5. Feoktistov, p. 237.
6. Gurko, p. 108.
7. Figner, vol. i, pp. 321–2.
8. *Ibid.*, p. 325.
9. Tikhomirov, *Neizdannyye zapiski*, p. 171.
10. Yarmolinsky, pp. 322–3.
11. Gernet, vol. iii, p. 129.
12. *Ibid.*, p. 130.
13. *Ibid.*, p. 121.
14. Yarmolinsky, p. 333.
15. Agafonov, p. 4.
16. *Ibid.*, p. 38.
17. Gerassimoff, p. 67; Gurko, p. 180.
18. Menshchikov, *Okhrana i revolyutsiya*, part ii, p. 23.
19. Wolfe, *Three who Made a Revolution*, p. 129.

CHAPTER 5: THE OKHRANA IN THE AGE OF ASSASSINATIONS

1. Nicolaievsky, *Aseff*, p. 44.
2. Gurko, p. 120.
3. Gerassimoff, p. 34.
4. Agafonov, p. 229.
5. *Ibid.*, p. 240.
6. Gerassimoff, pp. 199–200.
7. Nicolaievsky, *Aseff*, p. 73.
8. Greenberg, vol. ii, p. 43.
9. *Ibid.*, pp. 88–94.
10. Cohn, pp. 86–8.
11. Gerassimoff, p. 39.
12. *Ibid.*, p. 41.

13. *Ibid.*, p. 15.
14. *Ibid.*, pp. 23–5.
15. *Ibid.*, p. 65.
16. *Ibid.*, p. 63.
17. *Ibid.*, p. 77.
18. *Ibid.*, p. 137.
19. Gernet, vol. iv, p. 105.
20. *Ibid.*, vol. v, p. 68.

CHAPTER 6: THE DECLINE AND FALL OF THE OKHRANA

1. Wolfe, *Three who Made a Revolution*, p. 542.
2. *Ibid.*, pp. 553–4.
3. Smith, *The Young Stalin*, p. 8.
4. *Ibid.*, pp. 67–8.
5. E.g. R. H. Bruce Lockhart, p. 128.
6. Vassilyev, p. 151.
7. Massie, p. 333.
8. Vassilyev, p. 158.
9. *Ibid.*, p. 149.
10. Walkin, p. 70.
11. Nikitine, p. 24.
12. Vassilyev, pp. 229–30.
13. *Ibid.*, p. 265.
14. Wolfe, *Three who Made a Revolution*, p. 547.
15. Shchogolev, *Padeniye tsarskogo rezhima*, vol. iii, pp. 294–5.
16. Katkov, *Russia 1917*, p. 413.
17. Shchogolev, *Padeniye tsarskogo rezhima*, vol. iii, p. 17.
18. Nikitine, p. 19.
19. *Ibid.*, pp. 108–32.
20. *Ibid.*, p. 179.

CHAPTER 7: THE CHEKA

1. Schapiro, *The Communist Party of the Soviet Union*, p. 171.
2. Trotsky, quoted in Schapiro, *The Origin of the Communist Autocracy*, p. 112, note.
3. Scott, p. 7.
4. Ivo Lapenna in Schapiro and Reddaway, p. 253.
5. Wolin and Slusser, p. 4.

6. Scott, pp. 1–2.
7. Wolin and Slusser, p. 67.
8. Chamberlin, vol. ii, p. 67.
9. Peters, p. 99.
10. *Ibid.*, p. 97.
11. Sofinov, pp. 43–4.
12. *Ibid.*, p. 40.
13. Scott, p. 8.
14. *See* Carr, *The Bolshevik Revolution*, vol. i, p. 163.
15. *See* Katkov, 'The Assassination of Count Mirbach', *passim.*
16. Peters, p. 110.
17. Carr, *The Bolshevik Revolution*, vol. i, p. 166.
18. Scott, p. 9.
19. R. H. Bruce Lockhart, p. 201.
20. Sofinov, p. 96.
21. R. H. Bruce Lockhart, pp. 314–16.
22. *Ibid.*, pp. 321–2.
23. Sofinov, p. 102.
24. R. H. Bruce Lockhart, p. 329.
25. Latsis, quoted in Chamberlin, vol. ii, p. 74.
26. Denikine, p. 292.
27. Chamberlin, vol. ii, p. 75.
28. Alinin, p. 31.
29. *Ibid.*, p. 69.
30. *Che-Ka*, pp. 146–7.
31. *Ibid.*, p. 147.
32. *Ibid.*, p. 57.
33. *Ibid.*, p. 89.
34. *See* Ivo Lapenna in Schapiro and Reddaway, pp. 253–7.
35. Scott, p. 14.
36. Lewytzkyj, p. 55.
37. Scott, p. 14.
38. Sofinov, pp. 222–3.
39. Katkov, 'The Kronstadt Rebellion', pp. 65–6.
40. Sofinov, p. 226.
41. *Ibid.*, p. 218.
42. *Ibid.*, p. 217.
43. Wolfe, *The Bridge and the Abyss*, pp. 114–17.

CHAPTER 8: THE GPU/OGPU

1. Wolin and Slusser, p. 12.

2. Carr, *The Bolshevik Revolution*, vol. i, p. 181.
3. Carr, *Socialism in One Country*, vol. ii, p. 424.
4. Dallin and Nicolaevsky, p. 173.
5. Carr, *Socialism in One Country*, vol. ii, pp. 449–50; Dallin and Nicolaevsky, pp. 179–81.
6. Schapiro, *The Origin of the Communist Autocracy*, p. 168.
7. Trotsky, *Stalin*, pp. 359–61.
8. Carr, *The Interregnum*, p. 286.
9. Schapiro, *The Communist Party of the Soviet Union*, pp. 276–7.
10. Trotsky, *Stalin*, p. 418.
11. Ulam, *Lenin and the Bolsheviks*, p. 518.
12. Lewytzkyj, p. 73.
13. Bailey, pp. 38–41.
14. Lewytzkyj, p. 89.
15. Bailey, p. 57.
16. *See* Wraga, *passim*.
17. Carr, *Socialism in One Country*, vol. iii, part 1, pp. 267–9.
18. Trotsky, *My Life*, quoted in Lewytzkyj, p. 75.
19. Quoted in Swianiewicz, p. 123.
20. *Ibid.*
21. Fainsod, *Smolensk under Soviet Rule*, p. 240.
22. Conquest, *The Great Terror*, p. 22.
23. *Ibid.*
24. *See* Fainsod, *Smolensk under Soviet Rule*, pp. 280–93.
25. Schapiro, *The Communist Party of the Soviet Union*, p. 388.
26. Lewytzkyj, p. 76.
27. *See* Williams-Ellis *passim*.
28. Dallin and Nicolaevsky, pp. 224–5.
29. Tchernavin, p. 252.
30. G. Kitchin, quoted in Dallin and Nicolaevsky, pp. 226–8.
31. Orlov, p. 28.
32. Avtorkhanov, pp. 28–9.
33. Lyons, p. 117.
34. *Ibid.*, p. 370.
35. Abramovitch, pp. 384–6.
36. Schapiro, *The Communist Party of the Soviet Union*, p. 393.
37. Conquest, *The Great Terror*, pp. 551–2.
38. Tchernavin, pp. 199–204; Lyons, pp. 447–64.
39. Abramovitch, p. 355; Nicolaevsky, *Power and the Soviet Elite*, p. 30.

CHAPTER 9: THE NKVD UNDER YAGODA AND YEZHOV

1. Stalin, quoted in Conquest, *The Great Terror*, p. 36.
2. Khrushchev, quoted in Rigby, p. 38.
3. *See* L. Shaumyan, quoted in Rigby, p. 110.
4. Fainsod, *How Russia is Ruled*, p. 364.
5. *See* Nicolaevsky, *Power and the Soviet Elite*, pp. 93–4; Leonhard, *Kreml ohne Stalin*, pp. 95–6; Schapiro, *The Communist Party of the Soviet Union*, p. 403.
6. Rigby, p. 39.
7. Schapiro, *The Communist Party of the Soviet Union*, p. 404.
8. Orlov, pp. 167–8.
9. *Ibid.*, p. 179.
10. *See* Rigby, pp. 47–8.
11. *Ibid.*, p. 40.
12. Nicolaevsky, *Power and the Soviet Elite*, p. 22.
13. Orlov, p. 342.
14. *Ibid.*, p. 350.
15. Rigby, p. 70.
16. Conquest, *The Great Terror*, p. 195.
17. *Ibid.*, p. 194.
18. Rigby, p. 37.
19. Orlov, pp. 221–5.
20. Unger, p. 325.
21. *Ibid.*, p. 324.
22. Fainsod, *The Smolensk Archives*, p. 59.
23. Conquest, *The Great Terror*, p. 250.
24. Orlov, p. 232.
25. Bailey, pp. 227–67.
26. Schapiro, *The Communist Party of the Soviet Union*, p. 420.
27. Erickson, pp. 390–1.
28. Wolin and Slusser, pp. 126–30.
29. *Ibid.*, p. 197.
30. Erickson, p. 432.
31. Solzhenitsyn, quoted in Sakharov, p. 131.
32. Serge, p. 269.
33. Conquest, *The Great Terror*, p. 323.
34. *Ibid.*, p. 278.
35. Mandelshtam, vol. i, p. lxix.

36. Beck and Godin, pp. 149–66.
37. Conquest, *The Great Terror*, p. 532.
38. Herling, p. 3.
39. Conquest, *The Great Terror*, p. 308.
40. Gorbatov, p. 127.
41. Ivanov-Razumnik, p. 272.
42. *Ibid.*, p. 271.
43. *Ibid.*, p. 267.
44. Ginsburg, pp. 269–70.
45. Dallin and Nicolaevsky, p. 128.
46. Lipper, p. 95.
47. *Ibid.*, p. 108.
48. Anders, p. 108.
49. Dallin and Nicolaevsky, pp. 129–32.
50. Alliluyeva, *Twenty Letters to a Friend*, p. 105.
51. Wolin and Slusser, p. 194.
52. Herling, pp. 28–31.
53. Rupert, p. 97.
54. *Ibid.*, p. 101.
55. Weissberg, p. 425.
56. Deakin and Storry, pp. 199–203.
57. Beck and Godin, pp. 202–3.

CHAPTER 10: BERIA AND THE NKVD/NKGB

1. *Kommunist* (Armenia) 28 November 1963, quoted in Conquest, *The Great Terror*, p. 249.
2. Alliluyeva, *Twenty Letters to a Friend*, p. 16.
3. Lewytzkyj, p. 167.
4. Grey, p. 315.
5. Zawodny, p. 5.
6. Dallin and Nicolaevsky, p. 265.
7. *Ibid.*, p. 264.
8. Zawodny, *passim.*
9. *Ibid.*, p. 160.
10. *Ibid.*, p. 155.
11. *Ibid.*, p. 113.
12. Buber-Neumann, p. 179.

13. Dallin and Nicolaevsky, p. 38.
14. Herling, p. 59.
15. Conquest, *The Great Terror*, p. 430.
16. Anonymous, p. 27.
17. Erickson , pp. 585–6.
18. *Ibid.,* p. 587.
19. Grey, p. 325.
20. Fischer, pp. 5–6.
21. Anonymous, p. 32.
22. Artemyev, pp. 108–9.
23. Lewytzkyj, pp. 191–2.
24. Conquest, *The Great Terror*, p. 491.
25. Kravchenko, p. 405.
26. Conquest, *The Great Terror*, pp. 489–90.
27. Armstrong, *Soviet Partisans in World War II*, p. 131.
28. Anonymous, p. 21.
29. Anders, p. 114.
30. Conquest, *The Soviet Deportation of Nationalities*, p. 97.
31. Anders, p. 36.
32. *Ibid.*, p. 86.
33. *Ibid.*, p. 115.
34. Wolin and Slusser, p. 20.
35. Conquest, *The Soviet Deportation of Nationalities*, p. 51.
36. *Ibid,*, p. 91.
37. Rigby, p. 62.
38. Wolin and Slusser, pp. 23–4.
39. Duhnke, p. 364.
40. Sinevirsky, pp. 108–9.
41. *Ibid.*, p. 47.
42. Dallin and Nicolaevsky, p. 293.
43. Lewytzkyj, pp. 210–11.
44. Stypulkowski, p. 5.
45. Kravchenko, p. 4.
46. *Ibid.*, p. 399.
47. Gouzenko, p. 319.

Chapter 11: Beria and the MVD/MGB

1. Lewytzkyj, p. 217; Conquest, *The Soviet Police System*, p. 21.
2. Rigby, p. 63.

3. Duhnke, p. 363.

4. Struve, pp. 335–6.

5. Meissner, *Sowjetrussland zwischen Revolution und Restauration,* pp. 42–3.

6. Conquest, *Power and Policy in the USSR,* p. 100.

7. *Ibid.,* p. 100.

8. Ulam, *Titoism and the Cominform,* p. 83.

9. Dedijer, p. 268.

10. *Ibid.,* p. 284.

11. Swiatlo, p. 7.

12. Kaplan, p. 101.

13. Barton, p. 303.

14. *Ibid.,* pp. 286–7.

15. Philby, pp. 201–2.

16. Page, pp. 189–99.

17. Conquest, *The Soviet Police System,* p. 22.

18. Nicolaevsky, *Power and the Soviet Elite,* p. 169.

19. Lewytzkyj, p. 252.

20. Alliluyeva, *Tolko odin god,* p. 326.

21. *Ibid.,* p. 334.

22. *Ibid.,* p. 240; Conquest, *Power and Policy in the USSR,* p. 439; Baron, pp. 318–19; Alliluyeva, *Tolko odin god,* p. 134.

23. Armstrong, *The Politics of Totalitarianism,* p. 242.

24. Lewytzkyj, p. 256.

25. Rigby, p. 81.

26. Leonhard, *Kreml ohne Stalin,* p. 73.

27. Conquest, *Power and Policy in the USSR,* p. 164.

28. Leonhard, *Kreml ohne Stalin,* p. 76.

29. Rigby, p. 66.

30. Leonhard, *Kreml ohne Stalin,* p. 77.

31. Menon, p. 29.

32. Conquest, *The Soviet Police System,* p. 22.

33. Leonhard, *Kreml ohne Stalin,* p. 96.

34. *Ibid.,* p. 108.

35. Alliluyeva, *Tolko odin god,* pp. 357–8.

36. Yevtushenko, p. 95.

37. Payne, pp. 718–19.

38. *See* Hingley, 'Emergency Encyclopaedia', *Punch,* 2 June 1954.

CHAPTER 12: THE KGB UNDER KHRUSHCHEV

1. Leonhard, *Kreml ohne Stalin*, p. 114.
2. Nicolaevsky, *Power and the Soviet Elite*, p. 190.
3. Penkovsky, p. 193.
4. *Ibid.*, pp. 94–5.
5. Rush, p. 21.
6. *Ibid.*, p. 82.
7. Nicolaevsky, *Power and the Soviet Elite*, pp. 148–57.
8. Conquest, *Power and Policy in the USSR*, pp. 190–1.
9. *Ibid.*, p. 269.
10. Printed in Rigby, pp. 23–84.
11. Barton, *L'Institution concentrationnaire en Russie*, p. 362.
12. *Ibid.*, p. 378.
13. *Ibid.*, p. 335.
14. Barton, 'An End to Concentration Camps?', p. 39.
15. Quoted *ibid.*, p. 40.
16. Described in Lewytzkyj, p. 292.
17. *Ibid*, p. 295.
18. Dallin, *Soviet Espionage*, p. 358.
19. *Ibid.*
20. Khokhlov, p. 240.
21. Penkovsky, p. 81.
22. Petrov, pp. 329–30.
23. Lewytzkyj, pp. 324–6.
24. Penkovsky, p. 93.
25. *Ibid.*, p. 195.
26. Rigby, p. 102.
27. Conquest, *Courage of Genius*, pp. 107–23.
28. Barton, 'An End to Concentration Camps?', p. 41.
29. Kline, p. 70.
30. Tatu, p. 327.
31. *Ibid.*, p. 198.
32. Marchenko, pp. 156–9.
33. *Sunday Telegraph*, 5 October 1969.
34. Wynne, p. 124.
35. *Ibid.*, p. 131.
36. Tatu, pp. 247–9.

CHAPTER 13: THE KGB AFTER KHRUSHCHEV

1. Trevor-Roper, p. 24.
2. Deakin and Storry, p. 350.
3. Trevor-Roper, p. 24.
4. Philby, p. xxi.
5. Trevor-Roper, p. 25.
6. *Pravda*, 20 December 1967.
7. Labedz and Hayward, p. 36.
8. *Ibid., passim.*
9. *Problems of Communism*, July–August 1968, p. 44.
10. Reddaway, p. 94.
11. Tarsis, *Ward* 7, p. 15.
12. Reddaway, p. 92.
13. *Ibid.*, p. 112.
14. *Problems of Communism*, May–June 1969, pp. 59–60.
15. *Ibid.*, September–October 1968, p. 47.
16. *Ibid.*, p. 51.
17. Alliluyeva, *Tolko odin god*, p. 292.
18. Marchenko, p. 3.
19. *Ibid.*, p. xviii.
20. Szamuely, *passim.*
21. Brooke, *passim.*
22. Cookridge, *passim.*
23. Kuznetsov, *passim.*
24. Nabokov, p. 263.

CONCLUSION

1. Mihajlov, p. 112.
2. *Ibid.*, pp. 88–9.
3. Conquest, *The Soviet Police System*, p. 26.
4. Conquest, *The Great Terror*, p. 532.
5. Vassilyev, p. 39.
6. Gernet, vol. i, p. 34.
7. *Ibid.*, vol. ii, pp. 279–80.
8. Gernet, vol. i, p. 7.

9. Conquest, *The Great Terror*, p. 296.
10. McClosky and Turner, p. 488.

Bibliography

Abbreviations

ed. = edited (by)
n.d. = undated
SPB = St Petersburg
tr. = translated (by)

ABRAMOVITCH, Raphael R., *The Soviet Revolution, 1917–1939*
 (London, 1962)
AGABEKOV, G. S., *Ch. K. za rabotoy* (Berlin, 1931)
AGABEKOV, G. S., *G.P.U.: zapiski chekista* (Berlin, 1930)
AGAFONOV, V. K., *Zagranichnaya okhranka . . . s prilozheniyem ocherka
 'Yevno Azef' i spiska sekretnykh sotrudnikov zagranichnoy agentury*
 (Petrograd, 1918)
AKHSHARUMOV, D. D., *Iz moikh vospominany, 1849–1951* (SPB, 1905)
ALININ, K., *'Cheka': lichnyya vospominaniya ob Odesskoy chrezvychayke.
 S portretami zhertv ch. k.* (Odessa, 1919)
ALLILUYEVA, Svetlana, *Twenty Letters to a Friend*, tr. from the
 Russian by Priscilla Johnson (London, 1967)
ALLILUYEVA, Svetlana, *Tolko odin god* (London, 1969)
ANDERS, Wladyslaw, *Mémoires, 1939–1946*, tr. from the Polish by
 J. Rzewuska (Paris, 1948)
ANDICS, Hellmut, *Rule of Terror*, tr. by Alexander Lieven (London,
 1969)
Anonymous, 'Sovetskiye organy gosudarstvennoy bezopasnosti v
 gody Velikoy otechestvennoy voyny', *Voprosy istorii* (Moscow)
 May 1965, pp. 20–39
*Anti-Stalin Campaign and International Communism, The: a Selection of
 Documents*, ed. by the Russian Institute, Columbia University
 (New York, 1956)

ARMSTRONG, John A., *The Politics of Totalitarianism: the Communist Party of the Soviet Union from 1934 to the Present* (New York, 1961)

ARMSTRONG, John A., *The Soviet Bureaucratic Elite: a Case Study of the Ukrainian Apparatus* (London, 1959)

ARMSTRONG, John A., ed., *Soviet Partisans in World War II* (Madison, 1964)

ARONSON, Grigory, *Rossiya nakanune revolyutsii: istoricheskiye etyudy* (New York, 1962)

ARTEMYEV, Vyacheslav P., *Rezhim i okhrana ispravitelno-trudovykh lagerey MVD* (Munich, 1956)

Aspects of Intellectual Ferment and Dissent in the Soviet Union, US Government Printing Office (Washington, 1968)

AVREKH, A. Ya., *Stolypin i Tretya Duma* (Moscow, 1968)

AVTORKHANOV, Abdurakhman, *Stalin and the Soviet Communist Party: a Study in the Technology of Power* (London, 1959)

BAILEY, Geoffrey, *The Conspirators* (London, 1961)

BARBOUR, Philip L., *Dimitry Called the Pretender: Tsar and Great Prince of All Russia, 1605–1606* (London, 1967)

BARMINE, Alexander, *One who Survived: the Life Story of a Russian under the Soviets* (New York, 1945)

BARON, Salo W., *The Russian Jew under Tsars and Soviets* (New York, 1964)

BARTON, Paul, *L'Institution concentrationnaire en Russie, 1930–1957* (Paris, 1959)

BARTON, Paul, 'An End to Concentration Camps?' *Problems of Communism* (Washington), March-April 1962, pp. 38–46

BAZILEVSKY, B., ed., *Gosudarstvennyya prestupleniya v Rossii v xix veke: sbornik izvlechonnykh iz offitsialnykh izdany pravitelstvennykh soobshcheny* (SPB, 1906)

BECK, F. and GODIN, W., *Russian Purge and the Extraction of Confession*, tr. from the German by Eric Mosbacher and David Porter (London, 1951)

BEGIN, Menachem, *White Nights: the Story of a Prisoner in Russia*, tr. from the Hebrew by Katie Kaplan (London, 1957)

BELOV, G. A. and others ed., *Iz istorii Vserossyskoy Chrezvychaynoy komissii, 1917–1921 gg.: sbornik dokumentov* (Moscow, 1958)

BERKMAN, Alexander, *The Bolshevik Myth: Diary, 1920–1922* (New York, 1925)

BEZSONOV, no initial, *Dvadtsat shest tyurem i pobeg s Solovkov* (Paris, 1928)

BILBASOV, V. A., *Istoriya Yekateriny vtoroy*, 2 vols. (Berlin, 1900)

BOURDEAUX, Michael, *Religious Ferment in Russia: Protestant Opposition to Soviet Religious Policy* (London, 1968)

Brockhaus-Efron Encyclopedia, ed. I. Ye. Andreyevsky (SPB, 1890–1906)

BRODSKY, N. L., *A. S. Pushkin: biografiya* (Moscow, 1937)
BROOKE, Gerald, Articles in *The People* (London), 3, 10, 17 and 24 August 1969.
BRUCE LOCKHART, R. H., *Memoirs of a British Agent: being an Account of the Author's Early Life in Many Lands and of his Official Mission to Moscow in 1918* (London, 1932)
BRUCE LOCKHART, Robin, *Ace of Spies* (London, 1967)
BRUNOVSKY, Vladimir, *The Methods of the OGPU* (London, 1931)
BRZEZINSKI, Zbigniew K., *The Permanent Purge: Politics in Soviet Totalitarianism* (Cambridge, Massachusetts, 1956)
BUBER-NEUMANN, Margarete, *Als Gefangene bei Stalin und Hitler: eine Welt im Dunkel* (Stuttgart, 1958)
BULYGIN, Paul, *The Murder of the Romanovs: the Authentic Account* (London, 1935)
BUNYAN, J., *Intervention, Civil War and Communism in Russia, April–December 1918: Documents and Materials* (Baltimore, 1936)
BUNYAN, J. and FISHER, H. H., *The Bolshevik Revolution, 1917–1918: Documents and Materials* (Stanford, 1934)
BURTSEV, Vladimir, *Borba za svobodnuyu Rossiyu: moi vospominaniya 1882–1924 gg.* (Berlin, 1924)

CAMPESINO', Général 'El, *La Vie et la mort en U.R.S.S., 1939–1949* (Paris, 1950)
CARR, E. H., *A History of Soviet Russia: The Bolshevik Revolution, 1917–1923,* 3 vols. (London, 1952–4); *The Interregnum, 1923–1924* (London, 1954); *Socialism in One Country, 1924–1926,* 3 (4) vols. (London, 1958–64); also (with DAVIES, R. W.) *Foundations of a Planned Economy, 1926–1929,* 2 vols. (London, 1969)
CHAMBERLIN, William Henry, *The Russian Revolution, 1917–1921,* 2 vols. (New York, 1935)
Che-Ka: materialy po deyatelnosti chrezvychaynykh komissy (Berlin, 1922)
CHLENOV, S. B., *Moskovskaya okhranka i yeyo sekretnyye sotrudniki; po dannym Komissii po obespecheniyu novogo stroya* (Moscow, 1919)
CHORNOVIL, Vyacheslav, compiler, *The Chornovil Papers* (New York, 1968)
CILIGA, Anton, *The Russian Enigma* (London, 1940)
COHN, Norman, *Warrant for Genocide: the Myth of the Jewish World-Conspiracy and the Protocols of the Elders of Zion* (London, 1967)
CONQUEST, Robert, *Courage of Genius: the Pasternak Affair* (London, 1961)
CONQUEST, Robert, *The Great Terror: Stalin's Purge of the Thirties* (London, 1968)
CONQUEST, Robert, *Power and Policy in the USSR: the Study of Soviet Dynastics* (London, 1961)
CONQUEST, Robert, *Russia after Khrushchev* (London, 1965)
CONQUEST, Robert, *The Soviet Deportation of Nationalities* (London, 1960)

294   Bibliography

CONQUEST, Robert, ed., *Justice and the Legal System in the USSR* (London, 1968)

CONQUEST, Robert, ed., *The Soviet Police System* (London, 1968)

COOKRIDGE, E. H., 'The Strangest Trade in the World: Bartering Spies', *The Daily Telegraph Magazine*, London, 10 October 1969

COQUART, Armand, *Dmitri Pisarev (1840–1868) et l'idéologie du nihilisme russe* (Paris, 1946)

CUSTINE, Marquis de, *Russia*, abridged from the French (London, 1855)

CZAPSKI, Joseph, *The Inhuman Land*, tr. from the French by Gerard Hopkins (London, 1951)

DALLIN, Alexander, *German Rule in Russia, 1941–1945: a Study of Occupation Policies* (London, 1957)

DALLIN, David J., *Soviet Espionage* (New Haven, 1955)

DALLIN, David J. and NICOLAEVSKY, Boris I., *Forced Labor in Soviet Russia* (London, 1948)

DANIELS, Robert Vincent, *The Conscience of the Revolution: Communist Opposition in Soviet Russia* (Cambridge, Massachusetts, 1960)

DANIELS, Robert Vincent, *Red October: the Bolshevik Revolution of 1917* (London, 1967)

DEAKIN, F. W. and STORRY, G. R., *The Case of Richard Sorge* (London, 1966)

DEDIJER, Vladimir, *Tito Speaks: his Self Portrait and Struggle with Stalin* (London, 1953)

DENIKINE, General A., *The White Army*, tr. from the Russian by Catherine Zvegintzov (London, 1930)

DEUTSCHER, I., *Stalin: a Political Biography* (London, 1967)

DEWAR, Hugo, *The Modern Inquisition* (London, 1953)

DJILAS, Milovan, *Conversations with Stalin*, tr. from the Serbo-Croat by Michael B. Petrovich (London, 1962)

DREZEN, A. K., ed., *Tsarizm v borbe s revolutsiyey, 1905–1907 gg.: sbornik dokumentov* (Moscow, 1936)

DUHNKE, Horst, *Stalinismus in Deutschland: die Geschichte der sowjetischen Besatzungszone* (Cologne, 1955)

DUKES, Sir Paul, *The Story of 'ST 25': Adventure and Romance in the Secret Intelligence Service in Red Russia* (London, 1938)

DUMBADZE, Ye., *Na sluzhbe Cheka i Kominterna: lichnyya vospominaniya* (Paris, 1930)

EKART, Antoni, *Vanished without Trace: the Story of Seven Years in Soviet Russia* (London, 1954)

ELIOT, T. S., preface by, *The Dark Side of the Moon* (London, 1946)

ERICKSON, John, *The Soviet High Command: a Military-Political History, 1918–1941* (London, 1962)

FAINSOD, Merle, *How Russia is Ruled* (Cambridge, Massachusetts, 1956)

FAINSOD, Merle, *Smolensk under Soviet Rule* (London, 1959)

FEOKTISTOV, Ye. M., *Vospominaniya: za kulisami politiki i literatury, 1848–96* (Moscow-Leningrad, 1929)

FIGNER, Vera, *Zapechatlyonny trud: vospominaniya v dvukh tomakh*, 2 vols. (Moscow, 1964)

FISCHER, George, *Soviet Opposition to Stalin: a Case Study in World War II* (Cambridge, Massachusetts, 1952)

FLORINSKY, Michael T., *The End of the Russian Empire* (New York, 1961)

FLORINSKY, Michael T., *Russia: a History and an Interpretation*, 2 vols. (New York, 1947)

FOMIN, F. T., *Zapiski starogo chekista* (Moscow, 1962)

FOOTMAN, David, *Red Prelude: a Life of A. I. Zhelyabov* (London, 1944)

FOOTMAN, David, 'The Tambov Revolt, 1919–21', unpublished article, n.d.

GANKIN, O. H. and FISHER, H. H., *The Bolsheviks and the World War: the Origins of the Third International* (Stanford, 1940)

GERASSIMOFF, Alexander, *Der Kampf gegen die erste russische Revolution: Erinnerungen* (Frauenfeld, 1934)

GERNET, M. N., *Istoriya tsarskoy tyurmy*, 3rd edition, 5 vols. (Moscow, 1960–3)

GERSHENZON, M. O., ed., *Epokha Nikolaya I* (Moscow, 1910)

GINZBURG, Evgenia Semyonovna, *Into the Whirlwind*, tr. from the Russian by Paul Stevenson and Manya Harari (London, 1967)

GOLDMAN, Emma, *My Disillusionment in Russia* (London, 1925)

GOLIKOVA, N. B., *Politicheskiye protsessy pri Petre I: po materialam Preobrazhenskogo prikaza* (Moscow, 1957)

GOLIKOVA, N. B., 'Organy politicheskogo syska i ikh razvitiye v xvii–xviii vv.', in *Absolyutizm v Rossii, xvii–xviii vv.*, ed. N. M. Druzhinin (Moscow, 1964), pp. 243–80

GOLLWITZER, Helmut, *Unwilling Journey: a Diary from Russia* (London, 1953)

GORBATOV, A. V., *Gody i voyny* (continuation), *Novy Mir* (Moscow), April 1964, pp. 99–138

GOUZENKO, Igor, *This was my Choice* (London, 1948)

GRAHAM, Stephen, *A Life of Alexander II, Tsar of Russia* (London, 1935)

GREENBERG, Louis, *The Jews in Russia: the Struggle for Emancipation*, 2 vols. in one (New Haven, 1965)

GREY, Ian, *The First Fifty Years: Soviet Russia, 1917–1967* (London, 1967)

GRIERSON, Philip, *Books on Soviet Russia, 1917–1942: a Bibliography and a Guide to Reading* (London, 1943)

GURKO, V. I., *Features and Figures of the Past: Government and Opinion in the Reign of Nicholas II* (Stanford, 1939)

HEILBRUNN, Otto, *The Soviet Secret Services* (London, 1956)

HERLING, Gustav, *A World Apart*, tr. from the Polish by Joseph Marek (London, 1951)

HERZEN, A. I., *Byloye i dumy*, 2 vols. (Minsk, 1957)

HINGLEY, Ronald, *Nihilists: Russian Radicals and Revolutionaries in the Reign of Alexander II, 1855–1881* (London, 1967)

HINGLEY, Ronald, *The Tsars: Russian Autocrats, 1533–1917* (London, 1968)

IVANOV-RAZUMNIK, R. V., *Tyurmy i ssylki* (New York, 1953)

KAPLAN, Karel, 'Anatomy of a Show Trial', *Studies in Comparative Communism* (Los Angeles), April 1969, pp. 97–117

KATKOV, George, *Russia 1917: the February Revolution* (London, 1967)

KATKOV, George, *The Trial of Bukharin* (London, 1969)

KATKOV, George, 'The Assassination of Count Mirbach', *St Antony's Papers No. 12* (London, 1962), pp 53–93

KATKOV, George, 'The Kronstadt Rising', *St Antony's Papers, No. 6* (London, 1959) pp. 9–74

KEEP, J. L. H., *The Rise of Social Democracy in Russia* (Oxford, 1963)

KENNAN, George, *Siberia and the Exile System*, 2 vols. (London, 1891)

KENNAN, George F., 'Excerpts from a Draft Letter Written at some Time during the First Months of 1945', *Slavic Review* (New York), September 1968, pp. 481–4

KHOKHLOV, Nikolai, *In the Name of Conscience*, tr. by Emily Kingsbury (London, 1960)

KIZEVETTER, A. A., 'Imperator Aleksandr I i Arakcheyev', in his *Istoricheskiye ocherki* (Moscow, 1912)

KLINE, George L., 'Economic Crime and Punishment', *Survey* (London), October 1965

KLYUCHEVSKY, V. O., *Sochineniya*, 8 vols. (Moscow, 1956–9)

KOCHAN, Lionel, *The Making of Modern Russia* (London, 1962)

KOCHAN, Lionel, *Russia in Revolution, 1890–1918* (London, 1966)

KOLARZ, Walter, *Religion in the Soviet Union* (London, 1961)

KOLARZ, Walter, *Russia and her Colonies* (London, 1952)

KOLARZ, Walter, ed., *Books on Communism: a Bibliography* (London, 1963)

KORIN, A., *Sovetskaya Rossiya v 40–60 godakh* (Frankfurt/Main, 1968)

KOTOSHIKHIN, Grigory, *O Rossii v tsarstvovaniye Alekseya Mikhaylovicha: sochineniye Grigorya Kotoshikhina*, 4th edition (SPB, 1906)

KOZMIN, B. P., preface by, 'N. G. Chernyshevsky i III otdeleniye', *Krasny arkhiv* (Moscow), 1928, vol. 29, p. 175 ff.

Krasnaya kniga Vecheka, ed. P. Makintsyan (Moscow, 1920)

KRAVCHENKO, Victor, *I Chose Freedom: the Personal and Political Life of a Soviet Official* (London, 1947)

KRIVITSKY, W. G., *I was Stalin's Agent* (London, 1940)

KROPOTKIN, P. A., *Zapiski revolyutsionera* (Moscow-Leningrad, 1933)

KURLOV, Pavel Grigoryevich, *Gibel imperatorskoy Rossii* (Berlin, 1923)

KUZNETSOV, Anatoli (A. Anatol), 'Russian Writers and the Secret Police', *The Sunday Telegraph* (London), 10 August 1969

LABEDZ, Leopold and HAYWARD, Max, ed., *On Trial: the Case of Sinyavsky (Tertz) and Daniel (Arzhak): Documents* (London, 1967)

LABIN, Suzanne, *Stalin's Russia*, tr. by Edward Fitzgerald (London, 1949)

LAMPERT, E., *Sons against Fathers: Studies in Russian Radicalism and Revolution* (Oxford, 1965)

LANG, David Marshall, *The First Russian Radical: Alexander Radishchev, 1749–1802* (London, 1959)

LAPORTE, Maurice, *Histoire de l'Okhrana: la police secrète des Tsars, 1880–1917* (Paris, 1935)

LEITES, Nathan and BERNAUT, Elsa, *Ritual of Liquidation: the Case of the Moscow Trials* (Glencoe, Illinois, 1954)

LEMKE, M., *Nikolayevskiye zhandarmy i literatura 1826–1855 gg.: po podlinnym delam Tretyago otdeleniya Sobstv. Ye. I. Velichestva Kantselyarii*, 2nd edition (SPB, 1909)

LEMKE, M., *Ocherki po istorii russkoy tsenzury i zhurnalistiki xix stoletiy* (SPB, 1904)

LEMKE, M., *Politicheskiye protsessy v Rossii 1860-kh gg.: po arkhivnym dokumentam*, 2nd edition (Moscow-Petrograd, 1923)

LEONHARD, Wolfgang, *Child of the Revolution*, tr. by C. M. Woodhouse (Chicago, 1958)

LEONHARD, Wolfgang, *Kreml ohne Stalin* (Cologne, 1959)

LERMOLO, Elizabeth, *Face of a Victim*, tr. from the Russian by I. D. W. Talmadge (London, 1955)

LEROY-BEAULIEU, A., *L'Empire des Tsars et les Russes*, 3 vols. (Paris, 1881–1889)

LEWYTZKYJ, Borys, *Die rote Inquisition: die Geschichte der sowjetischen Sicherheitsdienste* (Frankfurt/Main, 1967)

LIDDELL HART, B. H., ed., *The Soviet Army* (London, 1956)

LINDEN, Carl A., *Khrushchev and the Soviet Leadership* (Baltimore, 1966)

LIPPER, Elinor, *Eleven Years in Soviet Prison Camps* (London, 1951)

LITVINOV, Pavel, *The Demonstration in Pushkin Square*, tr. from the Russian by Manya Harari (London, 1969)

Livre Blanc sur les procédés agressifs des gouvernements de l'URSS, de Pologne, de Tchécoslovaquie, de Hongrie, de Roumanie, de Bulgarie, et d'Albanie envers la Yougoslavie (Belgrade, 1951)

LONSDALE, Gordon, *Spy: Twenty Years of Secret Service* (London, 1965)

LOPUKHIN, A. A., *Nastoyashcheye i budushcheye russkoy politsii* (Moscow, 1907)

LOUKOMSKY, General, *Memoirs of the Russian Revolution*, tr. by Mrs Vitali (London, 1922)

LYONS, Eugene, *Assignment in Utopia* (London, 1937)

MCCLOSKY, Herbert and TURNER, John E., *The Soviet Dictatorship* (New York, 1960)

MACKENZIE WALLACE, D., *Russia*, 3rd edition, 2 vols. (London, 1877)

MAGARSHACK, David, *Turgenev: a Life* (London, 1954)

MANDELSHTAM, Osip, *Sobraniye sochineny v dvukh tomakh*, ed. Struve and Filippov, vol. 1 (Washington, 1964)

MARCHENKO, Anatoly, *My Testimony*, tr. by Michael Scammell (London, 1969)

MASSIE, Robert K., *Nicholas and Alexandra* (London, 1967)

MAZOUR, Anatole G., *The First Russian Revolution, 1825: the Decembrist Movement* (Stanford, 1937)

MEISSNER, Boris, *Russland im Umbruch* (Frankfurt/Main, 1951)

MEISSNER, Boris, *Russland unter Chruschtschow* (Munich, 1960)

MEISSNER, Boris, *Sowjetrussland zwischen Revolution und Restauration* (Cologne, 1956)

MELGUNOV, S. P., '*Krasny terror' v Rossii, 1918–1923*, 2nd edition (Berlin, 1924)

MELGUNOV, S. P., *Sudba imperatora Nikolaya II posle otrecheniya* (Paris, 1951)

MENON, K. P. S., *The Flying Troika: Extracts from a Diary* (London, 1963)

MENSHCHIKOV, L., *Okhrana i revolyutsiya: k istorii taynykh politicheskikh organizatsy sushchestvovavshikh vo vremena samoderzhaviya*, 2 parts (Moscow, 1925–9)

MENSHCHIKOV, L., *Russky politichesky sysk za granitsey*, part i (Paris, 1914)

MESHCHERSKY, V. P., *Moi vospominaniya*, part ii, 1865–81 (SPB, 1898)

MIHAJLOV, Mihajlo, *Russian Themes*, tr. by Marija Mihajlov (London, 1968)

MIKHAYLOV, M. I., *Zapiski*. 1861–2 (Petrograd, 1922)

MILYUTIN, D. A., *Dnevnik D. A. Milyutina*, 4 vols. (Moscow, 1947–50)

MODZALEVSKY, B. L., *Pushkin pod taynym nadzorom*, 3rd edition (Leningrad, 1925)

MONAS, Sidney, *The Third Section: Police and Society in Russia under Nicholas I* (Cambridge, Massachusetts, 1961)

MONAS, Sidney, 'Anton Divier and the Police of St Petersburg', in *For Roman Jacobson: Essays on the Occasion of his Sixtieth Birthday* (The Hague, 1956), pp. 361–6

MOORE, Barrington, *Terror and Progress USSR: some Sources of Change and Stability in the Soviet Dictatorship* (Cambridge, Massachusetts, 1954)

MOSSE, W. E., *Alexander II and the Modernization of Russia* (London, 1958)

NABOKOV, Vladimir, *Speak, Memory: an Autobiography Revisited*, revised edition (New York, 1966)

NECHKINA, M. V., *Dvizheniye dekabristov*, 2 vols., (Moscow, 1955)

NICOLAEVSKY, Boris I., *Power and the Soviet Elite: 'The Letter of an Old Bolshevik' and other Essays* (London, 1966)

NICOLAIEVSKY, Boris, *Aseff: the Russian Judas*, tr. from the Russian by George Reavey (London, 1934)

NIKITINE, B. V., *The Fatal Years: Fresh Revelations on a Chapter of Underground History* (London, 1938)

OLDENBURG, S. S., *Tsarstvovaniye imperatora Nikolaya II* (Belgrade, 1939)

ORLOV, Alexander, *The Secret History of Stalin's Crimes* (London, 1954)

PAGE, Bruce and others, *Philby: the Spy who Betrayed a Generation* (London, 1968)

PALEOLOGUE, Maurice, *Aleksandr II i knyaginya Yuryevskaya* (Petrograd, 1924)

PAYNE, Robert, *The Rise and Fall of Stalin* (London, 1968)

PENKOVSKY, Oleg, *The Penkovsky Papers*, tr. by P. Deriabin (London, 1965)

PETERS, Ya., 'Vospominaniya o rabote v VChK v pervy god revolyutsii', *Byloye* (Paris) No. 11, 1933, pp. 93–123

PETROV, Vladimir and Evdokia, *Empire of Fear* (London, 1956)

PHILBY, Kim, *My Silent War* (New York, 1968)

POLIYEVKTOV, M., *Nikolay I: biografiya i obzor tsarstvovaniya* (Moscow, 1918)

POPOFF, George, *The Tcheka: the Red Inquisition* (London, 1925)

PRESNYAKOV, A. Ye., *Apogey samoderzhaviya: Nikolay I* (Leningrad, 1925)

RAEFF, Marc, *Michael Speransky: Statesman of Imperial Russia, 1772–1839* (The Hague, 1957)

RAUCH, Georg von, *A History of Soviet Russia* (London, 1957)

REDDAWAY, Peter, 'The Soviet Treatment of Dissenters and the Growth of a Civil Rights Movement', in *Rights and Wrongs: some Essays on Human Rights*, ed. Christopher R. Hill (London, 1969) pp. 79–120

Régime of the Concentration Camp in the Post-War World, 1945–53: Four Investigations Conducted by the International Commission against Concentration Camp Practices (Paris, n.d.)

Report of the Royal Commission on Espionage, Commonwealth of Australia (Sydney, 1955)

RIASANOVSKY, Nicholas V., *Nicholas I and Official Nationality in Russia, 1825–55* (Berkeley, 1959)

RIGBY, T. H., ed., *The Stalin Dictatorship: Khrushchev's 'Secret Speech' and Other Documents* (Sydney, 1968)

ROBINSON, Geroid T., *Rural Russia under the Old Régime* (New York, 1949)

RUPERT, Raphael, *A Hidden World* (London, 1963)

RUSH, Myron, *The Rise of Khrushchev* (Washington, 1958)

SABLIN, V. M., publisher, *Petrashevtsy* (Moscow, 1907)

SAKHAROV, Andrei D., *Progress, Co-existence and Intellectual Freedom*, tr. by *The New York Times* (New York, 1968)

SAMOYLOV, V., 'Vozniknoveniye Taynoy ekspeditsii pri Senate', *Voprosy istorii* (Moscow), 1948, No. 6, pp. 79–81

SAVINKOV, Boris, *Memoirs of a Terrorist*, tr. by Joseph Shaplen (New York, 1931)

SCHAPIRO, Leonard, *The Communist Party of the Soviet Union* (London, 1960)

SCHAPIRO, Leonard, *The Origin of the Communist Autocracy: Political Opposition in the Soviet State, First Phase, 1917–1922* (London, 1955)

SCHAPIRO, Leonard and REDDAWAY, Peter, ed., *Lenin: the Man, the Theorist, the Leader: a Reappraisal* (London, 1967)

SCHEBEKO, Lieutenant-General, *Chronique du mouvement socialiste en Russie, 1878–1887* (SPB, 1890)

SCHIEMANN, Theodor, *Die Ermordung Pauls und die Thronbesteigung Nikolaus I* (Berlin, 1902)

SCHIEMANN, Theodor, *Geschichte Russlands unter Kaiser Nikolaus I*, 4 vols. (Berlin, 1904–19)

SCHOLMER, Joseph, *Vorkuta*, tr. from the German by Robert Kee (London, 1954)

SCHWARZ (SHVARTS), Solomon M., *Antisemitizm v Sovetskom Soyuze* (New York, 1952)

SCHWARZ (SHVARTS), Solomon M., *The Jews in the Soviet Union* (Syracuse, 1951)

SCHWARZ (SHVARTS), Solomon M., *The Russian Revolution of 1905: the Workers' Movement and the Formation of Bolshevism and Menshevism* (Chicago, 1967)

SCHWEINITZ, VON, *Denkwürdigkeiten des Botschafters General von Schweinitz*, 2 vols. (Berlin, 1927)

SCOTT, E. J., 'The Cheka', *St Antony's Papers No. 1* (London, 1956), pp. 1–23

SEMEVSKY, V. I., *M. V. Butashevich-Petrashevsky i petrashevtsy*, part i (Moscow, 1922)

SERGE, Victor, *Memoirs of a Revolutionary, 1901–1941*, tr. and ed. by Peter Sedgwick (London, 1963)

SETON-WATSON, Hugh, *The Decline of Imperial Russia, 1855–1914* (London, 1952)

SETON-WATSON, Hugh, *The East European Revolution* (London, 1950)

SETON-WATSON, Hugh, *From Lenin to Malenkov: the History of World Communism* (New York, 1953)

SETON-WATSON, Hugh, *The Russian Empire, 1801–1917* (Oxford, 1967)

SHCHOGOLEV, P. Ye., *Duel i smert Pushkina: issledovaniye i materialy* (Moscow–Leningrad, 1928)

SHCHOGOLEV, P. Ye., *Iz zhizni i tvorchestva Pushkina*, 3rd edition (Moscow-Leningrad, 1931)

SHCHOGOLEV, P. Ye., ed., *Padeniye tsarskogo rezhima: po materialam Chrezvychaynoy Sledstvennoy Komissii Vremennogo pravitelstva*, 7 vols. (Moscow-Leningrad, 1924–7)

SHCHOGOLEV, P. Ye., ed., *Petrashevtsy v vospominaniyakh sovremennikov: sbornik materialov* (Moscow-Leningrad, 1926)

SHILDER, N. K., *Imperator Aleksandr I: yego zhizn i tsarstvovaniye*, 4 vols. (SPB, 1904–5)

SHILDER, N. K., *Imperator Nikolay I: yego zhizn i tsarstvovaniye*, 2 vols. (SPB, 1903)

SHILDER, N. K., *Imperator Pavel I* (SPB, 1901)

SIMMONDS, George W., ed., *Soviet Leaders* (New York, 1967)

SINEVIRSKY, N., *Smersh: god v stane vraga* (Limburg, 1948)

SKRYNNIKOV, R. G., *Nachalo Oprichniny* (Leningrad, 1966)

SMITH, Edward Ellis, '*The Okhrana*': *the Russian Department of Police: a Bibliography* (Stanford, 1967)

SMITH, Edward Ellis, *The Young Stalin: the Early Years of an Elusive Revolutionary* (London, 1968)

SOFINOV, P. G., *Ocherki istorii Vserossyskoy chrezvychaynoy komissii, 1917–1922 gg.* (Moscow, 1960)

SOLOVYOV, S. M., *Istoriya Rossii s drevneyshikh vremyon*, 15 vols. (Moscow, 1959–66)

SOROKIN, Pitirim, *Leaves from a Russian Diary* (London, n.d.)

SOUVARINE, Boris, *Staline: Aperçu historique du bolchévisme* (Pari 1935)

SPIRIDOVITCH, Alexandre, *Les Dernières Années de la Cour de Tzarskoïe-Selo*, tr. from the Russian by M. Jeanson (Paris, 1928–9)

SPIRIDOVITCH, Alexandre, *Istoriya bolshevizma v Rossii; ot vozniknoveniya do zakhvata vlasti, 1883–1903–1917* (Paris, 1922)

SPIRIDOVITCH, Alexandre, *Histoire du terrorisme russe, 1886–1917*,
tr. from the Russian by Vladimir Lazarevski (Paris, 1930)

SQUIRE, P. S., *The Third Department: the Establishment and Practices
of the Political Police in the Russia of Nicholas I* (Cambridge, 1968)

STÄHLIN, Karl, *Geschichte Russlands: von den Anfängen bis zur
Gegenwart*, 4 vols. (Berlin, 1923–39)

STEINBERG, I. N., *In the Workshop of the Revolution* (London, 1955)

STEINBERG, I. N., *Spiridonova: Revolutionary Terrorist*, tr. by Gwenda
David and Eric Mosbacher (London, 1935)

STÖKL, Günther, *Russische Geschichte: von den Anfängen bis zur
Gegenwart* (Stuttgart, 1965)

STRUVE, Gleb, *Soviet Russian Literature, 1917–50* (Norman, Oklahoma,
1951)

STUDENIKIN, S. S. and others, *Sovetskoye administrativnoye pravo*
(Moscow, 1950)

STYPULKOWSKI, Z., *Invitation to Moscow* (London, 1951)

SWAYZE, Harold, *Political Control of Literature in the USSR, 1946–1959*
(Cambridge, Massachusetts, 1962)

SWIANIEWICZ, S., *Forced Labour and Economic Development: an
Enquiry into the Experience of Soviet Industrialization* (London, 1965)

SWIATLO, Jozef, *The Inside Story of the Bezpieka and the Party*,
unpublished typescript, n.d.

SZAMUELY, Tibor, 'New House of the Dead', *The Spectator*
(London, 23 August 1969)

TARSIS, Valeriy, *Ward 7: an Autobiographical Novel*, tr. by Katya
Brown (London, 1965)

TATU, Michel, *Power in the Kremlin: from Khrushchev's Decline to
Collective Leadership*, tr. by Helen Katel (London, 1969)

TCHERNAVIN, Vladimir V., *I Speak for the Silent: Prisoners of the
Soviets*, tr. from the Russian by Nicholas M. Oushakoff (London,
1935)

THORWALD, Jürgen, *Wen sie verderben wollen: Bericht des grossen
Verrats* (Stuttgart, 1952)

TIKHOMIROV, Lev, *Vospominaniya Lva Tikhomirova* (Moscow-
Leningrad, 1927)

TIKHOMIROV, Lev, 'Neizdannyye zapiski L. Tikhomirova', *Krasny
arkhiv* (Moscow, 1928) vol. 29

TOKAEV, G. A., *Betrayal of an Ideal* (London, 1954)

TREVOR-ROPER, Hugh, 'The Philby Affair', *Encounter* (London),
April 1968, pp. 3–26

TROTSKY, I. M., *Tretye otdeleniye pri Nikolaye I* (Moscow, 1930)

TROTSKY, Leon, *Stalin: an Appraisal of the Man and his Influence*,
tr. from the Russian by Charles Malamuth (New York, 1941)

TROTSKY, Leon, *Trotsky's Diary in Exile, 1935* (Cambridge,
Massachusetts 1953)

TROYAT, Henri, *Tolstoy*, tr. from the French by Nancy Amphoux (London, 1968)

ULAM, Adam B., *Lenin and the Bolsheviks: the Intellectual and Political History of the Triumph of Communism in Russia* (London, 1965)
ULAM, Adam B., *Titoism and the Cominform* (Cambridge, Massachusetts, 1952)
UNGER, A. L., 'Stalin's Renewal of the Leading Stratum: a Note on the Great Purge', *Soviet Studies* (Glasgow), January 1969, pp. 321–30
UTECHIN, S. V., *Russian Political Thought: a Concise History* (New York, 1964)

VALUYEV, P. A., *Dnevnik P. A. Valuyeva, ministra vnutrennikh del*, 2 vols. (Moscow, 1961)
VASSILYEV, A. T., *The Okhrana: the Russian Secret Police*, ed. René Fülöp-Miller (Philadelphia, 1930)
VENTURI, Franco, *Roots of Revolution: a History of the Populist and Socialist Movements in Nineteenth Century Russia*, tr. from the Italian by Francis Haskell (London, 1960)
VESELOVSKY, S. B., *Issledovaniya po istorii oprichniny* (Moscow, 1963)
VICKERY, Walter N., *Pushkin: Death of a Poet* (Bloomington, 1968)

WALKIN, Jacob, *The Rise of Democracy in Pre-revolutionary Russia: Political and Social Institutions under the Last Three Czars* (London, 1963)
WEISSBERG, Alex, *Conspiracy of Silence* (London, 1952)
WILLIAMS-ELLIS, Amabel, ed., *The White Sea Canal: being an Account of the Construction of the New Canal between the White Sea and the Baltic Sea* (London, 1935)
WITTRAM, Reinhard, *Peter I: Czar und Kaiser: zur Geschichte Peters des Grossen in seiner Zeit*, 2 vols. (Göttingen, 1964)
WOLFE, Bertram D., *The Bridge and the Abyss: the Troubled Friendship of Maxim Gorky and V. I. Lenin* (London, 1967)
WOLFE, Bertram D., *Khrushchev and Stalin's Ghost: Text, Background and Meaning of Khrushchev's Secret Report to the Twentieth Congress on the Night of February 24–25 1956* (London, 1957)
WOLFE, Bertram D., *Three who Made a Revolution: a Biographical History* (London, 1956)
WOLIN, Simon and SLUSSER, Robert M., *The Soviet Secret Police* (New York, 1957)
WYNNE, Greville, *The Man from Moscow: the Story of Wynne and Penkovsky* (London, 1968)

YAKOVLEV, B., *Kontsentratsionnyye lageri SSSR* (Munich, 1955)

YARMOLINSKY, Avrahm, *Road to Revolution: a Century of Russian Radicalism* (London, 1957)

YESIPOV, G. V., *Lyudi starago veka: razskazy iz del Preobrazhenskago prizaka i Taynoy kantselyarii* (SPB, 1880)

YEVREINOV, N., *Istoryia telesnykh nakazany v Rossii* (SPB, n.d.)

YEVSTAFYEV, P. P., *Vosstaniye voyennykh poselyan Novgorodskoy gubernii v 1831 g.* (Moscow, 1934)

YEVTIKHIYEV, I. I. and VLASOV, V. A., *Administrativnoye pravo SSSR: uchebnik dlya yuridicheskikh institutov i fakultetov* (Moscow, 1946)

YEVTUSHENKO, Yevgeny, *A Precocious Autobiography*, tr. from the Russian by Andrew R. MacAndrew (London, 1963)

ZAOZERSKY, A. I., *Tsarskaya votchina xvii v.: iz istorii khozyaystvennoy i prikaznoy politiki tsarya Alekseya Mikhaylovicha*, 2nd edition (Moscow, 1937)

ZAWODNY, J. K., *Death in the Forest: the Story of the Katyn Forest Massacre* (Notre Dame, 1962)

ZAYONCHKOVSKY, P. A., *Krizis samoderzhaviya na rubezhe 1870–1880–kh godov* (Moscow, 1964)

ZIMIN, A. A., *Oprichnina Ivana Groznogo* (Moscow, 1964)

Index

About the Author

RONALD HINGLEY was born in Scotland in 1920. During World War II he served in the Intelligence Corps of the British Army. He earned an Honors Degree in Russian at Oxford University and was awarded a doctorate at London University for a thesis on the Russian stress accent. After teaching at London University and serving as director of studies at the Joint Services Language Course there, he returned to Oxford in 1955 as University Lecturer in Russian, later becoming also a Fellow of Saint Antony's College. He has written numerous works on Russian literature and history, including *Chekhov: A Biographical and Critical Study*, *The Undiscovered Dostoyevsky*, and *The Tsars: Russian Autocrats, 1533–1917*. Mr. Hingley is editor and translator of *The Oxford Chekhov*.